www.wadsworth.com

wadsworth.com is the World Wide Web site for Wadsworth and is your direct source to dozens of online resources.

At *wadsworth.com* you can find out about supplements, demonstration software, and student resources. You can also send email to many of our authors and preview new publications and exciting new technologies.

wadsworth.com
Changing the way the world learns®

From the Wadsworth Series in Mass Communication and Journalism

General Mass Communication

Biagi, Shirley, *Media/Impact: An Introduction to Mass Media,* 5th ed.

Bucy, Erik, *Living in the Information Age: A New Media Reader*

Craft, John, Frederic Leigh, and Donald Godfrey, *Electronic Media*

Day, Louis, *Ethics in Media Communications: Cases and Controversies,* 3rd ed.

Dennis, Everette E., and John C. Merrill, *Media Debates: Great Issues for the Digital Age,* 3rd ed.

Fortner, Robert S., *International Communication: History, Conflict, and Control of the Global Metropolis*

Gillmor, Donald, Jerome Barron, and Todd Simon, *Mass Communication Law: Cases and Comment,* 6th ed.

Gillmor, Donald, Jerome Barron, Todd Simon, and Herbert Terry, *Fundamentals of Mass Communication Law*

Hilmes, Michele, *Only Connect: A Cultural History of Broadcasting in the United States*

Jamieson, Kathleen Hall, and Karlyn Kohrs Campbell, *The Interplay of Influence,* 5th ed.

Kamalipour, Yahya R., *Global Communication*

Lester, Paul, *Visual Communication,* 2nd ed.

Lont, Cynthia, *Women and Media: Content, Careers, and Criticism*

Sparks, Glenn G., *Media Effects Research: A Basic Overview*

Straubhaar, Joseph, and Robert LaRose, *Media Now: Communications Media in the Information Age,* 3rd ed.

Surette, Ray, *Media, Crime, and Criminal Justice: Images and Realities,* 2nd ed.

Whetmore, Edward Jay, *Mediamerica, Mediaworld: Form, Content, and Consequence of Mass Communication,* updated 5th ed.

Zelezny, John D., *Cases in Communications Law,* 3rd ed.

Zelezny, John D., *Communications Law: Liberties, Restraints, and the Modern Media,* 3rd ed.

Journalism

Adams, Paul, *Writing Right for Today's Mass Media: A Textbook and Workbook with Language Exercises*

Anderson, Douglas, *Contemporary Sports Reporting,* 2nd ed.

Bowles, Dorothy, and Diane L. Borden, *Creative Editing,* 3rd ed.

Catsis, John, *Sports Broadcasting*

Chance, Jean, and William McKeen, *Literary Journalism: A Reader*

Dorn, Raymond, *How to Design and Improve Magazine Layouts,* 2nd ed.

Fischer, Heintz-Dietrich, *Sports Journalism at Its Best: Pulitzer Prize–Winning Articles, Cartoons, and Photographs*

Fisher, Lionel, *The Craft of Corporate Journalism*

Gaines, William, *Investigative Reporting for Print and Broadcast,* 2nd ed.

Hilliard, Robert L., *Writing for Television, Radio, and New Media,* 7th ed.

Kessler, Lauren, and Duncan McDonald, *When Words Collide,* 5th ed.

Klement, Alice M., and Carolyn Burrows Matalene, *Telling Stories/Taking Risks: Journalism Writing at the Century's Edge*

Laakaniemi, Ray, *Newswriting in Transition*

Rich, Carole, *Workbook for Writing and Reporting News,* 3rd ed.

Rich, Carole, *Writing and Reporting News: A Coaching Method,* 3rd ed.

Photojournalism and Photography

Parrish, Fred S., *Photojournalism: An Introduction*

Public Relations and Advertising

Hendrix, Jerry A., *Public Relations Cases,* 5th ed.

Jewler, Jerome A., and Bonnie L. Drewniany, *Creative Strategy in Advertising,* 7th ed.

Newsom, Doug, and Bob Carrell, *Public Relations Writing: Form and Style,* 6th ed.

Newsom, Doug, Judy VanSlyke Turk, and Dean Kruckeberg, *This Is PR: The Realities of Public Relations,* 7th ed.

Sivulka, Juliann, *Soap, Sex, and Cigarettes: A Cultural History of American Advertising*

Woods, Gail Baker, *Advertising and Marketing to the New Majority: A Case Study Approach*

Research and Theory

Babbie, Earl, *The Practice of Social Research,* 8th ed.

Baran, Stanley, and Dennis Davis, *Mass Communication Theory: Foundations, Ferment, and Future,* 2nd ed.

Rubenstein, Sondra, *Surveying Public Opinion*

Rubin, Rebecca B., Alan M. Rubin, and Linda J. Piele, *Communication Research: Strategies and Sources,* 5th ed.

Wimmer, Roger D., and Joseph R. Dominick, *Mass Media Research: An Introduction,* 6th ed.

Global Communication

Edited by

YAHYA R. KAMALIPOUR

Purdue University Calumet

WADSWORTH ™

THOMSON LEARNING

Australia · Canada · Mexico · Singapore · Spain · United Kingdom · United States

WADSWORTH
THOMSON LEARNING ™

Publisher: Holly J. Allen
Assistant Editor: Nicole George
Editorial Assistant: Mele Alusa
Marketing Manager: Kim Russell
Marketing Assistant: Neena Chandra
Signing Representative: Bradley Kosirog
Project Manager, Editorial Production: Cathy Linberg
Print/Media Buyer: Judy Inouye
Permissions Editor: Stephanie Keough-Hedges
Production Service: G&S Typesetters, Inc.
Copyeditor: Rosemary Wetherold

Cover Designer: Qin-Zhong Yu, QYA Design Studio
Cover Images: (clockwise from top) Bridge arch/
   PhotoLink; US flag in front of Capitol dome/
   PhotoLink; WWW on monitor/PhotoDisc; Cur-
   rency exchange/Keith Brofsky; Singapore street
   celebration/PhotoLink; International flags/Photo-
   Link; Grand Central Station/PhotoLink; Newspa-
   pers ready for delivery/Annie Reynolds/PhotoLink;
   Blue Mosque of Amman/R. Strange/PhotoLink
Compositor: G&S Typesetters, Inc.
Printer: Webcom Limited

Printed in Canada

   2 3 4 5 6 7 05 04 03 02

For permission to use material from this text,
contact us by
Web: http://www.thomsonrights.com
Fax: 1-800-730-2215
Phone: 1-800-730-2214

**Library of Congress Cataloging-in-
Publication Data**
Global communication / edited by Yahya R.
   Kamalipour
      p. cm.—(Wadsworth series in mass
   communication and journalism)
   Includes bibliographic references and index.
   ISBN 0-534-56127-6
   1. Communication, International. I. Kamalipour,
Yahya R. II. Series
P96.15 G53 2001
302.2—dc21   2001026817

Wadsworth / Thomson Learning
10 Davis Drive
Belmont, CA 94002-3098
USA

For more information about our products, contact us:

Thomson Learning Academic Resource Center
1-800-423-0563
http://www.wadsworth.com

International Headquarters
Thomson Learning
International Division
290 Harbor Drive, 2nd Floor
Stamford, CT 06902-7477
USA

UK/Europe/Middle East/South Africa
Thomson Learning
Berkshire House
168-173 High Holborn
London WC1V 7AA
United Kingdom

Asia
Thomson Learning
60 Albert Street, #15-01
Albert Complex
Singapore 189969

Canada
Nelson Thomson Learning
1120 Birchmount Road
Toronto, Ontario M1K 5G4
Canada

✦

*For Mah, Daria, Shirin, and Niki and to my mother
and late father, who, despite having no formal education,
somehow understood and appreciated the value of education*

*All the particles of the universe
Speak to you, day and night.
We see, we hear, we delight,
But to you strangers, we're blight.*

Jalal ed-Din Rumi,
13th-century Persian poet

Contents

Foreword

The history of international communications and cultural interchange is as old as human civilization. A civilized society that has never been influenced by another culture does not exist. In ancient and medieval times, this influence was considered quite normal, and nobody complained about it. Only since the beginning of the 19th century have foreign cultural influences been regarded by some people as a problem. There are two major reasons for this attitude.

First, the pace and scale of foreign influences have increased significantly. As long as the introduction of foreign influence was slow and on a small scale, people did not seem to mind it too much. However, the development of mass communication in the 19th and 20th centuries changed things to such a degree that this phenomenon spawned a new word: *globalization*. If the speed and scale of foreign influence exceed a certain threshold, culturally and politically conservative people—especially the older generations—tend to resent it and to resist, complain about, and protest the rapid changes.

The second reason for this new attitude toward foreign cultural influences is the rise of nationalism. In ancient and medieval times, when the majority of the population was illiterate, no sense of nationalism existed—at least among the masses. In modern societies, in which most of the population is literate and is informed by national radio and television, leaders from all shades of the political spectrum (depending on the situation of the country) often attack foreign cultural and political influences in order to arouse the masses' sense of nationalism, to unify the nation against a perceived outside threat, or to gain mass support.

Whether foreign cultural influence is a problem—and, if it is, to what extent—depends on several factors, including those just mentioned. Some of these factors are quite subjective. It is, therefore, extremely difficult for outsiders to predict whether any particular nation would consider foreign cultural influence a problem.

For example, I have met several foreign graduate students and junior researchers who hypothesized that the contemporary Japanese must consider American or Western influence to be cultural imperialism and must worry about the loss of traditional Japanese culture. However, these students and researchers were soon disappointed when they learned that hardly any recent literature supported this hypothesis. What support there is was written in Japan in the 1930s and early 1940s by ultranationalists and other right-wing agitators. Most of them were not only "defenders" of traditional Japanese culture but also Japanese "cultural imperialists" who attempted to force Japanese culture on other East Asian nations.

Contemporary Japanese intellectuals no longer consider American or Western influences to be cultural imperialism, chiefly because the postwar Japanese, like the postwar Germans, have been disillusioned by nationalism and no longer respond to nationalistic appeals, and because the Japanese cultural influence on other nations, including Western nations, is significant enough to satisfy their self-esteem.

Although the modern Japanese seem quite tolerant regarding popular foreign cultural influences, they are quite sensitive to language issues. As in France, stubborn opposition exists in Japan to what is perceived as English-language imperialism. Yet some other East Asian countries are so tolerant regarding language that they have adopted English as their official language, although at the same time stubbornly opposing the incursion of foreign popular cultures. East Asians do not take religion very seriously, yet West Asians do. It seems, then, that the nature of the perceived problems caused by globalization differs from one nation to another.

In Japan, people who insist on preserving "cultural identity" and "cultural continuity" and condemn "Western cultural imperialism" tend to be right-wing nationalists in politics. In some other countries, especially Third World countries, they tend to belong to the progressive and left-wing reformist political group. In the West, those who espouse, let's say, a French, German, or Canadian cultural identity would belong to the right-wing nationalist group, but those who clamor for cultural independence and continuity in Third World countries and protest against Western cultural influence would belong to the left-wing reformist group.

Furthermore, arguments regarding these concepts are often based on wrong assumptions. The facts are as follows.

First, national cultures change not only because of foreign influences but also because of many endogenous reasons such as the development of technology. For example, the introduction of contraception technology has changed and will continue to change all human societies in a similar manner. Just as paper production technology is no longer Chinese, contraception technology is no longer exclusively Western. Superior technology soon becomes international and universal. The national culture in most civilized countries in the 18th century was different from that of the 9th century, and foreign influence is only one of the many reasons. Consequently, it is almost impossible to define the nature of a national culture throughout its entire history. If someone were to attempt to do this with the Japanese culture, I could easily embarrass that person by asking, "Which century of Japanese culture are you talking about?" My point is that "traditional culture" is something that each individual feels subjectively, based on his or her taste and interest, and is not something that can be defined in an objective way.

Foreign cultural elements, after some time, are combined with, adapted to, and incorporated in the traditional culture and become a part of the national identity. For example, red pepper is an integral part of the modern Korean cuisine, but it was originally brought to Korea in the aftermath of the Japanese invasion in the late 16th century. Japanese tempura is famous, but its origin is in Portuguese cuisine. Thousands of examples such as these are found throughout the world.

Of Godzilla, Pokemon, Walkman, Play Station, Tamagochi, karaoke, or the latest fad of "entertainment robotics" (such as robot dogs and robot cats), which ones are Japanese and which are Western? Japan at present is one of the few countries in the world where the export of technologies exceeds the imports. Japan's younger generation is proud of these popular cultural items and technologies, which now constitute a part of their cultural identity.

So-called cultural imperialism, or cultural domination, exists not only between different countries but also between different ethnic groups within the same country. In the former Soviet Union, Turkish tribes in the south were forced to use Russian characters instead of Arabic or Roman ones. In China, Tibetans, Uighurs, and Mongolians are feeling strong cultural pressure from the majority Han culture. Cultural imperialism can exist not only under the capitalist system but also under the communist or socialist system. Eastern European countries of the former Soviet system are examples.

Another development is that the simple categorization of countries in terms of the West and the non-West is becoming increasingly invalid. In fact, the definition of *the West* has always been ambiguous. It could mean the countries with a "Western civilization," countries in the (noncommunist) "Western bloc," or (more recently) Western Europe, North America, Australia, and New Zealand. The image of the "West" has been white, Christian, rich, and technologically developed. Whatever the formal definition may be, in order to fit this image, some Latin American countries (such as Argentina) and some Eastern European countries (such as Hungary and Poland) have sometimes been included and sometimes excluded from this category called the West.

Japan was long considered the only country in the non-Western world that had some "Western characteristics." Nowadays, however, Japan is no longer an exception. The national income levels of Singapore, Hong Kong, and Taiwan have reached those of major Western countries. The technological levels of these countries and South Korea are apparently higher than those of Eastern European and Latin American countries. Some Eastern European and Latin American countries, such as Rumania, Yugoslavia, Bulgaria, Albania, Bolivia, Colombia, Paraguay, El Salvador, and others, are economically and technologically closer to the Third World than to the "West," even though they have some "Western characteristics" such as Caucasian populations and Christian traditions.

The above facts indicate how difficult it is to discuss issues of cultural identity, cultural continuity, or cultural imperialism objectively and in systematic and general terms. The difficulty of theorizing about these subjects is also quite evident.

Today international communication experts better recognize the complexities of this issue than they did 30 to 40 years ago. Because of this recognition, no chapter in this book is based on any single "grand theory" or simple categorization of the West versus the non-West. Instead, some authors have suggested new, alternative ways of categorizing the countries of the world.

I have already pointed out similarities between Japan and Germany (disillusionment of nationalism) and between Japan and France (resistance against English-language imperialism). From a political and sociological viewpoint, the so-called First World may be divided into the "former-Allies First World" (the United States, the United Kingdom, France, and Canada) and the "former-Axis First World" (Japan, Germany, and Italy). For example, I have theorized elsewhere about the differences between "information societies with strong civil society traditions" (the United States, the United Kingdom, and France) and "information societies with weak civil society traditions" (Germany and Japan).[1] Or, given the importance of language in the developing age of globalization, these countries may be divided into the "English-speaking First World" and the "non-English-speaking First World." The conventional Second World and Third World also need reclassification based on several criteria, including those of language and religion.

A grand theory that encompasses all the issues regarding the influences of globalization is probably impossible. However, middle-range theories applicable to new categories (such as "non-English-speaking First World countries") may be possible. This book is a milestone leading in such a new direction.

Ito Youichi, Professor
Department of Policy Management
Keio University at Shonan Fujisawa (Japan)

NOTE

1. Ito, Y. (1994). Information societies with strong and weak civil society traditions. In S. Splichal, A. Calabrese, and C. Sparks (Eds.), *Information society and civil society:* *Contemporary perspectives on the changing world order.* West Lafayette, IN: Purdue University Press.

Preface

In the idiom of popular opinion, globalization means that instantaneous telecommunications and modern transportation overcome the barriers between states and increase the range of interaction across international limits. The cliché is that people are exposed to the same global media and consumer products, that such flows are making borders less relevant.

JAMES H. MITTLEMAN

Throughout the rise of the media business in the 20th century, the industry's version of globalization has been simple: the U.S. creates entertainment, and the rest of the world consumes it. The formula wasn't always easily swallowed overseas— as with the longstanding French resistance to American films and fast food—but it survived for decades.

BRUCE ORWALL

This book is organized around one of the major components of globalization, a post–Cold War phenomenon that is rapidly transforming economic, relational, social, cultural, political, and structural aspects of practically every nation of the world. That component, made possible by the marvels of telecommunication technologies, is global or international communication—a vast, diverse, dynamic, complex, interactive, and rapidly evolving discipline and enterprise. Hence, shifts in national, regional, and international media patterns of production, distribution, and consumption are a part of a much larger shift called globalization. Paradoxically, the world has grown both larger and smaller—everything has a global dimension, and everyone is electronically connected. In many ways, Marshall McLuhan's predicted "global village" has materialized.

DEFINITIONS

The concepts of *international communication, global communication, transnational communication, transborder communication, world communication, intercultural communication, cross-cultural communication,* and *international relations* are multidimensional and highly complex. Hence, any attempt at formulating a simple definition would be incomplete and certainly debatable. Nonetheless, in terms of meaning, the afore-mentioned first five concepts are interchangeable—they all refer to information flow that crosses geographical boundaries of nation-states. On the other hand, *intercultural communication* and *cross-cultural communication* refer to interpersonal relations among peoples of different cultures, races, and backgrounds, and *international relations* mainly refers to political (government-to-government) and economic (business-to-business) relations and activities.

A GROWING FIELD

Today an increasing number of universities in the United States and abroad stress what is commonly known as the internationalization of curricula, by offering new courses in international communication, international relations, international education, intercultural communication, and international business. Accordingly, in the last decade or so, the demand for books dealing with global issues and globalization has been increasing rapidly. This timely book, along with the supplementary Web sites, fills the gap between the high demand for teaching material for international communication and the serious shortage of such material.

SCOPE OF THE BOOK

The speed of change in global communication is such that no textbook can be entirely current or adequate, nor can it include all the issues and concepts related to this complex and fascinating field of study. To the extent possible, in terms of contents and scope, this book attempts to provide a comprehensive coverage of global communication.

In conceptualizing this book, I operated under a highly probable assumption that upper-level undergraduate and lower-level graduate students enrolled in an international communication course have already taken some mass communication courses, possess the basic information and knowledge about the field, and are already familiar with at least some (if not most) of the fundamental issues and concepts.

A unique feature of this book is that it brings together diverse issues and perspectives from some of the world's most notable and accomplished communication scholars. In addition to covering the essential concepts of international communication, this book includes several emerging and controversial topics, such as international public relations and advertising, recent trends in media consolidation, cultural implications of globalization, international broadcasting, information flow, governmental and nongovernmental organizations, international communication law and regulation, the impact of the Internet, and trends in communication and information technologies.

STRUCTURE OF THE BOOK

The 13 chapters of this book are organized in a relatively logical manner, evolving from theoretical paradigms to specific topics and issues. The order could be easily changed to suit the preferences of instructors who may wish to follow a topical or thematic pattern of instruction. The first two chapters offer students essential information about historical and theoretical aspects of global communication; thus, they should be assigned first. Thereafter, the order is not as important as tailoring the contents of the book to meet the particular needs of students.

Readers will note that the length of chapters varies, depending on the complexity of the topic. In brief, the book is organized according to the following broad themes: historical, theoretical, economic, legal and regulatory, institutional and structural, political, developmental, cultural, and pedagogical.

- Chapter 1 (Following the Historical Paths of Global Communication) provides a brief and succinct background for studying global communication. Historical evidence of communication across geographical space leads far back into early prehistory, from the mythical and symbolic images of ancient people in their maps and documents to the practical innovations for delivery of messages by royal couriers and pigeons. On the historical stage set by explorers, conquerors, and merchants, the mechanical and technological revolution arrived, bringing the printing press, telegraph, telephone, radio, and so forth. Each new development brought new patterns of communication across great distances. Over time, the technological revolution conquered boundaries of geographical space and time, creating the conditions for important new perspectives in the immediacy and transparency of today's networked world.

- Chapter 2 (Drawing a Bead on Global Communication Theories) focuses on the major theories of international communication and establishes a framework for interpreting the global patterns of communication, including the traditional normative theories of the press. Mainstream media theories such as agenda setting and functionalism, along with European critical theories are also discussed for their relevance to understanding international communication processes. The chapter also includes empirical illustrations drawn mostly from Russia and Eastern Europe over the past decade and demonstrates the critical gaps of various kinds that afflict media theory in the current era of globalization.

- Chapter 3 (Global Economy and International Telecommunications Networks) examines the structural patterns of global telecommunication networks. The British imperial telegraph network, the first global telecommunications network, was highly centralized and had few lateral connections. All lines led to London. If two neighboring colonized countries wanted to communicate with each other, the message had to be routed via London, which was perhaps thousands of miles away. Later, this pattern was carried over to the telephone network. After World War II, the center of the world moved across the Atlantic to the United States, and accordingly, global

telecommunications networks were reconfigured. Now all lines led to
New York. However, the overall structure of global telecommunications
networks remained unchanged. They continued to be highly centralized
networks with few lateral lines. Even today this pattern persists in telephone
traffic, computer-to-computer communication, media flows, monetary
flows, and other modes of global communication. This chapter examines
the economic, political, and historical forces that have created and sustained
this pattern. It also explores whether the seemingly unique qualities of the
Internet will disrupt the long-established pattern and restructure global
communications.

- Chapter 4 (The Transnational Media Corporation and the Economics of
  Global Competition) examines the status of transnational media corporations
  (TNMCs) and explains why they engage in foreign direct investments. The
  chapter then explores the business of transnational media ownership, refer-
  encing a few select characteristics that distinguish the TNMC from other
  kinds of transnational corporations. Other issues pertaining to media acquisitions and mergers, in a world that is becoming increasingly privatized, are
  also examined.

- Chapter 5 (Global Communication Law) begins by outlining the traditional
  role of freedom of expression in Western democracies. It then discusses
  international and national limitations on freedom of expression. Major areas
  of focus include censorship for national security reasons and censorship for
  moral and religious reasons. Existing international regulatory and policy-
  making bodies and their roles are examined. The chapter concludes with a
  discussion of the Internet and its impact on global communication law.

- Chapter 6 (Global News and Information Flow) discusses the traditional
  news operations of international print and broadcast news agencies and news
  organizations, and it reviews new directions in the packaging of news for
  online consumers. Opportunities offered by the Internet to facilitate the
  emergence of new international news agencies are also addressed. Finally, the
  chapter explores issues pertaining to the quality and quantity of the flow of
  news between the developed and developing countries.

- Chapter 7 (International Broadcasting) traces the history and development of
  international radio broadcasting from before World War I to the present and
  examines the growth of direct satellite television across borders by both governments and media companies. The development of direct and cross-border
  broadcasting between countries is also discussed. Furthermore, the chapter
  explains why nations and certain organizations aim their broadcasts at each
  other's populations and, at the same time, outlines some of the key concepts
  about propaganda and public diplomacy. The chapter also examines why
  audiences listen to across-border broadcasts and why governments are concerned about such broadcasts.

- Chapter 8 (Milestones in Communication and National Development)
  surveys the role of the international community and its organizations, espe-

cially the United Nations, in the evolution of communication for development practice since the end of World War II. The chapter isolates and discusses key institutions, personalities, and ideas associated with communication and national development, concluding with an examination of contemporary strategies.

- Chapter 9 (The Politics of Global Communication) provides a brief history of the politics of global communication, focusing on the domains of telecommunications, intellectual property rights, and the mass media. It analyzes the most important recent shifts as they affect these domains. The essential issues that will largely shape the future of global communication are discussed and analyzed in terms of the strongly divided and conflicting political agendas that define these issues. The chapter concludes with a proposal for the intervention by public interest coalitions in the arena of global communication politics.

- Chapter 10 (Global Advertising and Public Relations) examines the roles of public relations and advertising in the 21st century, arguing that these fields are not solely Western in their origins; cannot be practiced globally through an exclusively Western perspective; do not historically, nor inherently, represent exclusively corporate interests; and are not best practiced as manipulative agents. The author argues that public relations and advertising both have strong democratic traditions and capitalistic heritages and can help address social problems that will occur in the 21st-century technological, global, and multicultural world. This potential is possible not only through the practitioners' skills and expertise in communication management but also through an expanded role of these fields in solving society's problems. The author concludes that advertising and public relations can be used effectively to ameliorate social problems provided these professional occupations are embraced globally and are practiced not manipulatively but collaboratively, in the traditions of democracy.

- Chapter 11 (Communication and Culture) focuses on culture and the cultural impact of media products. Today mass media make up a major part of the culture industries around the world. While Hollywood products, produced by global corporations, dominate the world's television screens and cinemas, many countries have adopted measures to compete with those products. Some scholars have argued that because so many people watch American television programs and films, they have adopted American cultural values. But the technologies of satellite and the Internet have also made possible the distribution of a wider range of cultural products from ethnic minorities who may hold different values, making the impact of globalization less clear.

- Chapter 12 (Pedagogy, Critical Citizenship, and International Communication) uses a critical pedagogy framework to address some aspects of teaching international communication as a field of inquiry and the role that global communication technologies can play in the classroom. It is partly a report of an experience in teaching a class in international communication that introduced students to a set of theories and methodologies, with the goal of creating a critical awareness of the students' roles as media consumers of global communication. The class focused on the Cable News Network (CNN) as a phenomenon that embodies issues and problems that the course content intended to address. The chapter demonstrates that an international communication class can become more engaging if the content is approached in a topical and concrete fashion. Second, the content of such a class can draw from other communication classes (for example, television criticism), which allows for a more integrated approach to a communication curriculum. Third, students are able to study particular international communication phenomena (such as CNN) in their wider cultural, political, social, and technological contexts. Finally, the topicality of the approach renders the study of international communication more relevant to students by drawing from the context of their social life.

■ Chapter 13 (Patterns in Global Communication: Prospects and Concerns) challenges readers to think critically about current and future prospects and concerns of global communication. The purpose of this concluding chapter is threefold. First, the status of the communication industry's global infrastructure is reviewed; second, the issues of privacy and information warfare are examined; and third, the interdependent connections of global economics, transnational media corporations, and vanishing national culture in 21st-century media will be explored. Obviously, the idyllic society portrayed in 1950s television has completely disappeared, and the "Tiffany" network of "Walter Cronkite news" has splintered into hundreds of information channels. Undoubtedly, the information revolution has had profound effects on the world community and continues to alter the structure, speed, complexity, and nature of entertainment and information services at an alarming rate. Consequently, global communities and societies are faced with new challenges and opportunities as well as many questions about the end of the communications revolution. Is humanity better off as a result of this media transformation? Who are the winners and the losers in global changes? What social concerns should industry leadership address worldwide? What are the prospects for the future development of media and communication in the new world order?

INTENDED AUDIENCE

This book is mainly intended for upper-level undergraduate and lower-level graduate students in such courses as international communication, comparative telecommunication systems, international broadcasting, international journalism, and intercultural communication. Students enrolled in international relations, international politics, international business, and the like will also benefit from the contents of this volume. In addition, this book will be a valuable resource for researchers, journalists, international agencies, international enterprises, and libraries.

RESOURCES AND WEB SITES

To keep students and instructors abreast of the ever-changing developments in the field of global communication and to supplement the contents of this textbook, I have designed a Web site entitled Global Media Monitor (GMM) and an electronic magazine, Global Media Journal (GMJ). The GMM (http://www .globalmediamonitor.com) serves as a clearinghouse for numerous issues related to global communication, and the GMJ (http://www.globalmediajournal.com), published quarterly, includes articles by global media experts, book reviews, announcements, profiles, and commentaries.

In essence the GMM serves as an electronic media data bank that stores a wide range of information on international communication, including lists of global scholars, profiles, and their areas of expertise; lists of books, journals, and articles; links to international online radio and television stations; links to print media of various nations; and links to many nations' Web sites where instructors and students can obtain up-to-date cultural, political, economic, geographical, and other information about a specific country, region, or media corporation.

In addition, an electronic message board allows students and instructors to hold electronic conferences, post questions, discuss issues, or exchange ideas on topics covered in the textbook or discussed in their classes.

Furthermore, students and instructors have access to InfoTrac® College Edition (http://www.infotrac-college.com/wadsworth), an online university library with access to more than 700 publications. Wadsworth offers this invaluable service to instructors and students who use this textbook for their courses.

INSTRUCTIONAL BENEFITS

The textbook, in conjunction with the Web sites and instructors' guidance, can aid students in undertaking a variety of interesting and informative case studies related to international communication. Students can easily access the Web sites and listen to broadcasts in many languages, including English (for example, Voice of America, Radio Free Europe/Radio Liberty, British Broadcasting Corporation, Radio Canada International, International Broadcast Services of the Islamic Republic of Iran, Radio Beijing, and Radio Moscow). In the process, they become exposed to international broadcasting and learn about a wide range of issues, news, and global perspectives. Likewise, students can access numerous newspapers, journals, governmental and nongovernmental organizations, cultural centers, U.S. Central Intelligence Agency databases, United Nations databases, and others throughout the world. These comprehensive resources should keep students up-to-date and also satisfy the needs of practically any instructor who wishes to include a case-study approach in the study of international communication.

QUESTIONS FOR DISCUSSION

Intended to encourage classroom discussions and to promote critical thinking skills among students, the contributing authors have each posed five mainly open-ended questions at the end of their chapter. Students may use these questions for debating issues, assessing comprehension of chapter contents, preparing for examinations, writing research papers, and/or developing case-study projects.

ADVANTAGES AND DISADVANTAGES

One of the key advantages of an edited volume, such as this textbook, is that it offers students, instructors, and researchers broad and multidimensional perspectives that typically are absent, or presented one-dimensionally, in a textbook by a single author. You will note that throughout this book some authors explain certain concepts (for instance, globalization, cultural imperialism, and information flow) in different contexts. Ordinarily, a given perspective depends on where (location) an individual stands (orientation/affiliation) and how (from what angle/through what lens) he or she looks (perspective) at a given situation (context). Hence, some authors may explain the same or similar concepts differently in different contexts. Such explanations should be viewed not as redundancies but as repetitions that restate, explain or frame a point in a different context. Education experts seem to agree that repetition, when used judiciously, becomes a key factor in the process of helping students learn, understand, and retain information better. I have attempted to consistently reduce redundancies while using repetition judiciously.

One of the major disadvantages of an edited volume is that the writing styles and approaches may be varied and inconsistent. In some cases, authors may even offer contradictory arguments. My own belief is that, in teaching and studying international communication, even such disadvantages may be turned into advantages. They can lead to lively discussions, critical analysis, further research, exposure to diverse thoughts, exposure to diverse writing/communication styles, and an appreciation of the complexity of the field.

FINAL THOUGHTS

At this particular juncture in human history, regional unrest, political conflicts, and ethnic tensions threaten the unity not only of many nations but also of the entire world. The widely trumpeted promises of globalization have been certainly beneficial for global corporations, national economies of mainly industrialized countries, and the transfer of goods, services, labor, knowledge, information, and information technologies throughout the world. Territorial boundaries have become blurred or redefined in favor of regional cooperatives (such as the North American Free Trade Agreement, or NAFTA; the European Union; the Asia–Pacific zone; and others). Democratization processes that often favor free market economies, consumerism, or capitalistic tendencies are on the rise. On the other hand, the economic and information inequities between haves and have-nots, "East and West," and North and South have been increasing rapidly. In many ways, the so-called digital divide has replaced the old bipolar East–West divide.

My hope is that this textbook provides a reasonable and sufficient framework for generating meaningful discussions that will result in an appreciation for the immense scope, disparity, and complexity of global communication. Furthermore, I hope that such discussions will ultimately lead to action and positive change—peaceful coexistence, mutual respect, less conflict, increased cultural sensitivity, and better cooperation among the peoples and nations of the world.

Y.R.K.

Acknowledgments

In completing this volume, I have benefited from the kind support and cooperation of many friends and colleagues throughout the world. Foremost, I would like to offer my sincere gratitude to the contributing authors of this book, for without their genuine interest, support, and cooperation this project could not have come to fruition. Also, I would like to thank the contributing authors' colleges, universities, and organizations for providing financial, research, administrative, and secretarial assistance to the authors during the course of this project. Many colleagues at various universities have reviewed at least two earlier copies of this book manuscript: Craig Allen, Arizona State University; Mark D. Alleyne, University of Illinois; Fred L. Casmir, Pepperdine University; Don H. Corrigan, Webster University; Festus Eribo, East Carolina University; Junhao Hong, State University of New York at Buffalo; Kris Kodrich, Colorado State University; Shanti Kumar, University of North Texas; Jung-Sook Lee, University of Southwestern Louisiana; Drew McDaniel, Ohio University; Tom McPhail, University of Missouri; John J. Schulz, Boston University; Douglas P. Starr, Texas A&M University; and Karin Wilkins, University of Texas at Austin. My thanks to all of them for their constructive and helpful comments and suggestions.

Furthermore, I am grateful to the following individuals for their valuable moral support, feedback, encouragement, and assistance throughout this project: Dennis Barbour, head of the Department of English and Philosophy at Purdue University Calumet; Dan Dunn, acting dean of the School of Liberal Arts and Social Sciences at Purdue University Calumet; Kuldip Rampal, professor of mass communications at Missouri Central State University; Mehdi Semati, assistant professor at Eastern Illinois University; and Susan VanTil, my department secretary.

Of course, I am indebted to many wonderful people at Wadsworth, including Susan Badger, Deirdre Cavanaugh, Karen Austin, Stacy Purviance, Mele Alusa, Bradley Kosirog, the production and marketing teams, and others, for working with me on this book from conception to production, marketing, and distribution.

Without my wife and children's unconditional love, emotional support, and understanding, this project could not have materialized. I cherish and thank them!

Y.R.K.

About the Editor

Yahya R. Kamalipour (PhD, University of Missouri–Columbia) is professor and head of the Department of Communication and Creative Arts, Purdue University Calumet, in Hammond, Indiana. He has taught at universities in Ohio, Illinois, Missouri, Indiana, Oxford (England), and Tehran (Iran). His most recent books are *Media, Sex, Violence, and Drugs in the Global Village* (with K. R. Rampal, 2001); *Religion, Law, and Freedom: A Global Perspective* (with J. Thierstein, 2000); *Images of the U.S. Around the World: A Multicultural Perspective* (1999); and *Cultural Diversity and the U.S. Media* (with T. Carilli, 1998). He is coeditor of the State University of New York Press series in Global Media Studies. In addition to several significant awards, numerous invited speeches, and many mass media appearances and interviews, Kamalipour has published articles in professional and mainstream publications in the United States and abroad. He earned an MA at the University of Wisconsin–Superior and a BA at Minnesota State University. For further details, visit his personal Web site at http://www.kamalipour.com.

1

✺

Following the Historical Paths of Global Communication

ALLEN PALMER

Allen Palmer (PhD, University of Utah) is a faculty member in the Department of Communications at Brigham Young University, Provo, Utah, where his research is focused on international communication problems. He also has taught as a visiting professor in Mauritius, Benin, the Philippines, and Kosovo.

> The global village is more than ever a turbulent place.
>
> KARIN DOVRING

GEOGRAPHICAL SPACE: A BARRIER TO COMMUNICATION

For at least 3,000 years, people have sought to communicate across great distances. Elaborate courier systems were used in ancient China and Egypt. The Greeks announced the fall of Troy by lighting signal fires on the tops of mountains. A Roman emperor ruled his empire by sending messages in reflected sunlight off polished metal shields.

From its early beginnings, communication has evolved into today's elaborate technosystems and networks, transforming world communication. For the first

 For additional online resources, access the Global Media Monitor Web site that accompanies this book on the Wadsworth Communication Cafe Web site at http://communication.wadsworth.com.

time in millennia, physical space is no longer an insurmountable obstacle to human interaction in international communication. What was once the "geography of space" has become the "geography of experience" (Wark, 1994).

How did global communication evolve from such modest origins? Even though historians have long been interested in oral and written language traditions and technologies, the broader concept of communication is relatively new. It was introduced for the first time as recently as 1979 by medieval historians to examine the cultural and intellectual history of the Middle Ages (Mostert, 1999). Communication history is not just a question of new technologies; rather it involves questions of how those technologies arise from complex social conditions and, in turn, transform human interactions (see, for instance, Aitken, 1985; Beniger, 1986; Carey, 1989; McIntyre, 1987; Peters, 1999; and Winston, 1986). With faster and more far-reaching communication, important social and political developments occurred at the margins of technology and ideology, each interacting and expanding the potential outcomes of the other (Gouldner, 1982). In the broadest sense, technologies are cultural metaphors for prevailing social and cultural conditions.

In this review, we examine some of the forces at work in how early cultures created the conditions for communication. We begin in prehistory with the mythical images of ancient life. The fate of people in ancient times was, as often as not, violent, uncertain, cruel, and short. Human encounters with enemies, animals, and nature were fraught with hazards. In a symbolic view, this ancient world was enchanted, filled with otherworldly spirits, creatures, and images.

In time, migrant populations turned to agriculture and commerce, with trade routes extending outward to distant and unfamiliar lands. Science eventually disproved and displaced myths about the outside world. By the late Middle Ages, the "age of discovery" saw explorers traveling the edge of the known world, mapping their paths for others to follow.

Communication strategies and devices of many varieties were used to gain advantage in warfare and trade. Military conquests and religious crusades often resulted in unexpected consequences, including the intermingling of cultures and ideas. The ancient Chinese art of papermaking was carried to Europe by Arab soldiers, eventually making it possible for a German printer to develop movable metal type to print multiple copies of his Bible. The magnetic compass needle, similarly, was carried to Europe from Asia, leading to experiments on electric telegraph signals. The printing press and telegraph challenged the barriers of space and time, redefining individual identity and shrinking the world outside (Launius, 1996).

Scientists experimented with new devices to solve old problems, seeing every problem as just another closed door to swing open (Lindberg, 1992). These social processes, once begun, created the conditions in which technologies made sense at the moment they appeared. Collectively, they ushered society toward the industrial and electrical transformation of the late 19th century, and the information revolution at the close of the 20th century.

GEOGRAPHY AND THE MYTHICAL WORLD

Ancient people certainly must have regarded the world with a sense of awe and wonder, struggling to grasp—and control—the unexplained events of their lives. The Greeks used the word *mantic* to describe ideas, both mythical and supernatural, coming to people from somewhere beyond the immediate world, the "other" world, one not of their own making. These beliefs were part of the ancient mystification, more often implied in their worldview than expressed in their words, about the uncontrolled forces reaching beyond their mundane lives (Nibley, 1991).

Until relatively recently in history, perhaps within just the past century or two, most people knew life only as they saw it unfolding within a few square miles of their rural homes. Travel in most of the historical past was hazardous and unpractical. The vast world beyond one's immediate reach was grasped through magical or metaphysical images. Beliefs about the earth, heaven, and underworld were built around sacred and profane spaces (Eliade, 1987).

Images of these ancient mythic worlds are in the ancient lore of history. The Greek historian Synesius reported on peasants in the Aegean islands who believed in the existence of the Cyclopes, one-eyed giants (Mignc, 1857). Such images appeared in the work of early mapmakers, like the medieval cartographer Pliny, who illustrated his maps with fanciful creatures in strange foreign lands.

Monster sightings reported by mariners were used to enliven ancient map illustrations (Edson, 1997). Europeans believed that India and Africa especially were places where pygmies fought with storks, and giant humans battled griffins, winged creatures that could carry an elephant in their talons. Foreign lands were believed to be the bizarre and frightening places where gymnosophists contemplated the sun all day, standing in the hot rays first on one leg and then on the other; where humans lived who had feet turned backward and eight toes on each foot; and where others who had only one large leg could run as fast as the wind. There were cynocephali, humans with doglike heads and claws who barked and snarled, and sciapods, people who shaded themselves from the sun by lying on their backs and holding up a single huge foot. There were headless humans with eyes in their stomachs; people who could sustain themselves just on the odors of food; and monsters that had the body parts of several animals (Wright, 1965).

Myths surfaced in many places during the Middle Ages about the travels and exploits of a fictitious Christian king named Prester John, whose tales were repeated in music and poetry throughout Europe. Rumors circulated in the 12th century that he had written a letter addressed to the rulers in Europe, describing both his piety and his formidable conquests. According to the historian Albericus, the text of this epistle, spread across the countryside by troubadours and minstrels, contained accounts of a kingdom "beyond India . . . toward the sunrise over the wastes, and . . . near the tower of Babel" (Baring-Gould, 1885/1967, p. 38).

Prester John was believed to rule over a land inhabited by men with horns, along with giants and curious creatures, like Cyclopes. What frightened many

Europeans most of all was the threat, conveyed in this epistle, that Prester John could command his fearsome legions of soldiers, accompanied by cannibals and flesh-eating animals, to sweep across western Europe. Pope Alexander II in the 12th century even drafted a response to Prester John to be carried by his personal envoy. The messengers left Rome and never returned (Baring-Gould, 1967, p. 39).

Attila, king of the medieval Huns (406–353 C.E.), understood the psychological power of such mythical beliefs among his enemies and encouraged the circulation of such exaggerations in his campaigns throughout Europe in the 5th century (Cantor, 1999). Popular lore about dragons, sea serpents, and other creatures was repeated among different people through the late medieval age and early Renaissance, even though the stories were most prevalent among the poor and uneducated (Lecouteux, 1995).

The product of fear and imagination, these mythical ideas among ancient cultures were richly symbolic and were accompanied by expression in art, science, language, and ritual (Scheffler, 1997; Schuster & Carpenter, 1996). Art historians believe that even cave art, such as the 30,000-year-old drawings of prehistoric animals discovered at Vallon-Pont-d'Arc in the Ardennes region of southern France, were used for rituals associated with hunting. As historians described it, the metaphysical world was "no less 'real' to those societies than [was] the physical world of Western culture" (Harley & Woodward, 1987, p. xxiv).

ANCIENT ENCOUNTERS OF SOCIETIES AND CULTURES

When Greek and Arab philosophers and mathematicians sought to rise above mythical beliefs and to construct rational models of knowledge, they saw the world as measurable space, even suggesting the use of coordinates to divide geographical space. The earliest history of Western geography as a science began for the ancient Greeks of Ionia in the 12th century B.C.E., from whom both Plato and Aristotle inherited their vision of the physical world (Stahl, 1962).

The early Greeks regarded the remote islands to their west as the horizon of the known world. One of the momentous voyages of discovery in Greek history was recorded in the 4th century B.C.E. when the Greek explorer Pytheas sailed around Spain into what must have been to him a strange and alien world, along the coast of Gaul (France), around Britain, and into the Baltic regions. His astronomical and mariner records were used in Greece for several centuries as the basis for the earliest writings on mathematical geography and cartography.

Alexander the Great stretched the geographical boundaries of the European worldview even farther in the 4th century B.C.E. His empire covered a vast region from Egypt through the Balkans, and Asia Minor, east to the Ganges River in India. Trade routes established in his empire brought geographical knowledge from southern and eastern Europe, Africa, and Asia back to Alexandria. The accumulation of knowledge on papyrus rolls in the renown library of Alexandria, starting about 300 B.C.E., was a momentous achievement, but one soon lost because of the fragility of papyrus and the political upheavals that swept across the region. The library, founded by Ptolemy Philadelphus, was built through Alexander's conquests of Europe, Asia, and North Africa and, in an ironic turn of history, was destroyed by fire in the first millennium C.E. The library held half a million papyrus rolls, which constituted the largest library in antiquity (Thiem, 1999).

The learning of the Greeks survived the Roman Empire, being revived in Latin translations by the Byzantines in the 5th century. Arab translations of the Greek manuscripts appeared in the 9th century. Maimonides, a leading 12th-century Jewish scholar, also studied Aristotle's writing and helped spread his influence (Cantor, 1999).

GLOBAL EXPLORERS: MIGRANTS, HOLY PEOPLE, MERCHANTS

For ancient pre-agrarian societies in Europe, migration was a way of life. Changing climate conditions and food supplies required a nomadic life before 2000 C.E. Improvement of farming techniques and implements allowed many nomadic groups to settle on fertile lands, unless they were confronted by disease, invasion, or war.

Except for trade caravans and emissaries on state business with armed escorts, travel was always considered hazardous and difficult. Asians, for their part, did not travel far. The cultures of the Far East, especially the eastern parts of Asia governed by the hereditary monarchy of China (which encompasses today's China, Japan, Korea, and Vietnam), were loosely united by a Chinese worldview, while the western region of Asia responded more particularly to India's religious influences of Hinduism and Buddhism (Sivin & Ledyard, 1994).

By the 9th century C.E., Arab ships made regular trips from the Persian Gulf to China by sea routes. A North African scholar, al-Idrisi, wrote a document titled "Amusement for Him Who Desires to Travel Round the World" in 1153 C.E. Records show that Egyptian merchants engaged in trade in India and the Spice Islands at the end of the 13th century. Lamenting the sketchy knowledge of the East, one Arab writer noted:

> Writers on the customs and kingdoms of the world have in their works mentioned many provinces and places and rivers as existing in China . . . but the names have not reached us with any exactness, nor have we any certain information as to their circumstances. Thus they are as good as unknown to us; there being few travelers who arrive from these parts, such as might furnish us with intelligence, and for this reason we forbear to detail them. (Yule, 1915, p. 255)

After the fall of the classical Greek and Roman empires, substantive knowledge and curiosity about China and India ebbed among Europeans. Historians puzzle over the 1,000-year gap in East–West contact from the end of the late classical Greek period to the 17th-century Renaissance. Even though the period has long been described as static, brutal, and benighted, some historians now suggest that the so-called Dark Ages instead was a dynamic period when social and intellectual life was in transition (Cantor, 1991). "It is hard to believe that for almost two millennia people were any less curious about the construction of practical methods for long-distance communication . . . but the sobering fact is that throughout this period only occasional references were made" (Holzmann & Pehrson, 1995, p. 57).

The disappearance of Greek scholarship on geography left Europeans without many clues about the outside world, but their desire to explore would soon lead to the expansion of their knowledge of the shrinking world. Europeans were introduced in the 15th century to the Arab translation of *Geographia,* by Claudius Ptolemy, written in the first century B.C.E. Widely used as a reference by mapmakers despite its miscalculations and errors, it was a guide for Christopher Columbus in his search for a new western trade route to India. "The purpose of *Geographia* is to represent the unity and continuity of the known world in its true nature and location," Ptolemy wrote (Cosgrove, 1992, p. 66).

Among the known records of Jewish travelers are written accounts of the trade paths followed into the farthest reaches of the known world. Jacob ibn Tarik carried astronomical books from Ceylon to Baghdad in 820 C.E. Another traveler, Joseph of Spain, introduced Arabic numerals to the Western world from India. Jewish merchants from Persia brought goods from China to Aix-la-Chapelle (now Aachen, Germany) (Adler, 1966).

Radanite Jewish merchants also traveled overland routes from Spain across Europe, as far north as Kiev and east to India and China. An Arab geographer, Ibn Khurdadhebeh, composed the *Book of Roads and Kingdoms* in 847 C.E., tracing numerous trade routes throughout Europe, stretching from Spain to Asia. In the book, he described contact with "ar-Rus merchants," early ancestors of Russian-Scandinavians: "They are a tribe from among the as-Saqaliba . . . [who] bring furs of beavers and of black foxes and swords from the most distant parts of the [land] to the sea of Rum [Mediterranean]" (Boba, 1967, p. 27).

Vikings, or Norsemen, were known to have plied sea routes in the northern oceans, raiding cities in western Europe as far south as Seville and the Andalusia region in southern Spain in the 9th century. The population centers of Europe were long plagued with raids and incursions by these nomadic tribes. These tribes also settled western regions of the north Atlantic, including the coastal areas of Iceland, Greenland, and Newfoundland.

When Marco Polo's caravan ventured from Venice to the kingdom of the Mongols, and then to the court of the great Kublai Khan about 1260 C.E., European traders speculated much—but actually knew little—about life in Asia. Traders had an interest in obtaining silk from the East for European trade. Scholars now have grave doubts that the Polo family actually merited their far-flung reputation for bringing down barriers between Europe and Asia and instead attribute their good fortune to storytellers' exaggerations. By 1340 C.E., trade with

Asia was virtually cut off because of economic collapse in Europe and danger on the trade routes east (Larner, 1999).

MAPMAKERS IN THE MEDIEVAL WORLD

Mapmaking was an integral part of communication history. Maps were widely considered to be valuable keys to unlocking unknown worlds. Walter Ong (1982) describes how printed maps enabled exploration and discovery:

> Only after . . . extensive experience with maps . . . would human beings, when they thought about the cosmos or universe or "world", think primarily of something laid out before their eyes, as in a modern printed atlas, a vast surface . . . ready to be "explored." The ancient oral world knew few "explorers", though it did know many itinerants, travelers, voyagers, adventurers and pilgrims (p. 73).

Maps were closely guarded as state secrets by European royalty. Maps and charts from Columbus's first voyage to the Americas were deposited for safekeeping in Seville's most secure vaults. This extreme secrecy probably accounts for why the original maps used by Columbus, Cortez, and Magellan, among others, were lost. The reliability of maps was, in any case, rife with uncertainty. Columbus thought he was making landfall on the coast of Asia, instead of the Caribbean isles.

Mapmaking spurred empire building by some European powers, especially after the introduction of gunpowder (Hale, 1985). The information on most ancient maps reflected the mapmaker's cultural and religious orientations, and much of the information was estimated, distorted, or just plain wrong.

Maps served many purposes in ancient times, including maritime navigation, religious pilgrimages, and military and administrative uses. In the more symbolic view, "maps make the invisible visible" (Jacob, 1996, p. 193). Asian maps were drawn as art. Tibetan maps, by contrast, led travelers along a spiritual path through one of many possible universes, vertically ordered, from an imagined world of "desire" to a world of "non-forms" (Smith, 1964). Because maps were an intellectual tool of the most educated in ancient Greece and Rome, travelers and military leaders probably seldom had access to them or practical reasons to use them. Maps were used instead as intellectual tools among the Greeks, as objects for meditation.

After the fall of the Roman Empire, Europe was roughly divided by Islam in the south, the Christian kingdoms in the west, and the Christian Byzantine Empire in the east. Medieval geographers depicted the world on rough maps divided among three continents—Asia, Africa, and Europe. In one version of these ancient maps, the world was contained within a circle, with Asia, the largest of the three continents, filling the upper semicircle. In the lower half is a T dividing Africa on the right from Europe on the left by the Nile River (Larner, 1999).

Because travel involved venturing beyond safe and familiar terrain, it was often regarded as an act of religious devotion. Religious belief systems were directly reflected in many medieval European maps. Such maps were centered, explicitly or otherwise, on Jerusalem and were meant to be interpreted like scripture as a kind of "moralized geography" as much as an instrument of science (Cosgrove, 1992, p. 68). Such maps used a measured grid system that diminished in size around Jerusalem.

The relative isolation of the European populations in the Middle Ages between the 4th and 18th centuries C.E. was reflected in their incomplete road systems. According to a leading medieval historian, no real roads existed in 11th-century Europe other than the remnants of a few old Roman roads. Travel and commerce relied almost exclusively on a few navigable rivers, such as the Danube and the Rhine. Trade and commerce were hindered in France because of the lack of inland waterways (Cantor, 1991).

A new awareness of geography arose with the Christian Crusades, beginning at the end of the 11th century and continuing into the 15th century. The Crusades marked a new wave of exploration. During these military expeditions across Europe into the Balkans and the eastern Mediterranean, many Europeans became more familiar with distant languages, cultures, and locations (Constable, 1988; Riley-Smith, 1986). Crusaders developed a taste for goods they found during their travels, including goods from China and India. The Crusades constituted a major chapter in international communication, even though they had both complex and contradictory effects (Barnouw, 1989).

Ultimately, the Crusades began a chain of events extending the trading activity of European merchants, changing attitudes in Europe toward the outside world, and launching the "age of discovery" with 15th-century explorers like Columbus, Bartolomeu Dias and Vasco da Gama of Portugal, and others. Commercial centers, including Venice, became trade centers linking Europe and the Middle East.

Muslims, for their part, observed for 1,400 years the sacred direction toward their holiest shrine at Mecca, the edifice that symbolizes the presence of Allah. In the Middle Ages, they used two traditions to determine the sacred direction, one that sought to locate certain stars and the equinox of the sun, and the other using the direction of a circle on a terrestrial sphere. The Muslims were also responsible for acquiring ideas and devices from many lands. An Islamic proverb offered this insight into their transcultural consciousness: "Allah has made three marvels: the brain of the Greek, the hand of the Chinese, and the tongue of the Arab" (Strayer, 1988, p. 661).

Islam's scholars recognized that the earth was a sphere, and they used Ptolemy's *Geographia* to improve their measurements until they employed longitude and latitude by the mid-9th century. Such grid coordinates became the basis of extensive and elaborate mapping of Islamic regions and cities (King, 1997). Only later did innovators like Roger Bacon (c. 1220–1292) blend insights of both Greek and Islamic science in his encyclopedia of medieval science, *Opus Maius*. European scholars, such as Bacon, began to weigh the value of advancements from other cultures, borrowing elemental ideas for development of a telescope, gunpowder, air flight, and maritime navigation.

INVENTORS: SIGNALS AND SEMAPHORES

The historical succession of technologies used for communication is lengthy. A time line tracking the emergence of information technologies shows a bewildering array of conceptual and material inventions. The chronology of innovations can be atomized to discrete events (Desmond, 1978) or viewed from evidence of cultural continuities. One review has categorized them by their domains: either alphabet and mathematics, or optical and audio media (Schement & Stout, 1990).

At their simplest, most information technologies were solutions to tangible and immediate problems. The earliest known communication use of a simple signal system over distances employed fires or beacons. Aristotle (384–322 B.C.E.) described in *Peri Kosmon* an elaborate signaling plan in 500 B.C.E. to inform the Persian king within one day about everything of significance that took place in his empire in Asia Minor.

Three Greek writers—Homer, Virgil, and Aeschylus—described signal systems for military use. Aeschylus wrote in *Agamemnon* about the arrival of news of the conquest of Troy (1184 B.C.E.) in Mycenae, a distance of 400 miles: "Yet who so swift could speed the message here?" The message was conveyed, the writer answered, "beacon to beacon" across mountaintops and "urged its way, in golden glory, like some strange new sun" (Oates & O'Neill, 1938, p. 177).

The Greeks attempted to develop a more elaborate torch signal system based on letters of the alphabet, but it proved to be too cumbersome for practical use, according to the historian Polybius (c. 200–c. 118 B.C.E.) (Walbank, 1979).

Interest in signaling systems among the Greeks was based on potential military purposes. Homer wrote in the *Iliad* about 700 B.C.E.:

> Thus, from some far-away beleaguered island, where all day long the men have fought a desperate battle from their city walls, the smoke goes up to heaven; but no sooner has the sun gone down than the light of the line of beacons blazes up and shoots into the sky to warn the neighboring islanders and bring them to the rescue in their ships. (Homer, 1950, p. 342)

Roman rulers adapted a type of heliograph, or visual signal system using reflected sunlight. The emperor Tiberius ruled Rome (26–37 C.E.) from the island of Capri, sending signals from a mirror of polished metal. No records have been found of the code used for the reflected messages, raising doubts among skeptics about the practical value of the attempt. The Moors also used a type of heliograph in Algeria in the 11th century (Woods, 1965, p. 151).

In-transit message systems employed couriers both on foot and horse-mounted. In ancient Babylon, King Hammurabi (1792–1750 B.C.E.) dispatched messengers on a regular two-day route to Larsa, riding continuously day and night.

Egyptian scribes tracked the daily passage of messengers for military and diplomatic missions along the kingdom's Syrian and Palestinian border outposts. These messengers were wary of being attacked en route by Bedouin robbers, prompting the posting of royal guards at stations and the eventual use of fire-beacon signals on the frontiers.

Herodotus, a Greek historian, described in minute detail a pony express–style relay system during Xerxes' rule over Persia in 486–465 B.C.E., modeled after a torch race to celebrate the Greek ruler Hephaestus (Dvornik, 1974). King Cyrus the Great of Persia made significant improvements in the courier system.

> [Cyrus] experimented to find out how great a distance a horse could cover in a day when ridden hard, but so as not to break down, and then he erected post-stations at just such distances and equipped them with horses, and men to take care of them; at each one of the stations he had the proper official appointed to receive the letters that were delivered and to forward them on, to take in the exhausted horses and riders and send on fresh ones. They say, moreover, that sometimes this express does not stop all night, but the night-messengers succeed the day messengers in relays, and when this is the case, this express, some say, gets over the ground faster than the cranes. (Holzmann & Pehrson, 1995, p. 48)

The Greek historian Herodotus reported there were at least 111 courier relay stations between Sardis and Susa, a distance of about 1,800 miles. In the Battle of Marathon (490 B.C.E.) near Athens, in which Greek forces withheld an invasion of the Persians, the Persian king Cyrus dispatched a message to his field commanders, using the words later adopted as a slogan by the U.S. Postal Service: "There is nothing in the world which travels faster than these Persian couriers. . . . Nothing stops these couriers from covering their allotted stage in the quickest possible time—neither snow, rain, heat, nor darkness" (Herodotus, De Sélincourt & Burn, 1972, p. 556).

The Romans adapted the Persian courier and message systems, using the famous Roman highway system for moving troops, commerce, and communications. Both government and commercial services delivered correspondence throughout the Roman Empire. Messages were conveyed on papyrus, parchment, and wax tablets. The courier system used elaborate relay stations to sustain the rigors of overland travel. Each station maintained a stable of 40 horses and riders, known as strators, who carried special licenses from the emperor to obtain fresh horses. In this arrangement, mail could be delivered 50 to 100 miles per day. The system eventually collapsed over controversy about who would be responsible to supply horses and provisions.

Throughout the Middle Ages, regional commercial postal services were maintained about merchant centers, such as Venice and Bruges. Charlemagne directed a courier system among France, Italy, Germany, and Spain. In 1464, Louis XI of France reintroduced a network of relay stations with mounted couriers for official communiqués. England began a comparable service in 1481. Private commercial systems, based on royal franchises, began as early as the 15th century in Venice.

Reliability and speed of delivery through the medieval postal systems were remarkably good. Historians have found evidence that some messages traveled up to 150 miles in one day from the 15th to the early 19th centuries in Britain. By 1900 the delivery service offered one-day service within 350 miles.

The Chinese developed extensive networks of messengers and couriers as early as the Chou dynasty (1122–221 B.C.E.), but few historical details are known. Marco Polo described a relay system employed by the Mongols in the 13th century C.E., dispatching everything from diplomatic messages to fruit from surrounding regions. Each station, separated at 25- to 30-mile intervals, was stocked with at least 400 horses. Messengers could travel as far as 250 to 300 miles per day when required by emergencies. The Venetian merchant Polo observed, "The whole organization is so stupendous and so costly that it baffles speech and writing" (Polo, 1938, p. 150).

The Mongol ruler Genghis Khan used pigeons in the 12th century C.E. for communication in his kingdom, which covered a vast area, including almost all of central Asia, from the Aral Sea on the west to the China Sea in the east (Woods, 1965). Carrier or homing pigeons were also used by Egyptian pharaohs to announce the arrival of important visitors as early as 2900 B.C.E. News of the outcome of the Olympic games in ancient Greece was sent to Athens by bird carriers. The kings of Mesopotamia in 2350 B.C.E. gave a homing pigeon to each royal messenger to carry on dangerous routes. If the messenger was attacked, he released the pigeon to signal that the message had been lost and a new messenger should be dispatched (Neal, 1974).

The Incas in medieval South America, beginning about 1200 C.E., used an elaborate communication system with both smoke signals and a quipu, a cord with knots based on a numerical system, for messages. The numeric cord was sent by relay messengers as far as 150 miles in a day (Cantor, 1999).

Devices such as trumpets, drums, and even ordinary people's shouting were used by many different cultures to extend the reach of physical sounds. Diodorus Siculus, in the first century C.E., described the use of stentors, or shouters, to pass news across open fields (Woods, 1965).

Other communication innovations that were developed involved tapping codes on metal tubes with a hammer or blowing into cylinders to produce sounds. An Italian scholar, Giambattista della Porta, wrote in *Magia Naturalis* in 1553 C.E. about an acoustical device in which messages were shouted through so-called speaking tubes. The magnetic compass was introduced to Europe from China at the end of the 12th century. By the 16th century, experiments succeeded in transmitting a cryptographic code using a crude system of magnetic compass needles, leading to eventual development of the electric telegraph (Strayer, 1988).

The enthusiasm of Renaissance inventors for various inventions intended to communicate over distances had detractors. Galileo wrote about his response to one such proposed device in *Dialogus de Systemate Mundi* in 1632 C.E.:

> You remind me of a man who wanted to sell me a secret art that would allow me to speak to someone at a distance of 2–3 thousand miles, by means of the attraction of magnetized needles. When I told him that I would be

delighted to purchase the device, if only I was allowed to try it first, and that I would be satisfied if I could do so from one corner of the room to another, he answered that at such a short distance the effect would be barely visible. At that point I said farewell to the man and I told him I had no interest to travel to Egypt or Moscow before I could try the device, but if he wanted to move there I would be happy to remain in Venice and give the signals from here. (Galileo, 1953, p. 88)

A renewal of interest in signaling systems came in the 16th century as the French, Spanish, and Venetian navies began using flag signaling techniques from their ships. Then the subsequent development of the telescope in 1608 by Dutch spectacle-maker Hans Lippersley extended the range of observers.

Interest in optical signals resulted in experiments by the 18th century in Germany and Switzerland. German professor Johann Bergstrasser constructed an optical telegraph line that connected Feldberg, Homberg, and Phillippsuhe. A Czech musician, Joseph Chudy, devised a system of five lights that could be read by telescope at a distance, in effect, employing a five-bit binary code in 1786.

THE PRINTING PRESS, LITERACY, AND THE KNOWLEDGE EXPLOSION

Throughout the early Middle Ages, clerics were among the few literate people engaged in any task requiring writing. In addition to their religious duties, they drafted legal documents and letters for official dispatches. On occasions when written communication for diplomacy or commerce was necessary, the preferred means was through epistles.

The circulation of religious and diplomatic correspondence was an ancient practice but was expanded and refined in the high Middle Ages in the 12th through the 14th centuries, a time when western Europe exhibited dramatic changes in literature, as well as philosophy, government, and law. Literacy for the common public, however, required easy access to printed matter and the means to transport and circulate it widely; thus a printing press and a postal service were prerequisites. The complexity and diversity of the intellectual and cultural life created a marketplace ripe for information, stimulating the spread of literacy in Europe after the development of the printing press (McIntyre, 1987).

Printing presses had appeared in Asia as early as the 8th century, but the success of such presses was hindered by the vast collection of Chinese characters required to reproduce texts. When the Arabs defeated Chinese forces in Samarkand in 751 C.E., they captured Chinese papermakers and brought the innovative process to North Africa. Papermaking arrived in Spain around 1150, in Italy in 1270, and in Germany in 1390. France acquired the new process from Spain in the 12th century but did not produce paper until later in the 14th century.

Johannes Gutenberg's development of the press in Mainz, Germany, about 1450 C.E. stemmed from his concerted effort to print Bibles for use in local churches. Advances in metalwork in Germany made it possible for Gutenberg to fabricate metal type for only 50 letter characters. He also adapted his presses to allow printing on both sides of a sheet of paper and produced copies with much clearer print than had been possible with older block printing.

The social consequences of the printing press were far-reaching, eventually encouraging the practice of reading among common people and the reformation of medieval European institutions, religions, and governments (Eisenstein, 1979). Still, in 17th-century Europe almost nothing printed was trustworthy. The world of printing was notorious for its piracy, incivility, plagiarism, unauthorized copying, false attributions, sedition, and errors (Adrian, 1998). Books and other printed material eventually sparked social and political changes that gave rise to popular political consciousness and "public opinion" (Darnton, 2000).

The industrial revolution was not finished with printing technology with the advent of movable type. Even after Gutenberg's innovations, printers set type by hand for almost five centuries until the middle of the 19th century when Ottmar Mergenthaler introduced a machine, the Linotype, to set type in lines and columns with molten metal (Gardner & Shortelle, 1997). The changes set in motion by the printing press were profound. New literacy introduced new kinds of social relationships and networks among both learned and common people (Thomas & Knippendorf, 1990).

The postal service was an innovation patterned after older courier and messenger systems. Such a delivery regularized and routinized delivery of epistles and other correspondence at a cost accessible to a growing middle class, opening a market for pamphlets and newspapers (Robinson, 1953).

SCIENTISTS AND

INTERNATIONAL NETWORKS

Technological innovations in travel and the changing role of international science in the mid-19th century brought far-reaching changes in relations between nations. The melding of cordial relations between previously isolated countries into a coherent global network resulted from intermingling both their shared interests and intractable differences through the means of technology.

Introduction of the first user-friendly electric telegraph in 1844 was a breakthrough in the longstanding dilemma over development of two-way information exchange (Hugill, 1999). It also marked a shift between transportation and ritual modes of communication and permitted the dissemination of strategic information over great distances (Carey, 1989). The electric telegraph was soon followed by the telephone and wireless radio. These instruments opened the door to the subsequent social revolution that accompanied the information age.

Beginning with the railroad and the telegraph, towns and cities were brought closer together within a nation, regardless of whether participants were reluctant or enthusiastic to embrace these changes. Railroad and telegraph companies were built upon the era's unbridled optimism in empire building.

Oddly, national governments were usually ambivalent about scientific initiatives through the middle of the 19th century. Government cooperation on science often hinged on the preconditions that such projects "did not cost too much, that the scientists themselves were prepared to do the work, and that nothing in the commitment trenched upon national security or sovereignty" (Lyons, 1963, pp. 228–229).

Because of the strategic importance of communication for military and diplomatic purposes, communication between nations was regarded in most 19th-century political circles as strategic and proprietary. Tensions between nation-states even prevented the rise of international organizations until about 1850. One of the first modern intergovernmental organizations was the Central Commission for the Navigation of the Rhine, organized by the Congress of Vienna in 1851 (Barnouw, 1989).

France was positioned to emerge in a central role in negotiation of new international standards of exchange among colonial powers but had a history of guarding communication systems for strategic military objectives. France maintained one of the best-organized visual signal systems, involving a network of towers across the countryside. The semaphore code used by the French was considered a state secret until about 1850. Eventually, scientists sought to bridge national interests and obtain increased intergovernmental cooperation and support, and a few intergovernmental science ventures were launched by the end of the 19th century. One of the these projects was an initiative to measure the circumference of the earth, introduced in 1862 by the Prussian Institute of Geodesy, which changed its name to the International Geodetic Association in 1867.

The first standardization of a code of science occurred in 1860 when an assembly of chemists convened in Karlsruhe, Germany, to clarify the general usage of chemical symbols. Within a few years, similar congresses were convened to discuss international cooperation in the disciplines of botany and horticulture (1864), geodesy (1864), astronomy (1865), pharmacy (1865), meteorology (1873), and geology (1878). International agreements were being drafted to regulate postal and telegraph traffic. The International Telegraph Union was formed in 1865, and the Universal Postal Union was established in 1875.

By 1889 there were 91 international meetings held in conjunction with the Paris Universal Exhibition. By the late 1880s the Paris-based Association for Scientific Advancement (Alliance Scientifique Universelle) issued an identity card, or passport, called the *diplome-circulaire,* which scientists carried during their foreign travels (Crawford, 1992). From such scientific assemblies, 37 international cooperative agreements were drafted between 1850 and 1880. An international agreement was issued by the General Postal Union in 1974, and a treaty for the International Regulation of Sea Routes in 1879 (Mattelart, 2000).

One of the significant steps toward internationalizing the world was adoption of a global time system (Macey, 1989). An 1884 conference on international standards of time reckoning was held in Washington, D.C., to discuss reforming time standards and designating an international meridian.

The selection of Greenwich Observatory near London as the international meridian showed tacit acceptance among negotiators of a shift to a scientific center of global interests, in spite of France's objections to Greenwich because of French–British jealousy. French officials sought to barter an agreement, trading their acceptance of the proposal to make Greenwich the international meridian in exchange for British acceptance of the French metric system as the basis of international exchange. France promoted worldwide adoption of the metric system as early as 1792, calling the meter a "new bond of general fraternity for the peoples who adopt it" and the "beneficial truth that will become a new link between nations and one of the most useful conquests of equality" (Mattelart, 2000, p. 5). Officers in the American Metrological Society had accepted the challenge to promote the metric system. Their primary objective was universal adoption, especially in the English-speaking countries that had long resisted.

THE INTERNATIONAL
ELECTRIC REVOLUTION

The scientific innovations of the 19th century launched the world on a path to electrification of industry and commerce. Steam power led to what had once seemed to be startling speeds of travel, first by steamboat and then by railroad. The *Savannah* was the first steamboat to cross the Atlantic Ocean, under power of both paddle wheel and sails in 1819. The steam-powered railway system in England opened the first rail service between Liverpool and Manchester in 1830, reading speeds of 45 kilometers an hour.

Electrical experiments in England, Denmark, Russia, and Sweden led to the first use of a telegraph by Carl Friedrich Gauss and Wilhelm Weber in Göttingen in 1838. The railroad and telegraph systems were important in establishing international corporate empires that successfully brought technological innovations, linking the telegraph to the railway systems in England in 1839 (International Telecommunication Union, 1965).

Within 20 years of the general introduction of the telegraph in 1844, there were 150,000 miles of telegraph lines throughout the world, but mostly in Europe and North America. The transatlantic line eventually became a landmark step in bringing nations together in an international communication network.

One of the earliest proposals for a transatlantic cable line was mentioned in the *National Telegraph Review* in July 1853, but business promoters failed to attract sufficient backing. Cyrus Field and Frederick N. Gisborne considered the proposal again in 1854 and sought the backing by telegraph inventor Samuel F. B. Morse (Thompson, 1972). Consummating the project involved a series of difficult business agreements, including consolidation of then-independent U.S. telegraph systems into what would eventually become the American Telegraph Company. Morse was anxious to see the expansion of telegraph technology and promised to allow the use of his patents without charge on a line from the British provinces in Canada to New York and to transmit telegraph messages at half price.

The first transatlantic line did not work, and other attempts to lay lines either broke or failed. Eventually a line was fully operational by 1866. Backers of the project were primarily motivated by their desire to reduce the time required for news to travel from Europe to America by as much as 48 hours (Thompson, 1972).

Before the transatlantic project was begun, another entrepreneur, businessman Perry McDonough Collins, began promoting his ambitious scheme to tie the world together by telegraph. Collins wanted to lay a telegraph line from the western United States through British Columbia, Russian America (Alaska), under the Bering Strait, and overland again through Siberia to connect to a Russian line in eastern Asia. The endeavor also included construction of telegraph lines to Central and Latin America. Collins had obtained approval of both American and Russian governments to begin work on the Alaska–Russia line, and he had dispatched George Kennan to begin surveying a route through the Siberian tundra. The project was aborted in July 1866, upon the successful laying of a transatlantic cable (Travis, 1990).

Alexander Graham Bell, who considered his true vocation to be a teacher of the deaf, almost stumbled across the electrical signaling process used by the telephone in his effort to improve the telegraph. Bell sought to devise a system to send several simultaneous messages over a single wire without interference (Pool, 1977). When telephones were demonstrated at the Philadelphia Centennial Exposition of 1876, the public showed little enthusiasm for the device. Even some scientists, who saw the virtue of the science employed in the telephone, were ambivalent about its practical social uses (Gardner & Shortelle, 1997).

The telephone was a communication innovation that was adopted and managed differently in each nation. In the United States, the privately operated Bell Telephone Company oversaw its development. The company sought to sell the first phone patents to the Western Union Telegraph Company for $100,000, but the offer was refused. Later, Bell franchised rights to lease phones to private agents throughout the country.

Governments oversaw commercial phone development in Germany, France, and England, creating state monopolies. Sweden and a few other countries began with open markets, but eventually moved toward government control through regulation and licensing.

Once unleashed, the social uses of technologies follow their own paths of social and economic opportunity. One of the oldest news agencies, Reuters, began in 1850 when Paul Julius Reuter used 40 carrier pigeons to send stock market prices between Brussels and Aachen to compete with the inefficient European telegraph system. Reuters News Service eventually became a major source of international information because of its emphasis on the speed of information exchange, a value shared in other enterprises:

> Speed was prominent in the . . . growth of international wire services. But speedy information was most important for the military (because it meant the difference between victory and defeat, life and death) and international traders (because it meant the difference between profit and loss). International news agencies grew because they served this demand for speedy information. (Alleyne, 1997, p. 20)

Inventors of "aerial telegraphy," sending signals over the air without wires, filed for the first patent in 1872. Later, Thomas Edison and others developed the elemental ideas for wireless transmissions. Edison eventually sold his ideas and patents to Guglielmo Marconi and his Marconi Wireless Telegraph Company. The first coded trans–Atlantic radio signal was received in 1901 (Dunlap, 1937).

Broadcast inventor Lee De Forest, who is now remembered as the "father of radio," made significant advancement in the clarity of sound with his triode vacuum tube, making the transmission of sound—voice and music—possible. De Forest's vision of the social use of radio was based on his idea that transmissions to mariners at sea would be a kind of musical beacon. He disliked proposals to commercialize radio, believing until his death that the technology was destined for some higher, more transcendent use (De Forest, 1950).

Interestingly, others who devised new technologies for communication also saw hope in the new information machines for ushering in an age of more authentic connections in society (Peters, 1999). Their dreams, however, were soon displaced by the commercial imperatives and the expanding public appetite for information.

SUMMARY: GLOBAL IMMEDIACY
AND TRANSPARENCY

Communication across distance has been a catalyst for many changes in human relationships. Through a variety of mediated technologies, the cumulative effect of these changes was a redefinition of space and time, and increasing immediacy and transparency in global connections (Olson, 1999).

Echoes of continuity are found between what began in simple signal systems among the Greeks and Romans and the innovations in today's global society (Innis, 1950, 1951; Lasswell, Lerner, & Speier, 1979). Taken as a whole, these technologies accompanied the broad movement toward modernism and, later, its nemesis, postmodernism.

Communication is implicated in the sweeping social and political information-scape, including the shifting relations between capital and labor and the continuing struggle over old metaphysical symbols and obstacles. Others have placed these developments within predominant historical themes, such as war, progress, and culture (Mattelart, 1994). It has been too easy to overlook that communication is bound up in "the geopolitical consequences of human power struggles" (Cantor, 1999, p. 7) or in the rationalizing of the marketplace through techno-scientific networks of power (Mattelart, 2000). Significantly, one of the most penetrating studies of ancient communication practices is contained in a history of espionage (Dvornik, 1974).

Deciding what is—or is not—distinctive about today's global communication calls for synthesis of historical evidence. The challenge of understanding cultural transformation is only partly explained by technology. We fail to see other factors: "That our history has been shaped by the form and use of our tools in ways totally unanticipated by their inventors is, as always, conveniently forgotten" (Rochlin, 1997, p. 5). The emergence of international communication imposes new frames of meaning about the path of historical change.

For more information on the topics that appear in this chapter, use the password that came free with this book to access InfoTrac College Edition. Use the following words as keyterms and subject searches: communication history, Dark Ages, map-making, printing press, international agreements, communication revolution.

QUESTIONS FOR DISCUSSION

1. What strange images and myths did Europeans entertain about the people they believed lived in far-off places like India? Do such myths about strangers and distant lands persist today?

2. How did exploration and conquests by people like Marco Polo and Alexander the Great stretch the boundaries of the known world? Who are today's explorers?

3. What role did mapmakers and traveling merchants play in unlocking unknown regions of the world in the Middle Ages? Do mapmakers play an important role today?

4. Describe how the earliest known signal and messenger systems eventually evolved into modern communication across vast distances.

5. What were the consequences for international communication of the printing press? The telegraph? The clock? How might today's inventions change communication in the future?

REFERENCES

Adler, E. N. (1966). *Jewish travellers*. New York: Hermon Press.

Adrian, J. (1998). *The nature of the book: Print and knowledge in the making*. Chicago: University of Chicago Press.

Aitken, H. G. J. (1985). *The continuous wave: Technology and American radio, 1900–1932*. Princeton, NJ: Princeton University Press.

Alleyne, M. D. (1997). *News revolution: Political and economic decisions about global information*. New York: St. Martin's Press.

Baring-Gould, S. (1967). *Curious myths of the Middle Ages*. New Hyde Park, NY. (Reprinted from 1885, New York: J. B. Alden).

Barnouw, E. (1989). *International encyclopedia of communications*. Oxford: Oxford University Press.

Beniger, J. R. (1986). *The control revolution*. Cambridge: Harvard University Press.

Boba, I. (1967). *Nomads, Northmen, and Slavs*. The Hague: Mouton.

Cantor, N. F. (1991). *Inventing the Middle Ages*. New York: William Morrow.

Cantor, N. F. (1999). *Encyclopedia of the Middle Ages*. New York: Viking.

Carey, J. (1989). *Communication and culture*. Thousand Oaks, CA: Sage.

Constable, G. (1988). *Monks, hermits, and crusaders in Medieval Europe*. Aldershot, England: Variorum.

Cosgrove, D. (1992). Mapping new worlds: Culture and cartography in 16th-century Venice. *Imago Mundi, 44,* 65–89.

Crawford, E. (1992). *Nationalism and internationalism in science, 1880–1939*. Cambridge: Cambridge University Press.

Darnton, R. (2000). An early information society: News and media in 18th-century Paris. *American Historical Review, 105.* Retrieved November 15, 2000, from the World Wide Web: http://www.indiana.edu/~ahr/darnton

De Forest, L. (1950). *Father of radio: The autobiography of Lee De Forest*. Chicago: Wilcox & Follett.

Desmond, R. W. (1978). *The information process*. Iowa City: University of Iowa Press.

Dovring, K. (1997). *English as lingua franca: Double talk in global persuasion*. Westport, CN: Praeger.

Dunlap, O. E. (1937). *Marconi: The man and his wireless*. New York: Macmillan.

Dvornik, F. (1974). *Origins of intelligence services*. New Brunswick, NJ: Rutgers University Press.

Edson, E. (1997). *Mapping time and space: How Medieval mapmakers viewed their world*. London: British Library.

Eisenstein, E. L. (1979). *The printing press as an agent of change*. Cambridge: Cambridge University Press.

Eliade, M. (1987). *The sacred and the profane*. New York: Harcourt.

Galileo (1953). *Dialogue concerning the two chief world systems* (S. Drake, Trans.). Berkeley and Los Angeles: University of California Press.

Gardner, R., & Shortelle, D. (1997). *Encyclopedia of communication technology*. Santa Barbara, CA: ABC-CLIO.

Gouldner, A. W. (1982). *The dialectic of ideology and technology: The origins, grammar, and future of technology*. New York: Oxford University Press.

Hale, J. (1985). *War and society in renaissance Europe*. London: Fontana.

Harley, J. B., & Woodward, D. (1987). *The history of cartography*. Chicago: University of Chicago Press.

Herodotus, De Sélincourt, A., & Burn, A. R. (1972). *The histories* (A. R. Burn, Ed.). Baltimore: Penguin Books.

Holzmann, G. J., & Pehrson, B. (1995). *The early history of data networks*. Los Alamitos, CA: IEEE Computer Society.

Homer. (1950). *Iliad*. New York: Penguin Classics.

Hugill, P. J. (1999). *Global communication since 1844: Geopolitics and technology*. Baltimore: Johns Hopkins University Press.

Innis, H. (1950). *Empire and communication*. Oxford: Clarendon Press.

Innis, H. (1951). *The bias of communication*. Toronto: University of Toronto Press.

International Telecommunication Union. (1965). *From semaphore to satellite*. Geneva: ITU.

Jacob, C. (1996). Toward a cultural history of cartography. *Imago Mundi, 48*, 191–198.

King, D. A. (1997). Two Iranian world maps for finding the direction and distance to Mecca. *Imago Mundi, 49*, 62–82.

Larner, J. (1999). *Marco Polo and the discovery of the world*. New Haven, CT: Yale University Press.

Lasswell, H. D., Lerner, D., & Speier, H. (1979). *Propaganda and communication in world history*. Honolulu: East–West Center/University Press of Hawaii.

Launius, R. D. (1996). *Technohistory: Using the history of American technology in interdisciplinary research*. Malabar, FL: Krieger Publishing Co.

Lecouteux, C. (1995). *Démons et génies du terroir au Moyen Age*. Paris: Imago.

Lindberg, D. C. (1992). *The beginnings of western science*. Chicago: University of Chicago Press.

Lyons, F. (1963). *Internationalism in Europe, 1815–1914*. Leyden: A. W. Sythoff.

Macey, S. L. (1989). *The dynamics of progress: Time, method, and measure*. Athens: University of Georgia Press.

Mattelart, A. (1994). *Mapping world communication: War, progress, culture*. Minneapolis: University of Minnesota Press.

Mattelart, A. (2000). *Networking the world: 1794–2000*. Minneapolis: University of Minnesota Press.

McIntyre, J. (1987, Summer/Autumn). The Avvisi of Venice: Toward an archaeology of media forms. *Journalism History, 14*, 68–85.

Migne, J. P. (1857). *Patrologiae Cursus Completus: Series Graeca*. Paris: Migne.

Mostert, M. (1999). *New approaches to medieval communication*. Turnhout, Belgium: Brepols.

Neal, H. (1974). *Communication from stone age to space age*. New York: J. Messner.

Nibley, H. (1991). *The ancient state: The rulers and the ruled*. Salt Lake City: Deseret Book Co.

Oates, W. J., & O'Neill, E., Jr. (1938). *The complete Greek drama*. New York: Random House.

Olson, S. R. (1999). *Hollywood planet: Global media and the competitive advantage of narrative transparency*. Mahwah, NJ: Lawrence Erlbaum Associates.

Ong, W. (1982). *Orality and literacy: The technologizing of the word*. London: Methuen.

Peters, J. D. (1999). *Speaking into the air: History of the idea of communication*. Chicago: University of Chicago Press.

Polo, M. (1938). *The description of the world* (A. C. Moule & P. Pelliot, Trans.). London.

Pool, I. (1977). *The social impact of the telephone*. Cambridge: MIT Press.

Riley-Smith, J. (1986). *The first Crusade and the idea of crusading*. London: Athlone Press.

Robinson, H. (1953). *Britain's post office: A history of development from the beginnings to the present day*. New York: Oxford University Press.

Rochlin, G. I. (1997). *Trapped in the net: The unintended consequences of computerization*. Princeton, NJ: Princeton University Press.

Scheffler, I. (1997). *Symbolic worlds*. Cambridge: Cambridge University Press.

Schement, J., & Stout, D. (1990). A timeline of information technology. In B. Ruben & L. Lievrouw (Eds.), *Mediation, information, and communication: Vol. 3, Information and behavior* (pp. 395–424). New Brunswick, NJ: Transaction Publishers.

Schuster, C., & Carpenter, E. (1996). *Patterns that connect: Social symbolism in ancient and tribal art*. New York: Harry N. Adams Publishers.

Sivin, N., & Ledyard, G. (1994). Introduction to East Asian cartography. In J. B. Harley & D. Woodward (Eds.), *Cartography in the traditional East and Southeast Asian societies* (Vol. 2, Book 2; pp. 23–31). Chicago: University of Chicago Press.

Smith, C. D. (1964). Prehistoric cartography in Asia. In J. B. Harley & D. Woodward (Eds.) *Cartography in the traditional East and Southeast Asian societies* (Vol. 2, Book 2; pp. 1–22). Chicago: University of Chicago Press.

Stahl, W. H. (1962). *Roman science*. Madison: University of Wisconsin Press.

Strayer, J. R. (1988). *Dictionary of the Middle Ages*. New York: Charles Scribner's Sons.

Thiem, J. (1999). Myths of the universal library: From Alexandria to the Postmodern age. In M.-L. Ryan (Ed.), *Cyberspace textuality: Computer technology and literary theory* (pp. 256–266). Bloomington: Indiana University Press.

Thomas, S., & Knippendorf, M. (1990). The death of intellectual history and the birth of the transient past. In B. Ruben & L. Lievrouw (Eds.), *Mediation, information, and communication: Vol. 3, Information and behavior* (pp. 117–124). New Brunswick, NJ: Transaction Publishers.

Thompson, R. L. (1972). *Wiring a continent: The history of the telegraph industry in the United States, 1832–1866*. New York: Arno Press.

Thrower, N. (1972). *Maps and man*. Englewood Cliffs, NJ: Prentice Hall.

Travis, F. F. (1990). *George Kennan and the American-Russian relationship, 1865–1924*. Athens: Ohio University Press.

Walbank, F. W. (1979). *A historical commentary on Polybius*. Oxford: Clarendon Press.

Wark, M. (1994). *Virtual geography: Living with global media events*. Bloomington: Indiana University Press.

Winston, B. (1986). *Misunderstanding media*. Cambridge: Harvard University Press.

Woods, D. (1965). *A history of tactical communication techniques*. New York: Arno Press.

Wright, J. K. (1965). *The geographical lore of the time of the Crusades*. New York: Dover Publications.

Yule, H. (1915). *Cathay and the way thither*. London: Hakluyt.

2

Drawing a Bead
on Global
Communication Theories

JOHN D. H. DOWNING

John D. H. Downing (PhD, London School of Economics and Political Science) is John T. Jones, Jr., Centennial Professor of Communication at the University of Texas at Austin. He writes on international communication, radical alternative media and social movements, and ethnicity, racism, and media. He teaches African and Latin American cinemas, media in Russia, and media theory.

A "bead," as the word is used in the title of this chapter, is the small piece of raised metal at the far tip of a rifle barrel that enables accurate targeting. Theorizing has the same function, or it should. It is not an end in itself but a way of getting a phenomenon clearly in our sights—though hopefully not of killing it, which is where the analogy collapses.

This is why it makes sense to argue about different theories. It's one thing to have a "fact" staring you in the face. For instance, there are many times more telephones and TV sets per head in Japan than in the 50 nations of the African continent—but how did that happen, and what does it mean? We need to attempt an explanation, a theory. What did it mean at the turn of the last century and into this one to have a single corporation—News Corporation—own one of the four major TV networks in the United States; Star TV satellite television, which beamed programs to China and India (accounting for more than 40% of the world's

For additional online resources, access the Global Media Monitor Web site that accompanies this book on the Wadsworth Communication Cafe Web site at http://communication.wadsworth.com.

Six Normative Theories

Authoritarian theory can justify advance censor-ship and punishment for deviation. . . . the theory was likely to be observed in dictatorial regimes, under conditions of military rule or foreign occu-pation and even during states of extreme emer-gency in democratic societies. Authoritarian prin-ciples may even express the popular will under some conditions (such as in a nation at war or in response to terrorism). Authoritarian theory is generally designed to protect the established so-cial order and its agents, setting clear and close limits to media freedom. . . .

The second of the Four Theories . . . was la-belled **libertarian,** drawing on the ideas of clas-sical liberalism and referring to the idea that the press should be a "free marketplace of ideas" in which the best would be recognized and the worst fail. In one respect it is a simple extension to the (newspaper) press of the fundamental in-dividual rights to freedom of opinion, speech, re-ligion and assembly. . . . The nearest approxima-tion to truth will emerge from the competitive exposure of alternative viewpoints, and progress for society will depend on the choice of "right" over "wrong" solutions. . . .

Soviet theory . . . assigned the media a role as collective agitator, propagandist and educator in the building of communism. . . . The main principle was subordination of the media to the Communist Party—the only legitimate voice and agent of the working class. Not surprisingly, the theory did not favour free expression, but it did propose a positive role for the media in society and in the world, with a strong emphasis on cul-ture and information and on the task of economic and social development. . . .

Social responsibility theory involved the view that media ownership and operation are a form of public trust or stewardship, rather than an unlimited private franchise. For the privately owned media, social responsibility theory has been expressed and applied mainly in the form of codes of professional journalistic standards, ethics and conduct or in various kinds of council or tribunal for dealing with individual complaints against the press, or by way of public commis-sions of inquiry into particular media. Most such councils have been organized by the press them-selves, a key feature of the theory being its em-phasis on self-regulation. . . .

Development media theory . . . was in-tended to recognize the fact that societies under-going a transition from underdevelopment and colonialism to independence and better material conditions often lack the infrastructure, the money, the traditions, the professional skills and even the audiences. . . . it emphasizes the follow-ing goals: the primacy of the national develop-ment task (economic, social, cultural and politi-cal); the pursuit of cultural and informational autonomy; support for democracy; and solidarity with other developing countries. Because of the priority given to these ends, limited resources available for media can legitimately be allocated by government, and journalistic freedom can also be restricted. . . .

Democratic-participant media theory . . . supports the right to relevant local information, the right to answer back and the right to use the new means of communication for interaction and social action in small-scale settings of community, interest group or subculture. Both theory and technology have challenged the necessity for and desirability of uniform, centralized, high-cost, commercialized, professionalized or state-controlled media. In their place should be encouraged multiple, small-scale, local, non-institutional committed media which link send-ers to receivers and also favour horizontal pat-terns of interaction. . . . Both freedom and self-regulation are seen to have failed.

Note. Excerpted from *Mass Communication Theory: An Introduc-tion* (3rd ed.), by D. McQuail, 1994, Thousand Oaks, CA: Sage. Re-printed with permission.

population); a bunch of major newspapers in Britain and Australia; and a whole lot more media besides? Again, we need to attempt an explanation, a theory.

To answer such questions, someone has to produce a theory or at least spin some guesswork. Most of us would rather deal seriously with an idea that some-one has thought out carefully than with guesswork. Careful, focused thinking is what "theorizing," properly speaking, means. Thinking carefully and with focus doesn't mean that a theory is automatically right or even mostly correct. That's one reason we argue about theories. But theorizing is a serious attempt to think connectedly and deeply about something.

There are better theories and worse theories, just as there are smarter guesses and stupider ones. If we are to understand international media, we have to train ourselves to think through these theories and evaluate them. What follows is a start on doing just that. We will begin by reviewing critically the first systematic attempt to analyze media across the planet. In the second section, we will examine a different approach to the same task.

"NORMATIVE" THEORIES

One of the earliest attempts to think about media internationally was a book published in the 1950s entitled *Four Theories of the Press* (Siebert, Peterson & Schramm, 1956). Its authors set out to create what is sometimes called a taxonomy, which means dividing up all the various versions and aspects of a topic into systematic categories and sometimes subcategories as well. The taxonomy the authors proposed was that the world's various media systems could be grouped into four categories or models: authoritarian, Soviet, liberal, and social responsibility. It compared the systems with each other, which in principle makes it easier to see the differences and then to see each system's particular characteristics—all too often, familiar only with the media system with which we grew up, we assume it is the only imaginable way of organizing media communication. Comparisons are not just interesting for what they tell us about the rest of the world. They help us sharpen our understanding of our own nation's media system (see Sidebar, which cites a leading media scholar's summary of normative theories).

Authoritarian effectively meant dictatorial, and the authors had especially in mind the nightmare fascist regimes of Hitler in Germany and Mussolini in Italy. *Soviet* referred to the communist dictatorships at that time in Russia and its surrounding ring of client regimes in Eastern Europe, the Transcaucasus, and Central Asia. The prime difference between the Soviet bloc dictatorships and "authoritarian" regimes lay, the authors proposed, in the particular political ideology that undergirded the Soviet regimes, namely Communism, which claimed to show the way to construct a just and equal society.

By *liberal,* the authors meant not "left-wing," as in current American parlance, but free market–based, which is the sense of the term in current continental European parlance. The contrast with both of the first two categories was, clearly, between media systems ruled by state regulation and censorship, and media systems ruled by capitalist money-making priorities. By *social responsibility,* the authors effectively meant a different order of reality again, namely, media operating within a capitalist dynamic but simultaneously committed to serving the public's needs. These needs were for a watchdog on government and business malpractice and for a steady flow of reliable information to help the citizens of a democracy make up their minds on matters of public concern.

A strong underlying assumption in all four models was that news and information were the primary roles of media, a view that rather heavily downplayed their entertainment function, ignoring the significant informative and thought-provoking dimensions that entertainment also carries. Indeed, despite the title *Four Theories of the Press,* the book effectively even sidelined many types of print media (comics, trade magazines, fashion magazines, sports publications, and so on). Effectively, its obsession was with the democratic functions of serious, "quality" newspapers and weekly newsmagazines, with their contribution to rational public debate and policy making. The model the authors endorsed as the best was the social responsibility model.

These theories—of which we shall review two later ones in a moment—were what is called deontic, or normative. That is to say, they did not seek simply to explain or contrast comparative media systems but to define how those systems ought to operate according to certain guiding principles. In particular, by touting the social responsibility model as superior, the authors effectively directed attention to what they saw as the highest duties of media in a democracy. They did not, however, explain why media should follow that model other than as a result of the high ethical principles of their owners and executives. Whether media owners actually worked by such codes, and what might stimulate them to do so, were left unexplained. The social responsibility model was simply a series of ethically inspired decisions by owners and editors for the public good.

The two later categories/models (cf. McQuail, 1994, pp. 131–132) added still further variety. One was the development model; the other, the participatory/democratic model. The *development* model meant media that addressed issues of poverty, health care, literacy, and education, particularly in Third World settings. Media were defined as being vitally responsible for informing the public—for example, about more efficient agricultural methods or about health hazards and how to combat them. Radio campaigns against the spread of HIV and AIDS would be a typical example. Development media were also held to have an important role in fostering a sense of nationhood in countries with highly disparate groups in the population, territories often artificially created by European colonialists as recently as the late 19th century.

Participatory media, the sixth category/model, typically designated local, small-scale, and more democratically organized media, such as community radio stations or public access video, with their staff and producers having considerable input into editorial decisions. This alone sharply distinguished them from mainstream media of all kinds. But in addition, participatory media were defined as closely involved with the ongoing life of the communities they served, so that their readers or listeners could also have considerable influence over editorial policies. Sometimes these media shared the same development goals as the previous model cited, but not on any kind of authoritative top-down basis or as agents of government development policies. Public participation and a democratic process were central to their operation.

These six models did indeed cover a great variety of media structures internationally. Whether they did so satisfactorily is another matter. Let us look briefly at some of their shortcomings. Aside from their typical failure to engage with entertainment, already mentioned, their distinction among Soviet, authoritarian, and development models was very blurred in practice.

For instance, the mechanisms of Soviet and authoritarian media control were often very similar, and many Third World regimes hid behind "development priorities" and "national unity" to justify their iron control over any media critique of their behavior. The liberal model of free capitalist competition spoke to a by-gone age, already vanishing by the time the original *Four Theories* book was published, an age when many small newspapers and radio stations competed with each other. In the current era of global media transnational corporations—giants valued in tens, twenties, or even approaching hundreds of billions of U.S. dollars—it is quaintly archaic to be imagining still a free media market where all media are on a level playing field.

But perhaps the chief problem with the four (or six) theories approach goes back to the deontic, or normative, dimension of the theories. The two terms used above—*categories* and *models*—illustrate this problem, for though they can be synonyms, *model* implies something that ought to be followed. While media, like any cultural organization, clearly do follow certain guiding principles and do not reinvent their priorities day by day, what media executives claim those principles are and how the same media executives behave in actuality may often be light-years apart. Let us look at some examples.

Communist media in the former Soviet bloc claimed their purpose was to serve the general public, the industrial workers, and the farmers who made up the vast majority of the population. Yet when the opportunity arose in those countries in the late 1980s, public criticism of the cover-ups and distortions of Communist media became a tidal wave.

In the social responsibility model, objectivity is trumpeted as the journalists' core principle, the driving force of their daily investigation and writing. Yet as media researchers in a number of countries have demonstrated, journalists readily place patriotism above objectivity and define objectivity in practice as the middle point between two opposing views, often those of rival political parties, not troubling to question whether truth may lie somewhere else. In the 1990s and into the next decade, the pathetic U.S. news media coverage of battles over how to reconstruct the ever more problematic U.S. health care system offered a sadly accurate confirmation of the failure of objectivity once it was defined as the midpoint between the Republican and Democratic parties (Blendon, 1995; Fallows, 1996, pp. 204–234).

Development media, as noted, were often steered away from sensitive topics by arrogant, autocratic regimes in the name of national unity and the need to focus on bettering economic production. Even media activists working for peanuts in participatory media sometimes claimed a dedication to "the cause" that masked their own obsession with wielding petty power in their community.

In other words, media researchers need to penetrate well below the surface of media professionals' assertions that they are driven by distinguished values, such as development or social responsibility or the public good, and to examine the full range of forces actually at work in media. Not to do so is hopelessly naive and blots out the prime force in media at the beginning of this century all across the planet:

the ferocious elimination, as a result of the worship of market forces, of any ethical values in media save naked profitability.

COMPARING MEDIA GLOBALLY:
A DIFFERENT APPROACH

In this section, we will examine some lessons that can be drawn from the now extinct Soviet Russian media system in order to understand media internationally, rather than basing our examination on a single nation. The system lasted, in different forms, from the revolution late in 1917 to December 25, 1991, when the last Soviet president, Mikhail Gorbachev, formally signed a document dissolving the Soviet Union. Many people would agree that some of the USSR's principal features persisted well after that date, with new private banks supplanting the old Communist Party as media bosses. However, although the Soviet media system is extinct in its original form, its history has a lot to contribute to our understanding of media elsewhere in the world.

First, as noted, Soviet media had a strong overlap with media under other dictatorships and with so-called development media. As an illustration, in the first 40 years of Taiwan's existence as an entity separate from mainland China, following the end of Japanese colonial rule in 1945, the media system of Taiwan was that of a dictatorial one-party state (whose leader, Chiang Kai-shek, had been schooled in Soviet Russia). Chiang Kai-shek was fiercely opposed to Communism, but that certainly did not mean he gave his own media any freedom. Another example is India, which was not a dictatorship like Taiwan but a country where, until the beginning of the 1990s, broadcast media were government-owned in the name of national development and unity, and where the Soviet model of the state as the basic agency of economic development had held sway ever since independence from British rule in 1947. Thus the study of Soviet Russian media throws light on a variety of the world's media systems.

Second, those of us who live in economically advanced and politically stable countries are in a poor position to understand how media work on much of the rest of the planet. Most if not all of what we read is about research based on the United States or Britain, two nations with a considerable shared culture and the same majority language. We have little information even about media in Canada, France, Germany, Italy, or Japan—the other members of the elite Group of Eight (G8) countries—and least of all about Russia, the odd-man-out number 8 that is, as I will argue below, much more like the world at large.

In the world at large, issues of extreme poverty, economic crisis, political instability even to the point of civil war, turbulent insurgent movements, military or other authoritarian regimes, and violent repression of political dissent are the central context of media. To pretend that we can generalize about what all media are by just studying U.S. or British media, or even just media in the G8 countries minus Russia, is wildly silly. Statements such as "broadcasting is . . ." or "the Internet is . . ." or "newspapers are . . ." are inaccurate, however authoritative they may look at first glance—not because "every country is a bit different," but because of the major factors named at the beginning of this paragraph.

To be sure, some countries not in G8 are politically stable and economically affluent (Denmark and New Zealand, for example), even some crisis-torn nations have many positive dimensions that offset their acute problems (the Congo and Indonesia, for example). The media of affluent countries spend so little time on the constructive dimensions of other nations that the average media user in those countries can be forgiven up to a point for being unaware that there are any. But to return to the basic point here: Russia, the outsider in the G8 group, is a valuable entry point for understanding media in the world at large and thus for avoiding being imprisoned in superficial assumptions about what media are. I have argued this case elsewhere in much more detail than can be offered here (Downing, 1996), but let us see why, at least in outline.

At least the four following important issues must be considered—namely, how we understand the relation of mainstream media to (1) political power, (2) economic crisis, (3) dramatic social transitions, and (4) small-scale alternative media (such as samizdat, a term explained below). Each of the Russian examples below offers a contrast case to the usual U.S./U.K. profile of media and provokes a basic question about media in capitalist democracies.

Political Power

The relation between political power and Communist media always seemed a no-brainer. Communist media were seen as simple mirror-opposites of media in the West. Communism equaled repression and censorship, in the name of a forlorn ideal of justice, but capitalist democracy (the West) won out in the end, and over the years 1989–1991 the whole Communist system foundered, never to return. Soviet media were the favorite counterexample for proving what was right with Western media.

Now, it is indeed true that state control over media was extremely detailed in Soviet Russia, even more so than in some other dictatorships. The Communist Party's Propaganda Committee established ideological priorities. Its cell-groups in every newspaper, magazine, publishing house, and broadcast channel kept a close watch over any subversive tendencies. Media executives were chosen from a list of party members who had proven their loyalty. And the KGB (the political police) would quickly intervene if any trouble seemed evident or imminent. With all this, the official censorship body, known as Glavlit, had relatively little to do. Typewriters were licensed by the state, and a copy of the characters produced on paper by their keys—which were always slightly out of sync and therefore could be used to identify where a subversive document had originated—was on file with the local KGB. When photocopy machines came into use, access to them was governed in microscopic detail. Bugging technology was one of the most advanced aspects of Soviet industry.

This outrageous and unnerving machinery of control over communication did not, in the end, win. Many factors served to subvert it, including samizdat media (see below). But one factor perhaps was the least controllable of all—namely, the extreme difficulty of producing media that were credible or interesting inside this straitjacket. Communist Party members read *Pravda* (The Truth) daily because they knew they were expected to, not because they were convinced it was factually informative. People in general expected authentic news to arrive by conversational rumor, and honest opinion by samizdat. Only if that rumor confirmed what Soviet media announced did many people take the latter as reliable (and then only on the given topic).

Thus in the later decades of the Soviet system in Russia a dual-level public realm developed: official truths that the media blared out, that everyone mouthed, and that few believed; and an unofficial realism that was the stuff of everyday private conversation or samizdat. When Gorbachev came to power in 1985, intent on reform, he gradually introduced a new degree of frankness and directness in media (the famous glasnost policy), intended to reduce the gap between these two levels.

This media credibility dilemma is a significant one in any dictatorship. And perhaps the longer the dictatorship lasts, the worse the dilemma.

Question for Stable, Affluent Nations. The fascinating contrast is with the relatively ready trust in mainstream media, the bulk of which are owned by very large and unaccountable capitalist firms. Were Soviet media so bluntly and clumsily controlled that skepticism was a self-evident response? Are Western media sufficiently subtle, flexible, and savvy so that their message is much more attractive and their plausibility much tougher to question?

Economic Crisis

Economic crisis was a daily experience for the majority of Russians, especially from the time of the Soviet bloc's collapse up to the time of writing this essay, but it had been gathering momentum from the early 1980s onward. It continues to be a daily experience of citizens in many of the world's nations, including the impoverished sectors within the other G8 countries. The "Structural Adjustment Policies" of the International Monetary Fund, as the IMF so abstractly termed them over the 1980s and 1990s, blighted the lives of untold hundreds of millions in the countries to which the fund applied its ruthless capitalist logic. The health and housing and education prospects of children, women, the aged, peasant farmers, and slum dwellers have been sacrificed to the dictates of debt repayment to international banks, to the point that great chunks of national income go back to the banks in interest payments instead of to the public (cf. Nielsen 1995; Peabody 1996; Stein 1995; Weisbrot 1997).

"It's their governments' fault," cry the public relations specialists of the banks and the IMF, holding up their holy hands in pious denial. Their denial blots out the banks' full knowledge of what kind of governments they were dealing with at the time they contracted the loans in question: kleptocracies, or thief regimes, that spend a good chunk of the loan on themselves, and another chunk on buying weapons from the West's arms factories to put down civil unrest directed against their rule—or to manufacture wars with their neighbors in order to divert attention from their own abuses.

The Soviet and post–Soviet Russian experience of economic crisis has been profound, except during the 1970s and early 1980s, when oil revenues shot up on the world market. But during the 1990s, Russian life expectancy actually fell, which in turn meant that infant mortality increased, for the death rate among children under one year old is the prime factor in average life expectancy. Once again, among the G8 countries, Russia is the exception that stands in for much of the rest of the planet. Russian media, until the last few years of the old Soviet Union, were silent about this decline in living standards and stagnation in productivity and asserted that the capitalist countries were suffering from acute and irremediable economic problems. In the post–Soviet period, Russian media have often found it easier to point the finger at the IMF—not, it must be said, without reason—than to take aim at the Russian kleptocracy as well.

How do media in general deal with these economic crises? Do they explore them or avoid them? Do they blame them on distant scapegoats? On the IMF if theirs is the country affected? Or on Third World governments if they are in an affluent nation? Or on domestic scapegoats—immigrants, Gypsies, Chinese, Jews, refugees, Muslims?

Question for Stable, Affluent Nations. How thoroughly do media really explain economic crisis? How well do they explain strategies to deal with it that do not hit the poor and poorest much harder than the wealthy? Although global indices indicated that living standards in the United States in the 1990s were remarkably high and crisis was remote, wages had fallen way below what they were in real terms during the 1960s. Typically both parents had to work full-time to retain a stable income level, and single-parent households, a sizable proportion of the total number of households, mostly struggled to get by. The U.S. media at the turn of the millennium suggested universal prosperity, but the facts suggested a slow-burning invisible crisis, one in which the public, despite working many hours, was mostly one or two paychecks away from "welfare," a racially defined form of public humiliation that few embraced if they could avoid it. When did you last see a TV program or watch an ad or read a newspaper that got into these realities in a way that struck you?

Dramatic Social Transitions

The third issue is the relation of media to dramatic social transitions. Russia went through many transitions in the 20th century, beginning with the disastrous World War I, which opened the way to the 1917 revolution and the three-year civil war that followed the revolution. Next came the tyrannical and savage uprooting of Russian and Ukrainian farmers in 1928–1933 and Stalin's ongoing terror and vast prison camp population. Then came the loss of 20 to 25 million lives in the war against Hitler in 1941–1945, the severe economic disruptions of Gorbachev's attempt to reform the system in the late 1980s, and the economic chaos of the 1990s. This is a dimension that, with the exception of the two world wars, has not characterized the affluent nations' experience, but once again Russian experience in this regard has been much more characteristic of the world's. Colonial rule, invasion, war, vast social movements, civil war, entrenched ethnic conflicts, wrenching changes of government, and dictatorships were common experiences across the planet. Media in Russia also went through many transitions during the 20th century. Let us briefly note them.

Before the revolution, there was an active newspaper, magazine, and book industry, but it was restricted to people who could read, perhaps a quarter of the population at most, and they were nearly all concentrated in towns. Furthermore, the imperial censorship made it very risky indeed for anyone to print anything directly critical of the czars. Jail or exile in frozen Siberia were standard penalties for challenging the status quo, which included, during the war against Germany in 1914–1917, any criticism of the slaughter into which many Russian generals forced their troops. Came the revolution, the Bolshevik leadership sought peace with Germany, and criticism of the old status quo was everywhere. Literacy campaigns began, in part to enable the new revolutionary regime to get its message across. This was the first media transition.

At the time of the revolution, the arts in Russia were in ferment and had been for more than a decade. Some of the most inventive and spectacular artistic work in Europe was being done by a new generation of Russian artists. For the first 10 years or so of the revolutionary era, these artists were actively encouraged by the new regime to express their talents in theater, advertising, public campaigns, cinema, photography, and music, along with painting and sculpture. Russian media were on the cutting edge, especially in the then newer technologies of cinema and photography. However, with the rise of Stalin to power as Soviet dictator, this innovative work was shoved aside in the name of "Soviet progress." Those who did not bend to the new orthodoxy suffered at least disgrace and, at worst, prison camps or even death. This was the second media transition.

Next, for a period of about 25 years until Stalin's death in 1953, Russian media marched to the dictator's tread, looking neither right nor left. Not only did they follow the official line unwaveringly, but their language was also wooden, saturated with political jargon, endlessly grinding out the messages given them from above. Whenever the official line changed—when Stalin suddenly signed a pact in 1939 with the Nazi regime; when the Nazis invaded in 1941; when the United States supported the USSR in the Lend-Lease program; when, in the aftermath of the Nazis' defeat, Stalin annexed three Baltic and five east-central European countries, along with a chunk of eastern Germany; when Stalin began a comprehensive anti-Semitic campaign in the years just before he died—each time the media instantly changed their tune to support the switch. George Orwell's famous novel *1984* conveys some of the flavor of the way that media during the Cold War massaged such 180-degree reversals, including the World War II portrayal of Stalin in U.S. media as "friendly Uncle Joe" and the redefinition of him as a monster after the war.

In the decade that followed Stalin's death, some Russian media professionals made cautious attempts to open up the media, with intermittent encouragement from Khrushchev, Stalin's successor. A famous short novel, Aleksandr Solzhenitsyn's *One Day in the Life of Ivan Denisovich,* was the first publication of anything about the vast prison camp system Stalin had brought into being. It was in some ways the high point of the attempt to open up the media system, even just a little, but in 1964 Khrushchev was thrown out of office and the lid was jammed back on Russian media. Some other brave dissidents who tried to publish works critical of the regime were sentenced to long terms of hard labor in highly publicized trials meant to scare off any would-be imitators. Another media transition.

Only in the mid-1980s, as the Russian economic system began to grind to a halt, was there a push in favor of media reform, the glasnost era, led by the USSR's last leader, Mikhail Gorbachev. This ultimately led to an avalanche of media, which challenged the long-established status quo, even to the point, eventually, of attacking the original revolution in 1917 and thus the very foundations of the Soviet system. A further media transition.

Finally, after the collapse of the USSR in 1991, yet another media transition emerged: a print media sector that was mostly allowed to follow its own path and commercial dictates; a TV sector that was under heavy government surveillance and control; and a radio sector somewhere between. Independent media existed to a greater extent than under the Soviet regime, but Russians were still largely deprived of anything approaching a genuinely democratic media system.

This postage-stamp account of Russian media in the 20th century has shown the significant transitions through which they passed. Again, in much of the world, such wrenching changes in media have been an everyday experience. Many specifics might vary, but the Russian type of experience is not unique. In the stable nations of the West, with the exception of the Nazi era in Europe, this kind of experience of media was foreign. But we cannot take that minority experience as typical. If we are to think intelligently about media, the Russian experience is much more the norm. To assume that a particular media system is permanent or normal, that transition is not inherent in media, flies in the face of the media experience of most of humankind in the 20th century.

Question for Stable, Affluent Nations. Media seem so familiar, so much part of the landscape, so central in the way we entertain ourselves, that even rapidly changing delivery technologies—fiber optic cables, compression technologies, digitization, satellites—seem to promise only sexy new options. Yet what does the bewilderingly rapid concentration of media ownership into the hands of giant transnational corporations mean for our media future (Bagdikian, 2000; McChesney, 1999)? Is citizen influence over media, despite being an obvious necessity for a true democracy, due to dwindle slowly and imperceptibly away to nothing? We are in the midst of our own media transition, and we had better find out. And watch out.

Small-Scale Alternative Media

I have made several references to the term *samizdat media*. The term refers to the hand-circulated pamphlets, poems, essays, plays, short stories, novels, and, at a later stage, audio- and videocassettes *(magnitizdat)* that began to emerge in Soviet Russia and later in other Soviet bloc countries from the 1960s onward. They contained material that was banned by the Soviet regimes. Writing, distributing, or possessing these materials carried sentences in hard-labor camps. Samizdat contained widely varied messages—some religious, some nationalist, some eco-logical, some reformist, some revising the myths of official Soviet history, some at-tacking Soviet policies, some defending citizens victimized by arbitrary arrest and imprisonment. The term *samizdat* literally means "self-published," in contra-distinction to state-published, that is, approved by the Soviet regime as "safe."

These micromedia took a long time to make a dent in the Soviet system—more than a generation. But their impact was extraordinary, for up until the last year of the USSR, even when the east-central European regimes had already shaken off Soviet rule, the Soviet Union appeared to be one of those facts of life institutions that few observers imagined could collapse. Those Russians, Ukraini-ans, Poles, and others who labored over those decades to create samizdat, and of-ten paid a heavy price in jail for their pains, showed amazing spirit, determination, and foresight. They were aided by the foreign shortwave radio stations that broad-cast in the region's languages into Soviet bloc territory: the BBC World Service, Radio Liberty, Radio Free Europe, Deutsche Welle, and Voice of America. These stations would read samizdat texts over the air as part of their programming and thus amplified their message outside the major urban centers, which were nor-mally the only places where samizdat was circulated. Sometimes the Soviet bloc governments jammed their broadcasts but not always.

Historically and comparatively, small-scale radical media of this kind have been common (Downing, 2001). They have been used in the United States from the time of the War of Independence through the abolitionist and suffragist move-ments to the civil rights and the anti–Vietnam War movements. Yet their signifi-cant role in slowly rotting away at Soviet power flags their importance in devel-oping our own definition *media*. All too often, we mistake size and speed for significance, as if they were the only way that media can wield power. In relation to the dizzying speed with which transnational corporations are merging media ownership, it is all too easy to slip into a fatalistic acceptance that these colossuses are too much for us to take on. Yet the samizdat story and its parallels in many other parts of the world suggest a diametrically different conclusion.

Question for Stable, Affluent Nations. The Internet greatly expanded citi-zens' communication options in economically advanced nations during the 1990s. Can it (a) be extended to lots of ordinary citizens outside those nations and (b) be preserved from virtually total corporate control? Corporate control can take var-ious forms—for example, charging long-distance phone tariffs to Internet users, putting ever higher prices on access to informational Web sites, and reserving high bandwidth access to corporate users or wealthy clients. Can this trend be fought off successfully?

CONCLUSIONS

I set out in this essay to challenge the easy assumption that by studying media in just the United States or Britain, the currently dominant nations in media research publication, we can manage to "draw a bead" on media. In a deliberate paradox, I selected what seems to be a closed chapter in recent history—namely, the story of Soviet media—to illustrate some heavy-duty media issues that conventional theories fail to get in their sights. But, as I argued, those media issues are common in most of the contemporary world. I also argued that, in certain ways, they direct our attention back to pivotal media issues even in stable, affluent nations. Global comparisons need to be central to media research.

For more information on the topics that appear in this chapter, use the password that came free with this book to access InfoTrac College Edition. Use the following words as keyterms and subject searches: mass communication theories, normative theories, participatory media, Communist media, social transitions, alternative media.

QUESTIONS FOR DISCUSSION

1. What are the chief problems with deontic, or normative, theories of media?

2. Why does a study of Russian media, whether during or since the 1917–1991 Soviet era, help us understand our own media system more clearly?

3. How do our own news media present economic crises, either at home or in other parts of the planet?

4. What roles do media play in the sometimes wrenching process of transition from one type of government to another (for example, from a military government to a civilian one)?

5. What roles may alternative or underground media play in energizing active democracy and social movements?

REFERENCES

Bagdikian, B. (2000) *The media monopoly* (6th ed.). Boston: Beacon Press.

Blendon, R. J. (1995). Health care reform: The press failed to inform the public of alternative strategies. *Nieman Reports, 49*(3), 17–19.

Downing, J. (1996). *Internationalizing media theory: Transition, power, culture: Reflections on media in Russia, Poland, and Hungary, 1980–95.* London: Sage.

Downing, J. (2001). *Radical media: Rebellious communication and social movements.* Thousand Oaks, CA: Sage.

Fallows, J. (1996). *Breaking the news: How the media undermine American democracy.* New York: Pantheon.

McChesney, R. (1999). *Rich media, poor democracy.* Urbana: University of Illinois Press.

McQuail, D. (1994). *Mass communication theory: An introduction* (3rd ed.). London: Sage.

Nielsen, K. (1995). Industrial policy and structural adjustment: A case of planned versus creeping institutional change. *American Behavioral Scientist, 38*(5), 716–740.

Peabody, J. W. (1996). Economic reform and health sector policy: Lessons from structural adjustment programs. *Social Science and Medicine, 43*(5), 823–835.

Siebert, F., Peterson, T., & Schramm, W. (1956). *Four theories of the press*. Urbana: University of Illinois Press.

Stein, H. (Ed.). (1995). *Asian industrialization and Africa: Studies in policy alternatives to structural adjustment*. New York: St. Martin's Press.

Weisbrot, M. (1997). Structural adjustment in Haiti. *Monthly Review, 48*(8), 25–39.

3

❂

Global Economy
and International
Telecommunications
·Networks

HARMEET SAWHNEY

Harmeet Sawhney (PhD, University of Texas at Austin) is an associate professor in the Department of Telecommunications, Indiana University, Bloomington. He works on issues related to telecommunications infrastructure planning and policy. His research has been published in a variety of academic journals, including *Journal of Broadcasting and Electronic Media; Media, Culture, and Society;* and *Telecommunications Policy.* He is currently serving as the deputy editor of *The Information Society* journal.

We often hear the term *global economy* in news accounts of distant events such as Asian financial crises, International Monetary Fund loans, and free trade agreements. However, the global economy is not an abstraction. It affects our lives in personal ways. If we look at just the things that clothe our body at any point in time, we are likely to encounter products from all over the world. In my case, at the time I first wrote these words, I was wearing a shirt from Sri Lanka, pants from the United States, sandals from Mexico, a watch from Korea, and glasses from France. If we look beyond our personal possessions, we

For additional online resources, access the Global Media Monitor Web site that accompanies this book on the Wadsworth Communication Cafe Web site at http://communication.wadsworth.com.

will see that the influence of the global economy percolates down to the most mundane of our everyday activities. The price of gas is determined by global oil markets, the ups and downs of interest rates are prompted by global money flows, and the availability of jobs is greatly affected by activities of global corporations.

The global economy is also closely related to global communication, the focus of this book. They are inseparably intertwined, for the global economy requires global communication to control and coordinate global division of labor. To fully comprehend the relationship between the two, we will first look at the world before the advent of the industrial revolution. That will help us understand how global division of labor has transformed the world and in the process given birth to both the global economy and global communications.

PREMODERN WORLD

In the thirteenth century, the world was very different from the world of today. Among other things, the personal possessions of our predecessors were all made locally—not in a town 100 miles away but in the town or village one actually lived in. Foreign products were extremely rare. The only people who had access to them were kings, queens, and the rich. Even then, foreign products were basically exotic items—such as gems, silks, and spices—that were easy to transport because of their light weight and yet were of high value. Everyday goods were made by local shoemakers, tailors, blacksmiths, wheelwrights, goldsmiths, and other such artisans and craftsmen who worked more or less independently. For example, a shoemaker, working in a workshop next to his cottage, would process the leather, cut it, create the sole and the upper, stitch the different pieces together, make a lace and insert it into the eyelets to make a complete shoe. The shoe thus created would be custom-made and hence tailored to each customer's feet. However, since he had to do everything by himself from beginning to end, he would be able to make a limited number of shoes per day.

DIVISION OF LABOR

One of the things that distinguished the modern world from the premodern world was the extent to which division of labor was used in the production process. With division of labor, the shoemakers in a town no longer work independently at their own workshops. They instead work together as a group in a factory. Shoemaker A processes the leather, shoemaker B creates the sole, shoemaker C crafts the uppers, shoemaker D stitches the shoe together, and shoemaker E makes the lace and puts it into the eyelets. The overall number of shoes produced in the town will grow exponentially as division of labor creates specialization that in turn increases efficiency. Because shoemaker A only processes the leather day in and day out, he becomes an expert in leather processing and thereby is able to greatly enhance his output per day. Similarly with specialization, the expertise of shoemakers B, C, D, and E increases, and correspondingly, so does the overall output of shoes.

The flip side to division of labor is that it creates interdependencies. Whereas in the old system shoemaker A could wake up whenever he wanted and start working whenever it suited his mood, the new system based on division of labor requires coordination. All five shoemakers have to work in sync with each other. Even if just one of them performs suboptimally, the entire production process will slow down. Just imagine a situation where shoemaker B develops a tendency to be slow in the morning and fast in the afternoon. This skewed pattern will create a serious problem if shoemakers A, C, D, and E continue to work steadily throughout the day. Therefore the interdependencies created by the division of labor require coordination and control to keep the production going smoothly.

In many ways, division of labor is a devil's bargain. It increases productivity via specialization, which in turn creates problems of coordination and control. In the early stages of the industrial revolution, division of labor was first employed on a small scale in small factories. The problems created by division of labor were taken care of by managers who coordinated and controlled the activities of individual workers performing specialized tasks. In the shoe factory mentioned above, the manager would walk around the factory floor, keep track of the performance of each worker, and give his instructions to them to make sure they all worked in sync with each other. Within the confined space of a factory, coordination and control problems can be handled on a face-to-face level, but these problems become more severe when division of labor occurs across geographical space as companies seek to capitalize on the locational advantage of each place.

Henry Ford's automobile factory in Dearborn, Michigan, was a huge establishment employing more than 10,000 workers. It was said that iron, rubber, and sand went in from one end and the finished car came out from the other end. In other words, Ford made almost all the components of his car in the same factory. However, when business owners started realizing that some components could be made more cheaply in other parts of the country, they moved away from centralized production—for example, horns were made in Indiana, steering wheels in Ohio, and brakes in Illinois. The reasons for lower costs could vary from easier access to raw materials to availability of skilled labor to lower real estate costs. These days division of labor has even spilled over beyond national boundaries. In a modern car company, one component may be made in Korea, another in India, yet another in Brazil, and so on, and the final car assembled in the United States. All this would not be possible without the whole array of modern communication technologies, ranging from fiber optics to satellites.

Thus we see that the global division of labor is intricately tied to modern communication technologies. While telecommunications technologies allow for global coordination and control, transportation technologies move raw materials and products from one corner of the world to another. Whereas global trade in the past was limited to lightweight items, today tons of steels, oil, grain, and other commodities are routinely moved across the world. These movements affect not only the consumption of luxuries by the wealthy, as in the past, but also the consumption of everyday items by the common people.

The above discussion explains the changes brought about by global economy, global division of labor, and global communication in a purely conceptual way, as if they were abstract phenomena. These transformations, however, actually took place in the real world of international politics. In order to comprehend their impact on our own lives, we need to understand the historical context within which they occurred. The next section provides an overview of how the world changed with the rise of the industrial powers.

IMPERIALISM

In the 13th century, the world was multipolar. Multiple centers of power—China, Egypt, India, Italy, Iraq, and others—dominated decentralized trading circuits. Figure 3.1 captures the overall structure of the world system. Although most of the trading took place within each of the trading circuits, they were not isolated from one another. For example, considerable evidence suggests that India and Italy traded with one another via Egypt and Iraq. The world was interconnected but in a loosely coupled way.

The picture changed dramatically with the emergence of Portuguese, Spanish, Dutch, French, and British empires in the 14th and 15th centuries. The Western powers transformed the multipolar world into a monopolar one (Figure 3.2). The development of science in western European countries gave them technologically superior weaponry, such as guns, that simply overwhelmed the indigenous people of Africa, America, Asia, and Australia, who were still fighting with bows and arrows. Therefore the relatively small western European countries could subjugate other nations with much larger populations. Their empires were vast as they spanned the globe. It was said that the sun never set on the British Empire; that is, its empire was so extensive and far-flung that the sun was always shining on some part of its holdings. Britain alone controlled about a quarter of the world's landmass. In addition, the French, Spaniards, Portuguese, Dutch, and others had their own empires. This was the era of imperialism.

These new empires were not like earlier ones in history. First, they were far-flung and disjointed, unlike the old empires, which were created through the conquest of neighboring countries. For example, when Genghis Khan stirred the spirit of the Mongols in the 13th century, they went on to conquer China, central Asia, and Iraq and swept into Europe as far as Hungary. Because these empires were contiguous, the cultural differences between the conquerors and the conquered were relatively small, though significant. Although the Iraqis may not have liked the Mongols, they at least knew who they were. On the other hand, in the 16th century, the Aztecs knew hardly anything about their conquerors, the Spaniards. To them, they might as well have been aliens from another planet.

Second, the economic relationship between the imperial powers and the subject territories changed in the age of imperialism. Although this relationship has always been an exploitative one, the nature of exploitation was different now. In the past, exploitation consisted of plunder and tribute. The conquerors simply smashed the palaces and temples and took away gold, jewels, and other precious materials. In addition, they extracted tribute in the form of gifts, grain, or taxes every year. Although this form of exploitation still existed in the new empires, it was minor relative to what took place through the commercial means.

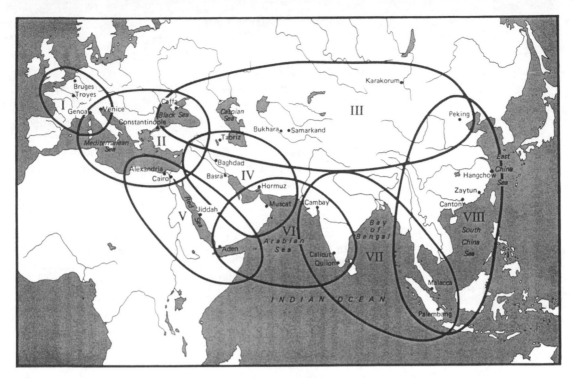

FIGURE 3-1 The Eight Circuits of the 13th-century World System.
From *Before European Hegemony* by Janet L. Abu-Lughod. Copyright
© 1989 by Oxford University Press, Inc. Used by permission of Oxford
University Press, Inc.

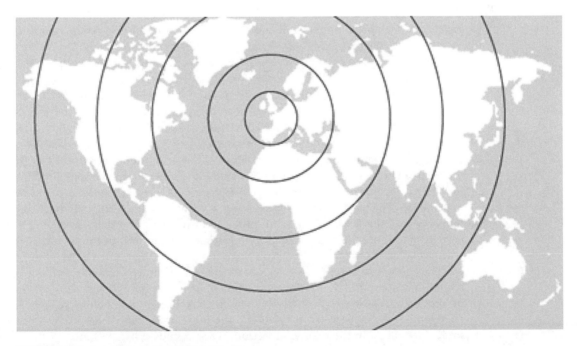

FIGURE 3-2 Euro-centered Monopolar World

One of the main reasons the imperial powers were interested in acquiring colonies was to gain access to raw materials for their growing industries. These industries needed cotton, rubber, tin, jute, indigo, and a whole range of other raw materials. After conquering new territory, the imperial powers soon set up plantations and mines and the means for transporting the raw materials to the factories in the mother country, especially railroads after they were invented. Once the raw materials were processed into finished goods, the empires used the colonies as captive markets for selling their factories' outputs. The colonies were thereby squeezed both ways as suppliers of cheap raw materials and captive markets for finished products.

How did the imperial powers maintain their control over their colonial possessions? It is important to ponder on this question before we start discussing contemporary global communications issues, because the past provides a good backdrop for understanding the present. Quite obviously, brute military power played a critical role in the creation and maintenance of empires. At the same time, a number of more subtle strategies were employed. One of them was to co-opt the native elite into the colonial administrative apparatus by educating them in the Western ways and then giving them positions of privilege in the administrative hierarchy. This co-opted class of people spoke the language of the colonial masters, attended schools modeled on European schools, went to the mother country for higher education, and in many other ways acquired European habits of the mind. At times, the effort to impose European culture on colonial subjects went beyond the native elites to the masses. The logic behind this strategy was quite simple: people who are culturally closer to the mother country than their own native traditions are less likely to revolt.

The imperial administrations also hampered collaboration among native groups so as to forestall the emergence of united opposition to colonial rule. On the one hand, they would often use the divide-and-conquer strategy and manipulate historical animosities among native groups to weaken potential opposition. On the other hand, administrators would create structural barriers among native groups with shared affinities to prevent any joint action by them. With this dynamic in mind, it is instructive to note certain characteristics of the global telegraph network that the British used to manage their vast empire (Figure 3.3). First, the network was totally London-centric, as telegraph lines from all over the empire converged onto the imperial capital. Second, lateral lines were rare. If people at any two points in the empire wanted to communicate with each other, they had to do so through London even if they were geographically adjacent to each other. This configuration is a classic structural characteristic of relationships between the power center and subjugated periphery. Typically, in a center-periphery relation, the center encourages centralized relationships and discourages lateral ones.

The above discussion sets the stage for us to examine the complexities of global communications. Today, in the eyes of many scholars, we have moved from an era of imperialism to one of electronic imperialism. Although this analogy suggests a degree of similarity between the past and the present, the word *electronic* suggests some differences. In the following section, we will study what they are.

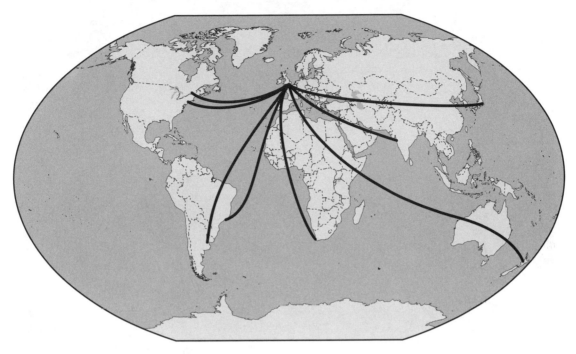

FIGURE 3-3 London-centric Telegraph Network

ELECTRONIC IMPERIALISM

Electronic imperialism is a broad concept that can encompass a wide range of issues. Here we will focus on two major issues—global media flows and international trade in services—so that we can attain a certain depth in our discussions.

Global Media Flows

After World War II, the age of imperialism came to an end as the colonies won independence one by one. The center of the world also moved across the Atlantic to the United States. The world was for the most part still monocentric (Figure 3.4). However, the way the center projected power over the periphery was qualitatively different.

The main source of U.S. power was its economic rather than its military strength even though the importance of the latter should not be discounted. Although the United States did not formally have an empire, in many quarters, the present world order, dominated by the United States, is believed to be no different. The only difference is that today the center—the United States—projects its power not brazenly, as imperial powers did in the days of gunboat diplomacy, but subtly through economic and more lately cultural means. Even if one does not agree with this point of view, one needs to be cognizant of it because it colors all discussions on global communication.

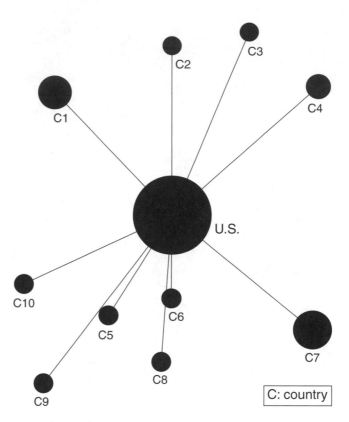

FIGURE 3-4
U.S.-centered
World System

Many scholars argue that although the formal empires have been dissolved, the global political structures created during the age of imperialism remain in place. These structures create a relationship of dependency between the rich and the poor countries (Galtung, 1971; McPhail, 1981; Schiller, 1969). For example, in Africa, even today, a telephone call to a neighboring country is often made via London or Paris or some other former imperial capital. This pattern of global communications is similar to the British telegraph network—monocentric with few lateral connections. The African telephone networks are basically a legacy of colonial times. Today the United States is the center, and we see a similar pattern with modern communication flows—films, TV programs, and other such cultural products.

The United States overwhelmingly dominates the cinema and television screens all over the world. No other country even comes near the U.S. presence on the world's electronic entertainment stage. Hollywood is correspondingly one of the top three export industries of the United States, generating more than $8 billion of trade surplus in theatrical films alone. The United States therefore tends to look at its media exports in purely business terms and argues that they are no different from other products.

Other countries, however, do not view films as simply a product, or Hollywood as simply an industry. They are more concerned about the cultural influence of films, fearing that imported films will shape people's attitudes and perceptions in accordance with alien ideas and values. In the developing countries, these fears are deeply rooted in their colonial experience, when their colonial masters imposed their language and culture on them. Developing nations consider the import of U.S. films to be a new kind of invasion—cultural invasion—that is more subtle and insidious. One can debate whether or not these fears and perceptions have any merit, depending on one's overall political position. Yet, one cannot ignore the fact that rich countries such as Canada and France share the concerns of developing countries about U.S. cultural dominance. Their stance on "electronic imperialism" gives the concerns of the developing nations some credence and suggests that those concerns do not stem from pure paranoia.

In fact, when we look at the global communication flows, we can easily see that they are disproportionately from the United States (the center) to the rest of the world (the periphery). The flow in the other direction and lateral flow between periphery countries is small. Critics have dubbed this pattern of communication *one-way flow*. In the 1970s a major debate began about this imbalance in global information flows. Many nations called for a new world information order (NWIO) that would change this asymmetrical pattern and make it more balanced. This idea sounds quite attractive as an abstraction but creates serious problems when implementation is attempted. First, it encourages regulation of information flows by governments, often undemocratic, which might attempt to control the national media for their own domestic political purposes. The NWIO would give them another excuse for their nefarious designs. Second, even if that is acceptable, regulating electronic communication flows is becoming increasingly difficult as the technology becomes ever more elusive to control.

The United States has been dead against the NWIO because it goes against the First Amendment to the U.S. Constitution, which guarantees freedom of the press. The United States not only opposes the NWIO but also pleads helplessness because the First Amendment makes it impossible for the government to legally do anything about it. However, some scholars have offered some thoughtful criticism of the First Amendment. They point out that it was written more than two centuries ago, when ordinary citizens could enter the newspaper business because the cost of setting up a printing press was low. In effect, ordinary citizens had a voice in the public forum or at least access to a mouthpiece. The newspapers and the electronic media have gradually become concentrated into large conglomerates as the media business has become exceedingly capital intensive. Ordinary citizens no longer have easy access to media, and now essentially a top-down communication, or one-way flow, situation exists even within the United States. In many ways the U.S. hinterlands have been colonized by Los Angeles and New York. In these current circumstances, the First Amendment basically protects the corporations that own the media rather than free speech itself (Carey, 1989; Innis, 1951; Schiller, 1974). What good is free speech when only a few people own loudspeakers? When we look at the current global situation, we can ask the same question: what good is a free flow of information when only a few countries have loudspeakers?

We see here a tussle between the First Amendment and its critics. The debate takes place within the backdrop of past colonial experience that has colored the responses of developing countries, which see a new threat to their sovereignty in the free flow of information.

Transborder Data Flow

Although the tensions are overt in the case of global flow of cultural products, similar, less obvious problems exist in other realms of international trade. With the improvement in transportation technologies, the international trade progressively moved beyond lightweight, high-value items to heavier and bulkier commodities. However, services such as accounting, insurance, and advertising remained local for the most part.

One of the main reasons that services changed little was that they required an intense amount of interaction between the service provider and the consumer. They were not like a product one could pick off a store shelf without ever knowing the manufacturer personally. The accountant could provide help only if the client shared the relevant information. Furthermore, this sharing of information took place over multiple interactions, because the accountant had to query the client often for additional information and clarification. Because this interaction previously took place mainly in person, the production and consumption of services were restricted to a small area. Modern communication and information technologies have radically changed all this. First, a computer software package such as Quicken can often perform functions that only a trained human being could previously do in person. Second, modern telecommunications networks can support a level of interaction between the service provider and the client that could be achieved only face-to-face in the past. The service provider and the client need no longer be in the same place. Even though they are at great distance from each other, even halfway around the world, they can do business via email, fax, and other communication technologies. These technological developments finally made even services tradable.

The trade in services assumes a great importance in the global economy. As the global division of labor has progressed, the manufacturing jobs have moved overseas from the United States to developing countries, where labor costs are much cheaper. This movement of industry across the globe in search of locational advantage is in many ways an extension of what happened in the United States. Earlier, the auto parts suppliers moved out of Detroit to other locations that offered a comparative advantage in either labor or raw materials costs. Today the same process is happening across national boundaries. The transportation and communications technologies, which made this dispersal possible within a country, are now making it possible across the world. In this new world of international division of labor, the United States is increasingly emerging as a world headquarters of sorts (Figure 3.5). While the corporations are moving the manufacturing facilities overseas, they are investing more and more in research and development, corporate services, management, and other coordination and control activities in the United States. The United States has thereby become the command and control node for global business activities.

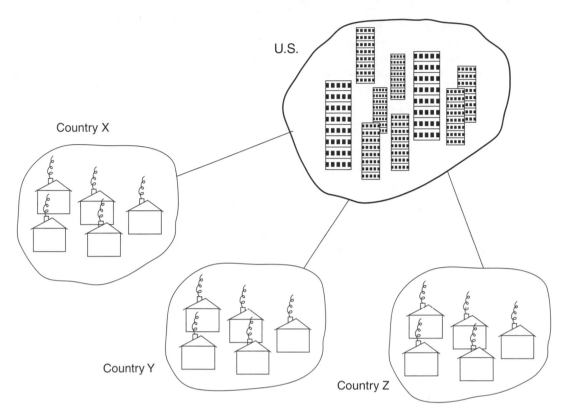

FIGURE 3-5 The United States as a World Headquarters

The perspectives and interests of the United States and the developing countries are quite different on issues related to the global economy. The United States favors both free trade and free flow of information. It promotes free trade because free trade leads to ever-increasing global division of labor as businesses keep seeking locations with cost advantages, which in turn increases overall productivity. At the same time, because the increasing division of labor leads to increasing interdependency, the United States also favors free flow of information, mostly over computer networks, to ensure coordination and control among the specialized units located in different parts of the world. For example, a large corporation like Proctor and Gamble needs unimpeded communication between its computers in its Cincinnati headquarters and those in its plants all over the world in order to operate a global enterprise successfully. This computer-to-computer communication across national boundaries is known as transborder data flow (TDF). From a purely business point of view, it is absolutely essential for the global corporations that this information flow take place in an unhindered manner.

The developing countries, on the other hand, have a different point of view. They are suspicious of both free trade and free flow of communication. They are suspicious of free trade because free trade among unequals more often than not leads to the exploitation of the weaker countries, which get relegated to being the source of cheap raw materials and labor for low value–added manufacturing activities. Furthermore, the structural relationships that develop leave them in a position of almost permanent dependency. If one were to use the brain-brawn analogy, the industrialized countries remain the brains of the world system and the developing countries the brawn. Finally, although the greater division of labor facilitated by free trade leads to greater productivity, there is no guarantee that the additional wealth thus generated will be shared equitably among the countries. In the case of the factory, which can be considered to be the cradle of division of labor, history has shown that the owners appropriate a disproportionate share of the additional wealth produced by specialization and leave the ordinary workers poorly compensated for their labor. A similar process is seen on the global scale. The industrialized countries take a disproportionate share of wealth generated by global division of labor, leaving the developing countries poorly rewarded for their contributions. Often, this exploitation does not take place in an overt manner but in many subtle ways. Among other things, all the high value–added activities like consultancy, advertising, research and development, and others take place in industrialized countries, and thereby a disproportionate part of the wealth created stays there.

This suspicion of free trade spills over onto issues related to the free flow of information. Although the U.S. and industrialized countries view free flow of information as a normal commercial activity essential for coordination and control of business processes, developing countries see it as a vehicle for foreign influence that undermines local centers of authority. In their perspective, free flow of information blurs national boundaries and thereby threatens national sovereignty. Consequently, transborder data flow has become a matter of heated debate. It can be argued that these concerns are ill founded. However, there is no denying that they are deeply rooted in historical experience. Among other things, as discussed earlier, the telegraph was used a means of maintaining imperial power. Therefore alien communication networks and the contents that flow over them are often viewed with suspicion.

The current imbalance in world trade further aggravates the problem. If one walks around a mall in the United States and looks at the labels of different products in the stores, one will come across products made in China, Korea, Malaysia, Brazil, Jamaica, Mexico, and many other countries but few made in the United States. This phenomenon is a reflection of the fact that most U.S. manufacturing has moved overseas, and most of the products needed in the United States have to be imported. Many of the manufacturing countries, particularly China, have huge balance of payments in their favor. On the other hand, what the U.S. exports is intangible products such as computer software, insurance, banking services, and films. So when the United States tries to close the balance of trade by exporting information products, in which it has a comparative advantage, it resents the opposition from other countries. The other countries, however, do not see these products are purely commercial products with no political or cultural implications. Their concern is that the unchecked inflow of these products will undermine their sovereignty.

So who is right? Perhaps both sides. The perceptions on both sides are shaped by their respective interests.[1] In the case of developing countries, their perceptions continue to be influenced by the colonial experience. The echoes of the past can be heard even today.

Our discussion of global media flows and trade in services shows one major similarity and one major difference between imperialism and electronic imperialism. The similarity is that they both exhibit a strong center-periphery relationship with few lateral connections among the periphery; in effect, the center almost totally dominates the periphery. The difference is today the center employs more subtle means to dominate the periphery than the brute force used in the past. Overall, we see significant continuity between imperialism and electronic imperialism. Will the newer technologies like Internet that are said to have decentralizing tendencies change the established center–periphery relationship? In the next section, we will explore the impact of emerging network structures on global communication.

EMERGING NETWORK STRUCTURES

The older technologies such as TV were amenable to centralized control. The high costs of program production and transmission make television a top-down mode of communication where the sources are few and the receivers many. However, newer technologies do not seem to follow the same logic, at least on the surface. The cost of production equipment has dropped sharply. Similarly, transmission costs have declined as bandwidths have significantly increased with the deployment of fiber optic and other broadband technologies. We have also seen the emergence of new transmission systems such as Internet that follow an entirely different logic in terms of organization. These days an ordinary citizen can shoot video with a camcorder and make it accessible via the Internet to anyone interested. Now the question arises, will the supposedly decentralizing technologies like the Internet strengthen or loosen U.S. control over world communications?

On the surface, the Internet looks like a democratic medium because nobody seems to control it. However, a closer examination reveals deeply embedded structural inequities. The rich countries, with only 16% of the world's population, have 97% of all Internet hosts. This inequity is even more striking when one considers that the 100 poorest countries have 20 times fewer Internet hosts than Iceland, a country with a population of only 250,000 (Petrazzini & Kibati, 1999). Furthermore, the global Internet exhibits a center–periphery relationship similar to that of the British imperial telegraph network and African telephone networks. An email from Stockholm to London goes there via the United States even though the direct physical distance between them is shorter (Cohen, 1999).

The U.S.-centric nature of the global Internet is also evident in the financial arrangements for international circuits. Unlike the telephone system, in which the cost of the international circuit connecting two countries is evenly split between them, the Internet service providers (ISPs) in other countries pay the entire cost of the circuit connecting them to the United States. The U.S. carriers are able to get away with this because of the leverage they have over overseas ISPs. They are willing to pay for the entire circuit because they need access to U.S. Web sites and exchange points that can connect them to other countries. This free ride by U.S. ISPs is particularly galling for the developing countries because the traffic flows over the international circuits are quite skewed. Typically, traffic from the United States to other countries is greater than the other way around. For example, the traffic from the United States to Ghana is twice that of the traffic from Ghana to the United States (Petrazzini & Kibati, 1999).

The network investment patterns suggest that in the future we will see the emergence of regional networks in Europe and Asia (Cohen, 1999). However, the change in the overall structure of the global Internet is unlikely in the near future. Even if the overseas ISPs try to create lateral connections among them, the economics of the entrenched infrastructure work heavily against them. Already so many high-capacity, U.S.-bound international circuits have been deployed that lateral connections between overseas ISPs, if created, will find it extremely difficult to survive the price competition with them. Thus it seems that the U.S.-centered structure of global Internet is here to stay, at least for the time being (Petrazzini & Kibati, 1999). The Internet, with all its lateral communication potentialities, is at present like the British imperial telegraph network and is likely to remain like that for the foreseeable future.

TOWARD A NEW WORLD SYSTEM?

Throughout history there have been centers and peripheries. However, the specific places (cities, countries, regions) that have played the roles of center and periphery have varied over time. During the colonial era, western Europe (England, France, Spain, and a few other countries) was the center, and the rest of the world was the periphery. After World War II the center moved across the Atlantic to the United States, and the rest of the world became the periphery. However, the nature of the center–periphery relationship has changed significantly. For one thing, we have a global division of labor on an unprecedented scale and enormous interdependencies that come with it. For another, the center—the United States—projects its power over the periphery in subtle ways instead of using the brute force seen in the empires of the past. One of these subtle ways includes international communication systems, the focus of this book. The existing systems that include the global Internet reflect the center–periphery relationship, and any major change in the structure of international communications systems is unlikely in the near future. However, as history provides ample evidence, the center–periphery relationship is bound to change over the long run, because nothing lasts forever. The question is that once the U.S. power declines, will the center merely pass from the United States to another country? Or will there be an emergence of a multipolar world like that of the 13th century?

For more information on the topics that appear in this chapter, use the password that came free with this book to access InfoTrac College Edition. Use the following words as keyterms and subject searches: global economy, division of labor, telecommunications technologies, imperialism, transborder data flow, new world information order, developing countries.

QUESTIONS FOR DISCUSSION

1. Explain what is meant by division of labor. How does division of labor increase productivity? What problems does it create? How do communications technologies help us manage these problems? What does division of labor have to do with the global economy?

2. Describe the structure of the British imperial telegraph network. Discuss why this configuration is a classic structural characteristic of relationships between the power center and subjugated periphery.

3. Explain what the term *transborder data flow* (TDF) means. Why has TDF become important over the last few decades? Why do industrialized countries want unrestricted TDF? Why are developing countries apprehensive about TDF?

4. Explain the economic forces that have shaped the structure of the global Internet. Is the U.S.-centric nature of the Internet a transitory phase in the Internet's growth curve, or will it harden into a long-term structure similar to that of the British imperial telegraph network?

5. In this chapter we saw how the multicentered world of the 13th century was transformed into a single-centered world system during the colonial era. Later the center moved across the Atlantic to the United States. How do you think the new communications technologies will affect the configuration of the world system? Will it remain single-centered or become multicentered? Why? Why not?

NOTE

1. In 1942, Kent Cooper, president of the Associated Press, bitterly complained,

So Reuters decided what news was to be sent from America. It told the world about Indians on the war path in the West, lynchings in the South and bizarre crimes in the North. The charge for decades was that nothing creditable to America ever was sent. American business criticized The Associated Press for permitting Reuters to belittle America abroad. (Cooper, 1942, p. 12)

Cooper's ire was directed against the British, who through their news agency Reuters were portraying America in a negative light. At that time, Britain was the center, and the United States was part of the semiperiphery. Today the tables have turned. Now that the United States is the center, the Americans find it difficult to understand the complaints of periphery countries about how they are covered by the U.S. media.

REFERENCES

Carey, J. (1989). *Communication as culture.* Boston: Unwin Hyman.

Cohen, R. B. (1999). Moving toward a non-US-centric international Internet. *Communications of the ACM, 42*(6), 37–40.

Cooper, K. (1942). *Barriers down.* New York: Farrar & Rinehart.

Galtung, J. (1971). A structural theory of imperialism. *Journal of Peace Research, 2,* 81–117.

Innis, H. A. (1951). *The bias of communication*. Toronto: University of Toronto Press.

McPhail, T. L. (1981). *Electronic colonialism*. Beverly Hills, CA: Sage.

Petrazzini, B., & Kibati, M. (1999). The Internet in developing countries. *Communications of the ACM, 42*(6), 31–36.

Schiller, H. I. (1969). *Mass communications and American empire*. New York: A. M. Kelley.

Schiller, H. I. (1974). Freedom from the "free flow." *Journal of Communication, 24*(1), 110–117.

4

✸

The Transnational Media Corporation and the Economics of Global Competition

RICHARD A. GERSHON

Richard A. Gershon (PhD, Ohio University) is a professor in the Department of Communication at Western Michigan University, Kalamazoo. He is cofounder of the telecommunications management program at Western Michigan, where he teaches courses in telecommunications management, law and regulations, and communication technology. He is the author of *The Transnational Media Corporation: Global Messages and Free Market Competition,* winner of the 1998 Book of the Year selected by the National Cable Television Museum. In 2000 the International Radio and Television Society gave Gershon the Steven H. Coltrin Professor of the Year Award for his work in communication and education.

The transnational corporation, as a system of organization, represents a natural evolution beyond the multinational corporation of the 1960s and 1970s. One distinctive feature of the transnational corporation (TNC) is that strategic decision making and the allocation of resources are predicated upon economic goals and efficiencies with little regard to national boundaries. What distinguishes the transnational media corporation (TNMC) from other types of TNCs

For additional online resources, access the Global Media Monitor Web site that accompanies this book on the Wadsworth Communication Cafe Web site at http://communication.wadsworth.com.

is that the principal commodity is information and entertainment. It has become a salient feature of today's global economic landscape (Albarran & Chan-Olmsted, 1998; Demers, 1999; Gershon, 1996; Herman & McChesney, 1997).

The TNMC is the most powerful economic force for global media activity in the world today. As Herman and McChesney (1997) point out, transnational media are a necessary component of global capitalism. They provide the informational and ideological environment that enables international free market trade to occur. Through a process of foreign direct investment, the TNMC actively promotes the use of advanced media and information technology on a worldwide basis. This chapter considers the underlying economic principles that help to explain the causes and consequences of transnational media ownership.

THE TRANSNATIONAL MEDIA CORPORATION

During the past two decades, scholars and media critics alike have become increasingly suspicious of the better-known, high-profile media mergers. Such suspicions have given way to a number of myths concerning the intentions of TNMCs and the people who run them. The first myth is that such companies operate in most or all markets of the world. Although today's TNMC is highly global in its approach to business, few companies operate in all markets of the world. Instead, the TNMC tends to operate in preferred markets with an obvious preference (and familiarity) toward its home market (Gershon, 1996, 2000). Thus, the company Bertelsmann A.G. describes its strategic planning philosophy as follows:

> Many years ago, Bertelsmann set as a strategic goal the establishment of an even balance among its businesses in Germany, other European countries and the United States. We have succeeded in this area as well; each of these regions accounts for just under a third of overall revenues. A smaller portion of our business is being generated in Asia. That's why we truly consider ourselves a European American media company with German roots. (Bertelsmann, 1998, p. 3)

A second prevalent myth concerning TNMCs is that such companies are monolithic in their approach to business. In fact, just the opposite is true. The business strategies and corporate culture of TNCs in general, and TNMCs in particular, often directly reflect the person (or persons) responsible for developing the organization and its business mission. The Sony Corporation, for example, is a company that was largely shaped and developed by its founders, Masaru Ibuka and Akio Morita. Together they formed a unique partnership that has left an indelible imprint on Sony's worldwide business operations. As a company, Sony is decidedly Japanese in its business values. Senior managers operating in the company's Tokyo headquarters identify themselves as Japanese first and entrepreneurs second. Their guiding principles are their overall responsibility to Japan, their responsibilities to their employees, and the need to be successful in business in order to fulfill the first two obligations. According to Morita, Shimomura, and Reingold (1986),

"The most important mission for a Japanese manager is to develop a healthy relationship with his employees, to create a family-like feeling with the corporation, a feeling that employees and managers share the same fate" (p. 130).

By contrast, Bertelsmann is a TNMC that reflects the business philosophy and media interests of its founder, Reinhard Mohn, who believed in the importance of decentralization. Bertelsmann's success can be attributed to long-range strategic planning and decentralization, a legacy that Mohn instilled in the company before his retirement in 1981. That philosophy is captured in the company charter, which stresses

- Entrepreneurial leadership and decentralization of operations
- Creativity and innovation at every level of the corporation
- Commitment to being a valued corporate citizen of the communities in which Bertelsmann companies operate (Bertelsmann, 1993, p. 7)

THE PURPOSE OF A
GLOBAL MEDIA STRATEGY

Most companies do not set out with an established plan for becoming a major international company. Rather, as a company's exports steadily increase, it establishes a foreign office to handle the sales and services of its products. In the beginning stages, the foreign office tends to be flexible and highly independent. As the firm gains experience, it may get involved in other facets of international business, such as licensing and manufacturing abroad. Later, as pressures arise from various international operations, the company begins to recognize the need for a more comprehensive global strategy (Gershon 1993, 1996; Robock & Simmonds, 1989). Historically, the TNMC begins as a company that is especially strong in one or two areas. At the start of the 1980s, for example, the Walt Disney company was principally in the business of children's animated films and theme parks, whereas NewsCorp Ltd. (parent company to Fox Broadcasting) was principally a newspaper publisher. Today both companies are transnational in scope, with a highly diverse set of products and services. In sum, most major corporations become foreign direct investors through a process of gradual evolution rather than by deliberate choice.

THE GLOBALIZATION OF MARKETS

The globalization of markets involves the full integration of transnational business, nation-states, and technologies operating at high speed. Globalization is being driven by a broad and powerful set of forces, including worldwide deregulation and privatization trends, technological change, market integration (such as the European Community), and the fall of communism. The basic requirements for all would-be players are free trade and a willingness to compete internationally. As Friedman

(1997) points out, "Globalization has its own set of economic rules—rules that re-volve around opening, deregulating and privatizing your company" (p. 8).

The Rules of Free Market Trade

To a greater or lesser extent, there is only one economic system operating in the world today. And that system is called free market capitalism. Whereas commu-nism provided a safety net for inefficient business practices, free market capitalism rewards only those who create new and innovative products and services. It is admittedly a fast-paced and uncertain world. According to German political the-orist Carl Schmitt, "The Cold War was a world of friends and enemies. The glob-alization world, by contrast, tends to turn all friends and enemies into competi-tors" (Friedman, 1997, p. 11).

A basic tenet of free market trade is that the private sector is the primary en-gine of growth. It presupposes that the nation-state can maintain a low rate of inflation and keep prices stable. It further attempts to keep the size of government small and to achieve a balanced budget, if not a surplus. The rules of free market trade adhere to the principles of deregulation and privatization of business. At the domestic level, free market trade attempts to promote as much domestic compe-tition as possible ("The New Economy," 2000). Free market trade opens up its banking and telecommunication systems to private ownership and competition and provides a nation and its citizens with access to a wide variety of choices.

The rules of free market trade extend internationally as well. Free market trade presupposes a willingness to open up one's domestic market to foreign direct in-vestment. It further attempts to eliminate, or at least reduce, tariffs and quotas on imported goods. Not all countries adhere to the rules of free market trade in the same way. Some countries tailor the rules to protect certain industries and/or cer-tain facets of domestic culture. As an example, Japan is highly protective of its banking industry ("Rebuilding the Banks," 1999), whereas France is highly pro-tective of its culture. In sum, free market trade in its varying forms provides the basic architecture for today's global economy.

Foreign Direct Investment

Foreign direct investment (FDI) refers to the ownership of a company in a foreign country. This includes the control of assets. As part of its commitment, the in-vesting company will transfer some of its managerial, financial, and technical ex-pertise to the foreign-owned company. In a transnational economy, media deci-sion making and FDI are largely based on economic efficiencies, with little regard for national boundaries (Gershon, 1993, 1996). The decision to engage in FDI is based upon the profitability of the market and future growth potential (Grosse & Kujawa, 1988). Let us consider five reasons why a company engages in FDI.

Proprietary and Physical Assets. Some TNCs invest abroad for the purpose of obtaining specific proprietary and physical assets. The ownership of talent or specialized expertise can be considered a type of proprietary asset. As an example, French media group Vivendi S.A. acquired Seagram Company Ltd. in 2001 at a cost of $43.3 billion. Seagram is home to Universal Studios and Polygram Records.

The purchase of Seagram now enables Vivendi to become a formidable player in music, film, and leisure entertainment. Instead of trying to enter the U.S. market by creating an altogether new company, Vivendi purchased proprietary assets in the form of exclusive contracts with those musicians and film producers who work for Universal Studios and Polygram Records. In addition, Vivendi has acquired Universal's production studios and theme parks, giving it control over an important set of physical assets.

Foreign Market Penetration. Some TNCs invest abroad for the purpose of entering a foreign market and serving it from that location. The market may exist or may have to be developed. The Sony Corporation employed the latter strategy when it formed Sony Corporation of America in 1960. The company established its first showroom in New York City. During the next few years, Sony established Sony Switzerland, Sony UK Ltd., Sony Deutchland, and Sony France. Early in his tenure, Akio Morita (president and cofounder) developed the kind of unique business skills that allowed him to successfully enter into foreign markets (Nathan, 1999). He did not initially have a global strategy in mind. Instead, he operated in those markets that he believed were important and where Sony's products would be most readily accepted. The United States clearly fulfilled both sets of objectives.

Production and Distribution Efficiencies. The cost of production and labor are important factors in the selection of foreign locations. Some countries offer significant advantages such as lower labor costs, tax relief, and technology infrastructure. Depending upon the country and/or technical facility, products and services can be produced for less cost and with greater efficiency. As an example, Ireland is fast becoming an important communications center for many high-tech companies. Thus, Dell Computer, for example, now centralizes all of its billing, inventory management, and distribution for its European operations by having the various functions flow through a single call center in Ireland. By centralizing these functions, the company is able to achieve significant cost savings.

Overcoming Regulatory Barriers to Entry. Some TNCs invest abroad for the purpose of entering into a market that is heavily tariffed. It is not uncommon for nations to engage in various protectionist policies designed to protect local industry. Such protectionist policies usually take the form of tariffs or import quotas. In 1998, for example, the seven leading international film exporters were U.S.-based companies (including Sony USA). They accounted for 85% of worldwide box office sales. In response to perceived U.S. dominance, many countries throughout the world—most notably, those of the European Community—have erected a variety of trade barriers designed to limit the import of U.S. television and film products (Litman, 1998). One way to overcome such regulatory barriers to entry is to promote joint partnerships and/or create foreign subsidiaries. A highly successful transnational company is one that smoothly integrates itself into the host nation's economy by becoming "national" in character and spirit. Consequently, many TNMCs form strategic partnerships with host nation companies as a way to circumvent tariffs and import quotas.

Empire Building. As Gershon (1993, 1996) notes, FDI can sometimes be prompted for reasons that go beyond simple business considerations. NewsCorp president Rupert Murdoch has sometimes been characterized as an "empire builder" in the tradition of the press barons of the 19th century (Shawcross, 1992; Smith, 1991). For CEOs like Murdoch (NewsCorp), Sumner Redstone (Viacom), Michael Eisner (Disney), and John Malone (Liberty Media), there is a certain amount of personal competitiveness and business gamesmanship that goes along with managing a major company. Success is measured in ways that go beyond straight profitability. A high premium is placed on successful deal making and new project ventures. The combination of respect and competitiveness can be seen in a comment made by Viacom's Sumner Redstone in an interview with *Fortune* magazine.

> There are two or three of us who started with nothing. Ted Turner started with a half-bankrupt billboard company. Rupert Murdoch started with a little newspaper someplace in Australia. I was born in a tenement, my father became reasonably successful, and I started with two drive-in theaters before people knew what a drive-in theater was. . . . So I do share that sort of background with Rupert. People say I want to emulate him [Murdoch]. I don't want to emulate him. I'd like to beat him. ("There's No Business," 1998, p. 104)

The Risks Associated with FDI

The decision to invest in a foreign country can pose serious risks to the company operating abroad. The TNC is subject to the laws and regulations of the host country. It is also vulnerable to the host country's politics and business policies. What are the kinds of risks associated with FDI? There are the problems associated with political instability, including wars, revolutions, and coups. Less dramatic, but equally important, are changes stemming from the election of socialist or nationalist governments that may prove hostile to private business and particularly to foreign-owned business (Ball & McCulloch, 1996). Changes in labor conditions and wage requirements are also relevant factors in terms of a company's ability to do business abroad. Foreign governments may impose laws concerning taxes, currency convertibility, and/or technology transfer. Dymsza (1984) writes that FDI can occur only if the host country is perceived to be politically stable, provides sufficient economic investment opportunities, and has business regulations that are considered reasonable. In light of such issues, the TNC will carefully consider the potential risks by doing what is called a country risk assessment before committing capital and resources (Gershon, 2000).

TRANSNATIONAL MEDIA OWNERSHIP

The decade of the 1990s witnessed an unprecedented number of international mergers and acquisitions that has brought about a major realignment of business players. Concerns for antitrust violations seem to be overshadowed by a general acceptance that such changes are inevitable in a global economy. The result has

Table 4.1 Transnational Media and Telecommunication Corporations

Companies	World headquarters	Principal business operations
AOL Time Warner	USA	Cable, magazines, publishing, music and film entertainment, Internet service provision
AT&T	USA	Long-distance telephony, cable television, wireless communication services
Bertelsmann A.G.	Germany	Book and record clubs, book publishing, magazines, music and film entertainment
British Telecom	United Kingdom	Telephony and other communication services
LM Ericsson	Sweden	Cellular telephony and telephone switching equipment
Mannesmann/ Vodafone	Germany	Telephony, wireless communication services
Microsoft	USA	Computer and Internet software
NewsCorp Ltd.	Australia	Newspapers, magazines, television and film entertainment, direct broadcast satellite
Nokia	Finland	Cellular telephone equipment
NTT DoCoMo	Japan	Cellular telephone equipment
Sony	Japan	Consumer electronics, video game consoles, music and film entertainment
Verizon	USA	Telephony, wireless communication services, Internet data transport
Viacom	USA	Television and film entertainment, cable programming, broadcast television, publishing, videocassette and DVD rental and sale
Vivendi S.A./ Universal	France	Television and film entertainment, music, theme parks
Walt Disney	USA	Theme parks, film entertainment, broadcasting, cable programming, consumer merchandise
WorldCom	USA	Long-distance telephony, Internet data transport

been a consolidation of players in all aspects of business, including banking, aviation, pharmaceuticals, media, and telecommunications. Table 4.1 identifies several of the world's leading transnational media and telecommunication corporations and includes information pertaining to their principal business operations.

Mergers, Acquisitions, and Strategic Alliances

Today's TNMCs are taking advantage of deregulatory and privatization trends to make ever-larger combinations. Starting in 1995, the field of media and telecommunications has undergone a new round of corporate consolidation, as evidenced by Walt Disney's $19 billion purchase of Capital Cities/ABC (1995), WorldCom's purchase of MCI Communication for $36.5 billion (1997), AT&T's $48 billion purchase of TCI Inc. (1999), and America Online's purchase of Time Warner for $183 billion (2001), to name only a few. Mergers, acquisitions, and strategic alliances represent different ways that companies can join (or partner together) to achieve increased market share, to diversify product line, and/or to create greater efficiency of operation. The goal, simply put, is to possess the size and resources necessary in order to compete on a global playing field.

Mergers. In a merger transaction, two companies are combined into one company. The newly formed company assumes the assets and liabilities of both companies (Ozanich & Wirth, 1998). A clear example is the February 2000 announcement that Vodafone, a British-based wireless telephone carrier, would merge with Mannesmann, a well-known German telecommunications company, at a cost of $190 billion, thus making it the largest media/telecommunications corporate merger to date. The merger is conceived as a global strategy whereby the combined company will offer mobile telephone service to an estimated 42.4 million customers in more than 25 countries, including the United States, Germany, Britain, and Italy ("A Vodacious Deal," 2000). The international growth rate of cellular telephones has increased significantly during the past several years. Cellular phones have proliferated throughout Southeast Asia, Latin America, and Europe, where building cellular systems is proving to be faster and more cost-effective than building (or reconstructing) traditional telephone systems.

Acquisitions. By contrast, an acquisition involves the purchase of one company by another company for the purpose of adding (or enhancing) the acquiring firm's productive capacity. During an acquisition, one company acquires the operating assets of another company in exchange for cash, securities, or a combination of both. A clear example of an acquisition was Viacom's 1999 decision to purchase CBS for $37 billion. For Viacom, the purchase of CBS represented an opportunity to obtain a well-established television network as well as a company that owns Infinity Broadcasting, representing more than 1,600 U.S. radio stations. For its part, Viacom is home to several well-established cable network services, including MTV, Nickelodeon, and Showtime. The purchase of CBS is expected to provide a steady distribution outlet for Viacom programs and to offer numerous cross-licensing and marketing opportunities ("CBS," 1999).

Strategic Alliance. A strategic alliance is a business relationship in which two or more companies work to achieve a collective advantage. The strategic alliance can vary in its approach and design, ranging from a simple licensing agreement to the actual combining of physical resources (Chan-Olmsted, 1998). A good example of a strategic alliance is a $10 billion joint venture between AT&T and British Telecommunications called Concert, which offers European telephone service.

In sum, mergers, acquisitions, and strategic alliances are the most direct ways for a company to expand or diversify into a new product line without having to undergo the problems associated with being a new startup. Table 4.2 identifies the major mergers and acquisitions of media and telecommunications companies in the United States (both pending and complete) for the years 1999–2001.

When Mergers and Acquisitions Fail

Not all mergers and acquisitions are successful. As companies feel the pressures of increased competition, they embrace a somewhat faulty assumption that increased size makes for a better company. Yet, upon closer examination, it becomes clear that this is not always the case. Often, the combining of two major firms creates

Table 4.2 Mergers and Acquisitions: Media and Telecommunication Companies (1999–2001)

Mergers and acquisitions	Description	Price (in billions of US$)	Year
Vivendi S.A. and Seagram (Universal and Polygram)	French media group Vivendi S.A. purchased Seagram Co. Ltd., which owns Universal Studios and Polygram Records.	43.3	2001
Vodafone and Mannesmann	Vodafone, a British wireless provider, and Mannesmann, a German-based telecommunications company, completed a merger.	190.0	2001
America Online and Time Warner	AOL acquired Time Warner Inc., the first combination of a major Internet service provider with a traditional media company.	183.0	2001
AT&T and MediaOne Group	AT&T purchased MediaOne, which in combination with its TCI cable holdings makes AT&T the largest MSO in the United States.	60.0	2000
Verizon— Bell Atlantic & GTE	Bell Atlantic purchased GTE in a major stock swap that allowed the company to enter the business of long-distance telephony. After the merger, the combined company was renamed Verizon.	52.8	2000
Viacom and CBS	Viacom purchased CBS Inc. Viacom has major investments in cable programming and film production.	37.0	2000
AT&T and TeleCommunications Inc. (TCI)	AT&T purchased TCI Inc., thus enabling AT&T to offer cable television, local and long-distance telephone service, and enhanced information services.	48.0	1999
SBC Communications & Ameritech	SBC purchased RBOC Ameritech, thus allowing SBC to increase its telephone network in the U.S. Midwest and East.	62.0	1999

Note. From R. Gershon and Company Reports.

problems that no one could foresee. A failed merger or acquisition can be highly disruptive to both organizations in terms of lost revenue, capital debt, and a decrease in job performance. The inevitable result is the elimination of staff and operations, as well as the potential for bankruptcy. In addition, the effects on the support, or host, communities can be quite destructive (Wasserstein, 1998).

There are four reasons that help to explain why mergers and acquisitions can sometimes fail. They include the lack of a compelling strategic rationale, failure to perform due diligence, postmerger planning and integration failures, and financing and the problems of excessive debt.

The Lack of a Compelling Strategic Rationale. The decision to merge is sometimes not supported by a compelling strategic rationale. In the desire to be globally competitive, both companies go into the proposed merger with unrealistic expectations of complementary strengths and presumed synergies. More often than not, the very problems that prompted a merger consideration in the first place become further exacerbated once the merger is complete.

Failure to Perform Due Diligence. In the highly charged atmosphere of intense negotiations, the merging parties fail to perform due diligence prior to the merger agreement. The acquiring company only later discovers that the intended acquisition may not accomplish the desired objectives ("The Case Against Mergers," 1995). Often the lack of due diligence results in the acquiring company's paying too much for the acquisition.

Postmerger Planning and Integration Failures. One of the most important reasons that mergers fail is bad postmerger planning and integration. If the proposed merger does not include an effective plan for combining divisions with similar products, the duplication can be a source of friction rather than synergy. Turf wars erupt, and reporting functions among managers become divisive. The problem becomes further complicated when there are significant differences in corporate culture. A research study performed by KPMG in 2000 reported that 83% of the 700 largest corporate mergers failed to boost the stock price, because of postmerger planning and integration failures.

Financing and the Problem of Excessive Debt. In order to finance the merger or acquisition, some companies will assume major amounts of debt through short-term loans. If or when performance does not meet expectations, such companies may be unable to meet their loan obligations. The said companies may be forced to sell off entire divisions in order to raise capital or, worse still, may default on their payment altogether. In the end, excessive debt can be highly destabilizing to the newly formed company.

MEDIA AND GLOBAL FINANCE

The business of media and telecommunications is an industry characterized by high startup costs and high risk. The decision to launch a direct broadcast satellite service or produce a new film is a high-risk venture with few guarantees. In order to obtain the necessary financing, today's media and telecommunication companies will either use their own money or seek the assistance of a financial lending institution. Researchers Ozanich and Wirth (1992) identify the importance of size and reputation of a TNC as the basis for being able to raise capital in a foreign market. The globalization of capital markets enables such companies to issue securities and obtain loans.

The Role of Global Capital Markets

What is a global capital market? What is its purpose? A global capital market brings together those companies and individuals who want to invest money and those who want to borrow it. For investors, the global capital market offers a much wider range of investment opportunities than can be found in purely domestic capital markets. For borrowers, the principal advantage of a global capital market is that it increases the supply of funds available for borrowing and decreases the cost of capital. If a company borrows strictly from a domestic capital market, the pool of investment sources is limited to one country. Moreover, the cost of borrowing money in a domestic market is often higher than in the international market.

Financial service groups serve as intermediaries between investors and borrowers. Such financial service groups include commercial banks (such as Citibank and US Bank) and investment companies (such as Merrill Lynch and Goldman Sachs). Commercial banks take the cash deposits from corporations and individual depositors and pay them a rate of interest in return. The banks, in turn, lend that money to borrowers at a higher rate of interest. The commercial banks make a profit based on the difference between the said interest rates. This difference is referred to as the interest rate spread. Investment companies bring investors and borrowers together and charge commissions for doing so. Investment companies are also portfolio managers, managing billions of dollars on behalf of mutual fund investors, pension funds, and insurance companies (Hill, 2000).

Capital Market Loans

Capital market loans are either equity loans or debt loans. An equity loan is made when a corporation sells stock to investors. A stock offering enables individual investors to purchase shares. A share of stock gives its holder a claim to a firm's profit stream. Investors purchase stock in anticipation of gains in the price of stock as well as possible dividends issued by the company. The money the corporation raises in return for its stock issuance can be used to purchase plant and equipment. Alternatively, debt financing requires the corporation to repay a predetermined portion of the loan amount (that is, principal + interest) at regular intervals for a specified period of time. Debt loans can be obtained from either cash loans made from a bank or funds raised through the sale of corporate bonds. In the latter case, the bondholder purchases the right to receive a specified number of payments over a set number of years until the bond maturity date.

Debt Financing

The TNMC, like any other company, needs to be able to invest in new product development as well as engage in potential mergers and acquisitions if and when it is deemed appropriate. To accomplish this, a company may finance the project venture by means of a debt loan, that is, borrowing money from various financial institutions. Banks, investment firms, and other financial institutions will loan money, using the borrowing firm's assets to secure the loan. If the firm's assets are not used as collateral, the lender may provide an unsecured loan at a higher interest rate. The length of the loan determines whether it is short-term, intermediate, or long-term debt. Short-term loans are used to meet immediate cash requirements, whereas long-terms loans (5 to 10 years) are used to underwrite the cost of business operations and expansion.

The problem is that too much debt load can be highly destabilizing to an organization. All too often the debt-driven deal will impose suffocating interest charges and repayment schedules on companies that were once financially stable.

As a consequence, the said companies are unable to withstand financial downturns in the marketplace, thus causing the value of their stock to decline significantly. In the worst-case scenario, excessive debt may force a company to default on its loans and seek Chapter 11 bankruptcy protection (Wasserstein, 1998).

Profiling NewsCorp Ltd. Rupert Murdoch, president and CEO of NewsCorp Ltd., is unique in his ability to structure debt and to obtain global financing. The Murdoch formula is to carefully build cash flow while borrowing aggressively. Throughout the early 1980s, Murdoch's excellent credit rating proved to be the essential ingredient to this formula. Each major purchase was expected to generate positive cash flow and thereby pay off what had been borrowed. Each successive purchase was expected to be bigger than the one before, thereby ensuring greater cash flow. In his desire to maintain control over his operations, Murdoch developed a special ability to manage debt at a higher level than most companies and organizations do (Gershon, 1996).

Throughout the 1980s, Murdoch's borrow-and-buy formula was bolstered by the fact that the market values of his media properties were growing faster than their underlying cash flows. The problem with NewsCorp's debt financing reached crisis proportions in 1991 when the company was carrying an estimated debt of $8.3 billion. The problem was compounded by the significant cash drains from Fox Television and the BSkyB DBS service. All this came at a time when the media industries (in general) were experiencing a worldwide economic recession. Murdoch was finally able to restructure the company's debt after several long and difficult meetings with some 146 investors. Murdoch was able to obtain the necessary financing but not before the divestment of some important assets and an agreement to significantly pare down the company's debt load. In summarizing Murdoch's business activities throughout the 1980s, *The Economist* (1990) wrote, "Nobody exploited the booming media industry in the late 1980's better than Mr. Rupert Murdoch's News Corporation—and few borrowed more money to do it" ("Murdoch's Kingdom," p. 62).

BUSINESS AND PLANNING STRATEGIES

As today's media and telecommunications companies continue to grow and expand, the challenges of staying globally competitive become increasingly more difficult. The main role of strategy is to plan for the future as well as to react to changes in the marketplace. Strategic planning is the set of managerial decisions and actions that determine the long-term performance of a company or organization. Strategic planning presupposes the use of environmental scanning whose purpose is to monitor, evaluate, and disseminate information from both the internal and the external business environments to the key decision makers within the organization. Environmental scanning requires assessing the internal strengths and weaknesses of the organization as well as the external opportunities and threats to the organization. Researchers like Wheelen and Hunger (1998) suggest that the need for strategic planning is sometimes caused by triggering events. A triggering can be caused by changes in the competitive marketplace, changes in the management structure of an organization, or changes associated with internal performance and operations.

Understanding Core Competency

The principle of core competency suggests that a highly successful company is one that possesses a specialized production process, brand recognition, or ownership of talent that enables it to achieve higher revenues and market dominance relative to its competitors. A good example of core competency can be seen with Cisco Systems, which specializes in the design and installation of Internet routers. Today, 80% of the world's Internet routers are made by Cisco Systems. To that end, Cisco is parlaying its core expertise to be a major player in the future of Internet networking ("Mr. Internet," 1999, p. 129). Core competency can be measured in many ways, including brand identity (Disney, ESPN, CNN), technological leadership (Cisco, Intel, Microsoft), superior research and development (Sony, Philips), and customer service (Dell, Gateway, Amazon.com). In sum, a company's core competency is something the organization does especially well in comparison with its competitors (Daft, 1997, p. 249).

Cross-Media Ownership

There are several ways that a major corporation can strategically plan for its future. One common growth strategy is vertical integration, whereby a company will control most or all of its operational phases. In principle, the TNMC can control an idea from its appearance in a book or magazine to its debut in domestic and foreign movie theaters, as well as later distribution via cable, satellite, or videocassette/DVD. The rationale is that vertical integration will allow a large company to be more efficient and creative by promoting combined synergies between (and among) its various operating divisions. One important substrategy for many of today's TNMCs is to engage in cross-media ownership, that is, to own a combination of entertainment, news, and enhanced information services. Cross-media ownership allows for a variety of efficiencies, such as the following:

- Sharing and recycling of news information
- Cross-licensing and marketing opportunities among company-owned media properties
- Bulk buying and group discount (that is, programming, and so on)
- Sharing of resources (including journalists, market researchers, computer equipment, newswire services, and so on)
- Offering of package discounts in advertising to clients (TNMCs like AOL Time Warner, Viacom, and NewsCorp routinely offer clients package discounts in advertising that cut across several company-owned print and electronic media outlets)
- Sharing of printing and distribution efficiencies

Profiling AOL Time Warner. The company that was once known as Time Inc. has been a party to three major business combinations since 1989. In July of that year, Time Inc. and Warner Communications completed a corporate merger that made it the largest media company in the world. The Time Warner merger was conceived as a global strategy that would enable the company to compete head-to-head with the world's leading media companies. At the time, company strategists believed that by the year 2000 there would be an international oligopoly of six or seven transnational media corporations (Saporito, 1989).

Both companies were highly complementary in their assets. Time Inc. brought to the merger agreement such notable magazines as *Time, Life, People, Fortune, Money,* and *Sports Illustrated.* In 1988 the magazine group was the largest magazine publisher in the United States. In addition, Time Inc. was America's leading pay-television programmer, with Home Box Office (HBO) and Cinemax. The company also owned America's second-largest cable (multiple system operator, or MSO), American Television and Communications.

Warner Communications brought to the merger agreement a major presence in television/film studio production, including Warner Brothers Studios (one of Hollywood's top three studios) and Lorimar Television Entertainment (a leading producer of television programs). In addition, Warner Brothers Studios was a key supplier of programming to the cable industry, including Time's very own HBO and Cinemax cable services. In the area of music entertainment, Warner Communications had a strong presence as well, including Warner Brothers Records, Atlantic Records, and Electra Entertainment (Clurman, 1992).

For several years, Time Inc. had wanted to acquire CNN. The opportunity presented itself in September 1995 when the newly created Time Warner Inc. acquired Turner Broadcasting Systems in a stock swap valued at $8 billion ("It's TBS Time," 1995). The rationale behind the purchase of Turner Broadcasting was to combine the news and programming assets of Turner Broadcasting with the highly complementary assets of Time Warner. According to Time Warner president and CEO Jerry Levin, "The complementary nature of the two organizations will allow us to maximize the value of our assets and distribution systems and position us as the leading media company in an increasingly competitive global marketplace" (Time Warner, 1995).

In January 2000, America Online (AOL), the largest Internet service provider in the United States, announced that it would purchase Time Warner Inc. for an estimated $183 billion. The deal was unique, given that AOL, with one fifth of the revenue and 15% of the workforce of Time Warner, was planning to purchase the largest TNMC in the world. Such is the nature of Internet economics, which allowed Wall Street to assign a monetary value to AOL well in excess of its actual value. During the next two years, most Internet startup companies would experience a significant decline in value. At the time of the original announcement, however, AOL president Steve Case recognized that his company was ultimately in a vulnerable position. It was only a matter of time before Wall Street would come to realize that AOL was an overvalued company. AOL did not have any recognizable brand content to speak of. Nor did the company have any major deals with cable companies for delivery. Instead, it was dependent on local telephone

**Table 4.3 AOL Time Warner Inc.'s Media
and Telecommunication Products and Services**

ENTERTAINMENT

Time Warner	**Turner Broadcasting**
Warner Brothers	TBS
(film, television, music)	Turner Network Television (TNT)
Home Box Office	Castle Rock Entertainment
(Cinemax, HBO international services)	Cartoon Network
Time Warner Cable	New Line Cinema
(cable operating system)	Hanna-Barbera Cartoons
	Atlanta Braves Baseball
	Atlanta Hawks Basketball

NEWS AND INFORMATION

Time, People, Sports Illustrated,	Cable News Network
Fortune (30+ magazines)	(CNN Headline News, international services)

INTERNET

America Online
(Internet service provision)

Note. From Time Warner Inc.

lines and satellite delivery. Time Warner clearly represented some of the most highly recognized media brands in the world.

In January 2001 the Federal Communications Commission gave final approval for AOL to acquire Time Warner Inc. Today, Time Warner Cable is the second-largest cable MSO in the United States. In the future, AOL Time Warner will look to combine the best features of old media and new media, including cable television, high-speed Internet access, and online music and film entertainment. In addition, AOL Time Warner is well positioned to engage in the cross-promotion of media entertainment and news products via AOL ("Showtime," 2001). In sum, AOL Time Warner has taken the philosophy of cross-media ownership to a whole new level in terms of strategic planning and operations. This can be seen in Table 4.3, which provides an overview of the company in terms of its media and telecommunications holdings.

Broadband Communication

The once-clear lines and historic boundaries that separated media and telecommunications are becoming less distinct. The result is a convergence of modes, whereby technologies and services are becoming more fully integrated. The main driving force behind convergence is the digitalization of media and information technology. It increases the potential for manipulation and transformation of data. A second important strategy for the future is the ability to own both software content and the means of distribution to the home. The term *broadband communication* is used to describe the ability to distribute multichannel information and entertainment services to the home.

Profiling AT&T. In June 1998, AT&T purchased TeleCommunications Inc. (TCI) cable for $48 billion. The stock and debt transaction gave AT&T direct connections into 33 million U.S. homes through TCI-owned and affiliated cable systems ("At Last," 1998, pp. 24–25). For AT&T the merger agreement represents an opportunity to enter the unregulated business of cable television. This comes at a time when AT&T is faced with the prospect of steadily declining market share in the business of long-distance telephony. The purchase of TCI will also allow AT&T to neatly circumvent both federal regulations and the local telephone companies' dominant control over the local exchange market. Currently, AT&T and the other long-distance carriers pay substantial access fees to the local exchange carriers (LECs) for the right to interconnect to the local exchange market.

In 2000, AT&T further strengthened its commitment to cable television by purchasing MediaOne Cable for $60 billion, thus adding 5 million subscribers to TCI's 12 million households. The purchase of TCI and MediaOne has made AT&T the largest cable MSO in the United States. AT&T's basic strategy requires the use of cable television as a primary conduit for offering broadband communication services to the home. According to AT&T CEO Michael Armstrong, "We will offer a full portfolio of services with one connection from one company" ("AT&T's Power Shake," 1998). AT&T's strategy further presupposes the ability to bundle, that is, to offer consumers various combinations of telecommunication service. The bundling of services will include cable television, local and long-distance telephone service, and high-speed Internet access.

AT&T's strategic plan hearkens a kind of back-to-the-future scenario in which the company can once again be America's full-service provider of communication services to the home. There is a difference, of course. AT&T now competes on a more competitive playing field than was the case before 1984. AT&T now competes with a host of other media and telecommunications companies. To date, the plan to deliver broadband residential services has proven to be a difficult strategy to implement. Although some services, such as local and long-distance telephony, seem to be natural partners, the issue of whether consumers want to get a full complement of services from the same company is not entirely clear. AT&T, for its part, has discovered that delivering enhanced information services to the home is both costly and time-consuming. In October 2000, president and CEO Michael Armstrong announced plans to divide AT&T into four separate companies. One of the said four companies will be AT&T Broadband, which will continue to implement its cable television strategy.

TRANSNATIONAL MEDIA AND
THE MARKETPLACE OF IDEAS

The combination of deregulation and privatization has transformed the conduct of international business. The TNMC of the 21st century is looking to position itself as a full-service provider of media and telecommunications products and services. Through a process of FDI, the TNMC actively promotes the use of traditional and advanced media technology. Such efforts have ignited the transborder flow of media products worldwide. The resulting globalization of media activity has forced governments and policy makers alike to consider the long-term implications. The concluding section of this chapter considers the issue of economic concentration and the marketplace of ideas. For this issue, above all others, will affect the cause of media diversity, product quality, and free expression.

Transnational Media and Economic Consolidation

In all areas of media and telecommunications, there has been a clear movement toward economic consolidation. In the United States the top 25 TV station groups (including the major networks) own or control 41.6% of all commercial TV stations; this is up from 35.9% in 1998 and 24.6% in 1996 ("Top 25 Television Groups," 2000). The four major U.S. networks (NBC, CBS, ABC, and Fox) are among the top 7 station groups. In cable television, the top three cable MSOs—AT&T, Time Warner Cable, and Charter Communication—control 60% of all U.S. cable homes (or 35.2 million subscribers) ("Top 25 Cable Operators," 2000). In newspaper communication, the top 15 newspapers are responsible for 50.6% of total daily circulation (Compaine & Gomery, 2000). In computer communication, Microsoft Inc. is responsible for 80% of the world's PC operating system software. The increase in group and cross-media ownership is the direct result of TNMCs' looking for ways to increase market share and promote greater internal efficiencies.

The Deregulation Paradox

In principle, deregulation is supposed to foster competition and thereby open markets to new service providers. The problem, however, is that complete and unfettered deregulation can sometimes create the very problem it was meant to solve—namely, a lack of competition. Instead of fostering an open marketplace of new players and competitors, too much consolidation can lead to fewer players and hence less competition (Demers, 1999; Gershon, 1996; Mosco, 1990). Researchers like Mosco (1990) call it the "mythology of telecommunications deregulation." Other writers, such as Demers (1999), refer to it as the "great paradox of capitalism." As Demers points out,

> The history of most industries in so-called free market economies is the history of the growth of oligopolies, where a few large companies eventually come to dominate. The first examples occurred during the late 1800s in the oil, steel and railroad industries. . . . Antitrust laws eventually were used to break up many of these companies but oligopolistic tendencies continue in these and most other industries. (p. 1)

The communications industry is no exception.

The Marketplace of Ideas

Numerous writers, including Bagdikian (1990), Herman and McChesney (1997), and Schiller (1990) argue that a small set of dominant media corporations exercises a disproportionate effect over the marketplace of ideas. According to Bagdikian (1990), the major issue is one of influence.

Market dominant corporations in the mass media have dominant influence over the public's news, information, public ideas, popular culture, and political attitudes. The same corporations exert considerable influence within government precisely because they influence their audiences' perceptions of public life, including perceptions of politics and politicians as they appear— or do not appear—in the media. (pp. 4–5)

Implicit in such arguments is that the TNMC should be treated differently from other TNCs because of its unique ability to influence public opinion. Corporate size is presumed to limit the diversity and availability of new media products and ideas, in favor of promoting some kind of corporate agenda. As McChesney (1997) argues,

A specter now haunts the world; a global commercial media system dominated by a small number of super-powerful, mostly U.S. based transnational media corporations. It is a system that works to advance the cause of the global market and promote commercial values, while denigrating journalism and culture not conducive to the immediate bottom line or long run corporate interests. (p. 11)

Do all such companies engage in anticompetitive behavior? Do they contribute to a lessening in media quality? Writers like Compaine (1985), Compaine and Gomery (2000), Poole (1983), Friedman (1997), and Gershon (1996) reject many of the traditional arguments associated with economic concentration. Compaine and Gomery (2000) would argue that greater media diversity does not necessarily translate into higher quality of content.

If the proliferation of television, books and Web sites reveals anything, it is that greater diversity means just that; more low brow shows, trash journalism, pandering politics to go along with opportunities for finding more thoughtful and quality outlets for analysis, entertainment and information. Diversity cuts all ways. (p. 578)

The above writers would further argue that advancements in new media technologies (including converging media formats and multiple distribution channels) preclude the possibility of a few dominant media companies controlling the marketplace of ideas. Since 1984 (and the breakup of AT&T), there has been a proliferation of new media and information technologies, including personal computers, cellular telephones, electronic mail, direct broadcast satellites, videogames, and the Internet, to name only a few. They are relatively "new" technologies and are the direct result of increased competition among large and small companies alike. The evidence would suggest that today's international business culture is more competitive and responsive to public needs and wants than at any time in history. Nowhere is this more evident than in the rapid growth of the Internet, which is moving well beyond any one company's (or person's) ability to dominate the content that is exhibited and exchanged among the millions of people who use it daily. Today the Internet is democratizing information access and is fundamentally rewriting the rules of global competition and business trade (Friedman, 1997).

Global Competition: What It Really Means

What are the real problems that face the TNMC in the years ahead? The answer to this question is not unique to the TNMC. Rather, the problems have to do with all companies that plan to operate in an increasingly deregulated and privatized world of business. Global competition has engendered a new competitive spirit that cuts across nationalities and borders. A new form of economic Darwinism abounds, characterized by a belief that size and complementary strengths are crucial to business survival. The relentless pursuit of profits (and the fear of failure) has made companies around the world ferocious in their attempts to right-size, reorganize, and reengineer their business operations. No company, large or small, remains unaffected by the intense drive to increase profits and decrease costs. The real issue is not the size or number of today's TNMCs. Rather, it has to do with business priorities where the pursuit of profits can sometimes promote egregious forms of media violence and lower the standards of quality journalism.

Transnational Media and Software Ambivalence

One of the more serious problems facing the public is that today's TNMC has to a large degree become software ambivalent. In a free market economy, profitability and market potential are often the true test of whether a creative work makes it. The TNMC, given its diverse worldwide media activities, is often unwilling to impose professional (or moral) restraints on the production of creative works, regardless of whether such efforts are obscene or violent or result in the invasion of privacy. Critics argue that the TNMC needs to recognize its civic responsibility when it comes to the production of music and films that are highly sexist, violent, and profane. Time Warner and Bertelsmann, for example, have come under increased scrutiny for their failure to exercise self-restraint when it comes to the marketing of select forms of hip-hop (or rap) music. In the area of journalism, this plays out in the crossing of the line between serious journalism and entertainment. Former CBS news anchor Walter Cronkite (1996) states the problem unequivocally:

> Will the journalism center hold in the changed economic environment of the future? In the last decade the networks have cut back news budgets while supporting in syndication the emergence of tabloid news shows, travesties of genuine news presentations. They bear the same relationship to the network news broadcasts as the *Enquirer* does to the *New York Times*. (p. 375)

What distinguishes the TNMC from other TNCs is that the principal commodity being sold is information and entertainment. It is a business mission that requires a greater degree of responsibility, given the media's unique power to inform, persuade, and entertain. A TNMC without a core business ethic is simply an organizational machine producing highly efficient products without considering the consequences. The direct fallout of such machinelike thinking is a kind of software ambivalence, with no company (or person) taking ownership for product quality and its potential impact on domestic and international audiences.

TNMCs and Nation-States

The problems cited become all the more complex at the international level. The TNMC possesses a level of power and influence that is second only to that of nation-states. Through a process of FDI, the TNMC actively promotes the use of advanced media and information technology. As a result, the geopolitical and cultural walls that once separated the nations of the earth are no longer sustainable. The resulting globalization of media activity has posed, and will continue to pose, a unique dilemma for many of today's host nations. On the one hand are the clear benefits of international free trade and the specific advantages that a TNMC offers, including jobs, investment capital, technology resources, and tax revenue. On the other are the problems associated with media imports, including cultural trespass, challenges to political sovereignty, and privacy invasion.

In the end, the goals of profitability and political sovereignty should not be considered mutually exclusive, but they do require a level of mutual cooperation and respect between the TNMC and the host nation. Host nations have a right and a responsibility to exercise appropriate controls when corporate behavior (or product quality) is deemed harmful or hazardous. Such rules, however, should be consistent and uniformly applied to all commercial traders. The decision to impose regulatory barriers to entry cannot be justified by a company's size or scale of operation. The host nation and the TNMC have a shared responsibility to create a system of globalization that is both desirable and sustainable.

For more information on the topics that appear in this chapter, use the password that came free with this book to access InfoTrac College Edition. Use the following words as keyterms and subject searches: transnational media corporations, global media, globalization, free market trade, media ownership, media mergers, global markets, cross-media ownership, global competition.

QUESTIONS FOR DISCUSSION

1. Why does a company engage in foreign direct investment? What are some of the risks associated with FDI, for the company as well as for the host nation?

2. Why do media and telecommunications companies engage in a mergers or acquisitions strategy? What are some of the reasons and more notable examples for doing so? Why does a mergers or acquisitions strategy sometimes fail?

3. As today's media and telecommunications companies continue to grow and expand, the challenges of staying globally competitive become increasingly more difficult. What does strategic planning mean? What are some of the more common strategies employed by today's TNMCs?

4. Do today's TNMCs control the marketplace of ideas? Consider the arguments from both a social and an economic standpoint.

5. In looking to the future, what are some of the responsibilities and obligations of today's TNMC in dealing with the general public and host nations?

REFERENCES

Albarran, A., & Chan-Olmsted, S. (1998). (Eds.). *Global media economics.* Ames: Iowa State University Press.

At last, telecommunications unbound. (1998, July 6). *Business Week,* pp. 24–25.

AT&T's power shake. (1998, July 6). *Time,* pp. 76–78.

Bagdikian, B. (1990). *The media monopoly* (3rd ed.). Boston: Beacon Press.

Ball, D., & McCulloch, W. H. (1996). *International business: The challenge of global competition* (6th ed.). Chicago: Irwin.

Bertelsmann A.G. (1993). *Bertelsmann: A world of experience* (press release). New York.

Bertelsmann A.G. (1998). *Annual report, 1998.* Retrieved from the World Wide Web: http://www.bertelsmann.de/english/geschber98/woessnerhtml

The case against mergers. (1995, October 30). *Business Week,* pp. 122–126.

CBS. (1999, April 5). *Business Week,* pp. 75–82.

Chan-Olmsted, S. (1998). The strategic alliances of broadcasting, cable television, and telephone services. *Journal of Media Economics, 11*(3), 33–46.

Clurman, R. (1992). *To the end of time.* New York: Simon & Schuster.

Compaine, B. (1985). The expanding base of media competition. *Journal of Communication, 35*(3).

Compaine, B., & Gomery, D. (2000). *Who owns the media?* (3rd ed.). Mahwah, NJ: Lawrence Erlbaum Associates.

Cronkite, W. (1996). *A reporter's life.* New York: Alfred A. Knopf.

Daft, R. (1997). *Management* (4th ed.). New York: Harcourt Brace.

Demers, D. (1999). *Global media: Menace or messiah?* Cresskill, NJ: Hampton Press.

Demers, D. (2000, Winter). Global media news. *GMN Newsletter, 2*(1), 1.

Dymsza, W. (1984). Trends in multinational business and global environments: A perspective. *Journal of International Business Studies,* pp. 25–45.

Friedman, T. (1997). *The Lexus and the olive tree.* New York: Farrar, Straus & Giroux.

Gershon, R. A. (1993). International deregulation and the rise of transnational media corporations. *Journal of Media Economics, 6*(2), 3–22.

Gershon, R. A. (1996). *The transnational media corporation: Global messages and free market competition.* Mahwah, NJ: Lawrence Erlbaum Associates.

Gershon, R. A. (2000). The transnational media corporation: Environmental scanning and strategy formulation. *Journal of Media Economics, 13*(2), 81–101.

Grosse, R., & Kujawa, D. (1988). *International business: Theory and application.* Homewood, IL: Irwin.

Herman, E., & McChesney, R. (1997). *The global media: The new missionaries of corporate capitalism.* London: Cassell.

Hill, C. W. (2000). *International business: Competing in the global marketplace* (3rd ed.). New York: McGraw-Hill.

It's TBS time. (1995, September 25). *Broadcasting and Cable,* pp. 8–10.

Litman, B. (1998). *The motion picture industry.* Boston: Allyn and Bacon.

McChesney, R. (1997, November/December). The global media giants: The nine firms that dominate the world. *Extra, 10*(6).

Mr. Internet. (1999, September 13). *Business Week,* p. 129.

Morita, A., Shimomura, M., & Reingold, E. (1986). *Made in Japan.* New York: E. P. Dutton.

Mosco, V. (1990, Winter). The mythology of telecommunications deregulation. *Journal of Communication, 40*(1), 36–49.

Murdoch's kingdom. (1990, August 18). *The Economist,* p. 62.

Nathan, J. (1999). *Sony: The private life.* Boston: Houghton Mifflin.

The new economy. (2000, January 31). *Business Week,* pp. 74–92.

Ozanich, G., & Wirth, M. (1992, April 12). *Trends in globalization: Direct foreign investments in media companies 1985–1991.* Paper presented at the 37th Annual Broadcast Education Association Conference, Las Vegas, NV.

Ozanich, G., & Wirth, M. (1998). Mergers and acquisitions: A communications industry overview. In A. Alexander, R. Carveth, and J. Owers (Eds.), *Media economics* (2nd ed.). Mahwah, NJ: Lawrence Erlbaum Associates.

Poole, I. S. (1983). *Technologies of freedom.* Cambridge, MA: Belknap Press.

Rebuilding the banks. (1999, September 6). *Business Week,* pp. 48–49.

Robock, S., & Simmonds, K. (1989). *International business and multinational enterprises* (4th ed.). Homewood, IL: Irwin.

Saporito, B. (1989, November 20). The inside story of Time Warner. *Fortune,* pp. 170–183.

Schiller, H. (1990). The global commercialization of culture. *Directions PCDS, 4,* 1–4.

Shawcross, W. (1992). *Murdoch.* New York: Simon & Schuster.

Showtime for AOL Time Warner. (2001, January 15). *Business Week,* pp. 57–64.

Smith, A. (1991). *The age of the behemoths.* New York: Priority Press Publications.

There's no business like show business. (1998, June 22). *Fortune,* pp. 92–104.

Time Warner Inc. (1995). Time Warner Inc. and Turner Broadcasting System Inc. agree to merge (press release). New York.

Top 25 cable operators (special report). (2000, May 1). *Broadcasting and Cable,* pp. 24–50.

Top 25 television groups (special report). (2000, April 10). *Broadcasting and Cable,* pp. 72–98.

A Vodacious deal. (2000, February 14). *Time,* p. 63.

Wasserstein, B. (1998). *Big deal: The battle for control of America's leading corporations.* New York: Warner Books.

Wheelen T., & Hunger, D. (1998). *Strategic management and business policy.* Reading, MA: Addison Wesley Longman.

5

Global
Communication Law

JOHN L. HUFFMAN
AND DENISE M. TRAUTH

John L. Huffman (PhD, University of Iowa) is a professor of communication studies at the University of North Carolina at Charlotte. He was formerly a professor of
mass communication at Bowling Green State University and director of the School
of Mass Communication there. He is one of the founders of the Communication
Law and Policy Division of the International Communication Association.

Denise M. Trauth (PhD, University of Iowa) was appointed provost and vice
chancellor for academic affairs at the University of North Carolina at Charlotte in
March 1997. Before 1997, she served as dean of the graduate school and professor
of communication studies at UNC Charlotte. Before coming to UNC Charlotte,
Trauth was associate dean of the graduate college at Bowling Green State University in Ohio. She serves on numerous civic and community boards.

The study of communication law and policy has, in large measure, traditionally been nation-specific except in those areas where particular technologies
or common goals mandated a degree of international cooperation. Thus,
freedom of speech and freedom of the press, prior restraint and censorship, libel
and slander, the right to privacy, free press–fair trial conflicts, freedom of information, obscenity, and advertising regulation were studied in the context of a particular nation. A global approach to the implementation of international law and

For additional online resources, access the Global Media Monitor Web site that
accompanies this book on the Wadsworth Communication Cafe Web site at
http://communication.wadsworth.com.

policy administered by an agency such as the International Telecommunication Union (ITU) was reserved for areas such as broadcasting. Radio and television signals, freely crossing international boundaries, had the potential to interfere with one another and destroy any utility the medium might have; they also had the potential to carry political and social messages that affected countries might object to. A global approach has also been embraced when mutual cooperation furthered social goals such as the protection of intellectual property rights—patents, trademarks, and copyrights—under the Berne Convention, the Universal Copyright Convention (UCC), and the General Agreement on Tariffs and Trade (GATT), and World Intellectual Property Organization (WIPO).

However, Marshall McLuhan's global village is inexorably if somewhat belatedly becoming more of a reality, and the unforeseen catalytic medium is the computer tied to the Internet. Suddenly, all of the aforementioned nation-specific areas of communication law and policy are going to have global dimensions as the Internet continues at breakneck speed to interconnect the planet and make gratuitous the physical boundaries formerly used by nation-states to control communication. This chapter will address the following issues:

- The traditional role of freedom of expression in Western democracies
- International and national limitations on freedom of expression
- Censorship and national security
- Censorship for moral and religious reasons
- Existing international regulatory and policy-making bodies and their roles
- The Internet and its impact on global communication law

THE TRADITIONAL ROLE
OF FREEDOM OF EXPRESSION

Conditions Accompanying Freedom

The term *freedom of expression* was made coherent and given substance by Yale law professor Thomas I. Emerson in his seminal work, *The System of Freedom of Expression,* published in 1970. Emerson saw freedom of expression in a modern democratic society as a set of rights. Among these were the right of citizens to think and believe whatever they wanted to and the right to communicate those thoughts and beliefs in any medium. Also residing in freedom of expression was a right to remain silent, a right to hear others and enjoy access to information, and a right to assemble with others for purposes of joint expression. More recent legal commentators embrace the same litany of rights constituting freedom of expression. According to Rodney A. Smolla (1992),

> A nation committed to an open culture will defend human expression and conscience in all its wonderful variety, protecting freedom of speech, freedom of the press, freedom of religion, freedom of association, freedom of

assembly, and freedom of peaceful mass protest. These freedoms will be extended not only to political discourse, but to the infinite range of artistic, scientific, religious, and philosophical inquiries that capture and cajole the human imagination. (p. 4)

Freedom of expression is assigned a primacy among social values in a modern democratic society. It is considered a foundational value, a core underpinning in such a society. Its importance stems from four resultant conditions that are essential to a true democracy and that are present in a society only when freedom of expression is present.

The first of these four resultant conditions is human dignity and self-fulfillment. U.S. Supreme Court Justice Thurgood Marshall spoke of the human spirit as "a spirit that demands self-expression" (*Procunier v. Martinez,* 1974, p. 427). Freedom to express one's self without externally imposed restraints leads to self-realization and self-identity, to growth and development as a human being. Without that freedom, individual evolution is stunted. It would be "an insult to the humanity of a mature adult that others (particularly the state) should presume to determine for him what expressions he will hear or see in forming his own conception of what is worthy in his life" (Murphy, 1997, p. 557). Self-fulfillment through free expression is, in a Lockean sense, a natural, intrinsic, and inalienable right that we are endowed with at birth.

The second of the four conditions that emanate from freedom of expression and are vital to a democratic society is a progression toward truth through an unfettered "marketplace of ideas." U.S. Supreme Court Justice Oliver Wendell Holmes argued that "the best test of truth is the power of the thought to get itself accepted in the competition of the market" (*Abrams v. United States,* 1919, p. 630). Rational human beings will, given time, reject that which is false and embrace that which is true. They can do so, however, only if truth is present in the marketplace; censorship poses the grave risk of removing truth as an alternative in the marketplace. An oft-quoted passage that English author John Milton wrote in an essay in 1644 entitled "Areopagitica" captures well the essential need for a marketplace of ideas:

> And though all the windes of doctrine were let loose to play upon the earth, so Truth be in the field, we do injuriously by licencing and prohibiting to misdoubt her strength. Let her and Falshood grapple; who ever knew truth put to the worse in a free and open encounter. (pp. 681–682)

The third of the four conditions that accompany freedom of expression and are essential to the operation of a modern democracy is the provision of the instrument, or means, of democratic decision making. In a democracy, the majority is charged with making the state's political decisions. Citizens must gather and analyze information and ideas in order to arrive at and render a reasoned judgment. The vehicle for this process is, obviously, their freedom of expression. "Freedom to think as you will and to speak as you think are means indispensable to the discovery and spread of political truth" (*Whitney v. California,* 1927, p. 375). Likewise, decisions that are made outside of the political realm in a democratic society—decisions about art, culture, music, science, and all conceivable areas of human endeavor—are enabled by freedom of expression. Without this freedom, democratic decision making is an oxymoron.

The fourth condition that is produced by freedom of expression is one in which conflict can take place without any necessary recourse to violence. As Emerson (1970, p. 7) points out, suppression of expression denies the opportunity for rational discussion and reasoned judgment, and leaves violence as a plausible alternative for those who passionately wish to change circumstances or develop new ideas. Expression can act, then, as a safety valve in a modern democracy. U.S. Supreme Court Justice Louis Brandeis saw this function of freedom of expression as one that motivated the framers of the U.S. Constitution:

> [They] knew that order cannot be secured merely through fear of punishment for its infraction; that it is hazardous to discourage thought, hope and imagination; that fear breeds repression; that repression breeds hate; that hate menaces stable government; that the path of safety lies in the opportunity to discuss freely supposed grievances and proposed remedies; and that the fitting remedy for evil counsels is good ones. (*Whitney v. California,* 1927, p. 375)

These four resultant conditions springing from freedom of expression thus provide the rationale underlying the paramount position of this freedom in a democratic society. Not all democratic societies value the conditions in the same manner or assign the same priorities to them as justifications for freedom of expression. In the United States, the U.S. Supreme Court has relied most heavily on the "marketplace of ideas" function in its 20th-century decisions supporting freedom of expression (Hall, 1992, p. 298). Uyttendaele and Dumortier (1998, pp. 915–918) note that the Council of Europe, on the other hand, has explicitly recognized the function of democratic decision making as the primary rationale underlying freedom of expression, and they argue that Europe has generally rejected both the marketplace of ideas rationale and the natural rights rationale. Regardless of the relative valuing of the four rationales by Western democracies, it should be apparent that, taken together, they represent a cogent argument for the presence of freedom of expression as a primary prerequisite for the existence of a truly democratic state.

INTERNATIONAL AND NATIONAL LIMITATIONS ON FREEDOM OF EXPRESSION

The United States

Although freedom of expression is a foundational value in a modern democracy, other societal values *at specific times and in specific circumstances* are equally important or of greater importance to democratic nation-states. National security is a societal value that is embraced by all nation-states. Likewise, protection of citizens' physical well-being and protection of property are universally important societal values. Even those democracies that most strongly champion freedom of expression will draw the line at expression that clearly puts the nation-state at risk or imminently endangers the life of its citizens or puts their private or commonly held property at jeopardy. Absolute freedom of expression is nonexistent; no nation-state is willing to allow highly classified national security materials to be passed without penalty to an enemy, nor to allow a conspiracy to murder a group of innocent citizens, nor to allow a leader at a demonstration to urge the burning of nearby buildings. Instead, lines are drawn by democratic governments: a citizen's speech is protected up to a particular point, but after that point, the citizen's speech can be suppressed or punished if it does occur.

Modern democracies differ both as to the critical societal values that must be balanced against freedom of expression and the formulas that are to be used in the balancing process. In the United States, where polls show that the citizens believe they have too much freedom of expression ("Survey Finds," 1999, p. 6), the modern Supreme Court has fashioned legal principles that balance the scales strongly in favor of freedom of expression in its conflicts with numerous social values. Thus, offensive, vulgar, uncivil, and indecent expression is protected. Even so-called hate speech and hate symbols such as swastikas and Ku Klux Klan robes are protected.

As a general rule, expression in the United States can be penalized only when it causes the following: (a) real injuries to individuals or property; (b) real injuries to social relationships that have traditionally been defined as important to society, such as the destruction of one's reputation [libel or slander]; (c) real injuries to business operations or business relationships, such as fraud or false advertising; (d) real injuries to confidentiality, both personal (invasion of one's privacy) or national (release of vital security information); and (e) real injuries to private and corporate ownership of intellectual property (copyright, trademark, appropriation). An exception to this general rule in the United States is the area of obscenity, which, while arguably causing no tangible or assessable harm, is nonetheless subject to legal sanctions by both the federal government and the individual states.

Punishment for expression that causes the real injuries outlined above usually occurs in the United States *after* the expression has taken place; prior restraint or classic censorship of expression has been constitutionally disfavored by the U.S. Supreme Court, which has said, "Any system of prior restraints of expression comes to this Court bearing a heavy presumption against its constitutional validity" (*Bantam Books, Inc. v. Sullivan,* 1963, p. 70). In order to justify any blocking of expression before it takes place, the government must usually prove that the projected injury done by the expression will be direct, immediate, and substantial, which is, at least in the majority of cases, an impossible task. Finally, expression in the United States can usually be penalized only when the definition of injurious speech is specific and understandable so that speakers are forewarned.

Thus, the United States allows much expression that is punished or banned in some modern democracies. Emotional or intellectual responses to expression by either the majority of society or minorities within society provide no legal grounds for punishment of that expression. Expression that engenders emotional distress or disgust, expression that causes embarrassment, expression that might be perceived as insulting, blasphemous, sexist, racist, vulgar or indecent—all are protected and tolerated as free speech in American society.

International Covenants

"The right of free speech stands as a general norm of customary international law," according to legal scholar Thomas David Jones (1998, p. 37). Indeed, provisions in all of the major international human rights instruments list freedom of expression as a fundamental human right. This is true of the Universal Declaration of Human Rights (1948), the European Convention for the Protection of Human Rights and Fundamental Freedoms (1953), the International Convention on the Elimination of All Forms of Racial Discrimination (1969), the International Covenant on Civil and Political Rights (1976), the American Convention on Human Rights (1978), and the Banjul Charter of Human and Peoples' Rights (1982). All of these instruments defend freedom of expression in language similar to that used in the Universal Declaration of Human Rights: "Everyone has the right to freedom of opinion and expression; this right includes freedom to hold opinions without interference and to seek, receive, and impart information and ideas through any media and regardless of frontiers" (p. 71). At the same time, these same instruments make patently clear that the freedom of expression they trumpet is not an absolute freedom but instead may be limited by the signatories to the instruments. Such limitations must under international law be legitimate, legal, and a democratic necessity (Turk & Joinet, 1992), but these terms intentionally allow a wide latitude of restriction by the signatories. Most human rights treaties signed by democratic countries overtly permit restrictions on speech to promote respect for the rights of others, national security, public order or safety, and public health and morals. Covertly, most of these treaties allow additional restrictions by means of provisions like that contained in the European Convention that "the exercise of these freedoms . . . may be subject to such formalities, conditions, restrictions or penalties as are prescribed by law" (p. 230). What happens, of course, is that these statements of formal law are filtered through disparate cultures and traditions and unique social structures as they are translated into nation-states' laws. The result is that while all democratic nation-states champion freedom of expression, the contours of that freedom vary in major ways from country to country.

National Limitations

Democratic nation-states diverge in significant ways in their respective limitations on freedom of expression. As noted above, in the United States expressions of racial hatred and group defamation are protected speech. Groups and individuals who openly engage in speech disparaging people of particular races, creeds, or colors can do so freely. They can even go so far as to advocate genocide as the ultimate solution to the problems they perceive as associated with the group they choose to hate. Such speech can be curtailed only if it is on the brink of resulting in direct physical harm to those who are being attacked. The laissez-faire attitude of the United States in the area of hate expression can be contrasted with that of Great Britain, Canada, India, and Nigeria, for example. These countries all regulate group defamation through restrictive legislation (Jones, 1998, p. 152), as does also Sweden (Swedish Penal Code, 1986).

Germany, a nation-state that formed much of its present legal system in large part as a reaction to its own historical experience with racial hatred, permits wide restrictions on extremist political speech, even to the point of prohibiting completely any writing or broadcast that incites racial hatred or "describes cruel or otherwise inhuman acts of violence against humans in a manner which glorifies or minimizes such acts" (Stein, 1986, p. 131).

Similar divergences by democratic nation-states in assigning the parameters of freedom of expression are readily apparent in areas such as prior restraint and censorship for national security purposes, the definition and treatment of libel and slander, a right to privacy, free press—fair trial conflicts, freedom of governmental information, and obscenity. One good example of such a divergence is the Mitterrand—Dr. Gubler affair, which occurred in France in 1996. Aspects of prior restraint, libel, a right to privacy, and a free press were all intertwined in this case. At the request of President François Mitterrand's widow and three children, a series of French judges upheld the censorship of a book and the punishment of its authors and publisher for divulging a "professional secret," a criminal offense in France. The book, entitled *The Great Secret,* disclosed that Mitterrand had contracted a fatal cancer in 1981 and that by 1994, though still in office, was in reality no longer capable of carrying out his duties. When the widow and children went to court in an attempt to preserve Mitterrand's reputation, a judge initially issued a preliminary injunction that halted all future sales of the book, even though the book had gone on sale the day before and sold 40,000 copies throughout France. A court of appeals affirmed this injunction, a subsequent criminal court convicted Dr. Gubler, his coauthor, and his publisher of violating the criminal code, and a trial court made the injunction permanent and awarded damages to the Mitterrand family (Sokol, 1999, p. 5).

In the United States, it is impossible to conceive of any of this happening. Judges conversant with First Amendment law would have been unwilling to issue the original preliminary injunction; if a judge could be found to issue the order, an appeals court would quickly stay it. There could have been no criminal conviction, because no parallel criminal privacy law exists in the United States. There could have been no damage award, because any civil privacy concerns would have been outweighed by the fact that the matter was of public concern. Such revelations are routinely published in the United States without even a hint of possible censorship or subsequent punishment.

When particular forms of expression strike at the most cherished values in a particular society, it is quite often the case that the society will opt for restrictions rather than open expression. Although it is impossible to deal with all areas of divergence adequately in a single chapter, the areas of censorship for national security purposes and censorship for moral and religious reasons are especially worthy of further examination.

CENSORSHIP AND NATIONAL SECURITY

The U.S. Situation

As mentioned previously, the general concept of censorship—that is, the concept of the government's taking overt action to prevent its people from having access to particular facts, ideals, and opinions—is constitutionally repugnant in the United States. This is true even when national security is advanced as the compelling reason that censorship must be enforced. In fact, the modern constitutional definition of what freedom of expression means in the United States had its genesis in a series of U.S. Supreme Court cases early in the 20th century that dealt explicitly with national security issues.

In cases such as *Abrams v. U.S.* (1919), *Gitlow v. New York* (1925), and *Whitney v. California* (1927), Justice Holmes and Justice Brandeis wrote decisions that crafted the country's modern-day approach to freedom of expression. These decisions, mainly in the form of dissents written against the majority reasoning of the Supreme Court and the dominant mood of the country as a whole, argued against a wide-ranging power on the part of the government to stifle protest and unpopular ideas in times of perceived national threat. Socialists, anarchists, radicals, and revolutionaries should enjoy freedom of expression up to the point where the national security was truly threatened. The line that they drew is known as the "clear and present danger" doctrine. Justice Brandeis defined the boundaries of the doctrine in a famous opinion written in *Whitney v. California* (1927):

> [N]o danger flowing from speech can be deemed clear and present, unless the incidence of the evil apprehended is so imminent that it may befall before there is opportunity for discussion. If there be time to expose through discussion the falsehood and fallacies, to avert the evil by the processes of education, the remedy to be applied is more speech, not enforced silence. Only an emergency can justify repression. (p. 377)

Thus, expression that condemns the United States, expression that attempts to thwart the aims of the United States, even expression that advocates the overthrow of the United States government by force or violence, is protected up to the point where the expression poses a large, imminent danger to the well-being of the United States.

In the United States, most recent charges of governmental censorship in the national security arena have centered on the treatment of the press during military operations. It is important to note that most of the charges have been leveled not on the basis of any denial of freedom to speak or freedom to publish but on the denial of access to information. The Supreme Court of the United States has been reluctant to grant the press any special First Amendment right of access to any information except in the limited context of criminal proceedings (*Richmond Newspapers v. Virginia,* 1980). The First Amendment, then, protects speaking and publishing but has not been generally interpreted as guaranteeing that the press has a coextensive constitutional recourse to government information and materials.

Complaints about limited access have been made by the press when the government militarily intervened in Grenada, Panama, and the Persian Gulf. Negotiations with the Department of Defense eventually resulted in a 1997 agreement between representatives of the press and the government that was mutually accepted as balancing national security needs with the duty of the press to inform American citizens (Terry, 1997, p. 1). The agreed-upon principles included open and independent coverage by the press, use of "pool" coverage when conditions mandate it, credentialing of journalists, access to all major military units, noninterference with reporting by public affairs officers, the provision of transport and communication facilities for journalists, and an "agreement to disagree" on the issue of security review of stories produced by the journalists, which is, of course, a problem area (Terry, p. 3–5). The deletion of certain stories and facts might well result from such a security review by the armed forces, and this would constitute prior restraint or censorship, which, as noted above, would traditionally be upheld by the courts only when the information at issue posed a clear and present danger to the armed forces. However, the conservative judicial philosophy of the present federal court system has resulted in an "extreme deference accorded the government and the military" (Jazayerli, 1997, p. 161) that might well work in favor of any governmental assertion of a threat to national security. An indication that the agreement between the press and government is now working to some degree can be found in the fact that relatively few charges of censorship were made by the press over recent U.S. military actions in Bosnia and Kosovo, although the situation might have been different had U.S. ground troops been involved in substantial numbers in a ground war.

In the absence of a constitutional right, the general notion of a right of the American people to have access to governmental information has been embedded in the federal Freedom of Information Act (FOIA, 1994, and Suppl. 1996) and in similar state statutes in almost every state. These laws affirmatively grant a right of access and affirmatively impose a duty for government agencies to make available and publish particular kinds of information. Although Congress and the courts are not covered by the laws, and the federal law and state laws do contain exceptions (such as, notably, national security information, internal agency rules, commercial secrets, and so on), freedom of information laws have proven to be an effective way of opening government operations to citizen scrutiny in the United States. The culture of a "right to information" has permeated American society since the original adoption of the FOIA in 1966. So, even without the umbrella protection of the First Amendment, American citizens are privy to much of the innermost workings of their government, and the court system stands by as arbiter and potential ally when the government does attempt to block the flow of information.

The World Situation

Censorship in the name of national security is prevalent throughout modern democracies. Great Britain provides a good example of a country that does not hesitate to curtail expression for what it claims are national security reasons. Britain does not have a written constitution that sets forth the respective responsibilities and rights of the government and the people. Rather than constitutional law, British law has developed in parliamentary statutes, common law, judicial decisions, and custom and tradition. Without a "First Amendment" to serve as a foundational guardian of free expression, and without a judiciary committed to such constitutionally mandated freedom as the supreme law of the land, Britain has evolved into what some commentators have described as "one of the most secretive democracies in the world today" (Silverman, 1997, p. 471).

In the year 2000, Britain incorporated the European Convention on Human Rights into its own domestic law, providing Britons with at least the opportunity to have a right of freedom of expression that can be enforced in the British courts.

Under Britain's Official Secrets Act (1911), it is a criminal offense to disclose official information without authority, and it is likewise a criminal offense to receive such information. All government information is presumed official and thereby not subject to disclosure. Local governments have adopted the national model and are perhaps even more secretive that the national government (U.K., *Parl. Deb.,* Commons, 6s, 72:547, 1985). Britain currently has no freedom-of-information law like that in the United States that would grant statutory presumptive access to government information, although a limited version of a freedom-of-information law is planned for implementation sometime in 2002.

The British government has, in numerous instances in recent times, blocked publication of information it posited as a threat to national security, even going so far as to censor information in Britain that had already been published in other countries (Silverman, 1997, p. 490). Any change to the British penchant for secrecy in the name of national security will most likely be incremental and gradual.

Germany provides another example of a democratic society that does not hesitate to censor in the name of national security. The German constitutional system, or Basic Law, establishes numerous individual rights, including the right to free speech. However, basic rights must give way if they are perceived to be a threat to the fundamental constitutional structure of the country. Laws are allowed to limit individual liberties if the "purpose of the law has a higher rank of importance than the individual liberty itself" (McGuire, 1999, p. 765). Some forms of political speech are viewed as dangerous expression that potentially can do great harm to the internal security of the nation. Thus, German laws exist that ban Nazi propaganda, the Hitler salute, and even radical political parties as national security threats.

And Britain and Germany certainly do not stand alone among modern Western democracies. The Japanese Supreme Court, which has a textual mandate to protect freedom of expression through judicial review, "has never struck down a local, prefectural, or national ordinance or law on free speech grounds" (Krotoszynski, 1998, p. 905) even though numerous Japanese laws that are justified by a national security claim would appear as censorship to American eyes. The Irish Constitution specifies that free expression by both individuals and the press is qualified and that "seditious" speech and speech undermining "public order" are subject to punishment and control, and the government employs official censors (O'Callaghan, 1998, p. 53). France has been described as a nation where "patterns of thought remain firmly rooted in a monarchical tradition, because the French establishment is fearful of an open society, and because in France much is hidden and confidentiality esteemed," a nation where "censorship prevailed because the press is weak, the broadcasting media fearful of a government which has historically owned and subsidized it," and a nation "where the judiciary is timid and impoverished" (Sokol, 1999, p. 45).

Although this appraisal seems somewhat harsh, nonetheless France has openly and almost disdainfully exercised censorship in the name of security. In October 1995, when France set off underground nuclear tests in the Pacific Ocean that resulted in anti-French demonstrations around the world, 25 Danish high school students visiting Paris were deported for the threat they posed to French security. The threat was that they were wearing T-shirts decorated with "Chirac Non" (Whitney, 1995, p. 10).

Britain, Germany, Japan, Ireland, and France represent relatively long-established democracies. If similar scrutiny were applied to more recently emerged democracies in various parts of the world, the tendency of nations to censor for perceived national security reasons would become even more apparent. When freedom of expression comes into conflict with nation-specific values that are identified as crucial to that nation's continued existence, freedom of expression may well be curtailed. And that continued existence need not necessarily be the nation's actual physical existence; a great deal of censorship in the modern world is engaged in by governments intent on preserving a particular moral or religious existence.

CENSORSHIP FOR MORAL
AND RELIGIOUS REASONS

American Censorship

As indicated before in this chapter, the American position with regard to obscenity is somewhat at odds with its general posture as the world's leading defender of freedom of expression. In the year 1896, the U.S. Supreme Court confronted the challenge of deciding an obscenity case for the first time. Rather than legally defining obscenity, the Court chose to dwell on what it was not. The Court's ruling was that vulgar and coarse language was not obscene, and that obscenity, whatever its definition might be, was a concept dealing with a message "of immorality which has relation to sexual impurity" (*Swearingen v. U.S.,* 1896, p. 446). The Court next mentioned the subject of obscenity in *Near v. Minnesota* in 1931. It did so in an almost offhanded way, noting that obscenity was one of the few areas of expression that could be censored without raising any kind of constitutional problem. Chief Justice Hughes offered no legal explanation why this was true, nor did he offer any further definition of the term *obscenity*. In *Chaplinsky v. New Hampshire* in 1942, the Court felt comfortable in citing the *Near* position on obscenity and declaring that it fell into that class of expressions "of such slight value as a step to truth that any benefit that may be derived from them is clearly outweighed by the social interest in order and morality" (p. 572), still without clarifying the term *obscenity*.

Finally, in 1957 the Supreme Court took on the task of legally defining obscenity and spent the next 16 years finding that it could not do so. Justice Brennan, writing in the 1957 case *Roth v. U.S.,* accepted the Near–Chaplinsky position that obscenity was valueless speech that had no constitutional protection and made an initial attempt to define it: "Whether to the average person, applying contemporary community standards, the dominant theme of the material taken as a whole appeals to prurient interest" (p. 476). The problem with this definition became quickly apparent to Court members as they attempted to apply it to material charged as obscene in subsequent cases. What was "a contemporary community standard"? How does "prurient interest" manifest itself? In case after case throughout the 1960s, the Court wrestled with the problem of making what was "obscene" clear and understandable to the judiciary and the American people. What resulted was dissension and frustration and confusion among both Court members and the American public, illustrated in the now-famous disgruntled observation of Justice Potter Stewart that he could not define obscenity but "I know it when I see it" (*Jacobellis v. Ohio,* 1964, p. 184).

No definition of obscenity could command a majority of the Court during the 1960s and early 1970s. When a new, more conservative Court led by Chief Justice Burger faced the issue in 1973, they reached a solution that was more practical than elegant: Give the states some general guidelines and turn the vexing problem over to them. The definition of *obscenity* did not have to be uniform from state to state and community to community. Individual juries could make the determination. This solution by the Court forms the core of obscenity regulation in the United States today. Citizens in the United States must confront the legal fact that a videotape that is legal entertainment in Oregon (which provides state constitutional protection for obscenity) could well be a felony crime in North Carolina.

The general guidelines provided by the Burger Court for juries and judges in 1973 were as follows: (a) whether the "average person, applying contemporary community standards" would find that the work, taken as a whole, appeals to the prurient interest; (b) whether the work depicts or describes, in a patently offensive way, sexual conduct specifically defined by the applicable state law; and (c) whether the work, taken as a whole, lacks serious literary, artistic, political, or scientific value" (*Miller v. California,* 1973, p. 24). The Court also offered some examples of sexual representations that states might find obscene, including "patently offensive representations or descriptions of ultimate sexual acts real or perverted, actual or simulated, and "patently offensive representations or descriptions of masturbation, excretory functions, and lewd exhibition of the genitals" (p. 25).

What the Court did in *Miller* was to provide somewhat hazy boundaries for what might be termed hard-core pornography and then allow the states, if they wished, to define the material within these boundaries as potentially obscene, subject to a final finding of obscenity by the local community. Some communities have become almost obscenity refuges, safe from any obscenity convictions. The last successful obscenity prosecution in Manhattan occurred in 1973 (*People v. Heller,* 1973). By contrast, a LexisNexis search of appellate courts in the U.S. shows that there were 189 obscenity convictions appealed across the nation in just the five-year period from 1994 to 1999. Considering that only a small percentage of such cases are appealed, it seems safe to assume that obscenity prosecutions and convictions are progressing at a brisk pace in those communities that define pornography as a danger to their moral fabric.

A much different position is taken in the United States with regard to censorship for religious reasons such as heresy, blasphemy or sacrilege, and dissenting views concerning private morality. In these areas, the United States steps back into its role of defender of free expression. Censorship in these areas is never allowed; such speech is fully protected under the First Amendment, and even though such speech is often verbally attacked by those serving in government positions, no laws banning or punishing such speech have been upheld in modern constitutional history.

Moral-Religious Censorship around the World

The American predilection to single out obscenity as an area of expression bereft of protection is not necessarily shared around the globe. "Such 'puritanism' in the United States stands in contrast to many European countries' views of the subject" (McGuire, 1999, p. 756). In Germany, for example, obscenity is not "as central a policy concern" (p. 756). Likewise, England takes a more permissive legal stance on obscenity than the United States, defining obscenity according to the type of person who may obtain the material. The U.K. Obscene Publications Act of 1959 states that if a viewer is likely to be depraved and corrupted by the material, then the material meets the standards for obscenity. Thus, the law is primarily aimed at the protection of children, and graphic sexual materials that are restricted to the adult population are not necessarily considered obscene (Edick, 1998, p. 437).

Sweden and Holland have virtually no laws restricting obscenity, and both of these countries have large pornography industries (Friel, 1997, p. 252). The same is true in Denmark, where the use of pornography by adults is completely unhindered (Ditthavong, 1996). In Italy a generally liberal legal position prevails for pornography. Obscenity laws are vague. Material featuring juveniles is a crime, as it now is in many European countries, but otherwise it is up to a local Italian judge to decide what can go on sale ("Controlling Pornography," 1998).

However, some countries engage in even more intense censorship of obscenity than the United States does. In Ireland, for example, "banning a book or periodical is alarmingly simple" (O'Callaghan, 1998, p. 57). The Irish Constitution explicitly allows censorship, and censorship boards can and do operate to protect traditional Catholic ideas of morality. Ireland also employs government censors for videos and film.

A global look at the reaction of nation-states to pornographic and obscene materials thus reveals the same divergences in policy and law that affect all other areas of expression. In some parts of the world, extremely strict laws banning obscene materials are combined with equally strict laws dealing with religious heresy or blasphemy. An example of this occurs in the Muslim countries of Iran and Saudi Arabia, both of which assert that Islam justifies and mandates a special approach to human rights, including freedom of expression, and that the traditional Western democratic approaches are not suitable in their societies (Mayer, 1994,

p. 307). These countries argue that concepts like individualism, liberty, democracy, free markets, and the separation of church and state are out of place in an Islamic civilization.

The claim to a unique and valid alternative position on human rights leads quite naturally to censorship in the name of Islam. The 1990 Cairo Declaration on Human Rights in Islam, which was issued in Iran, enumerates rights and freedoms on which Islamic qualifications have been imposed. No freedom of religion is afforded in the Cairo Declaration. "The Declaration assumed that Islam is the true faith and that adherence to Islam is natural, with the consequence that it effectively bans other faiths from proselytizing" (Mayer, 1994, p. 334). The declaration does not provide for freedom of the press; in fact, Islamic criteria are used to limit freedom of speech. Opinions must be expressed in a manner not contrary to Islamic law, and people can advocate only what is "right" and "good," as specified in Islamic tenets. The declaration "bars the exploitation of misuse of information 'in such a way as may violate sanctities and the dignity of Prophets, undermine moral and ethical values or disintegrate, corrupt or harm society or weaken its faith'" (Mayer, 1994, p. 334).

In a manner similar to the declaration emanating from Iran, the Basic Law of Saudi Arabia denies any right to freedom of expression that might counter Islamic tenets. No guarantee of freedom of expression is included in the Basic Law. The media and the people are called upon to adhere to all state regulations while supporting the unity of the country, contributing to Islamic education, and using courteous language, and they are forbidden to publish or disseminate ideas that could lead to strife or degrade man's dignity. The law endorses "the existing censorship standards, which are extensive and stringently enforced by the government" (Mayer, 1994, p. 361).

A rejection of the Western concept of human rights as some form of cultural imperialism, and an acceptance of Islam as the source of human rights, can give rise to censorship activities that seem quite foreign from a Western democratic perspective. Such was the now-famous case of Salman Rushdie, an Indian-born internationally acclaimed British writer who won the prestigious Booker Prize for literature in 1981 and was a candidate in 1999 for the Nobel Prize in literature. The year after Rushdie published his novel *The Satanic Verses* in 1988, Iranian Ayatollah Khomeini issued a "fatwa," or law, that read as follows:

> To God we belong and to Him we shall return. I inform all zealous Muslims of the world that the author of *The Satanic Verses*—which has been compiled, printed, and published in opposition to Islam, the Prophet, and the Qur'an—and all those involved in its publication who were aware of its content are sentenced to death. I call on all zealous Muslims to execute them quickly, wherever they may be found." (Chase, 1996, p. 375)

The novel was perceived to be an obscene and mocking insult that attempted to undermine the authority of Islam's founder and its founding text. And, in the context of Islam, Rushdie had committed sacrilege, blasphemy, and heresy so great that death was a suitable punishment, to be carried out by believers regardless of where Rushdie might be. Western countries reacted to the original death sentence with horror and shock, and many countries severed formal relationships with Iran. After years of living under protection and in constant fear of death, Rushdie finally received a reprieve of sorts in 1998 when the government and religious leaders of Iran chose to distance themselves from the death sentence.

What is obvious from the foregoing example is that some nation-states deny the universality of the Western democratic conception of human rights and the subsequent importance of freedom of expression. Arguing from a perspective of religious purity, ethnic purity, cultural purity, monarchical fiat, or dictatorial necessity, these nation-states reject external norms as irrelevant or antithetical to their societies and embrace censorship as a means to a greater end. On a global scale of freedom of expression ranging from total censorship to absolute freedom, nation-states can be found that occupy almost all available positions. However, it is worthy of note that as the world advances in the direction of the "global village," the direction of movement on the scale seems conclusively toward the freedom end.

EXISTING INTERNATIONAL REGULATORY BODIES

As mentioned in the introduction of this chapter, numerous international regulatory and policy-making bodies govern aspects of the global trade in information and ideas. For the most part, the scope of these agencies is limited to areas such as broadcasting, where radio and television signals spanning international boundaries have the capability of interfering with one another (as well as the potential to carry political and social messages that are at odds with national standards). This "traffic cop" role is perhaps the primary role of such agencies. International agencies have also been formed when mutual cooperation forwarded social goals such as the protection of intellectual property rights—patents, trademarks, and copyrights—under treaties and conventions. The roles of the major international agencies will now be examined.

International Telecommunication Union

The International Telecommunication Union (ITU) was formed in 1932, growing out of the International Telegraph Union, which was itself formed in 1865. In 1947 the ITU became a specialized agency of the United Nations, with its headquarters in Geneva. In various forms it has played a dominant role in international cooperation and standard setting throughout the history of telecommunications, presiding over the first radiotelegraph convention, the first provisions for international telephone service, the first trials of broadcasting, the first world space radiocommunication conference, and the first world telecommunication standardization conference. It has played an active role in the implementation of virtually all communication technologies through standardization, technical coordination, and regulation oversight. It now functions as the ultimate manager of the world's telecommunication resources, allocating radio frequencies and communication satellite orbital positions to its member nation-states (Allison, 1993, p. 45). It does so at periodic meetings of the World Administrative Radio Conference (WARC).

The ITU has its own convention, constitution, and operating regulations, all of which have the status of international treaties. Its membership is made up exclusively of nation-states and includes most of the members of the United Nations, but nonstate entities such as private telecommunication companies can become members of the individual sectors. It is governed by a full Plenipotentiary Conference meeting every four years, at which a 43-member council that meets annually is elected. A general secretariat exists for administrative and management functions, and there is a secretariat for each of the ITU's three sectors, the radiocommunication sector, the telecommunication sector, and the telecommunication development sector (two-thirds of ITU's membership consists of developing countries).

Two major criticisms currently threaten the continued dominance of the ITU in its role as global overseer of telecommunications (Cook, 1999, p. 672). The first deals with voting power. Every member state has one vote, as in the General Assembly of the United Nations. The second concerns financial contributions, "which can vary by as much as a factor of 640 between the lowest level of contribution and the highest" (Cook). A small minority of its members contributes the great majority of the ITU budget, yet the great majority of the voting power resides in those countries that contribute "less than ten percent of its finances" (Cook).

Yet another problem facing the ITU is the growing importance of nonstate actors, primarily large commercial telecommunication firms, on the world telecommunication scene. They are currently without full membership privileges in the ITU but obviously are major players in the telecommunication area. Some people fear that these firms might together form a new organization that would lessen the role and impact of the ITU.

INTELSAT

The International Telecommunications Satellite Organization (INTELSAT) was established by the United States and various European countries in 1964. Initially, like the ITU, INTELSAT was primarily an organization directed by its member nation-states, although state-designated telecommunication entities also were part of a multilevel governance scheme. Operated much as a commercial cooperative, with 143 current member countries, INTELSAT was and is a wholesaler of satellite communications and links the world's telecommunications networks together. INTELSAT has 213 investing entities and owns and operates a global satellite system that delivers public switched network, private and business networks, Internet services, and video services to more than 200 countries.

What is unique about this quasi-governmental consortium is that, as of this writing, it is in the midst of going private. In 1998, INTELSAT created an independent spin-off company called New Skies Satellites N.V. that will be its own international competitor. This was a first step in a plan for INTELSAT to become completely private by the year 2001.

The desire to go private is motivated by the satellite telecommunications industry's frustration with the lack of competition in the global marketplace. Approximately 70% of the INTELSAT signatories are government-owned monopolies that control the access to individual markets, precluding U.S. and European companies from competing.

An indication of the growing reluctance of INTELSAT to submit to external nation-state controls occurred in October 1999. INTELSAT, which is headquartered in Washington, D.C., announced that it was looking at alternative sites outside the United States. "Unfriendly signals" from Washington legislators about its privatization plan were cited as providing the impetus for the proposed move (Taverna, 1999, p. 38).

The Communications Satellite Organization (COMSAT), the U.S. signatory representing U.S. interests to INTELSAT, is also in the process of going completely private as of this writing. COMSAT provides satellite communications in and out of the United States for 700 international customers, including telephony providers (AT&T, MCI WorldCom, and Sprint), broadcasters, other corporations, and the U.S. government; it also operates an integrated group of telecommunications companies. To oversee COMSAT's multinational role, U.S. federal law currently restricts its ownership. In September 1999, Lockheed Martin received permission from the Justice Department and the Federal Communications Commission to acquire 49% of COMSAT's stock. Lockheed Martin wants to eventually acquire all of COMSAT's stock and is presently awaiting congressional legislation that will allow it to do so (Asker, 1999, p. 27).

World Trade Organization

The World Trade Organization (WTO) is a Geneva-based international organization of more than 130 nation-states dealing with the global rules of trade between nations. It presently has an impact on telecommunications policy and intellectual property rights and may have a greater impact in the future as telecommunications, satellite technology, and computer technology converge. The WTO came into being in 1995 as a successor to the General Agreement on Tariffs and Trade (GATT) that was established after World War II, and now it administers all GATT provisions.

Decisions in the WTO are typically made by consensus arrived at through negotiations, or "rounds," at ministerial conferences held every two years in various countries and then are ratified by the members' parliaments. The WTO has a dispute settlement process established to interpret agreements and commitments and to make sure that members' trade policies conform to them. In February 1997, 69 WTO member governments, including the United States and its major trading partners, agreed to wide-ranging liberalization measures in the area of telecommunications services. Three additional countries have since made similar commitments. Essentially, these members have agreed not to engage in anticompetitive behaviors and to open their telecommunications systems up to foreign investment and control. Members have made commitments toward increasing international competition in voice telephony, data transmission, facsimile services, fixed and mobile satellite services, paging, and personal communication services. Although many of the signatories are not yet in compliance with this agreement (Ku, 1999, p. 111), its emergence marks the entry of a new player on the telecommunications global regulatory scene. A ministerial conference was held in the United States in November 1999, with its major agenda item being trade issues arising from global electronic commerce. The impact of this meeting on the future of Internet commerce is still undetermined.

The WTO also now administers GATT intellectual property provisions covering patents, trademarks, and copyrights, which are contained in the 1994 Agreement on Trade-Related Intellectual Property Rights (TRIPS). The copyright provisions closely parallel the Berne Convention rules (discussed below), setting minimum standards for copyright protection.

World Intellectual Property Organization

The World Intellectual Property Organization (WIPO) is an intergovernmental organization headquartered in Geneva, Switzerland. It is one of the 16 specialized agencies of the United Nations system of organizations. WIPO is responsible for the promotion of the protection of intellectual property throughout the world through cooperation among nation-states. The organization also administers various multilateral treaties dealing with the legal and administrative aspects of intellectual property.

The intellectual property concerns of WIPO fall into two categories: industrial property, chiefly in inventions, trademarks, industrial designs, and appellations of origin; and copyright, chiefly in literary, musical, artistic, photographic, and audiovisual works. A substantial part of the activities and the resources of WIPO is devoted to development cooperation with developing countries. The number of nation-states that are members of WIPO was 177 as of March 2001.

Industrial property deals principally with the protection of inventions by patents, marks (registered trademarks and service marks) and industrial designs, and the repression of unfair competition. The laws of a nation-state relating to industrial property are generally concerned only with acts accomplished or committed in the nation-state itself. Consequently, a patent, the registration of a mark, or the registration of an industrial design is effective only where the government office granted them. It is not effective in other nation-states. In order to guarantee protection in foreign countries, in 1883 eleven countries established the International Union for the Protection of Industrial Property by signing the Paris Convention for the Protection of Industrial Property. Since that time, the number of the members of the Paris Union has been constantly growing. The convention has been revised several times.

The Paris Union and WIPO—which furnishes the secretariat of the union—pursue the aim of strengthening cooperation among sovereign nations in the field of industrial property. The aim is to ensure that such protection be adequate, easy to obtain, and, once obtained, effectively respected.

In copyright, as in industrial property, the laws of a nation-state are generally concerned only with acts accomplished or committed in the nation-state. In order to guarantee protection in foreign countries for their own citizens, 10 countries established the International Union for the Protection of Literary and Artistic Works in 1886 by signing the Berne Convention for the Protection of Literary and Artistic Works. By 2000, more than 120 countries had signed the Berne Convention, which requires member states to recognize the moral rights of integrity and attribution. A member country must already have copyright protection within its own legal system that provides protection without a requirement for copyright registration and without a requirement for a notice of copyright to appear on the work. The author's work may not be exploited. The Berne Convention explicitly grants economic rights—the author has exclusive right to translate, reproduce, perform, or adapt protected works and may bring suit in any member country for actual damages and other remedies.

WIPO, recognizing the dangers posed by the new global information system, in 1996 passed two new treaties. The first, the Copyright Treaty, was intended to strengthen the Berne Convention by including protection for cyberspace commerce. The provisions of the WIPO Copyright Treaty included protection for computer programs and mandated that nation-states develop legal remedies to preserve the integrity of "rights management information" (Andrepont, 1999, p. 9). The second WIPO treaty, the Performances and Phonograms Treaty, dealt with protection for sound recordings in a digital environment.

The two WIPO treaties update the existing Berne Convention protections for creators of intellectual property and make clear the illegality of encryption violations and the circumvention of copyright protections. They also increase the protection provided to online works such as music, software, movies, and literary works. The treaties specify the limits of liability for information service providers and the telephone companies that serve as carriers for the protected works. The treaties also deal with the limits of the fair use exception to copyright violation for educational institutions and libraries.

As of this writing, 22 countires had ratified the treaties. For the treaties to achieve full force in the international community, a minimum of 30 countries will have to adopt the guidelines.

The Internet and Its Impact
on Global Communication Law

The increasingly widespread use of the Internet, a borderless technology with no international boundaries, has called into question traditional approaches to communication law and regulation in Western democracies. The traditional approaches are to some measure, as has been pointed out in this chapter, idiosyncratic and nation-specific, tailored to the perceived needs of different societies and different cultural heritages.

As might be expected, the United States is endorsing the principle of self-regulation for the Internet. Grounded in a constitutional system that has produced broad principles of freedom of speech, the United States has proposed that the content of the Internet be subjected to the same minimal controls that are applied to traditional media such as newspapers and magazines in the United States (Clinton & Gore, 1998) and that the Internet be allowed to respond to free market demands.

In the wake of *Reno v. ACLU* in 1997, in which the U.S. Supreme Court struck down as unconstitutional the Communications Decency Act passed by the U.S. Congress, the Administration has apparently even relaxed attempts to police pornography on the Internet, instead supporting software filters as a way to protect children from indecent Internet content (Clinton & Gore, 1998). The law that Congress passed and President Clinton signed in 1999 to try to cure the defects of the Communications Decency Act—the Child Online Protection Act (COPA, 1999)—has also been declared unconstitutional in a federal district court decision that was upheld by the Ninth Circuit Court of Appeals. In June 2001 the U.S. Supreme Court agreed to hear the case. Two of the U.S. Circuit Court judges hearing the appeal of that case expressed the opinion that it is probably impossible to create legislation that satisfies the First Amendment while at the same time controlling children's access to harmful content ("Appellate Judges Slam Internet Censorship," 1999).

Suppliers and distributors of pornographic materials that reach the level of illegal obscenity under *Miller v. California* can, of course, still be punished (if they reside in the United States) in those communities that are able to successfully try and convict them, in the same manner as suppliers and distributors can be punished for obscene materials in traditional media such as magazines and videotapes (*United States v. Thomas,* 1996). Likewise, existing laws aimed at child pornography can be enforced against U.S. violators who use the Internet as a medium. However, half of the sexually explicit material available over the Internet originates outside of the country and is thus exempt from the laws of the United States (Merchant, 1998, p. 429).

Existing libel and slander laws can be applied, as can privacy provisions, advertising regulations, and all other aspects of existing U.S. communication regulation, as long as all parties to all disputes reside within the United States. Because the current system of communication in the United States is the freest in the world, the U.S. vision of Internet control endorses a largely unfettered medium.

Other nations are not so sanguine about a relatively uncontrolled and unrestricted Internet that passes through national boundaries and exposes citizens to ideas and images that their cultures reject. Germany compelled CompuServe Inc., an Internet service provider, to completely block 200 discussion groups to German web sites in reaction to pro-Nazi messages (Knoll, 1996). France has prosecuted a Web site owner for uploading a book bearing secrets about a former French president. Singapore punishes both Internet users and providers who download and upload politically and morally objectionable material and imposes proxy servers, or "censoring computers," that keep its people from accessing outside Web pages that are currently banned by the government. China, in an attempt to protect its people from Western influences, built an Intranet that blocks Chinese people from the Internet, substituting for it a Chinese version, and plans to use proxy servers like those employed in Singapore when it does allow its citizens to access the worldwide Internet. Malaysia has condemned the Internet because of its Western ideas that are alien to Malaysian society and culture (Hanley, 1998, p. 997).

Despite the best attempts of various countries to regulate the Internet, no country's method has been globally effective. Nation-states can to some extent seek out and punish violators of communication laws within their own national boundaries, but absent some kind of agreement that is binding in all parts of the world, they are powerless to control messages and images totally and effectively that emanate from other nation-states. To compound the problem, senders of messages increasingly have the power to encrypt the transmission so that the receiver of the message has no capability of knowing who sent it. Screening and filtering software is imprecise and at the same time overwhelmed by the vast amount of information traveling across the Internet and the time required to properly classify and filter all information. Network providers have neither the jurisdiction in most countries nor the physical capacity to actively and adequately censor the entire Internet. Proxy servers, as described above, could be employed to limit a nation's citizens to carefully selected Internet sites, but this solution obviates the major benefit of the Internet—worldwide communication—and isolates the censoring country from the rest of the world.

The only apparent regulatory solution for the Internet is international agreement on censorship of intolerable speech. This censorship does not now exist and probably never will, except perhaps in the area of protection of children. Satellite and telephone international agreements exist, but they are aimed at resolving technical problems, not on achieving a desirable level of censorship among countries with vastly different cultures and mores.

So, in the absence of a satisfactory method of global Internet control, nation-states have two major alternatives. They can either embrace the direction in which the United States is heading—that is, endorse self-regulation for the Internet and then for the most part leave it alone—or they can opt out of the free flow of information and ideas that is the Internet and substitute a heavily censored, governmentally approved version that is expensive and difficult to maintain and only partially effective.

The "borderless" nature of the Internet may end up having profound effects on traditional communication law and policy enforced within a nation-state's borders. For instance, with material that could be judged obscene in the United States available to a U.S. citizen on the Internet from hundreds of sites around the world, does it still make logical sense to prosecute similar material that is generated in the United States? If a libelous statement about a British citizen can be published with impunity on the Internet because the statement originates outside the borders of England, should a similar statement be subjected to civil penalty just because it originates in England? Communication law and policy that are unenforceable on one medium—the Internet—are tainted with unfairness when they are applied to another medium—books, newspapers, movies, and the like—simply because that medium is more susceptible to control.

Long range, it may well be that what the Internet will cause is the erosion and eventual disappearance of communication law and policy aimed at any kind of content control in those countries that embrace a free Internet. And if projections hold true and many or most of the traditional media such as telephone, broadcasting, and newspapers converge and fold into the Internet, and if the Internet does become the backbone of international commerce in the 21st century, it may also well be that nation after nation will have to drop Internet censorship if they are to function on an equal basis with the other nations of the world, and thus they also will have to face the problems of an ungovernable medium. Is it possible that the birth of the Internet may indeed have signaled the death of all censorship throughout the world? Well, we shall see.

For more information on the topics that appear in this chapter, use the password that came free with this book to access InfoTrac College Edition. Use the following words as keyterms and subject searches: global communication law, freedom of expression, international covenants, media censorship, Freedom of Information Act, media regulations, human rights, regulatory agencies, trade organizations.

QUESTIONS FOR DISCUSSION

1. Is it a worthwhile goal to work for a common approach to freedom of expression throughout the world?

2. What is the best course for nations to take when national security seems threatened by free speech?

3. What position should nations take with regard to religious and moral censorship attempts by other nations on their own populations?

4. Should the roles of existing international communication regulatory/policy-making bodies be expanded? How?

5. What are various impacts the Internet might have on global communication law?

REFERENCES

Abrams v. U.S., 250 U.S. 616 (1919).

Agreement on Trade-Related Aspects of Intellectual Property Rights, Apr. 15, 1994, Marrakesh Agreement Establishing the World Trade Organization, Annex 1C, The Results of the Uruguay Round of Multilateral Trade Negotiations—The Legal Texts 365 (1994), 33 I.L.M. 1197 (1994).

Allison, A. (1993). Meeting the challenges of change: The reform of the International Telecommunication Union. *Federal Communications Law Journal, 45*, 491–514.

American Convention on Human Rights, 1144 U.N.T.S. 143 (1978).

Andrepont, C. (1999). Legislative update: Digital Millennium Copyright Act: copyright protections for the digital age. *Journal of Art and Entertainment Law, 9*, 397–413.

Appellate judges slam Internet censorship law. (1999, November 11). *EPIC Alert, 6*(19), 4. Retrieved from the World Wide Web: http://www.epic.org

Asker, J. R. (1999, September 20). Merger mania. *Aviation Week and Space Technology, 151*, 27.

Banjul Charter of Human and Peoples' Rights, 21 I.L.M. 58 (1982).

Bantam Books, Inc. v. Sullivan, 372 U.S. 58 (1963).

Chaplinsky v. New Hampshire, 315 U.S. 568 (1942).

Chase, A. (1996). Legal guardians: Islamic law, international law, human rights law, and the Salman Rushdie affair. *American University Journal of International Law and Policy, 11,* 375–435.

Child Online Protection Act, 47 U.S.C.S. § 231, Title 4 (1999).

Clinton, W. J., & Gore, A. (1998). *A framework for global electronic commerce.* Retrieved November 11, 1999, from the World Wide Web: http://www.iitf.nist .gov/eleccomm/execsu.htm

Controlling pornography: Law/how Britain compares with other countries in dealing with the problem of obscenity. (1998, August 13). *The Guardian* (London), p. 4.

Cook, K. V. (1999). The discovery of lunar water: An opportunity to develop a workable moon theory. *Georgetown International Environmental Law Review, 11,* 647–706.

Ditthavong, K. (1996). Paving the way for women on the information superhighway: Curbing sexism not freedoms. *American University Journal of Gender and the Law, 4,* 455–509.

Edick, D. (1998). Regulation of pornography on the Internet in the United States and the United Kingdom. *Boston College International and Comparative Law Review, 21,* 437–460.

Emerson, T. I. (1970). *The system of freedom of expression.* New York: Random House.

European Convention for the Protection of Human Rights and Fundamental Freedoms, 213 U.N.T.S. 221 (1953).

Freedom of Information Act, 5 U.S.C. § 552 (1994) and Suppl. (1996).

Friel, S. (1997). Porn by any other name? A constitutional alternative to regulating "victimless" computer-generated child pornography. *Valparaiso University Law Review, 32,* 207–267.

Gitlow v. New York, 268 U.S. 652 (1925).

Hall, K. L. (Ed.). (1992). *The Oxford companion to the Supreme Court.* New York: Oxford University Press.

Hanley, S. M. (1998). International Internet regulation: A multinational approach. *John Marshall Journal of Computer and Information Law, 16,* 997–1024.

International Convention on the Elimination of All Forms of Racial Discrimination, 660 U.N.T.S. 195 (1969).

International Covenant on Civil and Political Rights, 999 U.N.T.S. 171 (1976).

Jacobellis v. Ohio, 378 U.S. 184 (1964).

Jazayerli, R. (1997). War and the First Amendment: a call for legislation to protect a press' right of access to military operations. *Columbia Journal of Transnational Law, 35,* 131–173.

Jones, T. D. (1998). *Human rights: Group defamation, freedom of expression, and the law of nations.* Boston: Martinus Nijhoff.

Knoll, A. (1996). Any which way but loose: Nations regulate the Internet. *Tulane Journal of International and Comparative Law, 4,* 288–301.

Krotoszynski, R. (1998). The chrysanthemum, the sword, and the First Amendment: Disentangling culture, community, and freedom of expression. *Wisconsin Law Review, 1998,* 905–922.

Ku, R. (1999). A GATT-analogue approach to analyzing the consistency of the FCC's foreign participation order with U.S. GATS MFN commitments. *George Washington Journal of International Law and Economics, 32,* 111–153.

Mayer, A. E. (1994). Universal versus Islamic human rights: A clash of cultures or a clash with a construct. *Michigan Journal of International Law, 15,* 307–403.

McGuire, J. F. (1999). Note: When speech is heard around the world: Internet content regulation in the United States and Germany. *New York University Law Review, 74,* 750–792.

Merchant, M. J. (1998). Establishing the boundaries of First Amendment protection for speech in the cyberspace frontier: Reno v. ACLU. *Villanova Sports and Entertainment Law Forum, 5,* 429.

Miller v. California, 413 U.S. 15 (1973).

Milton, J. (Orig. 1644/1950). Areopagitica. In *Complete poetry and works of John Milton*. New York: Modern Library.

Murphy, J. G. (1997). Freedom of expression and the arts. *Arizona State Law Journal, 29,* 549.

Near v. Minnesota, 283 U.S. 697 (1931).

O'Callaghan, J. (1998). Censorship of indecency in Ireland: A view from abroad. *Cardozo Arts and Entertainment Law Journal, 16,* 53–80.

Official Secrets Act (OSA), 1911 (England).

People v. Heller, 33 N.Y.2d 314 (1973).

Procunier v. Martinez, 416 U.S. 396 (1974).

Reno v. ACLU, 521 U.S. 844 (1997).

Richmond Newspapers v. Virginia, 448 U.S. 555 (1980).

Roth v. U.S., 354 U.S. 476 (1957).

Silverman, D. L. (1997). Freedom of information: Will Blair be able to break the walls of secrecy in Britain? *American University International Law Review, 13,* 471.

Smolla, R. A. (1992). *Free speech in an open society.* New York: Alfred A. Knopf.

Sokol, R. P. (1999). Freedom of expression in France: The Mitterrand–Dr. Gubler affair. *Tulane Journal of International and Comparative Law, 7,* 5–42.

Stein, E. (1986). History against free speech: The new German law against the Auschwitz:—and other—"lies." *Michigan Law Review, 85,* 277–324.

Survey finds lukewarm support for free speech. (1999, July 28). *EPIC Alert 6*(12), 6. Retrieved from the World Wide Web: http://www.epic.orig

Swearingen v. U.S., 161 U.S. 446 (1896).

Swedish Penal Code, ch. 16, § 8 (1986).

Taverna, M. A. (1999, October 11). IntelSat to U.S.: We might leave. *Aviation Week and Space Technology, 151,* 38.

Terry, J. P. (1997). Press access to combatant operations in the post-peacekeeping era. *Military Law Review, 154,* 1–26.

Turk, D., & Joinet, L. (1992). *The right to freedom of opinion and expression: Final report* (U.N. Doc. E/CN.4/Sub.2/1992/9). New York: United Nations Commission on Human Rights.

United Kingdom. (1985). *Parliamentary Debates,* Commons, 6th ser., vol. 72, col. 547.

United States v. Thomas, 74 F.3d 701 (6th Cir., 1996).

Universal Declaration of Human Rights, G.A. Res. 217 (III), U.N. Doc. A/810 (1948).

Uyttendaele, C., & Dumortier, J. (1998). Free speech on the information superhighway: European perspectives. *John Marshall Journal of Computer and Information Law, 16,* 905–936.

Whitney v. California, 274 U.S. 357 (1927).

Whitney, C. R. (1995, October 17). Anti-nuke shirts get under Paris's skin. *International Herald Tribune,* p. 10.

6

✿

Global News
and Information Flow

KULDIP R. RAMPAL

Kuldip R. Rampal (PhD, University of Missouri—Columbia) is a professor of mass communication at Central Missouri State University in Warrensburg. A widely published author, Rampal received the 1993 International Communication Award from the Republic of China on Taiwan for his writings on press and political liberalization in Taiwan. He has coauthored a reference book on Afro mass media worldwide and is coeditor (with Y. R. Kamalipour) of the State University of New York Press series in Global Media Studies.

At the beginning of the 21st century, global news and information flow is at a crossroads. In February 2000 about 200 million people around the world were subscribing to the Internet, universally characterized as a revolutionary medium because it has opened up an altogether new world of information and communication (BBC World Service, Feb. 14, 2000). Apart from using the Internet as a speedy means of communication for personal and professional reasons, subscribers are turning to this multimedia, interactive medium to specify and obtain the news, information, and entertainment they need from across the world. This need-based information consumption pattern facilitated by the Internet is radically different from the centuries-old model in which the consumer is at the receiving end of news and information selected and purveyed by traditional media gatekeepers.

Internet reach, however, has a long way to go before the Internet becomes a medium of choice for most people around the world. Although thousands of new

 For additional online resources, access the Global Media Monitor Web site that accompanies this book on the Wadsworth Communication Cafe Web site at http://communication.wadsworth.com.

subscribers are logging on every day, only one-sixth of humanity—about 1 billion people—will be on the Internet by the year 2005, two-thirds of them outside the United States (Keohane & Nye, 1998, p. 82). The numbers, however, have more to do with the logistics of hooking into the Internet than with the appeal of this remarkable medium. At the beginning of the 21st century, three-quarters of the world's population does not own a telephone, much less a computer and a modem. Those who are not faced with these barriers, however, are adopting the Internet at a rate unmatched by many other innovations in history.

Purveyors of news and information worldwide, therefore, are faced with difficult choices. The interactive attribute of the Internet naturally makes the online consumer of news and information use this medium to meet specific needs. To remain relevant to this new class of information consumers, producers of mass media have to find new ways to fulfill their specialized and varied needs. Yet for at least another decade, traditional media will remain the primary sources of news and information for those of the world's population who lack access to the Internet. Thus, a critical question facing mass media producers at the dawn of the 21st century is, Do you just glue on to the Internet the paper-and-ink version of the traditional newspaper or magazine, or do you go beyond that in view of the versatility of this revolutionary medium and the unique information needs of the online consumer?

This chapter will first discuss the traditional news operations of international print and broadcast news agencies and news organizations and then review new directions in the packaging of news for online consumers. The chapter will also explore issues of quality and quantity in the flow of news between the developed and developing countries.

ORIGIN AND EARLY HISTORY
OF NEWS AGENCIES

News and mercantile information needs of the mass market press that emerged in the first half of the 1800s on both sides of the Atlantic provided the incentive for the creation of at least three of the major Western news agencies—the Associated Press (AP), Reuters, and Agence France-Presse (AFP). The mass market press, generally known as the penny press, had emerged as advertising became a significant source of revenue in industrially expanding societies, and readership increased because of the rising literacy and economic levels.

Sociologist Michael Schudson (1978) attributed the mass market for news in 1830s America to the emergence of a "democratic market society." More Americans were interested in business and politics than ever before. In business, this movement was expressed in the growth of a capitalistic middle class; in politics, it was known as Jacksonian, or "mass," democracy. The French saw their own versions of the so-called cheap press in 1836 as a vehicle for the restive middle class to push for more democracy—only 200,000 people could vote under the limited monarchy of Louis Philippe. In Britain, decreased newspaper production costs due to the removal of the newspaper stamp tax enabled the penny press to emerge in the 1850s to cater to a large, urban middle class.

Because no newspaper at the time had the financial and technical resources to gather and transmit news from far-flung areas to satisfy readers' growing demand for news, the stage was set for the establishment of news agencies. By selling their product to many newspapers, news agencies could supply a large amount of news at less expense than a newspaper would have to incur if it were to gather the same amount of news on its own. News agencies also had greater financial resources than the average newspaper to invest in technical facilities, such as the telegraph, to transmit the news as quickly as possible.

Agence France-Presse

The oldest of what were to eventually become the four major Western international news agencies, the Agence France-Presse (AFP) was created by Frenchman Charles-Louis Havas in 1835. Known as the Havas Agency at that time, the Paris-based news agency grew out of a news distribution service, used mostly by merchants and government officials, that Havas had started 10 years earlier. With the demand for news substantially up because of the emergence of the "cheap press" in France, Havas expanded his operations by hiring more correspondents and using the newly invented telegraph for faster delivery of news. By 1860 his agency was reporting news from all over Europe, and newspapers in most parts of the continent were subscribing to his agency.

Faced with Nazi aggression, the French government purchased the agency's news branch in 1940 to set up a propaganda office. The victorious Germans took over the agency and turned it into a part of the official Nazi news agency, DNB. In 1944, following liberation from occupying Nazi forces, the Havas Agency was given its present name, Agence France-Presse. In 1957 the French parliament passed legislation guaranteeing independence to the AFP.

Associated Press

The Associated Press (AP) grew out of the Harbor News Association, formed by 10 men representing six New York City newspapers in 1848 to pool efforts for collecting international news and to offset the prohibitive cost of transmitting news by telegraph. The newspapers at that time competed by sending reporters out in rowboats to meet the ships as they arrived in New York harbor. Competition had grown so fierce and expensive that it was decided to form a news cooperative. Cooperation among newspapers continues to be the operational policy of today's AP. In 1849 the Harbor News Association opened its first overseas bureau in Halifax, Nova Scotia, to meet ships arriving from Europe. This step enabled the association to telegraph stories to newspapers before ships docked in New York. Nine years later, news from Europe was arriving directly by transoceanic cable.

Following its merger with another news agency, the Harbor News Association became the New York Associated Press in 1857. To cut telegraphic costs, the New York AP formed news exchange agreements with regional newspaper groups in other parts of the country, including Western Associated Press, Southern

Associated Press, and Philadelphia Associated Press. The New York AP distributed the most important news to them, including news from Washington, D.C., and overseas. To this, each group added regional coverage. The Western Associated Press withdrew from the cooperative in 1885 and went on to form the Associated Press (AP), incorporated in Illinois, in 1892. The New York AP, which had fought this reorganization, lost and went out of business that year. The AP expanded rapidly, with 700 newspapers subscribing to its service by the mid-1890s. In 1900, AP was reorganized and incorporated in New York, where its headquarters have been ever since.

Two major changes have taken place in AP organization since 1945. In a historic decision, the U.S. Supreme Court held illegal a clause in AP bylaws under which members could block the effort of a competitor in the same city to obtain AP news service by requiring election to membership. As a result of the court ruling, AP membership was opened to all qualified U.S. newspapers. In 1946, radio stations, for the first time, were granted associate membership in AP, which allowed them to subscribe to its regular service. Previously, radio stations could subscribe only to a subsidiary service designed exclusively for them.

Reuters

Paul Julius Reuter, a German-born immigrant who took British citizenship in March 1857, opened a London office in October 1851, which transmitted stock market quotations between London and Paris using the first undersea cable. Two years earlier he had started using pigeons to fly stock prices between Aachen and Brussels. By 1859, Reuter had extended his service to the entire British press as well as to other European countries, expanding its content to include general and economic news. Read (1999) says that Reuter rightly regarded his general news service as running in tandem with his commercial services (p. 28). "[Reuter] was well aware that reports of battles lost and won, of political crises, or even of bad weather could affect markets, and that, conversely, news of market crises often had political effects" (p. 28). Branch offices sprang up throughout Europe and beyond as the international telegraph network developed. By 1861, Reuter reporters were located in Asia, South Africa, and Australia. By 1874, Reuter had established a presence in the Far East and South America.

A family concern until 1915, the agency became a private company later that year with its current name, Reuters Limited. The Press Association, the U.K. press agency, took a majority holding in Reuters in 1925, and in 1939 the company moved its corporate headquarters to its present location at 85 Fleet Street in London. In 1941, following acquisition of a substantial amount of the Reuters stock by British press associations, the agency became cooperative property of the British press. A Reuter Trust was also formed that year to safeguard the neutrality and independence of Reuters. Reuters was floated as a public company in 1984 on the London Stock Exchange and on NASDAQ in the United States. Reuters share ownership is now spread around the world, with the most significant holdings in Britain and the United States.

United Press International

The United Press International (UPI) was born July 21, 1907, as the United Press Associations because its founder, E. W. Scripps, believed there should be no restrictions on who could buy news from a news service. Scripps was opposed to the restrictive membership rules of the AP, as they existed then, because member publishers could deny AP's service to new publishers.

His determination to fight this restriction caused him to organize the Scripps-McRae Press Association in the Midwest and the Scripps News Association on the Pacific Coast in the early 1900s. In 1906 he purchased control of the Publishers Press, a small news service in the East, and merged the three services the following year to form the United Press Associations. The news agency's name was changed to United Press International on May 16, 1958, when its facilities were joined with those of William Randolph Hearst's International News Service and International News Photos.

A significant highlight in UPI's history is that it was instrumental in freeing up news collection and dissemination worldwide by rejecting a cartel arrangement established by the other major Western news agencies in 1869. The AP, Reuters, AFP, and the German news agency Wolff had agreed to collect and distribute news exclusively in certain regions of the world and to exchange it among themselves for subsequent distribution to their subscribers. Soon after its creation in 1907, UPI challenged the cartel by selling its service abroad, first to Britain and then to Japan and South America. Not wanting to be left behind, the AP signed agreements with Havas in 1918 and Reuters in 1926 to sell its service in their exclusive zones. The closure of Wolff in 1933 and operational disagreements among the remaining three members led to the formal breakup of the cartel in 1934.

UPI, the world's largest privately owned news agency, eventually could not keep up with competing services and has gone through two bankruptcy reorganizations and five owners since being sold by the Scripps family in 1982. Under the control of a group of Saudi Arabian investors since 1992 ("UPI Sold," 1992, p. 9), UPI was sold in mid-May 2000 to News World Communications, which owns the *Washington Times* newspaper. UPI president and CEO Arnaud de Borchgrave told the agency's staff members that although some top officials of News World Communications are members of the Unification Church, led by the Rev. Sun Myung Moon of South Korea, the church has no formal ties to News World Communications ("Moonies Acquire UPI," 2000).

ITAR-TASS

Another of the world's largest news agencies is the Information Telegraph Agency of Russia (ITAR-TASS), the successor to the Soviet TASS news agency, whose origins date back to 1904. Concerned that false reports were being circulated abroad about Russia's economic state, Emperor Nikolai II gave the go-ahead on July 21, 1904, to establish the St. Petersburg Telegraph Agency (SPTA) "to make internal business developments widely known" (ITAR-TASS, 2000). The agency began work on September 1, 1904.

SPTA became a comprehensive news agency in 1909, and its name was changed to Petrograd Telegraph Agency (PTA) in 1914. After the Bolshevik revolution of 1917, PTA was merged with Press Bureau, another government agency, and became Russian Telegraph Agency (ROSTA). ROSTA was created to distribute official communiqués and news items, as well as to send out propaganda material to the press in areas under Bolshevik control. The Telegraph Agency of the Soviet Union (TASS), with its headquarters in Moscow, replaced ROSTA on July 10, 1925. Under the Soviet media structure, TASS provided federal, state, and foreign news to national media and to each Soviet state's local news agency.

After the breakup of the Soviet Union in late 1991, Russia adopted the "Law of the Press," which abolished censorship for the first time in Russian history. A number of media organizations, however, were classified as "official," to be financed by the state budget. TASS was identified as one such official organization, although its director-general expects it to operate in an objective and professional manner (Ignatenko, 1993). In February 1992 the agency's name was changed to ITAR-TASS, following TASS's merger with the Information Telegraph Agency of Russia. It has retained its status as the state central information agency.

INTERNATIONAL NEWS AGENCIES TODAY

News dissemination by international news agencies has come a long way from Teletype delivery at 60 words per minute in the early 1950s. Today, news agencies using state-of-the-art telecommunications facilities—telephone, radio, cable, satellite phones, photo uplinks with mobile antennas, laptop computers with wireless satellite uplinks, and the Internet—can transmit up to 10,000 words per minute between any two points on the globe. On a typical day, the Associated Press, for example, is said to deliver millions of words and hundreds of photos and graphics. Let us turn to the contemporary operations of international print and broadcast news agencies.

Associated Press

The AP says its mission is to provide factual coverage of news to all parts of the globe for use by the media around the world. "News bearing the AP logotype can be counted on to be accurate, balanced and informed" (AP, Feb. 9, 2000). The AP subscribes to the code of ethics written by the Associated Press Managing Editors Association. As a not-for-profit cooperative, AP is owned by its 1,550 U.S. daily newspaper members. They elect a board of directors that directs the cooperative. The AP serves 1,700 daily, weekly, non-English, and college newspapers; 5,000 radio and television stations in the United States; and 8,500 newspaper, radio, and television subscribers in 112 countries. It has 3,500 employees working in 240 bureaus around the world, including 500 staff members abroad and 150 in Washington, D.C.

The AP says it sends more than 20 million words and about 1,000 photos each day to its subscribers worldwide. It serves as a source of news, photos, graphics, audio, and video for more than 1 billion people every day. As a cooperative, the AP also reserves the right to distribute stories done by its member newspapers to all its subscribers. The AP news services are delivered in the form of state, national, and international wires. A story that runs on a state wire will be seen only by newspaper and broadcast members in that state. A story that also "moves" nationally can be used by AP's U.S. newspaper members. A story that appears on AP's international wire reaches all of its international subscribers. The international wire is available in five languages (AP, Feb. 10, 2000). The AP has also offered a separate sports wire since 1946.

AP Information Services, started in 1990, packages and delivers AP content via the Internet to corporations and government agencies, and licenses AP content to online service providers. AP Online, one of the services offered by this division, is a news wire for the average consumer, composed of real-time, national-interest, headline news stories. The coverage is separated into various categories, including politics, business, sports, entertainment, weather, medical, transportation, crime, automobile, energy, and environment. In conjunction with a company called Audio Highway, AP Information Services also offers audio programming on the Internet, including up-to-the-minute newscasts 24 hours a day, live sportscasts, entertainment reports, business reports, and lifestyle commentary. Other services of this division include a Health and Wellness Wire and a Lifestyle Wire (AP, Feb. 19, 2000).

United Press International

Stating that "the world does not need another traditional wire service," UPI president Arnaud de Borchgrave announced in August 1999 that UPI would be transformed into a leading supplier of knowledge-based products to the Internet, "the fastest growing segment of the global news and information services market." According to de Borchgrave, this new line of products would be available under the company's new Knowledge@Work umbrella, "designed to meet the appetite of today's Internet clients for on-demand news, analysis, expert advisories and guidance, investigative pieces, and practical intelligence" (de Borchgrave, 1999).

UPI's new Knowledge@Work products include Global Impact Net, WebLine, and Specialized Web Newsletters. According to de Borchgrave, Global Impact Net delivers in-depth reporting, investigative pieces, and news analysis—as well as background and context—so that readers in the United States and around the world will know how Washington-based events are likely to affect them.

WebLine promises to be a streamlined, high-value, basic news service that will be ideal for Internet clients, the fastest-growing segment of the market. "WebLine delivers what clients need, and only what they need: brief, real-time, breaking news stories from around the world, including sports and entertainment, but without volumes of extra material to plow through. WebLine gives you what you want, when you want it, in a form you can easily use," de Borchgrave said.

UPI says Specialized Web Newsletters are produced by experts in the fields they cover. Developed for professionals and businesses, these newsletters equip subscribers to take action by delivering privileged, hard-to-get information; practical, specialized, expert guidance and analysis; and "over-the-horizon" insights and trend alerts on both business and policy matters. They serve as a focal point on the Web with their links to key think tanks and research centers (de Borchgrave, 1999).

A pioneer in radio news wire, UPI got out of the broadcast news business in 1999 as part of its plans to devote attention exclusively to products for and delivered via the Internet. The Associated Press acquired the UPI broadcast wire service and radio division and its 400 subscribers in August 1999. At that time de Borchgrave said that UPI would shed 47 radio news jobs but add 26 positions for coverage of specialized fields such as Internet newsletters and more in-depth stories.

At the time of this writing in February 2000, no information was available from UPI on its revenue or the number of subscribers to its new line of services. UPI has a total of 157 employees, including 107 in the United States, 28 in London, 16 in Latin America, and 6 in Asia. Its reports are disseminated through contracts with about 150 "redistributors" throughout the world, such as the Kyodo News agency of Japan.

Reuters

Reuters dedicates the bulk of its resources to providing financial information to the global financial markets, although it is also heavily involved in supplying news services to media subscribers worldwide. Its information and news products include real-time financial data, collective investment data, numerical, textual, historical, and graphical databases plus news, graphics, news video, and news pictures.

According to information supplied by Reuters, more than 519,000 users in 57,720 locations access its information and news worldwide. Data are provided for more than 940,000 shares, bonds, and other financial instruments, as well as for 40,000 companies. Typically, Reuters updates 3,200 prices and other data per second, with 65 million changes handled daily. Financial information is obtained from 282 exchanges and over-the-counter markets, contributed by 5,008 clients (A. Wolf, Reuters-America, personal communication, February 7, 2000).

News organizations in 157 countries subscribe to the agency's news service either directly or through their national news agencies, which translate the Reuters copy into their own languages for distribution. More than 3 million words of Reuters's copy are published daily. Reuters employs 1,946 journalists, photographers, and camera operators in 183 bureaus around the world. As of June 1999, Reuters had a total of 16,898 staff members in 212 cities in 95 countries. News is gathered and edited for both business and media clients in 23 languages. Reuters says its services are delivered to clients over the world's most extensive private satellite and cable communications network.

Reuters is also using the Internet extensively for wider distribution of information and news. In addition to the traditional print and TV media, Reuters provides news and information to more than 225 Internet sites, reaching an estimated 12 million viewers per month and generating approximately 140 million pageviews. In October 1999, Reuters launched its first real-time news and information product delivered and supported entirely on the Internet. Under the umbrella name of Reuters Inform, the company's first category of Internet-based services is designed for global agrimarkets and the North American power market. The services will comprise comprehensive agrimarket prices, breaking news, charts, weather maps, and customer bulletin boards. These services are expected to help large numbers of market professionals make better business decisions.

According to Reuters, potential customers for the North American power and agrimarkets products include farmers, agricultural cooperatives, food processors, traders, utilities, and other participants in the electricity and gas markets. Reuters Inform plans to serve the commodities and energy markets. The agency finds that "the Internet is ideally suited to the needs of smaller and geographically dispersed markets throughout the world." Based on the e-commerce business model, Reuters says that its online services will have "significantly lower delivery and administrative costs, online customer support, easy product upgrades and direct billing by credit card" (Reuters, Oct. 5, 1999).

Reuters believes that its premier position as a global news and information group is based on a reputation for speed, accuracy, integrity, and impartiality, as well as continuous technological innovation (Reuters, October 1999). Because three fourths of the revenue of Reuters comes from services provided to financial markets, it invests heavily in the development of computer technology and software to improve the quality of such services. For example, Reuters launched Dealing 3000, the next generation of its computer software for currency dealers in January 2000 after trial and feedback in 10 countries. For the first time, traders have the ability to integrate core Reuters information services while running currency trading applications (Reuters, Jan. 19, 2000).

Agence France-Presse

Like Reuters, AFP continues to provide a variety of services for the traditional media but is also developing a new line of services for the online sector. With its headquarters in central Paris, AFP provides general, economic, and sports news services in English, French, German, Spanish, Portuguese, and Arabic, delivering 2 million words a day.

The flagship general news wire carries about 120,000 to 200,000 words a day on politics, diplomacy, economics, society, sports, science, medicine, culture, people, and human interest. Subscribers include the new and traditional media, businesses, universities, embassies, institutions, and public offices. AFX News is the economic wire, a joint venture of AFP and Britain's Financial Times Group. AFX News provides real-time economic and financial news in English. Its subsidiary, AFX-Asia, specializes in the Asian marketplace. Services in French include economic, financial, and commodity wires, as well as an Internet product for traders. Sports AFP provides sports news in six languages and is the only international agency to distribute in Arabic. AFP also provides the sports news service in English and French and on the Internet.

AFP has developed a niche among news agencies for its photo service, which is recognized in the industry for its unique angle on general, international, and sports news. The photo service carries an average of 250 color photos a day in real time, as well as feature packages. AFP's archives contain more than 7 million photos, dating back as far as 1930. AFP says it has set up a state-of-the-art photo server called ImageForum, which allows subscribers to download images directly or through the Internet. The digital photo service is supplemented with about 80 maps, charts, and other graphics daily (AFP, Jan. 28, 2000). AFP's subscribers include 650 newspapers and periodicals; 400 radio and television stations; 1,500 businesses, banks, and public and private organizations; and about 100 national news agencies around the world. In addition to its editorial staff, AFP employs 1,200 reporters, 200 photographers, and 2,000 stringers in 165 countries (AFP, Jan. 28, 2000).

In February 2000, AFP announced a partnership with France's Alcatel telecommunications company to distribute information services through any fixed or mobile Internet device, including mobile phones, screenphones, and set-top boxes for televisions. General, economic, and sports news from AFP will be reformatted by Alcatel and automatically modified for the appropriate user device, regardless of screen size or operating system. AFP said the new service will enable telecommunications carriers to provide their users with access to personalized information services anywhere, anytime, and on any device. They will have access to extensive personalization and filtering tools that focus on the individual user's profile and interests (AFP, Feb. 2, 2000).

Less than a month earlier, AFP had signed a similar agreement with Finland's Nokia Corporation to provide news and information services based on wireless application protocol (WAP) and available through mobile phones. WAP is becoming a de facto standard for Internet content and advanced telephony services in digital mobile phones and other wireless terminals. The Finnish company estimated that by year 2004 more WAP-compatible mobile telephones than personal computers will be connected to the Internet (AFP, 1999). In early 2000, AFP's Internet services on WAP devices were available in French and English, and services in other languages were being planned. The stories are constantly updated and are independent of mobile phone manufacturer, gateway server manufacturer, and network provider. Subscribers can also receive news on preselected topics through email.

ITAR-TASS

In existence since 1992, ITAR-TASS is the state-owned successor to the Soviet-era TASS news agency. Whereas TASS was a propaganda arm of the Soviet communist system, often providing its news service practically free to countries that were potential candidates for communism, ITAR-TASS is struggling to become a credible, mainstream international news agency. By its own admission, however, ITAR-TASS's transition to an independent, objective, and reliable agency is still far from complete. Vitali Ignatenko (1993), director general of ITAR-TASS, told the London-based International Press Institute that, despite the abolition of censorship and other official restraints over the media in Russia, the political desire to make use of the media remains. For example, the news agency was frequently accused of being biased toward Boris Yeltsin during his political campaigns and presidency (p. 50).

In its attempt to gain international credibility, ITAR-TASS is paying renewed attention to its journalistic practices. The agency says it has developed a new set of priorities designed to streamline and improve key aspects of its operation, including how topics are selected, expansion of news coverage, and timely delivery of news. ITAR-TASS has 74 bureaus and offices in Russia and other CIS countries, and 65 bureaus in 62 foreign countries. In addition to Russian, the agency's news service is available in English, French, German, and Spanish. The English-language service distributes about 200 stories daily. ITAR-TASS's photo service distributes pictures of current developments in Russia, the CIS, and world. The agency's news service is available on the Internet on a subscription basis. It also offers specialized reports on Russian political and economic life in English on a subscription basis by fax or email (ITAR-TASS, 2000).

ITAR-TASS is facing stiff competition from another Russian news agency called Interfax, which offers general and financial news services. Interfax established its credibility in covering the 1991 coup attempt in Russia, when, unlike TASS, it became a major source of accurate and reliable information. Interfax claims that its current credibility is reinforced by the kind of customers it draws, including "the most distinguished corporations, investment funds, brokerage houses, banks, institutions, federal agencies and government structures worldwide" (Interfax, 2000). The agency has about 1,000 staff members in more than 70 bureaus. It produces more than 1,500 stories a day.

SUPPLEMENTAL NEWS AGENCIES

Whereas traditional news agencies, such as the AP and Reuters, are excellent in providing spot coverage, newspapers needing more specialized fare—such as hard news exclusives, investigative reporting, political commentary, and concentrated business coverage—turn to supplemental wire services. David Shaw, media writer for the *Los Angeles Times,* says that reporters who like to write investigative stories or stories that challenge the establishment find little opportunity to do so with traditional wire services such as the AP or Reuters because they are in the business of mass marketing the news (Shaw, 1988).

The major supplemental services in the United States are the New York Times News Service, the Los Angeles Times–Washington Post News Service, and Dow Jones Newswires. Founded in 1917, the New York Times News Service is the world's largest supplemental news service, distributing news gathered by the Times and its 12 partner news organizations to 650 clients in more than 50 countries. In addition, the New York Times Syndicate serves more than 2,000 clients worldwide. The syndicate edits and distributes columns, special features, news and news services, magazines, and book excerpts from many different countries and points of view. The service is available in English and Spanish (New York Times News Service, 2000).

Subscribing to the Los Angeles Times-Washington Post News Service gives organizations access to the reports of 11 contributing publications. The service provides national and international news, analysis, and features and averages 110 stories a day. This service, also available on the Internet, has 600 clients in 56 countries (Los Angeles Times–Washington Post News Service, 2000).

Dow Jones and Company's rebranded news service, Dow Jones Newswires (DJN), is a leading supplier of real-time news and market information to the business and financial community worldwide. The service's 800 editors and reporters around the globe put out 1,500 stories a day, which are distributed to 317,780 terminals around the world (J. McGeady, DJN, personal communication, February 14, 2000). Dow Jones NewsPlus is an online branch of the service providing real-time financial information to the international business community. DJN also offers Dow Jones Interactive, a Web-based business intelligence service, provided jointly by Dow Jones and AP news wires.

BROADCAST NEWS SERVICES

Reuters and Associated Press Television News (APTN) are the two dominant video news agencies in the world today, after taking over the operations of Visnews and WTN, respectively, in recent years. Reuters claims to have the world's largest television news service, twice the size of CNN's international newsgathering operations (Wood, 1998). Reuters provides television broadcasters and Internet providers with international news video in the areas of breaking news, business, and sports categories. The agency's World News Service is the prime delivery vehicle for its news feeds and specialist services, such as Reuters Reports.

Updated every 6 hours, Reuters Reports provides the top 10 to 12 stories of the moment in ready-to-air format, with a total of 60 international news and sports stories each day. An English-language voiceover on one audio channel is complemented by natural sound on the other. A transcript of each voiceover is also provided to enable translation. Major breaking news stories are run alongside business news and feature items. Reuters Reports is also designed to serve the needs of Internet sites that wish to offer video news clips. The Reuters network of 184 bureaus in 163 countries forms the backbone of the video agency's newsgathering activities. Some 310 subscribers plus their networks and affiliates in 93 countries use Reuters television news coverage (Wolf, 2000).

APTN is the international television arm of the Associated Press since 1998 and the successor to APTV, a video news service launched in 1994. APTN provides video of the day's top news stories by satellite to major news organizations worldwide from 83 AP bureaus in 67 countries. A total of 330 international broadcasters receive AP's global video news service, APTN, and SNTV, a sports joint-venture video service. SNTV is offered in collaboration with Trans World International, an independent supplier of sports programming. SNTV serves more than 100 broadcasters worldwide (APTN, 2000).

The AP launched the AP Radio Network in 1974 to provide hourly newscasts, sportscasts, and business programs. In early 2000 the service was received by nearly

1,000 AP broadcast members. A digital 24-hour-a-day radio service, All News Radio (ANR), was started by AP in 1994. More than 70 radio stations are now ANR affiliates. In August 1999, AP acquired United Press International's broadcast news division and its 400 subscribers. The Wall Street Journal Radio Network offers the Wall Street Journal Report, with 18 two-minute hourly business and financial newscasts each weekday and 6 weekend reports. This network also offers the Dow Jones Money Report, which provides 16 one-minute news briefs on money news and consumer trends. CNN operates a national and international radio network known as CNN Radio Network. Beginning every hour, the network offers a 5-minute newscast, with the latest information on news in the United States and around the world. Stations have a choice of running 2 minutes, 3.5 minutes, or the full 5-minute newscast. The network also offers a 2-minute newscast at half past every hour. Affiliate stations are alerted ahead of time when this broadcast will be breaking news. CNN's other radio divisions provide sports and business news.

GLOBAL NEWSPAPERS, MAGAZINES, AND BROADCASTERS

Several international newspapers, magazines, and broadcasting organizations also play a significant role as purveyors of news globally. Three newspapers that are especially valued by opinion leaders around the world are the *New York Times,* the *Times* of London, and *The Guardian,* also from Britain. In 1999 the *New York Times* had a weekday circulation of just over 1.15 million and Sunday circulation of 1.65 million. The New York Times online had more than 10 million registered users in February 2000; 13% of the users were from abroad. This service recorded 92 million page views in November 1999. The London *Times* has a daily circulation of almost 1.3 million, and *The Guardian* sells 386,942 copies daily. Both British newspapers are available on the Internet as well. A truly global newspaper, although not as influential among global opinion makers as the preceding three, is the *International Herald Tribune,* which is American-owned and based in Paris. It is printed simultaneously via satellite at 10 locations worldwide and distributed globally. In early 2000 it had a daily circulation of 227,945, with a total readership of more than 600,000 in 181 countries. Much of its copy comes from the *New York Times* and the *Washington Post,* which, along with Whitney Communications, own this newspaper.

The *Wall Street Journal,* the flagship publication of Dow Jones and Company, is a global business daily. With the *Wall Street Journal Europe,* published in Brussels, and the *Asian Wall Street Journal,* published in Hong Kong, it has a worldwide circulation of about 1.9 million. Another prestigious global business newspaper is the *Financial Times* of London, which also publishes a North American edition via satellite. In 1999 it had a circulation of 50,000 in the United States and 308,744 elsewhere in the world.

Among newsmagazines, three stand out for their global reach—*Time, Newsweek,* and Britain's *Economist. TIME,* with its 1999 circulation of 4.10 million in the United States alone, sold an additional million-plus copies to readers overseas.

It publishes editions for Canada, Europe, the Middle East, Asia, Africa, and Latin America. *Newsweek*'s 1999 U.S. circulation was just over 3.2 million; in addition, the magazine sold about 1 million copies internationally through its editions for Europe, Japan, Latin America, the Pacific, and Southeast Asia. *The Economist,* with a strong reputation for its comprehensive coverage of global issues and good writing, had a worldwide circulation of 654,214 in 1999.

In international television news broadcasting, CNN International is a global, 24-hour news network, offering comprehensive news coverage from the CNN News Group's 34 worldwide bureaus since 1985. Programmed specifically for a global audience, CNNI transmits four separate feeds that broadcast to the Asian Pacific, Europe, Latin America, and the United States. Combined, CNN/U.S. and CNNI can be seen in more than 225 million television households in 212 countries and territories worldwide, including 82.5 million subscribers for the two services in the United States. The CNN News Group has a newsgathering network of 4,000 staff and 850 global television affiliates (CNN, 2000).

CNN International's biggest competitor today is BBC World, the British Broadcasting Corporation's international news and information television channel, broadcasting 24 hours a day around the world from its headquarters in London. In operation since 1991, BBC World is available in 71 million homes 24 hours a day, and in an additional 96 million homes during part of each day, in nearly 200 countries and territories worldwide. BBC World provides news, business, sports, and weather 24 hours a day, plus the best of the BBC's current affairs, documentary, and lifestyle programming. BBC claims that it is the world's largest and most trusted news organization. BBC News, which supplies news programming for BBC World, has 50 bureaus worldwide, with more than 250 correspondents and a staff of more than 2,000. BBC World is a commercial channel funded by advertising and subscription.

In the United States, BBC's U.S.-specific channel, BBC America, is received in nearly 10 million homes. This channel carries BBC World's half-hour news bulletins in addition to some other public affairs programming. Since a 1998 agreement with U.S. public television, BBC World news bulletins are also available to 45 million TV households in the United States. BBC World provides dedicated local programming for the channel's substantial audiences in Europe and India, plus 70 hours per week of Japanese translation. Partly for that reason, BBC World's reach in India in early 2000, for example, was double that of CNN International's (BBC World, Feb. 16, 2000). BBC World became available on the Internet in 1999, when it dedicated the world's first all-digital 24-hour newsroom in London.

Another significant player in international television news broadcasting is Deutsche Welle TV, the German public broadcaster's international satellite television channel. DW-TV broadcasts news and public affairs programming in German, English, and Spanish in rotating 2-hour time slots. Canada's Newsworld International, another emerging 24-hour news channel, has been available in the United States for several years by direct-to-home satellite television. As more countries take advantage of satellite communication technology, additional sources of television news are becoming available for international audiences. Among the countries operating 24-hour international channels that carry some news programming in English are Japan (NHK and Channel J), India (DD World), China (CCTV), Egypt (Nile News), and South Korea (Arirang TV World).

The flow of news internationally through radio has been a reality for several decades, although it has generally been viewed as propaganda because international radio broadcasting has been performed primarily by government-run stations. Two government-sponsored stations, however, have established their credibility as reliable sources of news to listeners worldwide. They are the BBC World Service and the Voice of America. The BBC World Service, which went on the air in 1932, broadcast in 1999 to an international radio audience of 143 million, including 3.5 million regular listeners in the United States, in 44 languages (BBC World Service, 1999). The service is also available on the Internet. Studies have shown that, in several countries, BBC World Service news is regarded as more credible than the native radio newscasts (Rampal & Adams, 1990).

The Voice of America, established as the international broadcasting service of U.S. government in 1942, reached some 91 million listeners worldwide in 1999. VOA puts out more than 900 hours a week of broadcasts in English and 52 other languages. A network of 40 VOA correspondents and 100 freelance reporters in major cities worldwide covers news events. Voice of America broadcasts programs over the Internet from all 53 of its language services (VOA, 2000). Other major international broadcasters include Radio Moscow, Radio Beijing, Deutsche Welle Radio, Radio France International, Radio Nederland, All India Radio, and Radio Cairo.

NEWS FLOW PATTERNS: OFFLINE AND ONLINE

Before turning to the implications of the Internet for global news flow, let us review the problems and patterns in the flow of news associated with the traditional media system. Developing countries have been long concerned because the four major Western news agencies control the bulk of the world's news flow, with an output of about 30 million words daily; the next five leading news agencies accounted for only 1.09 million words daily in early 1990s (Frederick, 1993, p. 128).

Developing countries have also raised specific concerns since the 1970s regarding the pattern of news flow emerging from the dominance of Western news agencies. First, people in developing countries are forced to see each other, and even themselves, through the medium of these agencies because they are major suppliers of news to the developing world. Second, Western information dominance confines judgments and decisions on what should be known, and how it should be made known, into the hands of a few, resulting in an inadequate, negative, and stereotypical portrayal of developing countries. Third, the flow of news is heavily imbalanced, with information moving predominantly from advanced Western countries to developing countries. The fourth area of concern is that the West exercises a kind of "soft power" by virtue of the strong appeal of its cultural fare—films, television, music, books, and magazines—in the developing world, to the detriment of local cultural traditions.

Some recent studies lend support to these concerns. A 1996 study on the Associated Press, the largest news agency, found that "the distribution of AP bureaus and correspondents seems to reflect American corporate and government priorities among core regions and glacial disinterest in peripheral Third World regions" (Schiff, 1996, p. 12). The "core regions" for the AP constituted western Europe and Japan, the sources of much of the AP output outside the United States. The study also found that the republics and satellites of the former Soviet Union, central and south Asia, central America, and Africa are undercovered by the AP. A content analysis study of the *New York Times* found that the foreign news hole was shrinking and that international news was increasingly being reported within the context of U.S. interests. Additionally, reports on Western industrial nations dominated, and coverage of developing nations had decreased (Riffe, 1996, p. 17).

The imbalance of news flow is not just a developed/developing countries phenomenon, however. A content analysis study of the *New York Times, Washington Post,* the three major newsmagazines, and the commercial network news found that Scandinavian coverage was mostly crisis oriented, "enough so as to conclude that the Third World has no exclusive right to complaints that the U.S. media largely overlook developmental stories in favor of spot crisis-oriented news" (Fridriksson, 1993). The study also found that, were it not for the reporting of various isolated crises, overall coverage of Scandinavia in the American media would be so scant as to be practically nonexistent.

In a 1998 article, Herbert Schiller notes that "the American state of ignorance of the rest of the world has been extended since the end of the Cold War." Schiller cites a television news study to prove his point:

> the number and length of foreign topics in the evening news have declined far below Cold War levels. As a percentage of all topics between 1970 and 1995, the share of foreign stories fell from 35 percent to 23 percent, and the average length of these stories dropped from 1.7 minutes to 1.2 minutes. Worse, while the networks devoted on average more than 40 percent of total news time to foreign items in the 1970s, that share had been cut to 13.5 percent of news time by 1995. (p. 189)

Support for developing countries' concern over "soft power" comes from a 1998 article in the *Washington Post,* which reports that international sales of American popular culture products totaled $60.2 billion in 1996. The article quotes sociologist Todd Gitlin, who calls American popular culture "the latest in a long succession of bidders for global unification." Gitlin continues, "It succeeds the Latin imposed by the Roman Empire and the Catholic Church, and Marxist Leninism imposed by Communist government" (Farhi & Rosenfeld, 1998, p. A1).

These studies and articles also support some earlier theories on international news flow. Hester (1973) posits that nations of the world have designated places in an international pecking order. Perceptions of positions in that order partially determine the flow, direction, and volume of news. Hester also argues that strong economic relations or cultural affinities will increase the flow of news among nations, as will the perception of threat between any two nations. Galtung (1971) says that there is a "center-periphery" pattern in the flow of international news. News, he notes, flows mostly from the "center," or dominant countries, to the "periphery," or dependent areas. Kariel and Rosenvall (1984) find that the "eliteness" of a nation as a news source is the most important criterion for news selection.

Developing countries have tried various ways to address their concerns regarding international news flow. Beginning in the mid-1970s, they pushed for a new world information order (NWIO) through UNESCO. Among a variety of actions proposed to address problems associated with international news flow, one proposal called for regulating collection, processing, and transmission of news and data across national frontiers. Western countries strongly rejected such a move, with the United States and Britain eventually pulling out of UNESCO when the NWIO debate was seen to be taking political overtones. Then, upon UNESCO's recommendation, developing countries moved to establish or expand their own regional and global newsgathering operations. As a result, the developing world saw a variety of regional news agencies, including the Non-Aligned News Agencies Pool, Latin America's Inter Press Service, Manila-based DEPTH, the Pan African News Agency, and the Caribbean News Agency. With the possible exception of Inter Press Service, none of these agencies has posed a serious challenge to the major Western news agencies or acquired significant credibility for its own news service.

The Internet offers the best hope to developing countries seeking a low-cost vehicle for news distribution and a more balanced flow of news globally. For example, Gopal Raju, publisher of the New York–based newspaper for the Indian community, *India Abroad,* started India Abroad News Service (IANS) in 1987. From serving a single subscriber free in 1987, IANS now has more than 45 newspapers as commercial subscribers in India and abroad. Almost every major newspaper group in India subscribes to IANS, which is headquartered in New Delhi and accredited with the Indian government as an Indian news agency. In addition, IANS has subscribers in the United Arab Emirates, South Africa, Bangladesh, Sri Lanka, Australia, and Canada. An IANS spokesman in New York said that such an operation would not have been possible without the Internet, which greatly reduces the cost of news distribution to subscribers. According to a news release from the agency, "For the first time, news about India or of interest to India from different countries is being reported by IANS with an Indian perspective and not seen through the prism of the State Department or Whitehall or through the tinted eye glasses of a Western reporter" (IANS, 2000).

The Internet, however, is not a panacea for tackling the various concerns that the developing world has raised about global news flow. Although the distribution of news by a news agency to its clients via the Internet is much cheaper than via the traditional telecommunications system, a budding news agency must meet other costs and challenges before it acquires the necessary credibility as a global news service. For an emerging news agency to offer a comprehensive and quality news service, it must have an adequate number of professionally educated and trained reporters around the world. The financing required to hire the necessary staff and maintain news bureaus around the world is beyond the reach of most developing countries. And then there is the issue of quality of information. In the glut of information available on the Internet, credibility will be a key source of power and influence. Keohane and Nye (1998) say that news organizations in the United States, Britain, and France have capabilities for collecting intelligent information that dwarf those of other nations, adding that "information power flows to those who can edit and credibly validate information to sort out what is both correct and important. . . . Brand names and the ability to bestow an international seal of approval will become more important" (pp. 88–89). Emerging news agencies will have a lot of catching up to do before they can compete with the established Western news agencies, and that will not be an easy task. As Keohane and Nye say, "In some commercial situations, a fast follower can do better than a first mover, but in terms of power among states, it is usually better to be first" (p. 88).

The Internet has a greater promise in serving as an equalizer in the skewed flow of news and information globally, another of the concerns raised by the developing world. The typical 8% of the news and editorial space devoted to international news by an average U.S. metro daily—or about 14% (just over 3 minutes) of news time for such news programmed by television networks in the United States—does not offer much of a window on the world. Now, at the click of a mouse, an Internet subscriber can be reading newspapers from across the world while at the same time taking in the audiovisual news services of an increasing number of Web-based international broadcasters, such as BBC World. For example, the *Washington Post* ombudsman noted with embarrassment that it took until November 12, 1999, for the *Post* to carry a comprehensive story from its Delhi-based correspondent about a cyclone that hit the east Indian state of Orissa at the end of October. The *Post* story on the cyclone, which had claimed 10,000 lives and affected 15 million people, was not on the front page; it ran, instead, on page A27. One reader, having found the news about the cyclone in a number of English-language Indian newspapers and other news outlets on the Web, wondered in a letter to the editor whether the *Post* was ignoring the story because "Orissa is not Europe and does not have oil underground" ("Where in the World?" 1999, p. B6).

Another component of the information age, international satellite television, is providing more international news and information than ever before. Dozens of countries are transmitting daily television programs around the clock from Europe, the Middle East, Asia, and Latin America to niche and ethnic markets in the United States and elsewhere in the world. The huge supply of digital channels is also bringing crystal-clear radio programming from scores of countries via both communication satellites and the Internet.

A significant dimension of news flow on the Internet is that people in nondemocratic states are beginning to have access to uncensored news, analysis, and discussions about political developments in their own countries, even though regimes in such countries are jittery about the free flow of information. For example, the *New York Times* reported on March 18, 1999, that in the Middle East every government has jammed radio broadcasts, intercepted publications, scuttled fax transmissions, barred mobile telephones, or prohibited satellite television at one time or another (Jehl, 1999). The *Times* story adds that with the arrival of the

Internet in the mid-1990s, many countries, including Egypt, Jordan, and Lebanon, have quietly conceded the fight, concluding that the benefits of the new technology far outweigh the cost. Other countries, such as Saudi Arabia, Iran, China, Malaysia, and Singapore ("Singapore Unveils," 1996, p. B8), have been in the news in recent years for taking action to keep politically objectionable material out of the reach of their Internet subscribers even as they embrace this technology for economic development and other uses. With new Web sites emerging every day, however, it is practically impossible to keep Internet users in authoritarian and totalitarian regimes from gaining access to freewheeling news and political discussions. Nye and Owens (1996) see a great opportunity in the Internet for the United States to "engage the people, keeping them informed on world events and helping them prepare to build democratic market societies when the opportunity arises" (p. 30).

With all the promise that the Web holds for addressing some of the asymmetries in the global news and information flow, there is a major problem. As mentioned at the beginning of this chapter, only one sixth of humanity will be on the Internet by 2005. Most people will not have access to the Internet, because of the underdevelopment of telecommunications infrastructure necessary for getting online. That only 100 million subscribers to the Internet were outside the United States in February 2000, however, indicates that, even when there are no infrastructure problems, millions of people are not able to get online. In a move to narrow the "digital divide" between countries with access to information technology and those without, the World Bank and a Japanese Internet investment group, Softbank, set up a fund in February 2000 to help developing nations expand Internet projects. James Wolfensohn, president of the World Bank, said that the $520 million fund will be used to help set up indigenous companies to promote the Internet in 140 developing countries (BBC World Service, Feb. 14, 2000).

THE OUTLOOK

The expansion of political and civil liberties, including press freedom, in several parts of the world bodes well for the collection and free flow of news. The emergence of democracy in Russia, Eastern Europe, Latin America, and a number of African countries, as well as the expansion of democracy in Asia, has considerably lessened, if not eliminated, the obstacles that news agencies and foreign correspondents encounter in covering news. The New York–based Freedom House, which annually publishes a report on the status of civil liberties and press freedom around the world, said in its 1998–1999 report that 88 of the world's 191 countries (46%) were rated as "free," meaning that they maintain a high degree of such freedoms. Although this is the largest number of free countries on record, the remaining 54% still pose a major challenge to unhindered collection and flow of news. Totalitarian holdovers and authoritarian governments in many countries continue to create several obstacles in the coverage of news, including restricted access, explicit or implicit censorship, and pressure against correspondents, extending as far as expulsion. Two publications, *International Press Institute Report* and

Index on Censorship, regularly chronicle the pressures and dangers that local and international journalists face in carrying out their duties.

Restricted access results in incomplete and unreliable information because information must be obtained from visitors and from radio broadcasts, which are mostly produced by state-run radio. Explicit censorship results in deletions or refusal to transmit correspondents' copy. Implicit censorship is less obvious but nearly as inhibiting to balanced news coverage. Often the most difficult official sources for the foreign correspondent to reach are those who can best explain the story of their countries to the world. Also, when the local press is restricted to publishing only government-approved news, foreign correspondents' access to balanced local information suffers. This makes more difficult the foreign correspondents' efforts to understand and explain the country to readers in distant places. Direct action against foreign correspondents is the most extreme and dangerous obstacle to free news coverage. Wire service correspondents are often expelled because the government objects to the reporting of specific news. With the expansion of democracy, the trend against such restrictions will continue to grow.

Economic growth and the opportunities provided by the Internet should make it easier for many developing countries to expand their newsgathering and news dissemination operations. The India Abroad News Service is a good example of such possibilities, as is Bernama, the Malaysian news agency, which has expanded its reach into the member countries of the Association of Southeast Asian Nations. Several developing nations—including India, China, Indonesia, Brazil, Mexico, and countries in the Arab League—have their own communication satellites, providing them added abilities to collect and disseminate news globally. Developing countries are also increasingly stationing their own correspondents in major news capitals of the world. These factors should facilitate the newsgathering abilities of a number of developing countries and help reduce their dependence on Western news agencies. But developing countries need more than the newsgathering and transmission infrastructure before they can be seen as credible purveyors of news at home or globally. They need to appreciate and have their news agency staff employ sound journalistic practices within the framework of democratic political systems, human rights, and press freedoms. Fifty-four percent of the world's nations do not operate under such a framework, which will make it difficult for them to have their own viable and credible news agencies.

As for global news flow, various technologies of the information age will alter the patterns of news and information flow as well as the packaging of media products. For the online consumer and the person willing to spend money to receive international television, patterns of news and information flow have already changed radically since the mid-1990s. Online consumers can go straight to the Web editions of newspapers and magazines and, increasingly, to radio and television news broadcasts from many countries to satisfy their information needs when they feel that the indigenous media are not meeting those needs. At the same time, satellite television allows viewers today to jump from CNN or BBC World to China's CCTV, India's DD World, or one of a host of other niche-oriented stations from around the world. Marshall McLuhan's "global village" is indeed upon us.

News and information packaging for the Internet generation is also changing. As noted in this chapter, every major news organization is putting its services online and looking for new ways to better serve the consumer using this interactive medium. UPI's decision to offer only Web-based specialized information services is a clear indication of the media industry's recognition that the Internet will become the primary source of information for people and that they will use it to fulfill specialized information needs. No wonder then that media organizations going online are constantly improving both the packaging and the diversity of their Web services. Online newspapers are updating the news frequently between editions and offering links, both text and broadcast, to related items or sites. They are also adding new special sections to serve the varied needs of consumers. Broadcast services on the Web, such as CNN's, are equally expanding the scope of their offerings, allowing consumers to have access to a news item from a geographical area of their choice. Media organizations are also offering news, information, and entertainment services adapted to the subscriber's interest profile, either through email or through a Web page created for the subscriber.

The media consumer fragmentation that accompanied the high-tech American economy starting in the 1970s is reaching altogether new levels in the age of the Internet. Media owners worldwide are learning their lessons and are reshaping the nature, quantity, and quality of their output. Clearly, at the dawn of the new millennium, the Internet is creating new opportunities in and putting altogether new demands on the collection and dissemination of news and information globally. The consumer of news, information, and entertainment is emerging as the winner from the new dynamics unleashed by the information age.

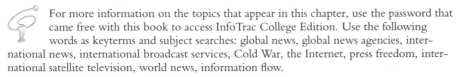 For more information on the topics that appear in this chapter, use the password that came free with this book to access InfoTrac College Edition. Use the following words as keyterms and subject searches: global news, global news agencies, international news, international broadcast services, Cold War, the Internet, press freedom, international satellite television, world news, information flow.

QUESTIONS FOR DISCUSSION

1. How will the traditional news agencies adapt their services to the Internet? Is UPI's decision to offer primarily Internet-delivered and subscriber-specific services the direction that all news agencies will have to take, making traditional newspapers and broadcast news services increasingly irrelevant? Why or why not?

2. Are online newspapers becoming more competitive with broadcast news by offering regular news updates? What new directions will broadcast news have to take to maintain its uniqueness and competitiveness in the new media environment?

3. Does the audience appeal, and therefore competitive success, of international television news networks, such as CNN and BBC World, depend on offering dedicated local programming in large countries like India? Why or why not?

4. Will the Internet make it more feasible for news agencies in developing countries to successfully compete worldwide with established Western news agencies? Why or why not?

5. Will the Internet facilitate an equitable flow of news between developed and developing countries? Why or why not? What direction will news flows take in the future?

REFERENCES

AFP. (1999, December 22). Nokia, AFP form WAP-based mobile news service venture. Retrieved from the World Wide Web: http://www.wash.afp.com/english/afp/?cat=new&page=index&release=nokia-wap

AFP. (2000, January 28). AFP: A world news agency. Information supplied by AFP.

AFP. (2000, February 2). Alcatel and AFP team up on mobile Internet content. Retrieved from the World Wide Web: http://www.afp.com/english/afp/?cat=new&page=index&release=alcatel

AP. (2000, February 9). Facts about AP. Retrieved from the World Wide Web: http://www.ap.org/pages/aptoday/index.html

AP. (2000, February 10). Frequently asked questions. Retrieved from the World Wide Web: http://www.ap.org/pages/aptoday/index.html

AP. (2000, February 19). AP information services. Retrieved from the World Wide Web: http://www.ap.org/is/index.html

APTN. (2000, February 16). About APTN. Retrieved from the World Wide Web: http://www.aptn.com/80256812004D9CF5/pages/About+APTN

BBC World Service. (1999). Annual review 1998/99. Retrieved from the World Wide Web: http://www.bbc.co.uk/worldservice/aboutus/annualreview/key.htm

BBC World Service. (2000, February 14). World business report. Retrieved from the World Wide Web: http://www.bbc.co.uk/worldservice/worldbusinessreport/

BBC World Service. (2000, February 16). Updated PAX 1999 India results. Retrieved from the World Wide Web: http://www.bbcworld.com/Content/About/pax.asp

CNN. (2000, February 16). CNN turns global village into a reality with millennium. Retrieved from the World Wide Web: http://www.turner-asia.com/cnni/cnni_highlights/index.html

de Borchgrave, A. (1999, August 6). Large-scale expansion to Internet services announced by UPI. Retrieved from the World Wide Web: http://www.upi.com/corp/press/990806.shtml

Farhi, P., & Rosenfeld, M. (1998, October 25). American pop penetrates worldwide. *Washington Post*, p. A1.

Frederick, H. H. (1993). *Global communication and international relations*. Belmont, CA: Wadsworth.

Fridriksson, L. (1993). *Coverage of Scandinavia in U.S. news media*. Paper presented at the Association for Education in Journalism and Mass Communication annual conference, Kansas City, Missouri.

Galtung, J. (1971). A structural theory of imperialism. *Journal of Peace Research, 8*(2), 81–117.

Hester, A. (1973). Theoretical considerations in predicting volume and direction of information flow. *Gazette, 19,* 238–247.

IANS. (2000, February 18). The global rise of India Abroad News Service.

Retrieved from the World Wide Web: http://www.indiaabroad.com/ians/ians.html

Ignatenko, V. (1993, June/July). *IPI Report, 42.*

Interfax. (2000, February 12). About Interfax. Retrieved from the World Wide Web: http://www.interfax-news.com/AboutInterfax/about.html

ITAR-TASS. (2000, February 12). Russian news agency. Retrieved from the World Wide Web: http://www.itar-tass.com/

Jehl, D. (1999, March 18). Riyadh journal: The Internet's "open sesame" is answered warily. *New York Times.* Retrieved from the World Wide Web: http://www.nytimes.com/

Kariel, H. G., & Rosenvall, L. A. (1984, Autumn). Factors influencing international news flow. *Journalism Quarterly, 61,* 509–516.

Keohane, R. O., & Nye, J. S., Jr. (1998, September/October). Power and interdependence in the information age. *Foreign Affairs, 77*(5).

Los Angeles Times–Washington Post News Service. (2000, February 14). All about us. Retrieved from the World Wide Web: http://www.newsservice.com/info.html

Moonies acquire UPI. (2000, May 15). Retrieved from the World Wide Web: http://www.auburn.edu/~lowrygr/moon.html

New York Times News Service. (2000, February 14). About the News Service. Retrieved from the World Wide Web: http://nytsyn.com/newsservice/about.html

Nye, J. S., Jr., & Owens, W. A. (1996, March/April). America's information edge. *Foreign Affairs, 75*(2).

Rampal, K., & Adams, W. C. (1990). Credibility of the Asian news broadcasts of the Voice of America and the British Broadcasting Corporation. *Gazette 46,* 93–111.

Read, D. (1999). *The power of news: The history of Reuters.* Oxford: Oxford University Press.

Reuters. (1999, October). Company information: General. Retrieved from the World Wide Web: http://www.reuters.com/aboutreuters/background/

Reuters. (1999, October 5). Reuters launches first Internet-based e-commerce product. Retrieved from the World Wide Web: http://www.reuters.com/aboutreuters/newsreleases/1999/Inform.html

Reuters. (2000, January 19). Reuters launches dealing 3000. Retrieved from the World Wide Web: http://www.reuters.com/aboutreuters/newsreleases/2000/Dealing3.html

Riffe, D. (1996, Spring). Linking international news to U.S. interests: A content analysis. *International Communication Bulletin, 31*(1–2).

Schiff, F. (1996, Spring). The Associated Press: Its worldwide bureaus and American interests. *International Communication Bulletin, 31*(1–2).

Schiller, H. (1998, April). Living in the number one society. *Gazette, 60*(2).

Schudson, M. (1978). *Discovering the news: A social history of American newspapers.* New York: Basic Books.

Shaw, D. (1988, April 3). The AP: It's everywhere and powerful. *LA Times Monograph.* Reprinted from the *Los Angeles Times.*

Singapore unveils sweeping measures to control words, images on Internet. (1996, March 6). *Wall Street Journal,* p. B8.

UPI sold to Arab firm. (1992, June 27). *Editor and Publisher, 125*(26).

VOA. (2000, February 16). Director's page. Retrieved from the World Wide Web: http://www.voa.gov/director/

Where in the world? (1999, November 28). *Washington Post,* p. B6.

Wood, M. (1998, March 19). In an interview with Deutsche Welle TV for a DW program on the history of Reuters.

7

International Broadcasting

JOSEPH D. STRAUBHAAR
AND DOUGLAS A. BOYD

Joseph D. Straubhaar (PhD, Tufts University) is associate dean for Academic Affairs of the College of Communication and the Amon G. Carter Professor of Communication, Radio-TV-Film Department, at the University of Texas at Austin. He previously taught at Brigham Young University and Michigan State University. He also worked as a Foreign Service officer in Brazil and Washington. Straubhaar coauthored *Communication Media in the Information Society* and *Video Cassette Recorders in the Third World* and has published extensively on international media studies.

Douglas A. Boyd (PhD, University of Minnesota) is director of the Office of International Affairs and a professor in the Department of Communication and School of Journalism and Telecommunications, University of Kentucky, Lexington. He is a former dean of the College of Communications and Information Studies, University of Kentucky. Boyd has received several significant awards (such as Ford Foundation, Japan's Hoso-Bunka Foundation, and UNESCO). He authored *Broadcasting in the Arab World* and is coauthor of *Video Cassette Recorders in the Third World*. He serves on the editorial boards of the *Journal of Communication* and *Journal of Broadcasting and Electronic Media*.

For additional online resources, access the Global Media Monitor Web site that accompanies this book on the Wadsworth Communication Cafe Web site at http://communication.wadsworth.com.

Countries and cultures have long been in communication across borders. However, in the 20th century, first radio and then television accelerated that process dramatically. National leaders are usually particularly unnerved when broadcasts come straight across borders, without any chance to stop, control, or mediate them. In the 1930s and 1940s, around World War II, and during the Cold War, radio seemed menacingly effective in propaganda across borders. Radio competitions and clashes, some miniature cold wars of their own, erupted among a number of countries, companies, and churches in Europe, the Mideast, Asia, North America, and Latin America. By contrast, broadcast television seemed comfortingly short range as it took preeminence from the late 1940s on.

Satellite television is the most recent technological development in international broadcasting. As early as the 1960s, the United Nations debated controlling broadcasts of television signals across borders via direct broadcast satellites (DBSs), because many countries feared that DBS, or direct-to-home (DTH), broadcasts would be used for propaganda or unwanted cultural influence. The global spread of satellite and cable TV channels in the 1990s has increased the outflow of American and European television programming and films to other countries.

Governments dominated activity in international radio, despite early developments and precedents from commercial international shortwave broadcasting prior to World War II. Why do private actors now dominate global television news and entertainment, instead of governments? Is the shift due to cost restraints or to a lack of consensus on need or desirability? What are the implications of a shift from government international radio broadcasting to private international satellite television? What are the relations between public diplomacy and private media actors, as well as concerns by receiving countries about the propriety of direct or even indirect satellite broadcasting that evades government controls?

FROM LOCAL TO GLOBAL

A variety of forms of international broadcasting take place, from accidental cross-border spillover to highly globalized systems that reach almost all people worldwide in various languages. The most local are the almost inevitable cross-border reaches of local radio on AM and FM and of local television on VHF and UHF. In fact, the rules of the International Telecommunication Union (ITU), which allocates radio frequencies to nations, officially reserves both AM and FM for purely domestic broadcasting and forbids using either to cross borders deliberately, although various stations on the U.S. border with Canada, Wolfman Jack's Tijuana station that covered much of the western United States in the 1960s, and stations like Radio Luxembourg in Europe have long ignored those rules, deliberately seeking audiences across borders for their advertisers.

Such commercial incursions across borders assume that a receptive audience, with similar language skills and cultural dispositions, waits on the other side. That is true in relatively few places, interestingly enough. Most radio audiences tend to be quite localized when given a choice, particularly with the spread of higher-fidelity

stereo FM broadcasts, which deliver the best available radio sound quality but seldom cover more than a limited metropolitan area. Radio stations may carry a great
deal of foreign music, but they do tend to broadcast from within national and even
local boundaries. From allocations given them by the ITU, national governments
distribute specific licenses to use certain frequencies, which gives governments a
powerful tool to try to keep national control over broadcasting.

Successful cross-border commercial operations tend to flourish only when local commercial competitors are few, as when Radio Luxembourg was one of the
few commercial rock music–oriented stations on the AM band in Europe in the
1960s and early 1970s. Similar cross-cultural spillover took place from expatriate
operations like the U.S. Armed Forces Radio–Television Service (AFRTS) in
South Korea and the Arab–American Oil Company (ARAMCO) television service for its North American employees in Saudi Arabia. Most governments try to
protect their commercial radio and television markets for their own advertisers,
which has led to clashes between the Canadian and U.S. governments, when the
former denied legal approval for tax deductions for advertising placed on U.S. stations targeted at Canadian listeners.

Both AM and shortwave have been used for deliberate international broadcasts
since the 1930s, mostly by governments and religious organizations. Radio Moscow, the Voice of America, Radio Havana, and other stations, mostly on shortwave, have become famous as vehicles of government propaganda. Their motives
and operations are discussed below. Governments began to try to use direct broadcast satellite television for similar purposes, but satellite television has come to be
dominated by private companies.

MOTIVATIONS FOR
BROADCASTING INTERNATIONALLY

Boyd (1986) has identified four major reasons that both state-run and private
organizations transmit directly across borders: to enhance national prestige, to
promote national interests, to attempt religious or political indoctrination, and to
foster cultural ties. Especially in the age of satellite-delivered television programming, a fifth reason may be added—to sell advertising for multicountry products.
A sixth is now to sell access to pay-TV broadcasts, either directly from satellite
(DTH) or by satellite-fed cable TV.

The main precedents for current cross-border satellite television broadcasts
come from international radio. Browne (1982) discusses international radio broadcasting within the context of purposes: as an instrument of foreign policy, as a mirror of society, as a symbolic presence, as a converter and sustainer, as a coercer and
intimidator, as an educator, as an entertainer, and as a seller of goods and services.
Almost all international broadcasting intends some variety of influence over the
audience, for no government or other major group broadcasts internationally
solely to entertain, without intent to sell or persuade.

Evidence of the importance that governments attach to international communication can be found in their total transmission hours; the major radio broad-

casters have been either single-party states or large Western democracies. Although no international broadcaster organizes programming for reception outside the originating country for only one purpose, every broadcaster has at least one of the motivations in mind as a major reason for transmitting.

WHY AUDIENCES LISTEN
OR VIEW ACROSS BORDERS

Until the 20th century, few people had been exposed on a frequent basis to direct contact with foreign sources of information. International flows of news and culture existed but were slower, less extensive, and more mediated by a series of personal sources and interpreters. However, the mass media have widened and sped up this process of contact and influence, creating the possibility for direct efforts to influence the thoughts and opinions of people within and across nations, or what has come to be considered public opinion.

According to the categories of listening motivations listed by Boyd (1986), audiences tune in to hear news and information, to be entertained, to learn, to hear religious or political broadcasts, to enhance their status, to protest, or to pursue a hobby. The U.S. Information Agency (USIA)/Voice of America (VOA) and the British Broadcasting Company (BBC) have conducted fairly extensive audience surveys in many countries, but the results are rarely published. Mytton (1993) does give some audience data as well as interesting overviews. Some audience data can also be found in the annual reports of the VOA, the BBC, and Radio Free Europe/Radio Liberty (RFE/RL), particularly about the size of the listening audience.

In most cases, one would have to conclude that, as with questions of media effects, the available studies show the effects of international radio to have been relatively limited. Nevertheless, two historical cases—Radio Free Europe's role in fomenting the Hungarian uprising of 1956, and what Frederick (1986) calls the radio war against Nicaragua—indicate that governments whose publics are the target of official radio public diplomacy are concerned about radio efforts to pursue ideological indoctrination or even to offer "information." This creates a strong aversion to the potential for similar public diplomacy on direct cross-border television, which is generally seen as an even more powerful medium.

CONCERNS ABOUT PUBLIC
DIPLOMACY AND PROPAGANDA

The need to influence public opinion as part of diplomacy is relatively new and still controversial. The new world information and communication order (NWICO) debate in UNESCO and other United Nations bodies looked at imbalances in the flow of media from the large Western countries, like the United States, to other countries. The debate also looked at the power that the United States and a few other countries exerted over others through international media. Within that debate, both Eastern European and some developing countries complained about direct attempts to influence publics in other nations via international radio broadcasts (mostly but not entirely on shortwave), advertising, and the like. They saw those as harmful propaganda and an infringement on national sovereignty (McPhail, 1987; Whitton, 1979). This debate has touched both official public diplomacy by governments and private information flows in the media. In fact, it is clear from what is most prominent in the NWICO debate that developing nations consider private media flows to be a much greater issue than official public diplomacy, although that has also been criticized. The developing countries' concern has focused primarily on commercially oriented media sales (film, news, music, television programs) that have flowed predominantly from the First World to the developing nations.

Beginning in the 1970s, the unequal nature of these radio broadcasts and flows of news, music, television programs, and films began to strike many researchers as an example of media imperialism (International Commission for the Study of Communication Problems, 1980; Nordenstreng & Varis, 1974; Schiller, 1971). While some research showed that flows of television and music were becoming less dominated by the United States in the 1980s and 1990s, film and news flows continued to be quite dominated by the United States. The onset of direct transborder satellite broadcasting in the 1980s also revived fears of unequal television flows, even in parts of the world like East Asia and Latin America, where nations had either begun to produce most of their own television or to import it from neighboring countries rather than from the United States. The Soviet and Eastern European governments' complaints focused somewhat more often on official government cross-border radio broadcasts, because U.S. and Western European official broadcasts were targeted at Eastern Europe and the USSR. Also, audiences for foreign radio broadcasts in Eastern Europe were much larger than foreign radio audiences elsewhere, according to research by VOA, RFE/RL, and BBC.

THE HISTORY OF
INTERNATIONAL BROADCASTING

Propaganda Radio and the World Wars

Most colonial powers started services in the 1920s to communicate with their nationals or citizens overseas. Holland started in 1927, Germany in 1929, France in 1931, and Britain in 1932 (Head, 1985). Effectively beginning with the efforts by various nations in World War I to influence publics in other nations—notably the Allied efforts to influence U.S. opinion toward entering the war—the idea of propaganda on radio gathered currency. British and German World War I propaganda on posters and other preradio media was seen as highly effective by early writers like Lippman (1965). Adolf Hitler seemed preoccupied with propaganda in *Mein Kampf,* his 1933 book that announced his plans for the takeover and governance of Germany. Propaganda continued to be directly associated with war or open conflict through World War II.

Pre–World War II
Commercial International Radio Efforts

With the exception of Radio Luxembourg's commercial broadcasts to other European countries, pre–World War II international radio in Europe did not develop along commercial lines. Rather, it evolved as a state activity (as for Germany and Italy), as a public corporation (like the BBC), or as a representative of other nongovernmental international interests, like Radio Vatican. In all these cases, the interests were noncommercial, educational, informative, and cultural, as the BBC intended to be. They became more openly persuasive, even propagandistic, in the case of wartime radio in Germany, Italy, Japan, and, to some degree, Great Britain.

However, in the Americas, things were different. Until World War II induced the United States to create the government-operated Voice of America, international radio was a commercial activity, based on a perception that profit could be made in international radio broadcasting. As the number of shortwave receivers increased in Europe and Latin America, the U.S. radio networks saw the possibility of an enormous foreign audience for American programming. To help foster international commercial broadcasting, the Federal Communications Commission (FCC) reworked the original classification of shortwave stations and ruled that they could provide an international service (Federal Communications Commission, 1936).

In 1938 the National Broadcasting Company (NBC) started an international division with 38 employees to transmit in five foreign languages plus English (*Hearings,* 1938). CBS also saw the commercial possibilities of shortwave programming, and in 1939 it established an international division that had 9 employees organizing programs for Europe and Latin America. Although primarily interested in the technical aspects of shortwave, General Electric by 1938 had a 10-person international staff at Schenectady, New York (*Hearings,* 1938).

In retrospect, Fejes (1983) and others believe that both private and public U.S. international radio broadcasting had considerable effects, particularly in Latin America. United States broadcasting, together with other private-sector public diplomacy, such as advertising, film exports, news wire service coverage, and book and magazine exports, seems to have reinforced both the official U.S. diplomatic agenda during World War II and the broader public and private agenda of drawing Latin America into close trade and investment ties favorable to the United States. They also reinforced the development of a commercialized system of broadcasting compatible with U.S. commercial interests.

World War II

The Soviet Union, which operated Radio Moscow, began a regular external service in 1929 "to explain [its] revolution to both sympathizers and opponents in the West" (Head, 1985). In 1935, Italy began broadcasting a shortwave service in Arabic to the Mideast. Great Britain countered with its own service in 1938 (Browne, 1982). The United States took over several existing private shortwave broadcasters aimed at international audiences and pulled them into the Voice of America in 1942. All of these broadcasters tried to influence third parties; examples include the German and American competition for influence in Latin America and the British–Italian radio war in the Mideast. Many of them also directly targeted each other, such as the Soviet–Nazi radio war, or each other's troops—for example, the way Tokyo Rose broadcast music and propaganda to American troops in the Pacific.

It was the declarations of war against both Germany and Japan that prompted the U.S. government to create the official Voice of America. Although broadcasters in the 1930s feared that a government-operated international station would create competition that would later have domestic broadcasting implications, that did not develop. However, the VOA did subsequently dominate international radio broadcasting. For years after World War II the government permitted only WRUL, later renamed WNYW, to operate, but eventually other stations received licenses. Most U.S. shortwave stations are now owned by religious organizations.

Cold War Radio

After World War II, as a less open but still intense ideological struggle between the United States and the Soviet Union began, U.S. policy makers began to talk about public diplomacy as a new but necessary addition to traditional diplomacy. Ideological struggle required a more explicit effort to reach and influence public opinion in other countries, those that were effectively being "fought" over.

For a time after World War II, governments, or public corporations sanctioned by the government (such as the BBC), had a monopoly on international broadcasting. Reasons for this situation involve both economics and technology: commercial radio broadcasters concentrated on the profitable domestic market rather than the uncertain international market. International radio was seen as precisely the domain of propaganda and public diplomacy.

At the peak of international radio propaganda, more than 80 countries had official international services aimed at other countries (Head, 1985). In one of the peak years, 1982, the largest operations were the Soviet Union, which broadcast more than 2,000 hours a week; the United States, which broadcast almost 2,000 hours; China, 1,300 hours; West Germany, almost 800 hours; and the United Kingdom, more than 700 hours (*BBC Annual Report,* 1983).

The primary U.S. international radio service has been the Voice of America, which has broadcast in dozens of languages to almost all parts of the world. The addition and deletion of language services over the years have reflected the list of countries with which the United States was politically preoccupied, dropping Brazilian Portuguese and adding hours to Arabic (targeting the West Bank and Gaza) in 2001, for example. The VOA has tended to concentrate on international news and on U.S. news, music, and culture. In contrast, the United States has also spent about half its broadcast time on several operations, sometimes called surrogate stations, which focus on providing some target country with news about itself (Head, 1985). Those stations have included Radio Free Europe (aimed at Eastern Europe), Radio Liberty (aimed at the former USSR), Radio (and TV) Martí (aimed at Cuba), and Radio Free Asia (aimed largely at China). These stations have been more controversial, although the stations aimed at the former Soviet Bloc have been complimented by post–Soviet era politicians, such as President Vaclav Havel of the Czech Republic, for bringing into those countries news that was unavailable under the previous regimes.

By the end of World War II, the BBC had evolved a quite different model from that of the VOA. Although the BBC had clearly served British government interests during the war and continued to do so during the Cold War, it was structured in a somewhat more independent manner than the VOA, which has always been under direct U.S. government policy control. BBC International is the overseas arm of the domestic BBC, which is carefully structured as an independent public corporation funded by license fees, whereas the VOA is directly funded by the U.S. Congress. Although the British Foreign Office helps fund the external service and set its policies, like which languages to broadcast in, the BBC has retained considerable editorial independence, which has increased its credibility to listeners abroad. USIA audience studies during the 1982 Falklands/Malvinas Islands war between the United Kingdom and Argentina found that even Argentine listeners turned to the BBC for accounts of the war (Head, 1985; U.S. Information Agency, 1982).

Radio Moscow began regular service in 1929, with the explicit mission of explaining and promoting the Soviet Revolution abroad. It expanded during World War II to focus on supporting the Soviet government in that conflict and continued to expand after the war, extending the languages and hours of broadcast into Eastern Europe and China and gradually into other developing countries, such as Cuba (after 1959) and elsewhere. At its peak, Radio Moscow broadcast in more than 80 languages, including relatively minor ones like Quechua (Head, 1985).

Government radio changed with the decline of the Cold War in 1989–1991 as Eastern European countries and then the Soviet Union moved away from communist governments. Much of the ideological rationale for international radio propaganda seemed to slip away, and the major broadcasters began to decrease the number of hours and languages they broadcast (Boyd, 1999). For example, the VOA has been using listener data as a basis for reducing language services that have small audiences or relatively low political priority, such as Portuguese and Turkish broadcasts. Cutting language services saved $4.2 million dollars, which was reallocated toward more current political priorities, like Arabic language services. The VOA had decreased the number of languages in which it broadcast to just over 30 in 2001 (VOA, 2001). Likewise, the Voice of Russia (formerly Radio Moscow) broadcast in 32 languages in 2001 (Voice of Russia, 2001). The BBC still maintains 43 language services in 2001 (BBC, 2001).

The structure of the broadcasting services was changed, along with this shift in emphasis. The VOA was put together with the former surrogate services— Radio Martí, VOA, RFE/RL, Radio Free Iraq, and Radio Free Asia—as the International Board of Broadcasters, itself under the supervision of the Board of Broadcast Governors. The official U.S. international broadcasters are now independent of the rest of the former USIA, which became the Educational and Cultural Bureau of the Department of State in 1998. The BBC international radio structure remains largely unchanged, although as we shall see below, the international BBC television operation has become increasingly privatized.

The use of radio in international broadcasting is changing decisively. Most of the international radio services are moving away from transmitting on shortwave radio and moving toward rebroadcasting or retransmitting on leased local FM facilities in the Arab world, Africa, Asia, and parts of Latin America. The BBC World Service Annual Review in 1998–1999 indicated that placement of BBC materials on FM stations around the world had become a top priority, with more than 1,000 FM stations carrying their programs by 1998 (BBC, 2000). For example, one can get the BBC World Service English 24 hours a day on local radio in Singapore. The VOA is also following similar paths away from reliance on direct international shortwave radio broadcasting.

Another major trend is for international broadcasters to put their signals out as streaming audio feeds on the Internet. This is a particularly significant move for small international broadcasters who have tracked their audiences' movement toward the Internet as a new convenient information source. For example, Jon Marks of Radio Niederland says that its priority is now Internet audio streaming (personal communication, April 2000). However, large broadcasters like the VOA and the BBC are also moving a number of their services onto the Internet. The BBC also highlights the need for Web presence and audio and video streaming services to supplement its traditional shortwave broadcasting as well as its new emphasis on local FM placements.

Cold War Propaganda, from Radio to Satellite

Except for cross-border transmissions such as those from the United States to Mexico and Canada, and Luxembourg's popular pan-European services, presatellite broadcasting technology did not permit direct international television communication without an investment that would have been impossible to recover. Satellites, however, have made the distribution of international television news and programming economically feasible and sometimes even profitable, especially from the mid-1990s with DTH satellite transmissions in Europe, Asia, and the Middle East.

For international television operations, perspectives are quite different from shortwave radio precedents. Television news by satellite is similar to shortwave in that it can be directly received anywhere in the satellite footprint by an appropriate receiver. However, access and control are issues. Access to direct-to-home (DTH) channels is severely limited in many countries by price. DTH access is limited in a number of other countries by national government prohibitions. China, Iran, Malaysia, Saudi Arabia, and others officially prohibit satellite television reception dishes (Boyd, 1999; Chan, 1994). Both types of limits on access are eased in some countries by offering satellite channels through cable TV systems. Cable is often cheaper than DTH service, and some governments allow cable but not DTH, because cable retransmission is more easily controlled. Most of the television news services are delivered for cable or broadcast retransmission, not for DTH.

In fact, the predominance of cable retransmission systems over DTH might remove some of the most glaring questions about national sovereignty and control in many countries, because some level of control over retransmission will or could exist on the ground in the receiving country. Still, some of the concerns about uncontrolled cross-border news influence are germane because several of the current services, such as Cable News Network International (CNNI), are being retransmitted on cable television in the Caribbean, Western Europe, Central America, and Japan without any editing or local control over content. Some of the services, again most notably CNNI, are also being directly received from satellites by homes with satellite dishes. Several of the current operations are intended for DTH news delivery, such as Britain's Sky Television, the British Broadcasting Corporation's World, CNN International, Asian Business News (Singapore), and the British-based, Arabic-language Middle East Broadcasting Centre.

The DBS Debate

The realization of direct international television broadcasting remained a distant possibility even after satellites were introduced to relay programs from one continent to another. Several factors—such as improved high-power satellite technology and abundant satellite transponders made possible by digital compression—resulted in inexpensive transmission time that increased the use of IntelSat and other existing international satellite systems for transmission of programs from one country or system to another. This led first to increased use of satellites for transmission of television news events, sports, and news footage. Next came transmission of entire newscasts on a regular basis, then cable system–oriented news channels, such as CNN. Only quite recently has DTH become a real possibility.

The technological possibilities of television news transmission via satellite created several policy issues. Long before satellite distribution of programs from one country or broadcasting/cable institution to another, and even longer before direct satellite broadcasting to small home dishes became a physical reality, the implications of international satellite television news for political propaganda were anticipated in debates among UNESCO, COPUOS (United Nations Committee on the Peaceful Use of Outer Space), and International Telecommunication Union (ITU) on DTH in the 1960s and 1970s.

Laskin and Chayes (1975) noted that most countries other than the United States feared not only political propaganda but also cultural influence and commercial consumer influence from advertising if DTH-type services were to flourish, unrestricted by international law. Still, it was primarily the prospect of having video versions of shortwave radio information and public diplomacy operations like VOA that worried many nations that did not like the idea of the direct flow of news and information. The Soviet Union and others had conducted extensive jamming of certain radio signals, such as those of Radio Liberty and Radio Free Europe, and they indicated in these debates that unrestricted DTH would be unacceptable (McPhail, 1987).

Despite U.S. protestations that restrictions would violate the principle of free flow of information, the United Nations General Assembly, based on a COPUOS working-group recommendation, voted 100 to 1 (the United States) in 1972 to establish restrictions. The essential condition was eventually established that before a country or company based in it could broadcast to another country, the receiving country had to give its prior consent (McPhail, 1987). The key point of the whole debate, emphasized by its taking place so long before the actual debut of DTH, is that policy makers in almost all countries other than the United States were concerned about the potential impact of both news and entertainment-oriented propaganda from cross-border television broadcasting. At least until recently, they have been unwilling to let a party beyond their borders make decisions about what might be telecast into the country.

However, despite all the attention given in the 1970s to creating international policies requiring prior consent by receiving nations for international satellite TV, relatively few nations, such as China, Saudi Arabia, and Malaysia, have officially restricted access to cross-border DBS (Boyd, 1999; Chan, 1994). This principle of prior consent has been honored only when pressed for by rigorous national policy, as in China. However, China's effective pressure on Murdoch's Star TV to discontinue showing BBC World television service has shown that determined leaders of a large country can force a major international satellite television operator to make major changes in hopes of thereby gaining approval for reception of their channels.

Experiments in Satellite TV News Flow

National political concerns about international television news services were also made clear by the operating principles of news exchange from the European Broadcasting Union (EBU) via Eurovision. Eurovision operates a television news exchange service primarily for Western Europe but, in fact, sends and receives material from other countries as well. However, member nations have never been willing to delegate news selection to a single country or a central staff. All member organizations, primarily national broadcasting companies or ministries, send stories about their countries to the exchange and use only what they want from what they take down from the satellite. All decisions are made nationally (Dizard, 1976; Eugster, 1983).

Another precedent comes from the role of international agencies in TV news flow and related concerns. Worldwide Television News (WTN)—formerly UPITN—and Visnews (both London-based), as well as Eurovision, have played a principal role in supplying news footage to television news operations around the world. The three U.S. commercial networks either have financial interests in the London-based television news organizations (ABC/WTN), or they have distribution agreements with WTN and Visnews ("NBC News," 1988; Paterson, 1996).

The major news agencies (UPI, AP, Reuters, Agence France-Presse, and TASS) also play a major part in supplying a variety of media with texts of news stories at a lower price for many countries where newscasts frequently are simply read without accompanying footage (Boyd-Barrett, 1980). Many broadcasters rely heavily on these services to supply international TV news, because even the biggest North American networks find it difficult to cover all world events with their own correspondents.

Some national information agencies, such as USIA, play a role similar to that of news agencies by supplying a variety of media with texts, photos, audiotapes (for radio), and film/video footage of news events, features, and cultural and scientific programs. These are widely used in the Third World and other places where resources make foreign newsgathering impossible, and even the purchase of commercial information services difficult. In many places, this disparity forces editors and programmers to take what they can get. For example, interviews in Mozambique in 1996 by one of the present authors found television news editors using satellite dishes to capture and record whatever images of current events they could find and then trying to connect them with whatever text sources they could find. One evening's take included news "footage" from USIA's WorldNet, Visnews, TV Globo (Brazil), CNN (as carried by Armed Forces Radio Television Service), and RTP (Portugal).

This mixture of seemingly hard and poor choices among sources for television news leaves many broadcasters with great ambivalence. This ambivalence was strongly reflected in the NWICO debate about letting foreign or international agencies set both the agenda and the substance of national newscast coverage of international events (Gerbner, Mowlana, & Nordenstreng, 1993; International Commission for the Study of Communication Problems, 1980).

Government Satellite TV

Despite the cautionary debates and research that have been conducted on previous forms of international television news flow, relatively little attention has been focused on two types of government or official international television news services. Those services are being made possible technically by satellites and are being brought closer to realization for both commercial and political motives.

Two international television news services have been offered, one by USIA and the other by the BBC World Service. This again raises the question discussed by receiving nations in the DTH debate about the appropriateness and acceptability of video news programs created by existing international radio broadcasters and government public diplomacy agencies. Both China and Saudi Arabia have forcefully protested the contents of BBC news and have succeeded in forcing the BBC channel off Star TV and Orbit, respectively (Boyd, 1999; Thomas, 1999).

Critics in both the United States and the United Kingdom have raised executive and legislative questions about the appropriateness and feasibility of such "official" international TV news services, looked at from the originating country's point of view. The goals, and the payoffs, would presumably be similar to those described above for international radio broadcasting: enhancing prestige, promoting national interests, fostering cultural ties, and, conceivably, attempting political indoctrination (Boyd, 1986). The British government refused to provide startup funds for BBC World because the government did not believe it could justify the expense to the British taxpayers. However, the BBC was successful in raising funds from the private sector through its commercial department. The U.S. government's WorldNet, after a several-year trial, was found to be too costly and was reduced to a fairly minor service for relaying existing public affairs programs and interactive videoconferences.

USIA's WorldNet.　As a public diplomacy agency, USIA is not new to television. It has been making and placing television news footage—and finished television features, documentaries, and discussion programs—for years. As a satellite television service, WorldNet was preceded and succeeded by a more modest, ad hoc series of USIA videoconferences. These typically featured a one-way video transmission of a speaker from the United States to one or several other countries and usually had two-way audio via international telephone lines so that local journalists or other audiences could ask questions. These conferences have been conducted since the late 1970s and continued under the WorldNet aegis, with greatly increased frequency under the Reagan administration. In the 1980s, substantial investment was made in satellite receiving dishes for a number of USIA posts overseas to foster this type of videoconferencing.

USIA's WorldNet was a major innovation of USIA during the Reagan administration. It was an expensive project and was canceled by the U.S. Congress, primarily for reasons of cost counted against benefit. The teleconferencing component (WorldNet Dialogues) is generally well regarded as cost-effective, because it tends to generate coverage in local media, and it has continued. The value of the regular news and magazine format transmissions, however, was challenged. In 1988, Congress required USIA to show evidence of effectiveness in the form of an audience of at least 2 million viewers in Western Europe ("Audience Survey," 1987) for funding to continue. A survey commissioned by USIA did not produce the mandated viewing numbers, and the television service was suspended when funding stopped in November 1988. Subsequently, VOA itself became a television service when it started regular satellite television transmissions in Russian and Farsi with the hope of creating a two-way dialogue, as viewers with home dishes were encouraged to call in during live telecasts. WorldNet was merged under VOA Radio and TV in 1998.

British Broadcasting Corporation.　BBC World, the BBC's international television news service, is also not new. BBC television news has been seen in other countries for more than three decades. BBC news is available either through the BBC's participation in the daily satellite news exchange of European Broadcasting Union, which was made available to many Western and developing countries, or via agreement with broadcasters to use some BBC domestic and international television news stories. Viewers in the Irish Republic and in the Netherlands, for example, see British television news either directly from transmission spillover or via retransmissions of over-the-air signals on local cable systems.

The development of an international television news service was one of the BBC World Service's objectives in the 1988–1993 five-year plan (Checkland, n.d.). Using the off-hour production capacity of the BBC London Television Centre and the foreign expertise of the World Service's journalists, the initial concept involved the production of several daily 30-minute news programs in English. Stations taking the service would have the option of using designated "windows"—

where international weather or financial news is featured—within the newscast for either commercial announcements or short local news items.

The British government was concerned about (a) an initial project request from World Service Television of between £6 and £10 million to fund the plan; (b) the technology, that is, whether such a service would be delivered only to broadcasters for retransmission or would also be available for satellite home reception; and (c) the blurring of the traditional lines of responsibility between the domestic service (financed by license fees paid by those owning television receivers) and the World Service (funded by an appropriation from the Foreign Office). In March 1988 the British government stated that it would not provide funds to start the service (Robert Wilson, senior international press officer, BBC World Service, personal communication, August 15, 1988). Subsequently, in August 1988, BBC announced that it would seek private funding for the international television news venture (Evans, 1988), and private funding was arranged in 1990 for a proposed 1991 start.

This commercial BBC channel has succeeded well in the United States and other English-speaking markets. BBC America, for example, is a 24-hour channel wholly owned by the BBC and distributed by Discovery Networks as part of a global alliance between the BBC and Discovery Channel International. It shows a mixture of documentaries, comedies, dramas, and news (http://www.bbcamerica .com/about.html). Increasingly, the BBC coproduces dramas and documentaries with international partners, like PBS and Discovery, while still producing its own news.

Commercial Satellite TV

Still other satellite news operations exist that have quite different motives. The U.S.-based Cable News Network and the British Independent Television News (ITN) have started internationally oriented news services for sale to European and other markets. These operations make a profit by selling advertising time on their services, primarily to be picked up by cable television systems. At least in the case of Time Warner's CNNI, there seem to have been motives beyond simply making money that might make CNNI a particularly active player in international public diplomacy. Time Warner cochairman and CNN founder Ted Turner himself was quoted as saying, "They are watching us in Moscow right now, in Havana, in London. . . . Within the next three years, virtually every leader in the world will be watching CNN with a satellite dish" (Schrange & Vise, 1986, p. H3). During the Reagan–Gorbachev summit in May 1988, CNNI was rebroadcast in Moscow on a UHF channel ("Rabbit Ears," 1988) and was thus available to those beyond the select few with satellite dishes (Gregg Creevey, special projects manager, CNNI, personal communication, August 15, 1988). Now CNNI can be seen in every part of the world.

CNN. Cable News Network (CNN) and its international service (CNNI) are commercial news operations, based in Atlanta, Georgia, and owned by U.S. media corporation Time Warner. CNN operates primarily in the United States on cable channels, although parts of its two 24-hour services, regular CNN and CNN

Headline News, are carried by some U.S. television stations. CNN created CNNI and began selling programming to Australia, then increased its overseas expansion to sell its services at about the same time as did other U.S. suppliers of cable television channels and programming who saw sales potential abroad. CNNI has been targeting hotels, cable systems, and airport departure lounges in Western Europe and Asia. CNNI is also retransmitted, often pirated, by some developing nation cable and television systems, primarily in the Caribbean and Latin America, because it can be picked up there from the same satellite used for distribution in the United States. CNNI is now carried legitimately by a scrambled UHF service in Brazil and by some cable operators in Latin America, and it has an agreement with Egypt to have the news service available via a scrambled UHF service in Cairo. CNNI programming reaches the Middle East via the Orbit Television and Radio network, a Rome-based, Saudi Arabian–owned DTH satellite service.

CNN also has the problem that it is offering to Europe, Asia, the Middle East, and Latin America regular news programming that is primarily designed for the U.S. market. Although CNN has had a distinct European edition via CNNI since 1985 (Dukes, 1985), it is acquiring more non-U.S.-specific content by originating news from its London and Hong Kong studios. It has also created much more localized versions in Spanish and Turkish.

CNNI seems to operate primarily as a straightforward commercial service, initiated in those markets, such as Western Europe, Latin America, and Asia, where a profit is projected. Further, the service operates under standard U.S. commercial news practices and editorial values. Those values, however, while familiar to U.S. television viewers, are not what European, Asian, or Latin American viewers often get from their own various government, public, and private television news services. Expanded world exposure to such news will probably have an impact on international news knowledge and opinion and hence on public diplomacy.

Turner seems to keep his hands off CNN and CNNI editorial policy, but projects such as the Goodwill Games and *World Report* (which shows news items created by local or national news services around the world)—and instances where CNN has juxtaposed BBC and Argentine reports on the Falklands War—indicate that he and CNN are somewhat more committed than many to the deliberate airing of other countries' points of view within an essentially U.S. commercial television news framework. This has interesting implications for public diplomacy. The importance of CNN in public diplomacy was further demonstrated in the 1990–1991 Gulf crisis. Saddam Hussein and George Bush were widely considered to be sending messages to each other's publics via CNN, a practice that continues in 2001 with Hussein and George W. Bush.

Murdoch and Sky News. A new competitor for the international satellite news audience has appeared: Rupert Murdoch's News Corporation. In 1989, Sky News, one of several Murdoch-owned satellite-to-home delivered services under British Sky Broadcasting (BSkyB), started operating a 24-hour CNN-type news service from London. Since then, News Corporation has expanded its worldwide television information and entertainment interests with the purchase of Asia's Star TV and ownership of JSkyB (Japan), LatinSkyB, ASkyB (North America), and Fox News, a New York–based 24-hour news channel. Clearly, Murdoch wishes to compete with Time Warner's CNN on an international level for news viewers, but his strategy seems to be a regional one of localizing news as well as entertainment programs for several regions. Increasingly, he works with local or regional partners, such as Zee-TV (India) for South Asia (Thussu, 2000), and TV Globo (Brazil) and Televisa (Mexico) for Latin America (Duarte, 2001).

Of course, the major satellite-delivered news services have primarily been in English and thus useful only to the elite or expatriates. An emerging trend is the regional satellite service, targeting those that can speak the majority language in the area. CNNI has finally decided to move beyond English-language service with a Spanish-language news channel to Latin America, where it must compete with national channels from Brazil (TV Globo) and Mexico (Televisa), which are becoming regional news channels, as well as a Turkish-language satellite news channel for Turkey and Central Asia. CNBC Asia from Singapore has established a presence in the Asian market, where financial news is important.

Orbit in the Mideast. The Saudi-owned, Rome-based Orbit Television and Radio Network soon learned that a news service over which it had no control was not good for business. Alexander Zilo, Orbit's CEO, has said that the former 8-hour service in Arabic provided by the BBC in London became a problem when it started devoting time to Saudi dissident Mohammed Al-Masari's specific objections to the way the Saudi royal family was running the country and that he had talked to the BBC about the coverage (A. Zilo, CEO Orbit Television and Radio Network, personal communication, January 3, 1995; Boyd, 1999). Coverage of Al-Masari's efforts peaked in late 1995 and early 1996 when he fought a court battle in London to stay there as a political refugee. However, the event that motivated Orbit to cancel its BBC contract was a *Panorama* program on Orbit's BBC Arabic Television News that showed film, secretly shot in Saudi Arabia, of the preparations for a double execution by beheading.

The Qatar-based Al Jazeera news channel seems to have picked up where Orbit's BBC Arabic television news stopped; it now offers the region a 24-hour daily television news broadcast. Though not only a news service, Saudi-owned Middle East Broadcasting Centre in London—and virtually every other Arab country except Iraq—offers some of form of regional satellite-delivered news in Arabic (Boyd, 1999).

International Radio, International DBS, and Isolated Audiences

Several decades of research on international radio audiences show that listening to BBC, VOA, and the others is highest among people who have few domestic options, like those in isolated areas. The numbers of such people have been steadily reduced by the increasing advance of domestic AM and FM radio in most countries. International radio is also sometimes sought by those who do not trust the local or national media that are available to them. That is still the case in a number of countries, but the number has been reduced by the fall of authoritarian regimes that exercised tight control over media contents in the former USSR, Eastern Europe, Asia, Africa, and Latin America.

Likewise, international television channels, whether brought in by DTH or cable TV, have shown certain patterns and limits in the audience research to date. Audiences for cross-border broadcast television, like those for radio, are largest in those areas where domestic television is not easily available. However, the number of such places is declining steadily. The same satellites that bring in international channels also permit the retransmission of national television channels to receiving dishes, cable head-ends, or rebroadcast transmitters. Studies by one of the authors in both urban and rural Brazil found that most owners of dishes, users of the satellite master antenna systems that serve urban apartment buildings, and cable subscribers primarily watched national channels (Straubhaar, 2000). Few (less than 8% of television households) subscribed to the pay-TV systems required to see international channels.

Again, as with international radio, some television viewers who are not satisfied with national programming or who seek news information to supplement or replace national news do turn to international channels. International political and economic elites are widely known to use CNN for fast-breaking news to supplement local sources. Many young people watch MTV, although MTV is increasingly presented in localized versions aimed at specific countries or regions and featuring local VJs and an increasing amount of local music. MTV also faces a host of local and regional competitors who tend to emphasize local, national, or regional music videos. Viewers dissatisfied with commercial entertainment channels often turn to various language versions of the Discovery Channel or the BBC.

Research by the present authors in Brazil, Saudi Arabia, and other locations has shown audiences of international television channels to be highly segmented. Few international channels have anything resembling a mass audience. Instead they have specific, small but important audiences segmented by interests in news, music, foreign movies, documentaries, sports, and so on (Duarte, 2001). These audiences tend to be smaller than the audiences for regular national broadcast television for several reasons. First, international channels require either a pay-TV DTH service or a cable subscription, whose prices tend to cut out nonaffluent viewers in many countries. In Brazil, where half of the population makes less than $200 a month, pay TV or cable TV tends to costs $20–30 a month. Second, research has shown that mass audiences tend to prefer national or nearby regional material because it is culturally more proximate or relevant to them (Straubhaar, 1991, 2000). Without the knowledge or cultural interest and awareness developed by international travel, second languages, or advanced education, most audience members find that national or nearby regional jokes are funnier, styles more pleasing, facial expressions more comprehensible, and the like (Straubhaar, 2000).

Public Diplomacy, International Communication, or Media Imperialism?

In current usage, most commonly among U.S. officials, public diplomacy is the use of mass communication and contacts with opinion leaders to influence international public opinion (U.S. Advisory Commission, 1998). Official public diplomacy is conducted by governmental information structures—including state-run news agencies, embassy, and other press offices, ministries of information, external radio and television broadcasting services, official exchange programs such as the Fulbright Program, and international communication organizations such as the U.S. Information Agency. Public diplomacy is an accepted, if still controversial, part of what governments do in the international diplomatic arena. Some would argue that these activities are best considered as simply the current phase of the evolution of propaganda, but U.S. practitioners at least have argued that such activities are open and public, an aboveboard adjunct to diplomacy (Hansen, 1984).

A more important reason for separately defining and studying public diplomacy, though, is that, by our definition at least, it intrinsically involves a whole series of public actors other than governments. Commercial mass media, tourism, academic exchanges, labor union contacts, political party ties, and church activities can all be considered as "private" transnational involvement in public diplomacy (Keohane & Nye, 1971). All of these entities are involved in trying to influence government policy (and sometimes private and corporate actions) by influencing general public opinion or selected publics who are particularly relevant to the issue at hand. For example, international environmental groups, like the World Wildlife Fund, give money to groups in countries like Brazil to create projects in part to attract attention in order to place issues on the agenda of local media and to gain coverage so as to influence local opinion.

Put another way, this is diplomacy in the public sphere, involving not only governments but also a variety of other actors who are trying to affect public opinion. In fact, it seems likely that in the shaping of current world opinion, governments are frequently much less important than key private actors. These include the wire services, which furnish much of the world's news; Hollywood films and television programs, which inform much of the world's interpretive framework about other nations; international television news services, which supply most of the current images people have about each other and events elsewhere; and most recently, globally oriented television news channels, such as CNN. However, critical scholars like Schiller (1971) note that governments frequently benefit greatly from the actions of what is public diplomacy in a technically private form. Joseph Nye (1990) has become famous in American policy circles for promoting the idea that the United States can benefit from the "soft power" of its cultural industries, software, and media.

As governments began to depart from traditional diplomacy—that is, direct government contacts—and began attempts to manipulate foreign publics so as to affect their governments' policies, then governments inadvertently opened up an area that other actors could more easily enter. While it is difficult, although not impossible or unheard of, for individuals or nongovernmental groups to conduct warfare or traditional diplomacy, it is much easier for nongovernmental actors to reach and influence public opinion. This is particularly true via mass media that can focus on whatever they decide is interesting or newsworthy. For example, modern terrorism can be considered "low-level warfare," but it is probably more often now thought of not as a means of achieving military-type objectives but more as a means of garnering media attention, and hence public attention for a cause.

So with the proliferation of publics to address, international electronic media to address them with, and groups with internationally focused causes to publicize, the use of international broadcasting for public diplomacy has great potential to proliferate. Equally likely is the continual increase in direct international broadcasting, particularly on satellite television, for less overtly political purposes of entertaining, informing, selling goods, and advertising.

 For more information on the topics that appear in this chapter, use the password that came free with this book to access InfoTrac College Edition. Use the following words as keyterms and subject searches: international broadcasting, cross-border broadcasting, propaganda, new world information order, international media, international TV news, international TV programming, international radio, International Telecommunication Union, satellite radio and TV, international communication organizations.

QUESTIONS FOR DISCUSSION

1. What are the main reasons why governments have been the main actors in international radio broadcasting?

2. How has international radio changed after the end of the Cold War?

3. Is public diplomacy a legitimate international activity of governments? Is public diplomacy any different from propaganda?

4. Why have commercial television companies emerged as the main direct satellite television broadcasters (DBS) instead of governments?

5. Is current DBS less of a threat to national cultures because it is largely carried out by companies instead of governments?

REFERENCES

Audience survey of WorldNet program. (1987, December 14). Cong. Rec. § 209, H11310.

BBC. (2000). *BBC World Service annual review.* Retrieved from the World Wide Web: http://www.bbc.co.uk/worldservice/aboutus/annualreview/chief.html

BBC. (2001). BBC World Service homepage. Retrieved from the World Wide Web: http://www.bbc.co.uk/worldservice/index.shtml

Boyd, D. A. (1986). International radio broadcasting: Technical developments and listening patterns in the developing world. *Space Communication and Broadcasting, 4*(1), 25–32.

Boyd, D. A. (1999). *Broadcasting in the Arab world: A survey of the electronic media in the Middle East* (3rd ed.). Ames: Iowa State University Press.

Boyd-Barrett, O. (1980). *The international news agencies.* Beverly Hills, CA: Sage.

Browne, D. R. (1982). *International radio broadcasting: The limits of the limitless medium.* New York: Praeger.

Chan, J. M. (1994). National responses and accessibility to STAR TV in Asia. *Journal of Communication, 44*(3): 70–88.

Checkland, M. (n.d.). *The next five years: 1988–1993.* London: BBC.

Dizard, W. (1976). Television's global networks. In H.-D. Fischer & J. C. Merrill (Eds.), *International and intercultural communication.* New York: Hastings House.

Duarte, L. G. (2001). *Looking south: American television networks enter Latin America.*

Unpublished doctoral dissertation, Michigan State University, East Lansing.

Dukes, A. (1985, September 30). Turner prepares to launch European edition of CNN. *Multichannel News,* p. 12.

Eugster, E. (1983). *Television programming across national boundaries: The EBU and OIRT experience.* Dedham, MA: Artech House.

Evans, R. (1988, August 11). BBC asks for private funds. *The Times* (London), p. 1.

Federal Communications Commission. (1936). *Second annual report.* Washington, DC: U.S. Government Printing Office.

Fejes, F. (1983). The U.S. in Third World communications: Latin America, 1900–1945. *Journalism Monographs,* no. 48.

Frederick, H. H. (1986, April 29). *Electronic penetration in low intensity warfare: The case of Nicaragua.* Paper presented at the 14th Annual Telecommunications Policy Conference, Airlie, VA.

Gerbner, G., Mowlana, H., and Nordenstreng, K. (1993). *The global media debate: Its rise, fall, and renewal.* Norwood, NJ: Ablex.

Hansen, A. (1984). *USIA, public diplomacy in the computer age.* New York: Praeger.

Head, S. (1985). *World broadcasting systems: A comparative analysis.* Belmont, CA: Wadsworth.

Hearings before a subcommittee of the committee on interstate commerce, Senate, on S. 3342. 75th Cong., 3rd Sess. (1938). Washington, DC: U.S. Government Printing Office.

Hitler, A. (1933). *Mein kampf, Zwei bande in einem band; ungekurzte ausgabe.* München: F. Eher.

International Commission for the Study of Communication Problems. (1980). *Many voices, one world: Communication and society, today and tomorrow.* New York: Unipub/UNESCO.

Keohane, R. O., & Nye, J. S. (1971). *Transnational relations and world politics.* Cambridge: Harvard University Press.

Laskin, P., & Chayes, A. (1975). International satellite controversy. *Society,* 12(6), pp. 30–40.

Lippman, W. (1965). *Public opinion.* New York: Free Press.

McPhail, T. L. (1987). *Electronic colonialism: The future of international broadcasting and communication.* Newbury Park, CA: Sage.

Mytton, Graham. (1993). *Global audiences: Research for worldwide broadcasting.* London: J. Libbey.

NBC news going worldwide with Visnews. (1988, November 21). *Broadcasting,* pp. 22–23.

Nordenstreng, K., and Varis, T. (1974). *Television traffic—a one-way street.* Reports and Papers on Mass Communication. Paris: UNESCO.

Nye, J. (1990). *Bound to lead: The changing nature of American power.* New York: Basic Books.

Paterson, C. (1996). *News production at Worldwide Television News (WTN): An analysis of television news agency coverage of developing countries.* Unpublished doctoral dissertation, University of Texas at Austin.

Rabbit ears and CNN's yours. (1988, June 1). *Variety,* p. 82.

Schiller, H. (1971). *Mass communication and American empire.* Boston: Beacon.

Schrange, M., & Vise, D. A. (1986, August 31). Murdoch, Turner launch era of global television. *Washington Post,* pp. H1, H3.

Straubhaar, J. D. (1991). Beyond cultural imperialism: Toward asymmetrical interdependence and cultural proximity. *Critical Studies in Mass Communication.*

Straubhaar, J. D. (2000). Cultural capital and media choices. In G. Wang, J. Servaes, & A. Goonasekera (Eds.), *The new communications landscape: Demystifying media globalization.* New York: Routledge.

Thomas, A. C. (1999). Regulating access to transnational satellite television: Shifting government policies in Northeast Asia. *Gazette, 61,* 243–254.

Thussu, D. K. (2000). *International communication: Continuity and change.* New York: Oxford University Press.

U.S. Advisory Commission on Public Diplomacy. (1998). *Publics and diplomats in the global communications age*. U.S. Advisory Commission on Public Diplomacy 1998 report. Washington, DC: U.S. Information Agency.

U.S. Information Agency. (1982). *Argentine international radio audiences during the Falklands War*. Washington, DC: USIA Office of Research.

VOA. (2001). Spring 2001–Autumn 2001 broadcast schedules. Retrieved from the World Wide Web: http://www.voa.gov/allsked.html

Voice of Russia. (2001). The Voice of Russia homepage. Retrieved from the World Wide Web: http://www.vor.ru

Whitton, J. (1979). Hostile international propaganda and international law. In K. Nordenstreng & H. I. Schiller (Eds.), *National sovereignty and international communication* (pp. 217–232). Norwood, NJ: Ablex.

8

✴

Milestones in Communication and National Development

VIBERT C. CAMBRIDGE

Vibert C. Cambridge (PhD, Ohio University) is an associate professor in the School of Telecommunications and director of the Communication and Development Studies program in the Center for International Studies at Ohio University, Athens. His current research interests are in entertainment-education and multicultural broadcasting in the United States. He has completed projects in communication for development in Africa, Asia, the Caribbean, and the United States.

In this chapter we explore the communication and development field. Several terms are used to describe the deliberate use of a social system's communication resources to promote, support, and sustain planned social change. Among the terms are *communication and national development, development communication, communication and development,* and *communication for development*. In this chapter the term *communication for development* is used to describe the systematic use of a social system's communication resources to stimulate, promote, and support human development. Fraser and Restrepo-Estrada (1998) offered a comprehensive definition of *communication for development:*

> Communication for development is the use of communication processes, techniques and media to help people toward a full awareness of their situation and their options for change, to resolve conflicts, to work toward

 For additional online resources, access the Global Media Monitor Web site that accompanies this book on the Wadsworth Communication Cafe Web site at http://communication.wadsworth.com.

consensus, to help people plan actions for change and sustainable development, to help people acquire the knowledge and skills they need to improve their condition and that society, and to improve the effectiveness of institutions. (p. 63)

Several strategies in communication for development are being used by community groups, national governments, regional and international organizations, and nongovernmental organizations to address the range of development challenges facing the world. Public awareness and information campaigns, community mobilization, folk media, social marketing, entertainment-education, and advocacy are among the dominant strategies being used to promote, support, and sustain projects aimed at agriculture, education, the environment, family planning and reproductive health, gender equality, nutrition, and public health. The attributes of these strategies are discussed later in this chapter.

Through an exploration of the contemporary origins of communication for development, especially the practices of the international community, we should develop an appreciation of the milestones associated with the field. Theory-based practice in communication for development is reaching vast populations around the world with critically needed information that could prevent HIV/AIDS infection and help women make informed choices about their reproductive health. Practitioners of communication for development are engaged in projects aimed at improving the economic, political, and cultural conditions of people all over the world. Practices and processes of communication for development are also facilitating community participation in the public discourses that nourish democratic systems of governance.

This deliberate application of a social system's communication resources to facilitate social change is not new. Humans have always used their communication capacity to bring about improvements in the quality of life. We can call this tendency *purposive communication*—the deliberate use of a social system's communication resources to encourage individual and collective movement in a preferred direction. This tendency is recognition of the power of communication. Purposive communication is necessary for the formulation and implementation of efforts to improve the quality of human life the 21st century.

Purposive communication must operate in accord with ethical principles. The totalitarian experiences of the 20th century demonstrate that a social system's communication resources can be appropriated for purposes that degrade humans.

That humans can speak and have languages influenced their social organization. The communally agreed-upon codes of speech permitted the sharing of information, and in the process those who spoke a common language developed a collective identity. Through speech and language, they could coordinate efforts to achieve common goals of the group, such as food gathering and security. The invention of writing, printing, and mass communication provided humans with additional communication capacity to bring about change. Historians have described these developments in human communication capacity as having civilizational consequences. Consider the role that writing played in the creation of the ancient Greek, Roman, Turkish, and Asian empires. Consider also the role that printing played in the spread of reformist ideas in Europe during the Renaissance. Today the mass media, especially print, broadcasting, and the Internet, play important roles in the delivery of formal and informal education in many societies. Lifelong education is essential for functioning in contemporary society.

In this chapter, the work of the international development community in the field of communication for development is emphasized. This community is made up of the United Nations system, development assistance agencies such as the U.S. Agency for International Development, global broadcasters such as the British Broadcasting Corporation, nongovernmental organizations such as Population Communication International, and academic institutions such as the Center for Communication Programs in Johns Hopkins University's School of Hygiene and Public Health. Of course, there are other players, but the focus here is on this particular community. The international development community is humanity's response to the human condition. This community works with national governments and regional organizations to improve the human condition. Contemporary development practice has its origins with the end of World War II and the creation of the United Nations in 1945.

POST–WORLD WAR II REALITIES

At the end of World War II, the human condition was bleak. The destruction caused by the war in Europe and the pervasiveness of poverty in Europe's colonies in Africa, Asia, and the Caribbean meant that millions of humans were living without adequate housing, health care, and food. The devastation caused by the war and the consequences of colonialism challenged the international community to do something about the unacceptable state of the human condition. By the late 1940s, humanity had a range of development challenges. The birth rate in Africa, Asia, and Latin America was almost three times larger than the birth rate in Europe. Infant mortality rates were almost five times higher in these regions than in Europe and the United States. Life expectancy for males and females in Brazil was about 37 years; in the United States it was 62 years for males and almost 66 years for females (United Nations, 1949).

The euphoria associated with the success of the Marshall Plan in the European reconstruction after World War II suggested that a similar model could be applied to the conditions that existed in Africa, Asia, Latin America, and the Caribbean. The Marshall Plan had demonstrated the effectiveness of management (a specialized communication system) in economic and social reconstruction (Drucker, 1985, p. 13). In a relatively short time, European industrial infrastructure was rehabilitated, and the quality of life improved rapidly. In retrospect, it was naive to think that the model could be transferred with similar success to other parts of the world. The objective circumstances were different. Development aid became an important item on the international relations agenda, and the development project became the primary vehicle for connecting aid with the individuals who needed it—the beneficiaries. Development projects in the early postwar years emphasized the transfer of technologies and techniques to support industrialization. Industrialization was generally accepted as the engine to drive social progress.

Development aid was not altruistic. According to Gerald Meier and Dudley Seers (1984),

> From the viewpoint of the governments of the major capitalist countries, there was grave danger that former colonies might, if there was little social progress, fall under communist domination: investment opportunities and access to markets and sources of raw materials would then be diminished. (p. 8)

The United States made major investments and funded substantial development aid programs in Iran, Turkey, India, Pakistan, and the other countries that bordered the Soviet Union. The aim was the containment of the Soviet Union.

At the end of World War II the United States and the Soviet Union emerged as the dominant world powers. Each sought to use its economic, military, and cultural (including communication) power to achieve its national interests. Among the primary national interests were national security and the expansion of spheres of influence. The term *spheres of influence* refers to the ability of powerful states to impose their will on other states through economic, cultural, and military means. The United States and its allies promoted and supported the achievement of progress through modernization by capitalism.

Like the field of development economics, the field of communication and development emerged as a "response to the needs of policymakers to advise governments on what should be done to allow their countries to emerge from chronic poverty" (Meier & Seers, 1984, p. 4).

The United Nations (UN) was created as a mechanism to prevent war and to coordinate the international community's response to the global pervasiveness of poverty, want, fear, ignorance, and disease in vast regions of the world. The preamble to the Charter of the United Nations includes a commitment "to employ international machinery for the promotion of the economic and social advancement of all peoples." The development project was the principal form of response. In the process, the UN has played a major role in the development of the field of communication for development.

WHAT IS DEVELOPMENT?

At the start of the 21st century, development is recognized as a complex, integrated, participatory process, involving stakeholders and beneficiaries and aimed at improving the overall quality of human life through improvements in a range of social sectors in an environmentally responsible manner. Stakeholders include national governments and politicians, international agencies such as the specialized agencies of the UN system, development assistance agencies such as the U.S. Agency for International Development (USAID), the private sector, nongovernmental organizations, and cultural leaders. Stakeholders have the power to help or hinder the development and implementation of development projects. The beneficiaries are the hundreds of millions of humans who need improvement in their quality of life.

At the start of the 21st century, the list of pressing development challenges facing humanity is intimidating. Among the challenges are the reduction and the elimination of poverty, provision of adequate housing, access to health care and lifelong education, food and nutritional sufficiency, adequate and functioning physical infrastructure, public health (including potable water, reliable sewerage, and waste disposal systems), roads, bridges, reliable transportation systems, protection of the environment, respect for human dignity and rights (including opportunities for self-actualization), access to the means of communication, and participation in the democratic governance of the society. These challenges are global in scope. They are no longer simply Third World problems.

Development is a profound form of social change. Everett Rogers, an influential theorist of the field, described development as

> a widely participatory process of directed social change in a society, intended to bring about both social and material advancement including greater equality, freedom, and other valued qualities for the majority of the people through their gaining greater control over their environment. (Rogers, 1962, cited in Singhal & Domatob, 1993, p. 98)

Development projects have been conducted around the world and have become synonymous with purposive social change. In the early postwar days many of these projects were the result of recommendations by external experts. The execution of these projects has had consequences—both intended and unintended. The huge hydroelectric dams like the Volta in Ghana and the Aswan in Egypt that were developed in the 1950s have been able to produce needed energy to power industries and provide electricity for homes—the intended consequences. However, these dams have also increased the spread of bilharziasis, a debilitating waterborne disease also known as snail fever—an unintended consequence.

New varieties of seeds associated with the green revolution of the late 1950s and the 1960s increased the yield of food grain, reduced hunger, and eliminated famine from India and large regions of Asia. However, the new seed varieties required extensive use of chemical fertilizers. An unintended consequence of the increased use of chemical fertilizers has been the pollution of water resources.

Questions of scope and relevance were also raised about many of these early development projects. Concerns were also raised about the inequitable distribution of the benefits of many of these early projects. Urban groups appeared to have benefited more than the rural poor.

Fifty years of engagement in the development arena by a number of players—the international community, national development agencies, and academics—has led to the acceptance that development was an "integrated, multidimensional and dialectic process" that had no universal recipe. There is some consensus on what constitutes development—"good change"—according to Robert Chambers (1994). Among the attributes are the following:

- Giving priority to the poor

- Aiming to meet basic needs

- Striving to be endogenous to a society—that is to say, it should originate from the society's values and its perceptions of its own future

- Making optimal use of natural resources, taking into account the potential of the local ecosystem, as well as the present and future limitations imposed by global considerations for the biosphere

- Basing the process on participatory and truly democratic decision-making practices at all levels of society (Fraser & Restrepo-Estrada, 1998)

According to Andrew Moemeka (2000), communication for development has two roles: support of social change that aims for higher quality of life, social justice, and correction of the dysfunctions from early development interventions; and socialization, creating an environment in which established values that support positive social change are maintained and, further, supporting the development of attitudes and behaviors needed to create a social system that benefits all citizens.

COMMUNICATION FOR DEVELOPMENT

Several forces have influenced the evolution of the field of communication for development. Among these are the growth of capitalism, advances in communication technology, and the ideological rivalries between the United States and the Soviet Union during the Cold War (1945–1992). Of central importance was the nature of the development challenges faced by the former European colonies in Africa, Asia, and the Caribbean that gained political independence during the 1950s–1970s and their subsequent involvement in international relations through mechanisms such as the Non-Aligned Movement, which promoted neutrality, solidarity, and self-reliance (Calvocoressi, 1982). This block was able to use the UN system to highlight the development problems of its member nations and recommend actions to alleviate them.

Of equal importance in the evolution of the field of communication for development were the influences of changing development paradigms and advances in communication theory, especially theories of mass media effects, persuasion, and behavior change. Since World War II, communication theory applicable to the field had grown substantially. Starting in 1930, U.S. and European émigré scholars in the United States have formulated a number of highly heuristic communication theories that have influenced communication for development practice. Among them are theories of persuasion, theories about the process through which ideas and innovations move through a social system (diffusion of innovations), and theories that explain mass media's ability to influence human behavior at individual, group, and societal levels. A chronicle of the development of these theories is provided in Everett Rogers's *History of Communication Study* (1994). Communication for development is the embodiment of Kurt Lewin's dictum, "Nothing is as practical as a good theory." Theory in the field of communication for development has been influential in mapping the scope and nature of development challenges, guiding research methods, and supporting transformative practice. These are the goals of practical theory (Barge, 2001, pp. 5–13).

Most of the early theories that guided the practice of communication for development emerged out of the modernization paradigm. A paradigm is defined as an overarching body of thought whose core assumptions are subscribed to by all who work under its rubric. These core assumptions inform and influence research methods, interpretation of data, and intervention strategies. During the Cold War the modernization paradigm not only guided the generation of communication theory but also influenced the foreign aid decisions of the United States and its allies. Details on the core assumptions of the modernization paradigm are provided below.

A few examples of interventions by communication for development from around the world—the United States, the former Soviet Union, Africa, and the Caribbean—are offered below not only to illustrate the scope of contemporary development challenges but also to suggest the factors that influence the choice of strategy.

Southeastern Ohio, USA

Southeastern Ohio is an example of mal-development and the process of underdevelopment. First settled as the Northwest Territories after the end of the U.S. Civil War in the late 18th century, contemporary southeastern Ohio is predominantly rural, with high levels of unemployment, high levels of physical inactivity, and substantial environmental degradation.

A recent study on physical inactivity in three Appalachian counties in southeastern Ohio revealed unemployment rates in excess of 10%. More than 30% of the population was overweight, and more than 20% obese (Cambridge, 2001). Overweight and obesity lead to early death from cardiovascular disease and some forms of cancer. The epidemic of overweight and obesity in Ohio has substantial consequences for the state's economy. Reducing overweight and obesity through regular physical activity is a public health goal for Ohio and the United States that is embodied in a program called Healthy Ohioans–Healthy Communities 2010. Social marketing is emerging as the dominant communication strategy to be used by the Ohio Department of Health in response to this public health crisis.

In the late 19th and early 20th centuries, coal mining, clay mining, and logging industries fueled economic development in southeastern Ohio. The coal mines supplied coal for the steel industry in Pittsburgh, and the clay mines provided the raw materials for the manufacture of bricks that were used to build the cities of Ohio and other states. The logging industry fed the paper manufacturing plants and the building industries. By the 1960s most of these industries were closed, leaving in their wake unemployment, polluted watershed areas, and other manifestations of environmental degradation. These economic and environmental realities have stimulated out-migrations to urban areas.

A consequence of the economic and environmental degradation in southeastern Ohio is low levels of individual and collective efficacy among some sectors of the population, especially the poor and those who did not graduate from high school. Efficacy is an individual or community's belief in its capacity to resolve a problem. The recently mentioned physical inactivity crisis can be considered as a manifestation of the low levels of individual and collective efficacy (Bandura, 1995). Community groups, such as Rural Action and the Monday Creek Watershed Improvement Committee, have been working to improve the economy and the environment by facilitating participatory practices and processes aimed at sustainable development. They use a range of communication resources—traditional channels, such as county fairs; interpersonal channels, such as group meetings; and traditional mass media and the Internet to build a voluntary coalition of citizens that strives to influence the formulation of policies to support sustainable development by local, state, and federal governments.

The concepts *participatory* and *sustainable* are central to contemporary communication for development practices. Participation refers to the involvement of citizens/beneficiaries in defining, designing, implementing, and evaluating development interventions. Participation is not simply a means for the design and implementation of development interventions. Participation is an end in human development. It is a requirement for the construction of democratic societies and a requirement for sustainable development (Dervin & Huesca, 1997, p. 46). The term *sustainable development* is used to describe an intervention whose outcomes are environmentally and culturally sound and can be continued by the community after the end of any resources that may have been provided by external agencies.

Turkmenistan

Communication for development interventions is also evident in the transitional societies that have emerged since the breakup of the Soviet Union. In Turkmenistan the National Puppet Theater, a new state-supported organization, is using a traditional communication channel (puppets), along with the mass media (radio, television, newspapers, and magazines) to create a sense of national identity and to address a number of pressing social problems such as drug abuse. Turkmenistan, formerly a republic in the Soviet Union, became an independent state in 1992. The government sees the building of national identity and the nurturing of national pride as important elements in the construction of individual and collective efficacy (Cambridge & Sleight-Brennan, 2000).

Eritrea

In Eritrea and other parts of Africa, modern communication technologies (computers and satellites) are being used to create distance education systems aimed at improving access to formal education and the management of the economy (Cambridge & Belinesh, 1995).

The Caribbean Community

In the English-speaking Caribbean, the Pan American Health Organization (PAHO) is working in collaboration with the Caribbean Community (CARICOM) and regional communication organizations, such as the Caribbean Broadcasting Union (CBU) and the Caribbean News Agency (CANA), to educate citizens on containing and eradicating mosquito-borne diseases such as dengue and malaria. These diseases induce high morbidity rates that undermine worker productivity and can make the Caribbean less attractive as a tourist destination. Tourism is a major source of income for Caribbean nations.

THE MODERNIZATION MODEL

The literature of communication for development identifies three development paradigms that have exerted substantial influence on the field since the end of World War II. Scholars have referred to them as the dominant paradigm (or modernization model), the dependency paradigm (or dependency critique), and the alternative paradigm (another development, or participatory, model) (Singhal & Sthapitanonda, 1996, pp. 10−25). What follows is a brief, general survey of the evolution and application of these paradigms, including some reflection on the core assumptions and the roles played by select individuals and institutions in this evolution. Readers are encouraged to refer to the primary sources identified in this survey.

Modernization through Capitalism

At the end of World War II, two ideas contended for dominance in the discourse on development and human progress: modernization through capitalism, and communism. The modernization perspective held that human society progresses in a linear fashion from traditional societies to modern systems of social organization and that they will continue to do so in an evolutionary manner. Traditional systems are characterized as predominantly rural, providing limited social and geographic mobility, and subscribing to cultural practices that do not support materialism or capital as a form of wealth. Traditional societies, according to modernization theory, tend to be oriented to maintaining a status quo dominated by ascribed status. Fatalism, or lack of self-efficacy, has also been identified as an attribute of traditional societies.

A modern society, on the other hand, is characterized by "materialism, the dominance of capital as a form of wealth, consumerism, rational–legal authority, sub-cultural diversity, and positive evaluation of change" (Weinstein, 1997, pp. 358−359). Modernization theorists argued that the process of becoming a modern society could be accelerated through the introduction of new ideas and practices. Modernization represented progress.

Modernization's core assumptions are also informed by Talcott Parsons' functionalist theory. This formulation holds that "human society is like a biological organism" whose constituent institutions—economy, government, law, religion, family, and education—play key roles in maintaining the social stability required for progress in a society. In the advanced, modern societies, progress is maintained through the increased consumption of material goods made possible by high incomes and higher standards of living (So, 1990). Walt Rostow, David McClelland, Daniel Lerner, Wilbur Schramm, and Everett Rogers were also influential modernization theorists.

Walt Rostow and David McClelland subscribed to the idea that the cause of underdevelopment was to be found exclusively in internal factors. They provided economic and psychological models of the modernization process. Walt Rostow identified four stages he considered necessary for progressing from a traditional to a modern society: the pre-takeoff stage, the takeoff stage, the road to maturity, and the mass-consumption society. A society must experience these stages before it becomes a modern society (Rostow, 1990). David McClelland emphasized the importance of a motivated populace if a society is to become modernized. His recommendation was to stimulate the individual need for achievement (nach) (McClelland, 1964). The ideas of these two men guided influential development aid projects funded by the United States and the UN.

Modernization scholars such as Daniel Lerner, Wilbur Schramm, and Everett Rogers emphasized the importance of broadcasting in the development process. Mass communication, especially broadcasting, was seen as a vehicle that would accelerate the behavioral and structural changes required for modernization. We will examine the contributions of these theorists below.

Communism

The Soviet Union and its allies promoted and supported efforts to achieve progress through revolutionary socialism. Revolutionary socialists contended that true progress could occur only in a socialist society. Socialist transformation would replace inequitable economic practices with more egalitarian ones—for example, equitable distribution of wealth and equity in access to education, health, and nutrition. In the process, the society would progress materially and spiritually, leading ultimately to "withering away of the state."

Information and communication had a special role in revolutionary socialist practice. In the 1970s, Soviet intellectuals posited,

> Communications among people, social groups, classes, nations and states contribute to the development of a scientific outlook by individuals. They assist them in arriving at their own understanding of the diverse phenomena and processes that are taking place in social life, in increasing their level of culture and their general education, in assimilating and carrying out laws and general principles, and in struggling with bourgeois and revisionist ideologies that are foreign to socialist norms. (Afanasyev, 1978)

The tensions between these two approaches—modernization through capitalism and progress through socialism—influenced practices of communication for development within the international development community. This chapter argues that this superpower tension did not undermine the field of communication for development. Instead, it contributed to the sharpening of the theory and practice of communication for development. The interplay of ideology, theory, practice, and ethics during the 1980s has influenced the contemporary practice of communication for development.

THE 1980S: DEVELOPMENT SUPPORT COMMUNICATION AND PROJECT SUPPORT COMMUNICATION

The work done by United Nations organizations has contributed much to the field of communication for development. Of special importance is the work of the UN Development Program (UNDP) and the UN Children's Fund (UNICEF) in establishing the importance of communication as a necessary ingredient in implementing development projects. UNDP and UNICEF pioneered communication planning for development at the Development Support Communication Service (Asia) in Bangkok, Thailand. This research and application service was established in 1967 and was led by Erskine Childers. The unit's mission was to provide communication strategies and materials to UN-funded projects in Asia. The approach was termed development support communication, or project support communication. Communication's role in this formulation was to accelerate the installation of the engines of modernization, especially the industrial infrastructure to facilitate economic growth. In these early days, development emphasized economic development (Fraser & Restrepo-Estrada, 1998).

The development support communication (DSC) approach arose out of dissatisfaction with the ineffectiveness of many of the UN-sponsored development projects in Asia and other parts of the developing world. Many of these projects were defined and designed outside of the developing world and tended not to reflect the needs of the beneficiaries. Further, these modernization-oriented projects also failed to take into account culture and context. As a result, there was waste, dissatisfaction, and underutilization.

For Childers (1973), development support communication meant "the use of communication techniques to elicit the voluntary and active participation of people in development planning and action." By 1980, UNICEF was actively promoting project support communications (PSC) around the developing world. UNICEF staff were actively assisting governments around the world in designing communication plans to support development (Tuluhungwa, 1981, p. 1). Table 8.1 identifies the scope and nature of a selection of the development support communication programs fostered by UNICEF in 1980.

Development support communication interventions by the Food and Agriculture Organization (FAO) demonstrated the essential role of communication in its projects aimed at improving food security and the empowerment of citizens, especially women and farmers. The green revolution of the 1950s and 1960s increased food security in many nations in Asia, Africa, Latin America, and the Caribbean.

Table 8.1 UNICEF's Development Support Communication Programs, 1980

Country	Nature of project support communication intervention
Republic of Korea	Developing a health education strategy and plan for primary health care
	Establishing a PSC clearinghouse through the Saemul Undong (New Village Movement)
Nigeria	Developing a PSC plan for establishing a Development Support Communication Unit in the Federal Ministry of Social Development, Sports, Youth and Culture
Rwanda	Retraining of radio producers by the Ministry of Information and increasing community-based radio programs to support basic services
Zambia	Establishing an interministerial communication committee for facilitating intersectoral communication cooperation at the community level
Indonesia	Establishing provincial communication units
Syria	Establishing a DSC unit in the Ministry of Information to train extension workers
Vietnam	Establishing an audiovisual production center to produce and distribute materials to schools and health facilities
Malawi	Developing a production and distribution system with the Extension Unit of the Ministry of Agriculture

Note. From "Highlights of PSC Activities in 1980," by R. Tuluhungwa, June 2, 1981, *Project Support Communications Newsletter,* 5(2), pp. 1–2.

The World Health Organization (WHO) demonstrated the centrality of purposive communication in its work to eradicate polio and other diseases. Similar effectiveness has been demonstrated by the UN Children's Fund in its work on immunization and diarrheal diseases. In all of these interventions, broadcasting was assigned an important role.

Broadcasting

In the 1930s, radio in the United States and Europe was used to persuade citizens to become more educated and to consume more goods and services. In Nazi Germany, radio and other mass media mobilized citizens for hate. In the 1950s, radio and television were mobilized to support development. Daniel Lerner, Wilbur Schramm, and Everett Rogers were influential modernization theorists who emphasized the importance of broadcasting in the development process.

Daniel Lerner's theorizing on broadcasting's role in national development emerged out of a research project conducted for the Voice of America in the Middle East and was associated with the United States' Soviet containment strategy. According to Lerner, broadcasting would serve as a psychic mobilizer, facilitating the modernizing process and preventing the adoption of Soviet ideology and practices. His research was published as *The Passing of Traditional Society: Modernizing the Middle East* (1958).

Wilbur Schramm emphasized the essential role of broadcasting in nation building (Schramm, 1964). For Schramm, broadcasting was key in constructing national identity and national unity and in mobilizing the society to execute the development goals designed by the political elites who dominated underdeveloped countries.

Everett Rogers is internationally acclaimed for his work on diffusion theory. This theory describes the process through which new ideas and technologies—innovations—are diffused in a society (Rogers, 1962). Broadcasting played an essential role in diffusion theory, by making the influential early adopters aware of the innovation. These early adopters, through interpersonal channels, set in motion a process that led to the acceptance of the innovation by the remainder of the society.

Broadcasting has remained central to the practice of communication for development. In times of stress (a constant condition in developing countries), people tend to increase their consumption of media for orientation and the clarification of societal ambiguities. This increased dependency creates the conditions that facilitate individual and collective behavioral change (DeFleur & Ball-Rokeach, 1989).

Collectively, these modernization theorists—Rostow, McClelland, Lerner, Schramm, and Rogers—concluded that it was internal factors that needed to be fixed. External models, especially those found in the industrialized West, were the models to be emulated if progress was to be achieved in the newly independent nations of the developing world. Communication, especially broadcasting played a major role in the process (Lerner & Schramm, 1967).

As indicated earlier, socialists held similar ideas about human progress. They contended, however, that capitalism had deformed and derailed human progress, resulting in human exploitation. Progress should allow individuals to achieve their full potential for the benefit of society—a collective versus an individualistic orientation. The end state of socialist progress was communism. According to socialists, capitalism-led modernization, with its gradualism, was really a strategy of appeasement, a strategy for maintaining the exploitative status quo. Socialists argued for a radical transformation, a revolution that would destroy all former patterns of exploitative relationships and replace them by a more egalitarian practice. Socialists argued for self-reliance and regional solidarity.

By the 1960s, developing nations that had followed the modernization route had demonstrated marginal improvements in meeting the basic needs of their citizens. In addition, unacceptable levels of waste, corruption, and human rights abuses were associated with the model. Criticisms against the model, especially from Latin America, became shriller.

The Dependency Critique

By the 1960s, the modernization approach was under attack from several fronts—operational and ideological. The critique of modernization emerged from two intellectual sources: "one rooted in neo-Marxism, or structuralism; the other, in the extensive Latin American debate on development associated with the United Nations' Economic Commission for Latin America" (Servaes & Malikhao, 1994).

Among the influential theorists were Andre Gunder Frank, Raul Prebisch, and Immanuel Wallerstein (Rhodes, 1970).

Dependency theorists demonstrated that the existing pattern of global economic relations, one dominated by the industrialized North, was contributing to the underdevelopment of the developing regions of the world. Dependency theorists contended that the broadcasting and other mass media systems that were put in place in the developing world to support modernization were actually undermining the possibilities of establishing equitable development. These broadcasting systems, they argued, were antidevelopment, as they tended to promote the agenda of political elites and relied on external sources for programming. Further, the broadcasting systems tended to marginalize indigenous modes of expression, thus undermining the development of national culture and identity. In addition, they encouraged demands for lifestyles that could not be provided by the economy. In this sense, the broadcasting systems were undermining development, a phenomenon that Howard Frederick has termed development sabotage communication (Frederick, 1990).

As stated earlier, these national broadcasting systems in many developing countries were excessively dependent on external entertainment programming, especially from the United States. This programming privileged individualism, consumerism, patriarchy, white male dominance, and many other themes that were considered counterproductive by political, religious, and cultural leaders of the developing world.

In the 1970s, concerns with the imbalanced state of international communication flows coincided with concerns about the inequities in the prevailing global economic system. The desires for change were articulated in UN resolutions calling for a new world economic order (United Nations, 1974) and a new world information and communication order (UNESCO, 1980).

By the 1970s the former colonies of Europe—now sovereign states—and other developing nations in Asia and Latin America had become an influential bloc in the UN system. This bloc is referred to as the Third World. Although the term now generates images of conflict, poverty, and disease, it initially represented resistance to domination by both the United States and the Soviet Union.

> It was a Third World because it rejected the notion of a world divided into two, a world in which only the United States and the USSR counted and everybody else had to declare for one or the other. It feared the power of the superpowers, exemplified and magnified by nuclear weapons. It distrusted their intentions, envied (particularly in the American case) their superior wealth and rejected their insistence that, in the one case in democratic capitalism and in the other in communism, they had discovered a way of life, which others need do no more than copy. (Calvocoressi, 1982, p. 95)

Dependency theorists have been criticized for offering a critique of the modernization model without offering prescriptive measures. However, the critique raised questions that have influenced contemporary practice of communication for development. The dependency critique focused attention on successful grassroots practices in Latin America, while drawing attention to the lack of genuine participation by citizens in the development process. In Latin America it was demonstrated that a benefit of genuine participation was more sustainable improvements in the quality of human life (Borda, 1988; Freire, 1983).

The dependency critique of modernization sharpened two essential ideas for communication and development practitioners: the importance of the programming of broadcasting in development; and the importance of practices of participation, not only for achieving a development project goal but also as a crucial element in nurturing democratic practices.

ANOTHER DEVELOPMENT

The dependency idea also emerged at a time when it was obvious that our world was interdependent and that development decisions in a nation-state or region had global significance. This recognition led to the "another development" formulation. This new perspective on development was initially articulated by the Dag Hammarskjöld Foundation in Sweden and has three fundamental pillars: development should strive to eradicate poverty and satisfy basic human needs, priority should be given to "self-reliant and endogenous change processes," and development should be environmentally responsible (Servaes & Malikhao, 1994, p. 10). Further, it was recognized that the need for development did not exist only in the Third World. Substantial regions of the industrialized world and the recently developed world were also in need.

With the winding down of the Cold War in the 1980s, this interdependent orientation took root. The round of world conferences organized by the United Nations during the 1990s reaffirmed the perspective on interdependence and called for increased global cooperation to deal with the global development crisis.

THE WORLD CONFERENCES

During the late 1980s and the throughout the 1990s the international community organized or reconvened a number of conferences that focused on the development challenges facing an interdependent world. Conferences focused on the environment (Rio de Janeiro, 1992), population and development (Cairo, 1994), social development (Copenhagen, 1995), women (Beijing, 1995), and food (Rome, 1996). These conferences revealed that despite marginal improvements in some sectors, the human condition continued to be unacceptable. Further, because of the interrelated and interdependent nature of global society, the development problems faced by a society had global consequences. The conferences reaffirmed the role of communication in the development process and called for its increased use.

CONTEMPORARY STRATEGIES IN COMMUNICATION FOR DEVELOPMENT

Exciting new strategies in communication for development have emerged over the past three decades. Public awareness campaigns, social marketing, entertainment-education, and advocacy have been effective in communication for development projects. These theory-driven strategies all subscribe to systematic planning. Six planning phases are identifiable: formative research, project design, pretesting of materials, implementation, monitoring, and evaluation. These strategies are integrative, incorporating a wide range of theory, demonstrating ethical awareness, applying powerful methodological strategies, and demonstrating commitment to participation (Piotrow, Kincaid, Rimon & Rinehart, 1997; see also http://www.comminit.com).

Public Awareness Campaigns

Public awareness campaigns systematically draw upon the power of the mass media, especially broadcasting, to create awareness in societies about the development intervention. Awareness is considered to be the first step in creating behavior change (Piotrow et al., 1997). Public service announcements (PSAs) are among the dominant artifacts used in this process. PSAs played an important role in awareness development and reinforcement in the "designated driver" anti–drunk driving campaign in the United States.

Social Marketing

Social marketing is the application of commercial marketing ideas to promote and to deliver pro-social interventions. Central to the social marketing approach is harmonizing the four essential elements of the social marketing—price, product, promotion, and place. Social marketing strategies have been applied extensively in the areas of family planning and reproductive health, immunization, and childhood diseases (Piotrow et al., 1997). In Ohio, interventions based on social marketing are being developed to increase the levels of physical activity (Cambridge, 2001).

Entertainment-Education

Entertainment-education has been defined as the systematic embedding of pro-social educational messages in popular entertainment formats. In recent years, this strategy has been used to address a wide range of development challenges, including agricultural improvement, adult education, domestic violence prevention, family planning and reproductive health, HIV/AIDS prevention, and peace and reconciliation (Sherry, 1997; Singhal & Rogers, 1999; Soul City, 1999). More than 160 entertainment-education projects were developed between 1990 and 2000. Included in this list is *New Life, New Hope,* a radio soap opera that is broadcast by BBC External Service. This soap opera promotes peace and reconciliation among Afghanis (Bosch & Ogada, 2000).

Advocacy

When stakeholders and beneficiaries in the development process promote the interventions by reporting on their positive experiences and benefits, the credibility of the communication increases. Advocacy for development does just that. An excellent recent example of effective advocacy is the project called Arab Women Speak Out, jointly conducted by Johns Hopkins University, the Center of Arab Women for Training and Research in Tunisia, and Population Initiative for Peace, a London-based nongovernmental organization. The project involved women in Lebanon, Palestine, Egypt, Tunisia, and Yemen who were engaged in agitating for women's rights in reproduction health decisions. These women became influential agents for social change (Piotrow et al., 1997). For details on these and other strategies, visit the Web site for the Communication Initiative (http:/www .comminit.com).

CHALLENGES IN THE 21ST CENTURY

The development challenges of the 21st century are profound. In a report to the Millennium Conference of the United Nations, Secretary-General Kofi Annan (2000) identified some of the challenges facing humanity at the start of the 21st century:

- Reducing the extreme poverty faced by 1.2 billion people who have to live on less than $1 per day
- Improving the lives of 100 million slum dwellers by 2020
- Ensuring that all children complete primary schooling
- Reducing HIV/AIDS infection in young people by 25% by 2010
- Improving agricultural productivity in Africa
- Preserving forests, fisheries, and biodiversity
- Reducing the threat of global warming by reducing by 60% emissions of carbon and other "greenhouse gases"
- Confronting the water crisis
- Defending the soil
- Preventing conflict

Windahl, Signitzer, and Olson (1992) have reminded us that the field of communication for development is not only systematic but also creative. This creativity will be stretched in the 21st century.

LESSONS LEARNED

The field of communication for development has grown in importance since World War II and is now accepted as a necessary element in development. To be effective, communication for development interventions require systematic planning and the involvement of stakeholders and beneficiaries in all aspects of the process—problem identification, design, pretesting of materials, implementation, monitoring, and evaluation. New communication technologies provide designers of communication for development with opportunities to support interactivity and knowledge sharing.

The development challenges facing mankind require increased global cooperation as the consequences of these challenges transcend the nation-state. In addition to addressing specific problems, the practice of communication for development can contribute to the creation and maintenance of the structures required for sustainable development and democratic life.

Today communication for development interventions, especially those that rely on broadcast media, must be aesthetically competitive if they are to be effective in the global communication environment, which is dominated by slick entertainment programming from the United States and other production centers in Europe and Latin America. Entertainment programs account for more than 60% of all broadcast schedules globally. Practitioners of communication for development must take this reality into consideration as they work with beneficiaries to plan, design, implement, monitor, and evaluate purposive social change.

 For more information on the topics that appear in this chapter, use the password that came free with this book to access InfoTrac College Edition. Use the following words as keyterms and subject searches: communication and development, U.S. Agency for International Development, the Marshall Plan, dominant paradigm, dependency paradigm, modernization, communism, UN Development Program.

QUESTIONS FOR DISCUSSION

1. Identify and discuss the phases in the development and implementation of a communication for development project.

2. What was the Marshall Plan?

3. What is a paradigm? Isolate and discuss the attributes of the modernization and another development paradigms.

4. Visit the Web site of the Communication Initiative (http://www.comminit.com) or the Johns Hopkins University Center for Communications Programs (http://www.jhuccp.org/), and select and study a social marketing intervention and an entertainment-education intervention. Prepare a report on the similarities of their design approaches.

5. How has the dependency critique contributed to improvements in the practice of communication for development?

REFERENCES

Afanasyev, V. (1978). *Social information and the regulation of social development*. Moscow: Progress Publishers.

Annan, Kofi A. (2000). *We the peoples: The role of the United Nations in the 21st century*. Report for the United Nations

Millennium Summit. Retrieved October 6, 2000, from the World Wide Web: http://www.un.org/millennium/sg/report/summ.htm

Bandura, A. (1995). Exercise of personal and collective efficacy in changing societies. In A. Bandura (Ed.), *Self-efficacy in changing societies*. Cambridge: Cambridge University Press.

Baran, J., & Davis, D. (1995). *Mass communication theory: Foundations, ferment, and future*. Belmont, CA: Wadsworth.

Barge, J. K. (2001). Practical theory as mapping, engaged reflection, and transformative practice. *Communication Theory* 11(1), 5–13.

Borda, O. (1988). *Knowledge and people's power: Lessons with peasants in Nicaragua, Mexico, and Colombia*. New Delhi: Indian Social Institute.

Bosch, T. E., & Ogada, J. O. (2000). *Entertainment-education around the world (1989–2000): A report to the third international conference on entertainment-education and social change*. Athens: Communication and Development Studies, Ohio University.

Calvocoressi, P. (1982). *World politics since 1945*. London: Longman.

Cambridge, V. C. (2001). *Formative research for social marketing–based interventions to increase physical activity in Ohio: A study in five counties (Adams, Meigs, Scioto, Defiance, and Lorain)*. Report to Ohio Department of Health's Bureau of Health Promotion and Risk Reduction. Athens: Communication and Development Studies, Ohio University.

Cambridge, V., & Araya, B. (1997). The rehabilitation of "failed states": Eritrea as a beta-site for distance education technologies. In *Educational Technology 2000: A global vision for open and distance learning* (pp. 325–337). Vancouver, British Columbia: The Commonwealth of Learning.

Cambridge, V. C., & Sleight-Brennan, S. (2000). *Report to UNESCO on workshop on entertainment-education held for Central Asian media professionals held in Ashgabat, Turkmenistan*. Athens: Communication and Development Studies, Ohio University.

Chambers, R. (1994). *Poverty and livelihoods: Whose reality counts?* Overview paper prepared for the Stockholm roundtable on global change, July 22–24, 1994.

Childers, E. (1973, February 20). *Draft guidelines and instructions for development support communication in country programming, project formulation, and implementation and evaluation*. Document circulated for consideration and revision at RBAFE training workshop and regional meeting.

DeFleur, M. L., & Ball-Rokeach, S. (1989). *Theories of mass communication* (5th ed.). New York: Longman.

Dervin, B., & Huesca, R. (1997). Reaching for the communicating in participatory communication: A meta-theoretical analysis. *Journal of International Communication* 4(2), 46–74.

Drucker, P. (1985). *Management: Tasks, responsibilities, practices*. New York: Harper & Row.

Fraser, C., & Restrepo-Estrada S. (1998). *Communicating development: Human change for survival*. New York: I. B. Tauris.

Frederick, H. (1990). *Global communication and international relations*. Belmont, CA: Wadsworth.

Freire, P. (1983). *Pedagogy of the oppressed*. New York: Seabury Press.

Lerner, D. (1958). *The passing of traditional society: Modernizing the Middle East*. New York: Free Press.

Lerner, D., and Schramm, W. (1967). *Communication and change in the developing countries*. Honolulu: University Press of Hawaii.

McClelland, D. (1964). Business drive and national achievement. In A. Etzioni & E. Etzioni (Eds.), *Social change* (pp. 165–178). New York: Basic Books.

Meier, G., & Seers, D. (1984). *Pioneers in development*. New York: Oxford University Press for the World Bank.

Moemeka, A. (2000). *Development communication in action: Building understanding and creating participation*. Lanham, MD: University Press of America.

Piotrow, P., Kincaid, D. L., Rimon II, J. G., & Rinehart, W. (1997). *Health communi-*

cation: Lessons from family planning and re-productive health. Westport, CT: Praeger.

Rhodes, R. (Ed.). (1970). *Imperialism and underdevelopment*. New York: Monthly Review Press.

Rogers, E. (1962). *Diffusion of innovations*. New York: Free Press.

Rogers, E. (1994). *A history of communication study: A biographical approach*. New York: Free Press.

Rostow, W. (1990). *The stages of economic growth: A non-communist manifesto* (3rd ed.). Cambridge: Cambridge University Press.

Schramm, W. (1964). *Mass media and national development: The role of information in developing nations*. Stanford, CA: Stanford University Press.

Servaes, J., & Malikhao, P. (1994). Concepts: The theoretical underpinnings of approaches to development communication. In *Approaches to development communication*. Paris: UNESCO.

Sherry, J. (1997, December). Prosocial soap operas for development: A review of research and theory. *Journal of International Communication, 4*(2), 75–101.

Singhal, A., & Domatob, J. (1993, December). The field of development communication: An appraisal. A conversation with Professor Everett M. Rogers. *Journal of Development Communication, 2*(4), 97–101.

Singhal, A., & Rogers, E. (1999). *Entertainment-education: A communication strategy for social change*. Mahwah, NJ: Lawrence Erlbaum Associates.

Singhal, A., & Sthapitanonda, P. (1996, June). The role of communication in development: Lessons learned from a critique of the dominant, dependency, and alternative paradigms. *Journal of Development Communication, 1*(7), 10–25.

So, A. (1990). *Social change and development: Modernization, dependency, and world-system theory*. Newbury Park, CA: Sage.

Soul City (1999). *Edutainment: How to make edutainment work for you*. Houghton, South Africa: Soul City.

Tuluhungwa, R. (1981, June 2). Highlights of PSC activities in 1980. *Project Support Communications Newsletter, 5*(2) 1–2.

UNESCO. (1980, June 7). *Resolution on the new international information order of the 4th Meeting of the Inter-governmental Coordinating Council of Non-aligned Countries for Information*. Baghdad.

United Nations. (1949). *Statistical yearbook 1948*. Lake Success, NY: United Nations.

United Nations (1974, May 1). *Declaration on the establishment of a new international economic order*. New York: United Nations.

Weinstein, J. (1997). *Social and cultural change: Social science for a dynamic world*. Boston: Allyn and Bacon.

Windahl, S., Signitzer, B., & Olson, J. (1992). *Using communication theory: An introduction to planned communication*. London: Sage.

9

✳

The Politics of
Global Communication

CEES J. HAMELINK

Cees J. Hamelink (PhD, University of Amsterdam) is professor of international communication at the University of Amsterdam, The Netherlands. He is the editor in chief of the *International Journal for Communication Studies: Gazette*. He is also honorary president of the International Association for Media and Communication Research, founder of the People's Communication Charter, and board member at large of the International Communication Association. Hamelink's major publications include *Cultural Autonomy in Global Communications* (1983), *Finance and Information* (1983), *The Technology Gamble* (1988), *The Politics of World Communication* (1994), *World Communication* (1995), and *The Ethics of Cyberspace* (2000).

THE THREE SUBSTANTIVE DOMAINS

Since the mid–19th century, global communication has developed into an important concern on the agenda of the international community. Over the past 150 years the players in this field (governments, commercial firms, and professional practitioners) have designed and adopted rules (by legislation or by self-regulation), institutions, and practices that provide limits and incentives for their conduct. During all these years the substantive domains of global communication politics have largely remained the same. They encompass the fields of telecommunication (now including data communication), intellectual property rights, and the mass media.

By and large, the core issues of today's communication politics are still to be found in these three domains. Technological developments have obviously added new dimensions to these issues. In the area of telecommunication the main issues

 For additional online resources, access the Global Media Monitor Web site that accompanies this book on the Wadsworth Communication Cafe Web site at http://communication.wadsworth.com.

continue to involve accessibility, allocation, and confidentiality. Today the accessibility issue refers not only to basic telephony but also to advanced computer networks. In addition to frequencies and settlement rates, the allocation issue today involves the new field of domain names for the use of the Internet.

The confidentiality issue has gained increased urgency through the global proliferation of data networks, data collection activities, and new forms of electronic surveillance. The issues in the domain of intellectual property rights have acquired more urgency through the application of new technologies that make large-scale copying of copyrighted materials easy. In the domain of mass media contents the basic controversy is still focused upon the tension between harmful content and free speech. The regulation of content on the Internet is today an urgent new issue on the agenda of global communication politics.

Global communication politics is initiated, amended, debated, and implemented by a variety of multilateral forums, including both governmental and nongovernmental organizations. For specific issues, distinct multilateral institutions have become responsible. Global communication in the 1990s confronted the world political arena with complex and controversial policy concerns that demanded resolution through multilateral bargaining. A major challenge for the 21st century is the inclusion of actors from global civil society in these bargaining processes.

THE BEGINNINGS

The politics of global communication emerges in the mid-19th century in the domains of telecommunication, intellectual property rights, and mass media.

Telecommunication

In 1868 Heinrich von Stephan, a senior official in the postal administration of the North German Confederation, prepared a proposal for an international postal union. Through his government this plan was submitted to a plenipotentiary conference that was held at the invitation of the Swiss government at Berne on September 15, 1874. The 22 countries present at the conference founded through the Treaty of Berne the General Postal Union.[1] The treaty of this convention entered into force on July 1, 1875. In 1878 the name of the organization was changed to Universal Postal Union. The 1874 Berne conference introduced basic norms and rules that still hold today. Among these were the guaranteed freedom of transit within the territory of the union, and the standardization of charges to be collected by each country for letter-post items addressed to any part of the union's territory.

By 1865 the need was felt to substitute a multiplicity of bilateral, trilateral, and quadrilateral arrangements for a multilateral agreement. In that year France invited the European states to an international conference that became the founding meeting of the International Telegraphy Union (May 17, 1865). With the establishment of this predecessor of today's International Telecommunication Union (ITU), the first treaty to deal with world communication was adopted: the International Telegraphy Convention. The original text of the convention's treaty stated that the signatories desired to secure for their telegraphy traffic the advantages of simple and reduced tariffs, to improve the conditions of international telegraphy, and to establish a permanent cooperation among themselves while retaining their freedom of operation.[2]

The convention adopted the Morse code as the first international telegraph standard. Among the other norms that were adopted were the protection of the secrecy of correspondence, the right of everybody to use international telegraphy, and the rejection of all liability for international telegraphy services. The contracting parties also reserved the right to stop any transmission that they considered dangerous for state security or to be in violation of national laws, public order, or morals.

Intellectual Property Rights

The Berne meeting of the International Literary and Artistic Society adopted the draft for a multilateral treaty entitled Convention Establishing a General Union for the Protection of the Rights of Authors in Their Literary and Artistic Works. This draft was sent to "all civilized countries" through the Federal Council of the Swiss Confederation, with the plan for a diplomatic conference in 1884 to adopt a formal treaty. The third diplomatic conference (September 6–9, 1886) adopted the earlier drafts for a convention, an additional article, and a final protocol. These three texts were signed by Belgium, France, Germany, Great Britain, Haiti, Italy, Liberia, Spain, Switzerland, and Tunisia. These founder members created a union that was open to all countries. The Berne treaty provided international recognition for the national treatment principle. As article 2(1) stated,

> Authors who are subjects or citizens of any of the countries of the Union, or their lawful representatives, shall enjoy in the other countries for their works, whether published in one of those countries or unpublished, the rights which the respective laws do now or may hereafter grant to natives.

In the field of copyright the Berne convention treaty remained the only multilateral treaty until 1952. Since 1886 it has been revised at diplomatic conference in 1896 (Paris), in 1908 (Berlin), in 1928 (Rome), in 1948 (Brussels), in 1967 (Stockholm), and in 1971 (Paris).

In the development of author's rights the basic principles have been to ensure remuneration for an author by protecting his or her work against reproduction (for 50 years after the author's lifetime); to demand respect for the individual integrity of the creator; to encourage the development of the arts, literature, and science; and to promote a wider dissemination of literary, artistic, and scientific works.

Mass Media

With the proliferation of printed and especially broadcast media (in the late 19th and early 20th centuries), serious concerns about the social impact of the mass media emerged. The positive, constructive contribution of the media to peaceful international relations generated considerable excitement. Such positive expectations were expressed in the 1933 Convention for Facilitating the International Circulation of Films of an Educational Character. This treaty of this convention was signed at Geneva on October 11, 1933. The contracting parties to the convention, which was registered with the secretariat of the League of Nations, considered the international circulation of educational films that contribute "towards the mutual understanding of peoples, in conformity with the aims of the League of Nations and consequently encourage moral disarmament" to be highly desirable. To facilitate the circulation of such films, the signatories agreed to exempt their importation, transit, and exportation from all customs duties and accessory charges of any kind.

However, the negative social impact of the mass media was also a serious concern. A moral, educational concern was expressed regarding the spread across borders of obscene publications. This concern resulted in the adoption of the 1910 and 1924 treaties on traffic in obscene publications. The 1924 International Convention for the Suppression of the Circulation of and Traffic in Obscene Publications declared it a punishable offence "to make or produce or have in possession (for trade or public exhibition) obscene writings, drawings, prints, paintings, printed matter, pictures, posters, emblems, photographs, cinematograph films or any other obscene objects." Also punishable was the importation or exportation of obscene materials for trade or public exhibition, and persons committing the offence "shall be amenable to the Courts of the Contracting Party in whose territories the offence . . . was committed."

Concern about the negative impact of the mass media also arose from the increasing use of the mass media in the course of the 19th century as instruments of foreign diplomacy. Although this was particularly the case with newspapers, the development of wireless radio widened the potential for this new form of diplomacy. Increasingly, diplomats shifted from traditional forms of silent diplomacy to a public diplomacy in which the constituencies of other states were directly addressed. In most cases this behavior amounted to propagandistic abuse of the medium. During the World War I, the means of propaganda were used extensively. This psychological warfare continued after the war ended, as international shortwave radio began to proliferate.

In the immediate postwar period the League of Nations initiated discussions about the contribution of the international press to peace. In 1931 the league asked the Institute for Intellectual Cooperation (the predecessor of UNESCO) to conduct a study on all questions raised by the use of radio for good international relations. In 1933 the study, *Broadcasting and Peace,* was published, and it recommended the drafting of a binding multilateral treaty. Under the war threat emanating from Germany after 1933 the treaty was indeed drafted, and on September 23, 1936, it was signed by 28 states. The fascist states did not participate. The International Convention Concerning the Use of Broadcasting in the Cause of Peace entered into force on April 2, 1938, after ratification or accession by nine countries: Australia, Brazil, Denmark, France, India, Luxembourg, New Zealand, the Union of South Africa, and the United Kingdom. Basic to the provisions of the treaty was the recognition of the need to prevent, through rules established by common agreement, the use of broadcasting in a manner prejudicial to good international understanding. These agreed-upon rules included the prohibition of transmissions that could incite the population of any territory "to acts incompatible with the internal order or security of contracting parties" or which were likely to harm good international understanding by incorrect statements. The contracting parties also agree to ensure "that any transmission likely to harm good international understanding by incorrect statements shall be rectified at the earliest possible moment." In 1999 the treaty was still in force and had been ratified by 26 member states of the United Nations.

The New Multilateral Institutions

After 1945, global communication politics received a new impetus through the establishment of the United Nations. With the creation of the United Nations and its specialized agencies, a crucial group of institutions for multilateral policy evolution and policy coordination entered the international system. The General Assembly of the UN (particularly through the International Law Commission and several subcommissions) and the International Court of Justice became the primary movers in the progressive development of the norms and rules that make up the current system of international law.

The UN General Assembly has contributed to global communication politics through a vast number of resolutions that address such divergent issues as the jamming of broadcasts, the protection of journalists on dangerous missions, direct satellite broadcasting, and human rights aspects of science and technology.

Among the key standard-setting instruments adopted by the General Assembly that are pertinent to world communication are the basic human rights covenants, declarations and conventions against discrimination, and treaties on outer space law. Among the various organs of the UN General Assembly, special attention for communication matters is located in the Third Committee of the General Assembly (responsible for social, humanitarian, and cultural matters) and the Economic and Social Council. The Economic and Social Council was established as the principal organ to coordinate the economic and social work of the UN and its specialized agencies. In the subsidiary bodies of the council, communication issues are addressed, especially in the case of the Commission on Human Rights or the Commission on Transnational Corporations.

Of particular importance was the establishment by the General Assembly in 1959 of the Committee on the Peaceful Uses of Outer Space. This body became the focal point for UN standard-setting in outer space law, with important references to world communication politics through regulatory instruments addressing satellite broadcasting.

In 1966 the General Assembly established the Commission on International Trade Law (UNCITRAL), with the mandate to facilitate the harmonization of the laws of international trade. With the increasing importance of computer technology in international transactions, the commission has been required to address such problems as legal validity of computer records and liability in electronic funds transfers.

In 1978 the UN General Assembly established the Committee on Information, which received its mandate through a resolution adopted on December 18, 1979. The committee has contributed to a series of resolutions on the new international information order and the public information activities of the UN.

Specialized Agencies

Multilateral policy is also made by the specialized agencies of the United Nations, and several of these became important regulators for the field of communication, especially the ITU; the Universal Postal Union (UPU); the UN Educational, Scientific, and Cultural Organization (UNESCO); and the World Intellectual Property Organization (WIPO). To a far lesser extent, the International Labor Organization (ILO) became involved through employment questions relating to communication professionals; and the World Health Organization (WHO) and Food and Agriculture Organization (FAO), through work in the field of standards for advertising and marketing of health and food products.

Standards affecting world communications are also set in the International Civil Aviation Organization (ICAO), which has adopted rules for aircraft telecommunications systems, and the International Maritime Organization (IMO), which has addressed issues of maritime communications.

In addition to the already existing multilateral forums that became UN specialized agencies, new regulatory bodies were also established, such as the now defunct Intergovernmental Bureau for Informatics (IBI) and the UN Conference on Trade and Development (UNCTAD), which has adopted standards in such fields as intellectual property and transfer of technology.

An important multilateral organization that does not belong to the United Nations family is the General Agreement on Tariffs and Trade (GATT). Among the other important multilateral bodies with participation of national governments are the organizations that have been established for the operational application of space telecommunications technology. These are primarily Intelsat and Inmarsat, intergovernmental satellite systems established by treaty.

Three other intergovernmental multilateral institutions should be mentioned, although they are not as broadly representative and in fact are more regionally oriented. However, they have made significant contributions to world communication politics. These are the Organisation for Economic Co-operation and Development (OECD), the Conference on Security and Co-operation in Europe (CSCE), and the Council of Europe. In such fields as freedom of information and protection of transborder flows, the standard-setting work of these organizations has had important impacts on the world.

The Nongovernmental Organizations

In the post-1945 phase of the evolution of world communication politics, an important contribution was offered by a rapidly growing group of international nongovernmental organizations (INGOs). INGOs are partly international, in terms of membership and activities, and partly nationally based. Obviously, they do not have the legal power to issue binding decisions, but they can influence the policy-making processes of the intergovernmental organizations as expert groups or as lobbying agents. They can also define standards for their own conduct that may have a political significance beyond the members of the group they represent. Illustrations are the efforts of the international professional bodies in journalism to arrive at a self-regulatory code of conduct, or the self-regulatory codes that are adopted by the International Public Relations Association and the International Advertising Association.

The United Nations and its specialized agencies have from their inception involved nongovernmental organizations in their policy-making processes. In the development of international human rights law, for example, INGOs have played an important role. INGOs such as Amnesty International have contributed to a crucial instrument for the implementation of human rights standards: "the mobilization of shame." Another example is provided by those INGOs that keep the World Health Organization informed of acts by multinational companies that violate the WHO code on the marketing of breast-milk substitutes. In the field of development cooperation, new policy insights have been forced upon public institutions through INGO pressure regarding concerns about women, population, health, and the environment. Various resolutions by the UN General Assembly have accorded special significance to the contributions of organizations representing scientists, employers, and workers' unions in negotiations on a code of conduct for transnational corporations. In UN agencies such as the ITU, WIPO, and UNESCO, INGOs have made significant contributions to the formulation of world communication politics.

Shifts in Global Communication Politics

Over the past decade the arena of global communication politics has seen major changes. Among the most important ones are the following:

- The international governance system for communication operated during the past 100 years mainly to coordinate national policies that were independently shaped by sovereign governments. Today's global governance system to a large extent determines supranationally the space that national governments have for independent policy making.

- Global communication politics is increasingly defined by trade and market standards and ever less by political considerations, with a noticeable shift from a predominantly political discourse to a largely economic-trade discourse. Evidence of this can be found in the growing emphasis on the economic importance of intellectual property and the related priority of protection for investors and corporate producers. In the telecommunications field the standards of universal public service and cross-subsidization have given way to cost-based tariff structures. In the area of transborder electronic data flows, politics has changed from political arguments about national sovereignty and cultural autonomy to such notions as trade barriers and market access.

- The most powerful private players have become more overtly significant. The invisible hand of the economic interests that have all along guided political decision making became in recent years more and more visible. Transnational corporations became prominent players in the arena and played their role explicitly in the foreground. The locus of policy making shifted from governments to associations of private business actors.

The recent developments in connection with the proposal for a charter on global communication demonstrates the reversal of roles. During the Interactive Conference of the ITU in September 1997, EU commissioner Martin Bangemann proposed the idea of a charter with key principles for the information society. The charter was to be a nonbinding agreement on a framework for global communications in the 21st century. The idea was further elaborated during a Group of Seven (G7) meeting in Brussels in October 1997.

On June 29, 1998, Commissioner Bangemann invited some 50 board chairpersons and corporate presidents from 15 countries to a roundtable discussion on global communications. Among the companies invited were Microsoft, Bertelsmann, Reuters, Polygram, IBM, Siemens, Deutsche Telekom, Sony, Toshiba, and VISA. On the agenda were questions such as, What are the most urgent obstacles to global communications, and what are the most effective means to remove them?

Intellectual property rights, taxation, tariffs, encryption, authentication, data protection, and liability were identified as urgent issues. The business participants proposed that regulation must be kept to a minimum because the global nature of the online economy makes it impossible for any single government or body to regulate. The industry expressed a clear preference for self-regulation. The meeting proposed to set up a Business Steering Committee to ensure that the initiative would be led by business. The industrialists announced that they would begin a new global business dialogue, to which governments and international organizations would be invited.

Ironically, the initial Bangemann plan was for a political declaration that would launch a dialogue between governments and companies on the global electronic marketplace, the goal of which would be a market-led approach in which the private sector would actively participate through a consultative process with governments and international organizations to shape global communications policy. This process has now been taken over by the private sector, which will—when it sees fit—invite governments and international organizations to participate in the shaping of a self-regulatory regime.

The World Trade Organization

Global communication policies were traditionally made in such intergovernmental forums as UNESCO, the World Intellectual Property Organization, and the International Telecommunication Union. These organizations were relatively open to the sociocultural dimension of developments in information and communication technologies. Moreover, they offered a platform where the interests of developing nations could also be voiced. In recent years the position of these international governmental organizations, or intergovernmental organizations (IGOs), was considerably weakened, as the major players began to prefer a forum that was more conducive to their specific interests. This forum is the successor to the General

Agreement on Tariffs and Trade: the World Trade Organization (WTO). The WTO was established as one of the outcomes of the GATT Uruguay Round of multilateral trade negotiations, which was completed in December 1993.

The WTO is generally more favorable to the trading interests of the major industrial countries than are other intergovernmental bodies. Among its main policy principles are the worldwide liberalization of markets and the nondiscrimination principle, which provides for national treatment of foreign competitors in national markets and for treatment as most favored nations. Actually, it should surprise no one that communication politics has shifted to this trade forum, given the increasing economic value of communication networks and information services. Today's global communications market generates more than US$1,600 billion annually. Together with the fact that the major communication and information corporations provide the essential support structures for commodity and financial markets, the governance of communication issues is now largely destined to be subject to a global trade regime. This implies that the rules of "free" trade are applied to the three main components of the world communications market: the manufacturing of hardware, the production and distribution of software (computer programs and contents), and the operation of networks and their services.

CURRENT PRACTICES

The Domain of Telecommunication

The prevailing pattern of thought that guides global politics in relation to telecommunication infrastructures is based on the following assumptions:

- Telecommunication infrastructures are essential to development.
- The installation and upgrading of infrastructures is expensive.
- Private funding is needed.
- To attract private funding, countries will have to liberalize their telecommunication markets and adopt pro-competition regulatory measures.

The global management of telecommunication is in fact left to freely operating private entrepreneurs. The basic thought is that a country's telecommunication infrastructure can be managed by private companies and that, whenever parts of the network are unprofitable, the state can provide the public means to secure that no citizen is disenfranchised.

In the course of the 1980s, deregulation became the leading principle for public policy. Its main aim of "less state and more market" has begun to affect more and more social domains and, in many countries, now also reaches out to primary facilities such as the provision of water and energy, thus rendering access and use of these facilities problematic for those with little income.

For national and global telecommunication markets the new policy implied privatization and liberalization. According to the deregulators, the creation of competitive markets and the shift from public to private ownership would facilitate the universal accessibility of telecommunication and information services. The key policy principles for global telecommunication are "liberalization of the market" and "universal service."

Combining these principles suggests that they are complementary and mutually reinforcing. That, however, remains to be demonstrated. Signals from different parts of the world indicate that leaving markets to private commercial and competitive forces does not necessarily lead to accessibility and affordability of telecommunication infrastructures.

Judging from the growing participation of the private section in telecommunication negotiations and the increase in market-opening commitments, the conclusion is that more and more countries believe that liberalizing their telecommunication markets is beneficial to them. The real political issue is no longer whether countries will liberalize but when they will do so. Yet opinions continue to differ, as the ITU's *World Telecommunication Development Report* observes: "Market access, for example, will be viewed by some as an opportunity, while others that are attempting to develop their own domestic telecommunication service industry might see it as a challenge and a threat to nascent local operators" (ITU, 1997, p. 102). In some countries, revenues for domestic operators will increase as a result of liberalization, but in other countries most revenues may accrue to foreign entities. As the ITU report rightly notes, "there will be winners and losers" (p. 106).

As part of the opening up of their markets, many countries have also begun to privatize their public telecommunication operators (PTOs). Whereas liberalization can be defined as the opening of markets to competition, privatization refers to the transfer of state-owned institutions or assets to various degrees of private ownership. These two processes can be in conflict with each other. Liberalization may clash with the desire of governments to get the highest price for their monopoly PTOs, and privatization may conflict with market liberalization when the incoming operator wants monopoly control for an initial period.

Governments pursue privatization and/or liberalization policies for quite different reasons. These policies—especially in poorer countries—may be more related to troublesome economies than to the desire to improve and upgrade telecommunication services. They may be related to the political wisdom of the day (for example, neoliberalism) or to the hope of getting technology transferred in the process. The new policies are neither an unequivocal recipe for disaster nor a guarantee of successful economic and technological performance. Results will be different in different countries, and much more study is needed to establish what social conditions determine benefits and costs.

Privatization has been implemented in a fairly large number of countries; 44 PTOs were privatized between 1984 and 1997 (ITU, 1997, 2). These privatizations have raised some $159 billion. The 12 major privatizations in 1996 raised more than $20 billion. These investments were roughly 50% domestic and 50% foreign. The overall trend has been that more than 30% of the invested capital comes from foreign sources. As the ITU reports, the PTOs themselves are usually the most active investors. However, in 1997, majority shares in 29 of the top 40 international carriers were still owned by states: "Rather than full privatization, it is corporatization of state-owned telecommunication companies that has instead proceeded across all regions" (ITU, 1998a, p. 9). Also liberalization has not proceeded so as to create competitive markets across sectors in all countries. In many countries, basic telecommunication services are not open to competition. Most liberalized are markets for mobile telephony, but even in this sector several countries do not yet allow competition.

The arguments that are used to support privatization point to the expansion and upgrading of networks, the improvement of services, and the lowering of tariffs for access and usage of networks. Experiences are varied, however. One of the results of privatization often is the expansion of the telecommunications network. In several countries (for example, Peru and Panama in 1997), privatization considerably improved teledensity. According to the ITU (1998b), "One reason is that network expansion targets have increasingly been made a requirement of privatization concessions" (p. 71). The added telephone lines of course benefit those users who can afford the service. The privatization scheme does not enlarge the group of citizens who have the purchasing power that is required for the use of telecommunication networks.

In several countries tariffs have gone down, but mainly for big corporate users, whereas the telephone bills for ordinary consumers have hardly benefited. Experiences with the provision of services are also differentiated. This is partly because the expectation of more competition and more choice as a result of privatization was not always fulfilled. As a matter of fact, in smaller and less advanced states, national telecommunication operators have lost against big global coalitions, the new monopolists. It is highly questionable whether markets controlled by a few global operators will actually benefit the consumer. It remains dubious how much competition will remain in the end. The reduction of prices and the increase in investments for technological innovations tend to shake competitors out of the market, and as a result, market liberalization almost everywhere tends to reinforce market concentration. This follows the historical experience that free markets inevitably lead to the formation of monopolies because competitors will shake contenders out of the market or will merge with each other.

The WTO Telecommunication Treaty

In 1994 the Marrakech Agreement Establishing the World Trade Organization (WTO) completed the eighth round of multilateral trade negotiations held under the GATT (Uruguay Round). Part of the final treaty was a General Agreement on Trade in Services (GATS). The most elaborate annex concerned the trade in telecommunications. The annex defined basic telecommunication services and networks as follows:

- Public telecommunications transport service: any telecommunication transport service required, explicitly or in effect, by a Member to be offered to the public generally.
- Public telecommunication transport network: the public telecommunication infrastructure which permits telecommunications between and among defined network termination points.

Of the 125 signatory countries of the Marrakech Agreement, some 60 made commitments to open their markets for telecommunication services, although most did not commit themselves on the issue of basic telecommunications. The commitments range from full competition for all telecommunication services to exceptions for basic telecommunication services or cellular services or for local services.

The Marrakech meeting established the Negotiating Group on Basic Telecommunications (NGBT), which was to deal with telecommunication services and conclude its work by April 1996. The NGBT failed to reach agreement by this date. Several issues remained inconclusive, such as the liberalization of satellite services and the settlement arrangements for international telecommunication rates. The negotiations did lead, however, to an agreement on some basic rules that were provided in a so-called Reference Paper, which deals with competitive safeguards, interconnection, universal service obligations, transparency of licensing criteria, independence of the regulator, and allocation and use of scarce resources.

A new group, called the Group on Basic Telecommunications, continued the work after July 1996. The main mandate of the group, which was open to all WTO member states and held monthly meetings, was to stimulate more countries to make commitments, to deal with the issue of liberalizing satellite services, and to solve a number of issues related to the provision of telecommunications services.

The new series of negotiations focused on the matter of restrictions on foreign ownership, among other things. The U.S. government pushed particularly hard for allowing maximum foreign ownership in domestic telecommunications. In making their commitments, restrictions on foreign ownership were fully waived by many countries; others, however, retained between 25%–80% of domestic control. Whereas some countries consider foreign ownership an opportunity to attract necessary foreign investment (ITU, 1997, p. 102), others perceive it as a threat to national sovereignty. Although national governments have full control over the scope, the phasing, and the timing of their commitments, once they have made those commitments, they cannot in the future change their concessions. A complex matter for the negotiations became the issue of mobile services provided through satellites. Although the allocation of satellite frequencies is the responsibility of the ITU, a trading aspect arises when national governments use national procedures for spectrum allocation as barriers to trade. Following the provisions of the GATS, such procedures should not be discriminatory.

On February 15, 1997, the Fourth Protocol of the General Agreement on Trade in Services was signed by 72 WTO member states (representing some 93% of the world trade in telecommunication services). On February 5, 1998, the protocol entered into force. This World Telecommunications Agreement demands that participating states liberalize their markets. They are allowed some leeway to implement universal access in ways they deem desirable, but significant qualifications in the agreement seriously limit the national political space.

The agreement has far-reaching implications for the governance of the basic infrastructures of telecommunications. On the issue of universal service, it states,

> Any member has the right to define the kind of universal service obligation it wishes to maintain. Such obligations will not be regarded as anti-competitive per se, provided they are administered in a transparent, non-

discriminatory and competitively neutral manner and are not more burdensome than necessary for the kind of universal service defined by the member.

This seriously limits the space for independent national policy making on access. Since foreign industries cannot be placed at a disadvantage, the national standards for universal service have to be administered in a competitively neutral manner. They cannot be set at levels "more burdensome than necessary." If a national public policy would consider providing access to telecommunication services on the basis of a cross-subsidization scheme rather than on the basis of cost-based tariffs, this might serve the interests of the small users better than those of telecommunication operators. Foreign market entrants could see this obligation as "more burdensome than necessary." As a consequence, the policy would be perceived as a violation of international trade law. It would be up to the largely obscure arbitration mechanisms of the WTO to judge the legitimacy of the national policy proposal.

The focus of the agreement is on the access that foreign suppliers should have to national markets for telecommunication services, rather than on the access that national citizens should have to the use of telecommunication services. The simplistic assumption is that these different forms of access equate.

As a result, social policy is restricted to limits defined by the commercial players. Trade interests rather than sociocultural aspirations determine national telecommunication policy. The WTO has suggested that, if the agreement is followed, an almost worldwide open market (probably up to 93%) for basic telecommunication services will be achieved by the year 2004, because most trading partners have agreed to liberalize their domestic markets. The establishment of worldwide free markets for any type of services does not, however, necessarily imply the availability of such services or the equitable use of these services for all who could benefit from them.

The Domain of Intellectual Property Rights

At present the essential governing institutions in the field of intellectual property rights are the World Intellectual Property Organization and the World Trade Organization. The WTO plays an increasingly important role because it oversees the execution of the legal provisions of the agreement on Trade-Related Intellectual Property Rights (TRIPS). This global agreement emerged under the GATT negotiations (as Annex 1C to the General Agreement on Tariffs and Trade in the Uruguay Round of multilateral trade negotiations, 1993). TRIPS contains the most important current rules on the protection of intellectual property rights (IPRs). It is implemented within the WTO regulatory framework. In this agreement the economic dimension of IPR protection is reinforced. As Venturelli (1998) correctly summarizes, "The balance has tipped entirely toward favoring the economic incentive interests of third-party exploiters and away from both the public access interests of citizens and the constitutional and human rights of creative labor" (p. 63). As IPRs have achieved a prominent place among the world's most important tradable commodities, the current trade-oriented IPR-regime favors the corporate producers (publishers, broadcast companies, music recording companies, advertising firms) against individual creators. The provisions of the TRIPS agreement protect the economic rights of investors better than the moral rights of creative individuals or the cultural interests of the public at large. For the dissemination of their products, the performing artists, writers, and composers increasingly transfer their rights to big conglomerates with which they sign contracts. Ultimately, these companies determine how creative products will be processed, packaged, and sold.

One of the serious problems with the current trend in IPR protection is that the emerging regulatory framework stifles the independence and diversity of creative production around the world. The regime is particularly unhelpful to the protection of the "small" independent originators of creative products. It establishes formidable obstacles to the use of creative products because it restricts the notion of fair use, under which—traditionally—these products could be freely used for a variety of educational and other purposes. The narrow economic angle of the current trend focuses more on the misappropriation of corporate property than on the innovation of artistic and literary creativity.

A particularly worrying phenomenon is that the current rules provide that once knowledge in the public domain is put into electronic databases, it will come under IPR protection. This will imply a considerable limit to freely accessible sources. Moreover, the present system of governance threatens to transform the new global forum that cyberspace potentially offers (through the new digital technologies) into a marketplace where a controlled volume of ideas will be traded.

The one-dimensional emphasis upon the commercial facets of copyright protection is reinforced by the progressive shifting of negotiating forums from the WIPO to the WTO. In this process the protection of intellectual property becomes part of the global free trade agenda. This implies that the public interest is secondary to the economic interest of the largest producers of intellectual property. The social value and common benefit of cultural products are not on the transnational corporate agenda.

These products (such as knowledge) tend to be seen as commodities that can be privately owned. A different point of view would contest this and propose that knowledge is part of the common heritage of humankind and cannot be the exclusive property of a few members of the community. The emphasis in the emerging system is rather exclusively on the rights of knowledge producers and almost completely bypasses the duties of rights holders. Such duties include the obligation of disclosure—the obligation to provide information and supporting documents concerning corresponding foreign applications and grants. The rights holder can be obliged to work a patent in the country where the patent was granted and can be required to refrain from engaging in abusive, restrictive, or anticompetitive practices.

Current intellectual property rights tend to benefit only the industrial nations, but they can also stimulate free innovation in poorer nations. Rather than strengthening the control of transnational corporations over technology and reinforcing the monopolistic rights of technology providers, the technological capabilities in the developing countries could be strengthened. The pressure to create a uniform global system of IPR protection constrains the flexibility that developing countries need in order to adapt the IPR system to their specific needs and interests. One can expect that in the years to come the domain of intellectual property rights will continue to be a crucial battlefield of conflicting interests.

The Domain of Mass Media

The main issues in relation to the mass media concern concentration of ownership and the trade in media products. The mega–media mergers of the 1980s and early 1990s renewed in many countries concerns about media concentration. On the international level, only minimal concern is being expressed. The essential guideline for policy makers seems to be the deregulation of the marketplace. The common argument in favor of an unregulated marketplace in the provision of information is that it guarantees creative and competitive forums that offer a diversity of contents. Abundant empirical evidence, however, suggests that concentration in the mass media promotes market control by a few companies that tend to produce a limited package of commercially viable contents only.

The World Trade Organization's rules, for example, stress the need for competition. However, the major concern is that public policies should not be anticompetitive in the sense of hampering free access to domestic markets. Current competition rules mainly address the dismantling of public services and the liberalization of markets, not the oligopolization of markets or the conduct of the dominant market parties.

The WTO Basic Telecommunications Agreement of February 15, 1997, governs market access but has little to say about the conduct of parties on the market. It does not guarantee that an effective, open competition between commercial actors. The nondiscrimination principle that provides for most-favored-nation treatment of foreign competitors is inadequate to secure competition on domestic markets.

The WTO provisions on anticompetitive practices do not exclude the possibility that local media markets would be controlled by only three or four foreign suppliers. The lack of a serious competition policy supports unhindered market concentration and reinforces foreign ownership of essential market domains, particularly in developing countries.

One of the main policy issues is the question of whether the info-com market is substantially different from markets for other commodities (such as automobiles or detergents) that it should be treated in a different way. Is the question whether public intervention for cultural products should be different from that for food products? Could it be that even if the shopping mall functions best when the state does not intervene, this does not necessarily apply if the mall is the main provider of information and culture?

Moreover, is a genuine international competition policy (Holmes, Kempton & McGowan, 1996, p. 755) that governs anticompetitive conduct of market parties a realistic option? Such a policy would imply more regulation and would thus clash with the predominant concern of the major market players to reduce regulation. Serious global governance to curb the formation of cartels will in any case be difficult. The approaches to cartels differ widely across national legal systems and traditions, and most free trade supporters believe that free markets will eventually create open competition and that anticartel rules create trade barriers.

In an economic environment where mega-mergers are almost natural and are loudly acclaimed by financiers and industrialists, the tendency toward public control is likely to be minimal. The European Commission does indeed stop and prohibit industrial mergers, but in a limited and modest way. The commission may propose demands that make companies decide not to merge. According to Jean Paul Marissing (of Caron & Stevens/Baker & McKenzie), who is a legal expert on mergers, out of several thousands of mergers that have been registered with the commission, only 10 were really prohibited (NRC Handelsblad, July 22, 1998).

One factor for low rate of merger prohibition is that mergers are considered serious problems only when consolidated companies may control more than 40% of a market. European regulation can prohibit abuse of monopoly positions, but not the development of market monopolies. Equally, in U.S. regulation a merger is considered a threat to competition only if the two companies after their merger control more than 60% of a market.

The phenomenon of media concentration is generally acknowledged, but its implications are not of universal concern. Political, industrial, and academic positions on the issue are widely divergent. Scientific research on concentration, for example, tends to focus on the question of effects of media concentration upon media contents. Such research often finds it "very difficult to demonstrate any link between the two" (McQuail, 1992, p. 125). This would be relevant if media contents were the core issue. It is, however, more important to question whether consolidation of media ownership guarantees sufficient independent locations for media workers, enough channels for audience reception and/or access, adequate protection against price controls on oligopolistic markets, and opportunities for newcomers on media markets. Even if the oligopolist could demonstrate quality, fairness, diversity, critical debate, objectivity, investigative reporting, and resistance to external pressures in his offerings to the marketplace, there would still be reason to provide regulatory correction, because the marketplace would effectively be closed for newcomers and thus not constitute a free market.

The players that argue for multilateral regulation of the issue constitute a heterogeneous collective of politicians, academicians, and professionals. They have a variety of motives for the conclusion of a multilateral accord. One motive is to protect the labor conditions of employees in the media industries. This motive addresses both employment opportunities and the quality of work in the media. The freedom of the workers on the information market is heavily dependent upon the strength of the agreements they can negotiate with their employers. Generally, in cases of market concentration the freedom of their professional position is under threat. The need to accommodate the commercial purposes of the company and the political idiosyncrasies of the ownership inevitably implies forms of direct and indirect censorship.

Another motive is constitutional. Several U.S. Supreme Court decisions, for example, have asserted that the freedom of the press is undermined, because the media have become so oligopolistic that censorship powers lie in private hands. An important motive addresses the extent of independence in information provision and cultural production. Industrial concentration inevitably implies the establishment of power. The megacompanies are centers of power that are at the same time subject and object of media exposure. Moreover, the information industry as power center is linked into other circuits of power, such as financial institutions, military establishments, and the political elite. A specific problem is posed in situations in which mass media that provide news and commentary are part of an industrial conglomerate.

The conglomerate may engage in activities that call for critical scrutiny by the media, but the controlling actors may prefer to protect those activities against exposure. The concern about concentration is also motivated by the threat that oligopolization erodes the diversity of informational and cultural production. In cases where consolidation occurs as vertical integration, meaning that production and distribution are controlled by the same actors, the real danger exists that they will exclusively offer their own products to the market. A common example is the newspaper that, as part of a conglomerate, places mainly reviews of its own books. The growing influence of institutional investors and commercial interests not genuine to the information sector tends to lead to an emphasis on the profitability of the commodity, rather than on its sociocultural quality. As a result, products that can be rapidly sold on mass markets are preferred. Illustrative is the tendency among film production companies and recorded music producers to concentrate on blockbusters. This "Rambo" and "Madonna" tendency reinforces a homogenization of markets, as the less profitable products are avoided.

On the issue of media concentration, the positions taken are conflicting. The preference for strict regulation clashes with the preference for no regulation at all. The pro-regulation position is defended with the following arguments. Antitrust legislation in the media field is defensible because concentration diminishes competition, and as a consequence, diversity on the information market is affected negatively. Moreover, anticartel–type measures promote competition, diversity, and freedom. Against this position is the oft-repeated suggestion that mergers lead to stronger companies with more power to protect information freedom. However, mergers are not always successful. They often occur without adequate careful weighing of assets and liabilities. They may be motivated by the personal interests of top management or the short-term interests of small stockholders. On average, of 10 major acquisitions, 4 or 5 will be sold again. Often the aims that a merger is expected to achieve are not met. It is quite possible that, after the consolidation, profits do not increase, market segments do not expand, and the innovative potential of the firms may even diminish. As a result of unsuccessful mergers, companies may collapse and disappear.

Oligopolization in the information industry may also undermine the civil and political fundamental right to freedom of expression. This is the case when concentration actually diminishes the number of channels that citizens can use to express or receive opinions. In oligopolistic markets the controlling interests may more easily refuse to distribute certain opinions. For example, in such situations, refusing certain forms of advertisement is easier.

Oligopolists always have the tendency to use their market power to price-gouge consumers. This may easily mean that the access to information and culture becomes dependent upon the level of disposable income. It can be attractive for the oligopolist to bring competing products on the market. This is, for example, quite common in such sectors as cosmetics or detergents. The implication of this intrafirm diversity is that it erects quite effective obstacles against the entry of newcomers into the market. This outcome is important because often a considerable contribution to market diversity originates with new entrants, although large firms may support loss-making operations by compensating for the losses elsewhere in the company accounts. In this way newspapers, for example, that otherwise would have disappeared can be maintained. However, the length of time this compensation will be acceptable to shareholders (and in particular institutional investors) is limited. Moreover, losses accumulate over time, and in the middle to longer term, products that are not profitable will have to be removed.

The key arguments against attempts to regulate media concentration are the following. There is no empirical proof that concentration has indeed such negative effects. On the contrary, it can be argued that strong consolidated companies can offer much more diversity and can mobilize more independence in their dealings with governments than smaller companies can. Moreover, strong media can "rescue" loss-making media that otherwise would disappear, and thus their contribution to diversity is retained. It is also argued that more competition does not guarantee more diversity, because competitors may all try to reach the largest share of the market with a similar product. Even if regulatory measures against industrial consolidation would be successful in stimulating more competition, an increase in product diversity is not guaranteed. Markets tend inevitably toward identical, though marginally distinct, products because, of necessity, they address the largest possible number of buyers. A problem is that allowing competition on the marketplace does not necessarily lead to more diversity. There is some evidence that the deregulated, competitive broadcast systems of Western European countries reflect less diversity in contents than the formerly regulated public monopolies. This type of situation occurs largely because the actors in a competitive market all try to control the largest segment by catering to rather similar tastes and preferences of that market segment.

The trading of media services has become global business with an expanding and profitable market. In the years ahead the international media market is generally expected to reach the $3 trillion mark. This expanding market is to a large extent due to the concurrent processes of deregulation of broadcasting and the commercialization of media institutions. These developments imply a growing demand for entertainment. The related important process is globalization—in terms of markets, but also in terms of products and ownership.

Worldwide a clear trend toward an increasing demand for the American-brand entertainment is seen. An important feature of the trend toward globalization is that the trading by the megacompanies is shifting from the international exchange of local products to production for global markets.

Concerns with regard to the world market in media services have been expressed in connection with the 1986–1993 Uruguay Round of multilateral trade negotiations. The special focus of these concerns is television programs and films and the existing and/or potential constraints to trading them across the world. The concerns focus on forms of national regulation that restrict imports of media services or national policies that protect national media industries. Other concerns focus on trade constraints related to the structure of the international media market, particularly to the large share of market control held by only few transnational operators.

Perspectives on the issue of traded media services diverge. Some players assert that this trade should be unhindered and that foreign markets should be freely accessed. Others are concerned that, without restrictions on media imports, local cultural industries cannot survive, and local cultural heritage gives way to McDonaldization. The leading media production companies, their associations (such as the Motion Pictures Export Association), and governments of exporting countries (especially the United States) have been concerned about barriers to media trade. The concern about the lack of controls is largely articulated by small producers and by governments of importing countries (Third World countries, Western European countries, Canada). Their preference for import restrictions is largely motivated by the desire to economically and culturally protect their own media industry. This desire is reinforced by the fear that transnational control over local distribution and exhibition mechanisms will exert a decisive influence on what cultural products are locally available.

The contending positions are liberal-permissive claims versus protectionist-restrictive claims. The liberal position prefers an arrangement that permits total liberalization of market access for media services. The more protectionist position favors levels of protection from media imports as instruments to support local media industries or to protect local culture.

One of the complexities of addressing media services in a trade context is that not all of them have commercial purposes. A part of mass media production is typically oriented toward noncommercial, educational, artistic, or sociocultural goals. Although this is recognized in Article IV of the GATT accord, the big media exporters define their product in terms of a commercial commodity only. This implies the collision of the claim to the opportunity to increase markets for a profitable commodity with the claim to rightfully regulate media imports and protect national media markets for a variety of reasons.

For developing countries another problem with the liberalization claim is that because media products are finished products, it is not likely that liberalization increases labor or technology inputs for them. Contrary to, for instance, tourism, media services do not bring employment or training. That market access is likely to be a one-way street is also a problem. The economic realities of media production and distribution allow for little chance of exports from the Third World countries.

At present it looks as if the most likely provisions to emerge for the world trade in media services are GATT rules pertaining to traded services and intellectual property rights. The emerging practice of multilateral trade cooperation will be based upon a binding and robust GATT accord. The question remains, however, as to the appropriateness of such an arrangement, given the distinctions between media services and services at large. First, the production of a film or television program resembles manufacturing. An actual physical product is generated, composed of labor- and capital-intensive inputs. So, in comparison with services such as tourism or construction, where employment occurs and value is added at the final destination of the service, films and television programs are finished products that are merely distributed at their final destination. The distancing of production and distribution in these industries virtually eliminates possibilities for technology transfer or highly skilled employment at the point of distribution. In comparison with some services in which developing countries could compete on the basis of a comparative labor-cost advantage, the manufacture of media products is organized in such a way that almost all labor inputs—and certainly all skilled labor inputs—occur in centralized locations far removed from the distribution point. Second, all the costs in making the product are incurred in turning out the first copy of the film or the television program. Additional copies can be produced very inexpensively. So profitability in this sector depends on timing and strategic control of the release of the film or program, a process that has become more complicated as the number of different types of potential distribution outlets has multiplied worldwide. This constraint on potential profit intensifies the need to control distribution tightly, for example, ownership of distribution networks (Christopherson & Ball, 1989, pp. 250–251).

Another complication is that film and television programs are both a good and a service. Contents may be transmitted in tangible formats, but also through intangible media such as airwaves. Moreover, as several studies have noted, it is quite difficult to measure in any reliable manner the actual trade volume (Guback, 1969; Widman & Siwek, 1988). Also, whether a GATT arrangement would permit certain trade barriers in the light of cultural policies remains to be seen. This process is allowed in the OECD Code of Liberalization of Current Invisible Operations (Annex IV to Annex A of the code), which provides, "For cultural reasons, systems of aid to the production of printed films for cinema exhibition may be maintained provided that they do not significantly distort international competition in export markets."

The GATT accord that was concluded in mid-December 1993 did not include the sector of audiovisual services. The most powerful players were divided among themselves and clashed on a free trade perspective promoted by the United States and a cultural policy perspective defended by the European Union. The discord is only of marginal significance. The opponents have no basic disagreement about the commercial nature of culture and information as marketable commodities. European politics has already for some time established that broadcasting, for example, is a traded service and is subject to the rules on market competition of the European Economic Community (EEC) Treaty. The European desire to exempt culture from international trade rules is not motivated by deep principles. In the bargaining, at some point a deal is likely to be struck, and a global trade agreement might emerge. For the time being, the major players have agreed to disagree. In February 1994 both key U.S. actors (such as the MPEA) and the European Commission indicated a desire to reconcile their divergent positions on the issue of traded media services.

For the trade negotiations at the WTO Seattle conference (November 1999), the U.S. government proposed the removal of broadcasting and audiovisual products from the exemptions to the existing agreements on the liberalization of telecommunications. The current exemptions are part of the Fourth Protocol of the General Agreement on Trade in Services that was mentioned above. The European public broadcasters rejected this proposal. Their position was considerably strengthened by the protocol on public service broadcasting that was appended to the European Union Amsterdam Treaty of June 1997. The EU agreed that public service broadcasting is related to democratic, social, and cultural needs and to the need to preserve media pluralism. The social and cultural significance of public broadcasting was acknowledged by allowing it to function outside the regime of free market funding. In the WTO negotiations the issue of traded media services continues to be controversial.

LESSONS FROM A KEY PROJECT
IN THE DOMAIN OF
GLOBAL MASS MEDIA POLITICS

During the 1970s a coalition of politicians, media activists, and communication researchers committed itself to the creation of a New International Information Order (NIIO), also referred to as New International Information and Communication Order or new world information and communication order (NWICO). This concept is described in more detail elsewhere in this book. The coalition aspired toward a new order that would be democratic, that would support economic development, enhance the international exchange of ideas, share knowledge among all the people of the world, and improve the quality of life.

This aspiration was first publicly expressed through a meeting of Non-Aligned Heads of State in 1973 at Algiers. This meeting started a project that—after several years of much commotion and anger and little concrete achievement—would again disappear from the world's political agenda. Among the various factors that contributed to the NIIO failure, the most critical one was the lack of people's participation.

The effort to democratize communication in the 1970s was never a very democratic process. The debate was mainly an exchange among governmental and commercial actors. Ordinary people were not on the playing field. The whole project was engineered by political and intellectual elites. Little or no attention was given to people's interests or even to the need to involve ordinary people in the debate.

The NIIO debate was firmly rooted in the realist paradigm of international relations. This paradigm conceived the world as a state-centric system and failed to take serious account of the numerous nonstate actors that had become essential forces in world politics. As a result the NIIO debate never explicitly promoted the notion that the effective protection of democratic rights could not be guaranteed under the conventional nation-state system. A critical problem was that the realist paradigm glossed over the internal dimension of state sovereignty while focusing on external factors. As a result, the nation-state was seen as protecting the liberties of its citizenry against external claims made by other states. However, the outwardly sovereign state tends also to appropriate sovereign control over its citizens in the process. This follows the vision of the philosopher Thomas Hobbes (1638–1709), who proposed that only the absolute sovereignty of the state (which he referred as the Leviathan) can control the eternal strife among civil actors. This position ignores that state sovereignty represents more than the emancipation from the powers of emperors, popes, and nobility.

The development of legitimate sovereign states went together with the development of egalitarianism, in which subjects became citizens. The French Revolution and the American Revolution gave birth both to independent nation-states and to citizens with basic civil rights. As a matter of fact, the French Revolution recognized the primacy of the people's sovereignty. This recognition was not taken up in the NIIO project. It was not a people's movement. Insofar as it aspired toward a democratic order, it was a "democratization from above." Just like the NIIO project, today's popular project for the construction of a Global Information Infrastructure (GII) is steered by the interests and stakes of governments and corporations. It is the bilateral playing field of "princes" and "merchants," and ordinary people are occasionally addressed as citizens or consumers, but they play no essential role.

A concern for the GII elite is actually that people may not be as excited about the digital future as the elite themselves are. It may be that ordinary men and women are not eagerly waiting to believe that virtual reality can resolve the problems of their daily lives. Therefore many of the official reports on the information society stress the need to promote awareness among consumers. A key concern of the constructors of the information superhighway is that consumers may be hesitant about adding digital services to the present media supply, certainly if they have to pay for them.

The GII project therefore needs to persuade people that the information society will bring them great improvements in lifestyle, comfort, and general well-being. This makes people important targets for propaganda and marketing. However, no serious involvement of people's movements is present in the making of the GII. No trilateral negotiations are taking place between governments, industrialists, and social movements to share decision making on our preferred common future. Like the project of the 1970s, the GII project is about "democratization from above" and is unlikely to be effective in making world communication more democratic.

GLOBAL COMMUNICATION
POLITICS TODAY

Current global communication politics is dominated by a set of eight essential issues that will largely shape the future of global communication. The governance of these issues is complicated because the political agendas in the world community are strongly divided and conflicting and define these issues in very different ways. The neoliberal political agenda is commercially oriented and market-centered. This agenda proposes the liberalization of national markets, the lifting of trade restrictions, and the strengthening of the rights of investors. Opposed to this, one finds a humanitarian political agenda that puts the interests of citizens at the center of global policy making and that wants human rights to be taken as seriously as property and investment rights in global communication politics.

Access

The neoliberal agenda perceives people primarily as consumers and aspires to provide them with access to communication infrastructures so they can be integrated into the global consumer society. The humanitarian agenda perceives people primarily as citizens and wants them to be sufficiently literate so that communication infrastructures can be used to promote democratic participation.

Knowledge

On the neoliberal agenda, knowledge is a commodity that can be processed and owned by private parties, and the property rights of knowledge producers should be strictly reinforced. On the humanitarian agenda, knowledge is a public good that cannot be privately appropriated.

Global Advertising

The neoliberal agenda has a strong interest in the expansion of global advertising. This implies, among other things, more commercial space in media (mass media and the Internet), new target groups (especially children), more sponsorships (films, orchestras, exhibitions), and more places to advertise (the ubiquitous billboards).

The humanitarian agenda is concerned about the ecological implications of the worldwide promotion of a consumer society and the growing gap between those who can shop in the (electronic) global shopping mall and those who can only gawk. Moreover, the humanitarian agenda has a strong interest in defending public spaces against their commercial exploitation.

Privacy

The neoliberal agenda has a strong interest in data mining: the systematic collection, storage, and processing of masses of data about individuals to create client profiles for marketing purposes. The humanitarian agenda has a strong interest in the protection of people's privacy and the creation of critical attitudes among consumers to guard their personal information more adequately.

Intellectual Property Rights

The neoliberal agenda has a strong interest in the strict enforcement of a trade-based system for the protection of intellectual property rights that provides a large degree of freedom for the transnational commercial rights owners to exploit those rights. Equally these IPR owners have an interest in expanding the period of protection as well as the materials that can be brought under this protection.

The humanitarian agenda is concerned that the present system sanctions the grand-scale resource plunder of genetic information (biopiracy) from poor countries and serves the interests of corporate owners better than the interests of local communities or individual artistic creators. This agenda has a strong interest in protecting the interests of communal property of cultural resources and in protecting resources in the public domain against their exploitation by private companies.

Trade in Culture

The neoliberal agenda has a strong interest in the application of the rules of international trade law to the export and import of cultural products. Under these rules countries are not allowed to take measures that restrict cultural imports as part of their national cultural policy. The humanitarian agenda is interested in having culture exempted from trade provisions and in allowing national measures for the protection of cultural autonomy and local public space.

Concentration

The neoliberal agenda has a strong interest in creating business links (acquisitions, mergers, joint ventures) with partners in order to consolidate controlling positions on the world market and wants to create a sufficiently large regulatory vacuum in which to act freely. The humanitarian agenda is concerned that today's global merger activities have negative consequences for both consumers and professionals in terms of diminishing diversity and creating the loss of professional autonomy.

The Commons

The neoliberal agenda wants the private exploitation of such commons as the airwaves and promotes the auctioning of these resources to private parties. The humanitarian agenda wants retain the public property of the human common heritage so that public accountability and community requirements remain secured.

Civil Advocacy

At present the battle between these two conflicting agendas is fought with inequality of arms. The commercial agenda is supported by a strong constituency of the leading members of the WTO and powerful business lobbies (such as the Business Software Alliance and the Global Business Dialogue). The humanitarian agenda, although increasingly active in the economic arena, is still in search of an active constituency in the global communication arena. Although civil advocacy would be up against formidable opponents, a global movement could pose a serious political challenge. It would represent the interests of democratic citizenship and thus present a stronger claim to credibility than business firms. Because it would be inspired by such fundamental notions as universal human rights, it would have a moral authority, which is superior to those who are driven by commercial interests. It could use the court of public opinion more effectively than corporations and use this to get major concessions from its commercial opponents. A global civil movement would be made up of citizens who at the same time are consumers and thus clients of the media industries, which would make them a forceful lobby.

On December 20, 2000, the *International Herald Tribune* used for one of its articles the following lead: "Small Advocacy Groups Take Big Role as Conscience of the Global Economy." In the same way, it should be possible to state: "Small Advocacy Groups Take Big Role as Conscience of Global Communication Politics."

The intervention by public interest coalitions in the arena of global communication politics will not come about spontaneously. It demands organization and mobilization. A modest beginning has been made to achieve this through the Platform for Cooperation on Communication and Democratization. The platform that was established in 1995 is at present made up of AMARC, APC, Article 19, CENCOS, Cultural Environment Movement, GreenNet, Grupo de los Ocho, IDOC, International Federation of Journalists, IPAL, International Women's Tribune Center, MacBride Roundtable, MedTV, One World Online, Panos, People's Communication Charter, UNDA, Vidéazimut, WACC, WETV—Global Access Television, and Worldview International Foundation. Members of the platform have agreed to work for the formal recognition of the right to communicate. They emphasize the need to defend and deepen an open public space for debate and actions that build critical understanding of the ethics of communication, democratic policy, and equitable and effective access.

The right to communicate is also the central concern of the so-called People's Communication Charter (http://www.pccharter.net). The People's Communication Charter is an initiative that originated in 1991 with the Third World Network (Penang, Malaysia), the Centre for Communication & Human Rights (Amsterdam, the Netherlands), the Cultural Environment Movement (United States), the World Association of Community Radio Broadcasters (AMARC), and the World Association for Christian Communication. The charter provides the common framework for all those who share the belief that people should be active and critical participants in their social reality and capable of governing themselves. The People's Communication Charter could be a first step in the development of a permanent movement concerned with the quality of our cultural environment.

Eventually this movement could develop into a permanent institution for the enforcement of the PCC, perhaps in the form of an ombudsman's office for communication and cultural rights. This idea largely follows a recommendation made by the UNESCO World Commission on Culture and Development, chaired by Javier Pérez de Cuéllar, in its 1995 report *Our Creative Diversity*. The commission recommended the drawing of an International Code of Conduct on Culture and—under the auspices of the UN International Law Commission—the setting up of an International Office of the Ombudsperson for Cultural Rights (World Commission, 1995, p. 282). As the commission writes,

> Such an independent, free-standing entity could hear pleas from aggrieved
> or oppressed individuals or groups, act on their behalf and mediate with gov-
> ernments for the peaceful settlement of disputes. It could fully investigate
> and document cases, encourage a dialogue between parties and suggest a

process of arbitration and negotiated settlement leading to the effective re-
dress of wrongs, including, wherever appropriate, recommendations for legal
or legislative remedies as well as compensatory damages. (p. 283)

Ideally the proposed ombudsman's office would have full independence both
from governmental and from commercial parties, and as an independent agency
it would develop a strong moral authority on the basis of its expertise, its track
record, and the quality of the people and the organizations that would form
its constituency. Given the growing significance of the global communication
arena and the urgency of a humanitarian agenda for its politics, the building of
this new global institution constitutes one of the most exciting challenges in the
21st century.

For more information on the topics that appear in this chapter, use the password that
came free with this book to access InfoTrac College Edition. Use the following
words as keyterms and subject searches: global communication, International Telecommunication Union, intellectual property rights, international relations, human rights,
Commission on International Trade Law, communication and politics, telecommunication.

QUESTIONS FOR DISCUSSION

1. By and large, the core issues of today's communication politics are the same
   as a century ago. What new dimensions have technological developments
   added to these issues?

2. The arena for global communication politics has considerably expanded over
   the years. Which actors have entered the arena in addition to nation-states?

3. Are the recent shifts in global communication politics also reflected in the
   national communication politics of your country?

4. The New International Information Order (NIIO) was a project of "democratization from above." How feasible today is a project to democratize global
   communication from below?

5. Could you design a future Global Ombudsperson's Office for Cultural
   Rights? What, in your opinion, should be its main tasks, and how should
   it operate?

NOTES

1. The countries present at the conference
were Austria, Belgium, Denmark, Egypt,
France, Germany, Great Britain, Greece,
Hungary, Italy, Luxembourg, the Netherlands, Norway, Portugal, Rumania, Russia,
Serbia, Spain, Sweden, Switzerland, Turkey,
and the United States.

2. The following states attended: Austria,
Baden, Bavaria, Belgium, Denmark, France,
Hamburg, Hanover, Italy, the Netherlands,
Norway, Portugal, Prussia, Russia, Saxony,
Spain, Sweden, Turkey, and Würtemburg.
Great Britain was excluded because its tele-
graph network was privately owned. The
unions also decided in 1858 that French and
German were to be the official languages for
international telegrams.

REFERENCES

Christopherson, S., & Ball, S. (1989). Media services: Considerations relevant to multilateral trade negotiations. In *Trade in services: Sectoral issues* (pp. 249–308). Geneva: UNCTAD.

Guback, T. H. (1969). *The international film industry.* Bloomington: Indiana University Press.

Holmes, P., Kempton, J., & McGowan, F. (1996). International competition policy and telecommunications: Lessons from the EU and prospects for the WTO. *Telecommunications Policy, 20*(10): 755–767.

ITU. (1997). *World telecommunication development report 1996/97: Trade in telecommunications.* Geneva.

ITU. (1998a). *General trends in telecommunication reform 1998: World* (vol. 1). Geneva.

ITU. (1998b). *World telecommunication development report: Universal access.* Geneva.

McQuail, D. (1992). *Media performance: Mass communication and the public interest.* London: Sage.

NRC-Handelsblad (Daily Newspaper), Rotterdam, July 22, 1998.

Venturelli, S. (1998). Cultural rights and world trade agreements in the information society. *Gazette, 60*(1), 47–76.

Widman, S. S., & Siwek, S. E. (1988). *International trade in films and television programs.* Cambridge: Ballinger.

World Commission on Culture and Development. (1995). *Our creative diversity.* Paris: UNESCO.

10

Global Advertising
and Public Relations

DEAN KRUCKEBERG

Dean Kruckeberg (PhD, University of Iowa) is an APR, Fellow PRSA, and coordinator of the mass communication division at the University of Northern Iowa. He is coauthor of the books *Public Relations and Community: A Reconstructed Theory* and *This Is PR: The Realities of Public Relations*. A recipient of several national awards, he is a cochair of the Commission on Public Relations Education and a board member of the Public Relations Society of America. Kruckeberg's teaching and consulting have included work in the United Arab Emirates, Latvia, Russia, and Bulgaria.

Newsom, Turk, and Kruckeberg (2000) say that public relations practitioners are intermediaries between the organizations that they represent and all of their organizations' publics. They note, "As a management function, *public relations involves responsibility and responsiveness in policy and information to the best interests of the organization and its publics*" (p. 2). They further define public relations as "the various activities and communications that organizations undertake to monitor, evaluate, influence and adjust to the attitudes, opinions and behaviors of groups or individuals who constitute their publics" (p. 533). Noting that the strategy of advertising is to create desire and to motivate demand for a product, the authors say that designing advertisements, preparing advertisements' messages, and buying time or space for their exposure are the tasks of advertising. They further observe,

For additional online resources, access the Global Media Monitor Web site that accompanies this book on the Wadsworth Communication Cafe Web site at http://communication.wadsworth.com.

Advertising has been defined as paid-for time or space, except in the case of public service announcements (PSAs) where the time and space are donated to a nonprofit organization. (p. 372)

Both advertising and public relations—when examined on a global scale—must be comparatively considered within a context that includes historical and evolutionary factors that have influenced their development regionally. Full appreciation must be given for the diverse cultural, governmental/regulatory, economic, geographic, and technological factors that have differently influenced the development of advertising and public relations in various parts of the world, as well as the range of dominant ideological beliefs that have mitigated their development and contemporary practice.

Advertising and public relations are changing rapidly throughout the world, arguably becoming more "global" in their practice. Such globalism is partly in response to rapidly developing transnational media and global communication systems that are both creating and becoming increasingly dependent upon global markets to sustain them, as well as in response to a corresponding multiculturalism—all of which have come about because of previously unimaginable technological advances that are changing how and why people communicate.

This chapter provides a brief historical analysis and a prognosis of the continuing development—and role—of advertising and public relations worldwide, together with the implications of this development as well as of the future challenges in the mission, role, and function of both advertising and public relations.

BRIEF HISTORY OF ADVERTISING AND PUBLIC RELATIONS WORLDWIDE

Incorrectly so, laypeople in the United States oftentimes associate advertising and public relations solely as (1) Western, if not U.S., in origin; and (2) corporate in purpose, that is, representing primarily wealthy and powerful corporations that sell consumer products and services, increasingly to a global market. Too, laypeople often associate both advertising and public relations as (3) manipulative in their role, function, and intent.

These assumptions not only are simplifications but indeed in themselves constitute gross inaccuracies. However, more credence can be ascribed to the common contentions that both advertising and public relations are (4) democratic in their traditions, and (5) capitalistic in their heritages.

Western in Origin?

Campbell (2000) notes that advertising has existed in the Middle East since 3000 B.C., when Babylonian shop owners began hanging signs outside their stores. Early Egyptian merchants hired criers to announce the arrival of ships, and the walls of ancient Pompeii had advertisements painted on them; by 900 A.D., town criers in European cities were directing customers to stores. English booksellers used brochures, bills, and posters to announce new books in the 1470s, and advertisements in English newspapers began appearing in 1622.

In public relations, Kruckeberg, Badran, Ayish, and Awad (1994) make compelling arguments that the public relations role and function in the Middle East date at least as far back as Mohammed, and popular U.S. public relations textbooks point to public relations–like activities throughout the world that extend back into antiquity.

Indeed, although public relations in its contemporary sense is frequently regarded as a 20th-century U.S. phenomenon, a German organization had—if not the first—at least one of the earliest internal public relations departments. By 1890, Alfred Krupp's company had a "news-bureau" composed of as many as 20 staff members ("The German public relations business," 1987).

However, Mallinson (1991) notes that U.S. public relations was exported to post–World War II Europe primarily through Great Britain, in great part because of the two countries' historical and linguistic ties but also as an outcome of the U.S.-British military alliance in World War II that had preceded this postwar U.S. overseas investment.

Nevertheless, although no corner of the globe can exclusively claim the origins of public relations, and while sophisticated public relations in its most contemporary sense is being practiced throughout the world, Kruckeberg (1999) observes,

> The common presumption is that North American public relations is most sophisticated and thereby most deserving of emulation. Not only are North American strategies, tactics and techniques held in global esteem, but base cultural and ideological assumptions of North American public relations are unquestioningly accepted as normative to modern public relations practice, i.e., contemporary public relations practice is assumed to be predicated on specific North American social, political and economic ideologies. Public relations practice in North American society extends from philosophical foundations that hold in particular reverence the right to expression of public opinion and to freedom of the press, as well as a social tradition that is far more individualistic than historically has been that of many indigenous cultures in other parts of the world. Finally, public relations is based on—and inherently assumes—a sophisticated communication infrastructure that has evolved in North America, both politically and technically.

Despite the apparent widespread emulation of U.S. public relations practice elsewhere in the world, Ovaitt (1988) argues that public relations may be even more culture-bound than is either marketing or advertising—making it harder to conduct public relations programs based on concepts that extend across international boundaries.

For example, Tsetsura (2000a) observed that public relations in Russia had existed for little more than 15 years but nevertheless was well on its way to achieving respect in that country. Especially during the past few years, many specialized public relations agencies have been established in that country, and internal PR departments also have been created in many Russian companies. Furthermore, Russian scholars have been actively examining the theories and practice of public relations, according to Tsetsura, and the author's research indicates that American public relations theory has had a significant impact on Russian public relations theory. However, her research found the following:

> In general, American textbooks were more theoretically oriented than the Russian textbooks. Russian textbooks, in their turn, were primarily written for practitioners and students who are, most likely, unfamiliar with the public relations phenomenon. . . .
>
> Another tendency that should be noticed is a high concentration on political relations and election campaign strategies. Today, for many practitioners and even scholars, public relations is associated only with politics . . . or with integrated communications. (p. 60)

Significantly, Tsetsura's research found that Russian public relations textbook authors either were not familiar with—or chose to ignore—some major theoretical concepts of contemporary American theory. They tended to focus more on practice than on theory and on suggestions for practical suggestions, tactics, and practical tips rather than on theoretical explanations. Tsetsura (2000b) further suggests that misleading explanations of the goals of public relations in the past, which had been promulgated in the early 1990s by Russian scholars who were not educated in public relations, had contributed to a negative image of public relations in Russia.

Al-Enad (1990) sees a difference between Western practice of public relations and what is appropriate practice in less developed countries. He contends that public relations practice in Third World nations might also apply to Europe's less developed former Eastern Bloc countries. Al-Enad observes that whereas Western public relations literature places public relations between an institution and its publics or environment, public relations in developing nations is located between material and nonmaterial aspects of the culture.

Regardless of diverse regions' historical or contemporary influence, Kruckeberg (1994) concludes,

> Suffice it to say, there is growing appreciation for public relations professional practice worldwide. Countries previously unfazed—or at least unmoved—by negative public opinion are becoming cognizant of the benefits of good public relations to fulfill increasingly obvious needs. Aggressively, a range of public and private organizations and institutions are seeking both the knowledge and the means to enable these countries' total infrastructures to practice "good public relations." (p. 2)

Advertising, if not "global" in its commonality of strategies and tactics and in the availability of like media worldwide, most certainly is used extensively throughout the world. However, it is often tailored to indigenous—rather than global—tastes and perspectives; indeed, some advertising would be questionable, if not disastrous, if used elsewhere. For example, Vietnamese television viewers who were watching the Euro 2000 soccer matches saw a commercial for Binh Tien Consumer Goods Company's shoes, an advertisement produced by Chicago advertising agency Leo Burnett Company that contrasted the footwear of Vietnamese soldiers in the "American War"—that is, sandals made of tires—with the latest athletic shoes made by the Vietnamese manufacturer.

Burnett's headquarters says its partnership with a Vietnamese advertising agency wasn't trying to exploit a painful chapter in the history of Vietnam and the United States; it was just trying to sell shoes using images familiar to Vietnamese. "Anyone who has seen the ad realizes it does not exploit the war," says a Burnett representative. "Rather, it employs historical achievements that have meaning to the Vietnamese people" (Flagg, 2000, p. A19). Although the advertisement was well received in Vietnam, its use in the United States would have been unthinkable.

Swedish furniture company Ikea's latest campaign in the United Kingdom features "hapless Ikea employees who are forced to sniff a colleague's armpit." Another commercial employs tattooed thighs to help sell the company's furniture (Beck, 2001). A British advertising agency caused an uproar by using Holocaust images to promote an Imperial War Museum exhibit, with one poster reading, "Come and see what man can achieve when he really puts his mind to it" (Ellison, 2000b).

The importance of understanding international strategies and tactics and appreciating indigenous sensitivities becomes quickly evident to advertising agencies whose clients themselves have obtained their resources globally, including tapping into a worldwide labor pool. Such clients want an advertising agency that can provide services worldwide and that is sensitive to the nuances of regional markets throughout the world.

Effective advertising today must operate in a multicultural world that is unforgiving of marketers' cultural insensitivity to and lack of understanding of cultures other than their own. For example, John Hancock Financial Services aired a television spot in July 2000 that featured two Caucasian women at an airport holding an Asian baby. Although viewers could not positively identify the baby's ethnicity from this advertisement, adoption agencies nevertheless protested—fearing that Chinese government officials would assume that the child was from China and that the implied homosexuality of the two women parents was being tolerated by American adoption officials, an attitude the Chinese government did not share concerning prospective adopting parents (Gubernick, 2000).

Nike pulled a magazine advertisement for a running shoe after disabilities-rights groups objected to the advertisement's reference to people having such challenges as being "drooling and misshapen" (Grimes, 2000)—a characterization that one might hope would be a faux pas in any culture. The 2000 Super Bowl commercial that showed a walking Christopher Reeve brought derision for its perceived exploitation of a celebrity tragedy (O'Connell, 2001). Families of murder victims objected to the "We, on Death Row" advertising supplement that featured pinups and in-depth interviews with inmates awaiting execution to raise consciousness about the death penalty as well as about the Benetton's label of fashion clothing (Dumenco, 2000). A study by a global advertising agency found that many Europeans were being put off by a proliferation of technical advertisements; instead of enticing Europeans to enter this market, new product announcements were persuading them to wait until the onslaught of technology development slowed to a manageable pace (Ellison, 2000c). A German wife accused her husband of unfaithfulness when a postcard arrived at their home from "Your Sweetie" that thanked her husband for the flowers; days later, a second postcard revealed that the mailing was an advertising campaign from the German flower industry (Aalund, 2000). Meanwhile, an Internet animation series, "Lil' Pimp," featuring a 9-year-old street hustler, may have a growing audience, but presently has attracted little advertising revenue (Mathews, 2000).

In sum, it is highly naive to think of advertising and public relations as Western phenomena, either in their evolution and development or especially in their effective practice in a global but highly multicultural world.

Corporate in Purpose?

Seemingly compelling evidence suggests that advertising has been strongly—if not overwhelmingly—corporate in purpose, that is, accompanying the growth of large corporations as national and global institutions and enjoying the steady growth of consumerism as a worldwide social and economic phenomenon. Major clients of advertising agencies disproportionately include large corporations that sell goods and services, not only within the borders of their own countries but increasingly also to international markets. Although many corporations have marketed their products and services globally throughout most of their histories, others are now looking more closely to find opportune niches in international sites. For example, Unilever PLC has only recently launched a skin lotion for black women in Brazil, a nation that North Americans might be surprised to learn has the world's largest black population next to Nigeria, but members of this population do not necessarily identify themselves as being black (Ellison & White, 2000a). Procter and Gamble sends 4.5 million copies of its promotional magazine *Avanzando con tu familia* [Getting Ahead with Your Family] to Hispanic families in the United States (Porter & Nelson, 2000).

Public relations has not been as restricted to primarily supporting corporations that sell products and services. Popular U.S. textbooks point to governmental and nongovernmental organizations' social programs that were promoted in the 20th century through public relations. Nevertheless, Heath (2000) observes that "from its birth, public relations has been seen as a tool used largely by corporate managements to get their way" (p. 70).

Indeed, while both advertising and public relations historically have been widely used by corporations, U.S. governmental and nongovernmental organizations have also long used advertising, as well as public relations. Historically, patriotic World War II posters from the U.S. government come readily to mind, as do the various "poster" causes of charities and other nongovernmental organizations. Of course, political campaigning and agendas throughout the world, both in democratic and totalitarian countries, have included both advertising and public relations techniques. For example, consider the propaganda of wartime Germany under propaganda head Paul Joseph Goebbels (Boehm, 1989). Furthermore, scholars today contend that professional public relations practice in particular should be available for all publics.

Contemporary scholars see historic inequities that can be corrected through the use of public relations. Grunig (2000), for example, argues that a set of principles must be developed to overcome the problem of a possible imbalance in power between clients of public relations practitioners and the publics with whom they communicate. Further, considerable attention today is being paid to public relations for activist groups. Indeed, Holtzhausen (2000) contends,

> The fact that public relations as activism receives so little attention supports the theory that public relations has become part and parcel of the maintenance of metanarratives and domination in society. In fact, activists are often portrayed as the enemy of organizations and government, although they are actually the real voices of democracy. (p. 100)

The advertising industry in recent years has paid increasing attention to the concept of "relationship marketing," which has much potential, not only for corporations' relationships with customers and other publics but also for a variety of governmental, nongovernmental and charitable organizations. As an example, Hollywood has responded to charges that the entertainment industry is marketing violence to children by airing on network television public service announcements against youth violence (Bravin, 2000).

Manipulative in Their Role, Function, and Design?

Manipulative is a pejorative word, but there is little question that advertising—both consumer advertising to sell products and services, and public relations–oriented "institutional" advertising to sell ideas or to garner support for an organization—is most commonly persuasive in nature. The role, function, and design of public relations, however, are more complex. Grunig (2000) acknowledges that most people seem to view public relations as a "mysterious hidden persuader working for the rich and powerful to deceive and take advantage of the less powerful," and he further observes that some critical scholars and many practitioners view public relations as "a manipulative force in society." However, Grunig contends that most scholars and professionals believe that public relations plays an essential role in a democratic society. He argues,

> Public relations will have its greatest value to client organizations, to publics, and to society if it views collaboration as the core of its philosophy and makes collaboration the focus of research to develop a body of knowledge to guide public relations practice. Furthermore, . . . public relations brings an essential element of collectivism into the commonly individualistic world view of most Western organizations and . . . collaboration, as the core of what political scientists call societal corporatism, is the key element of democratic societies. (p. 25)

Contemporary advertising and marketing executives, particularly those engaged in "relationship marketing," appreciate that satisfactory relationships with customers and others, developed through quality products and service tailored to individual needs as well as through responsible corporate citizenship, have proven far more effective than crude attempts at manipulation.

Democratic in Tradition?

Both advertising and public relations are highly democratic in tradition, the former because advertising by its nature suggests the availability of consumer choice—that is, a marketplace democracy and the ultimate consumer determination of the relative benefits of these choices—and the latter because of an inherent supposition of the importance and value of public opinion within democratic forms of government.

Holtzhausen (2000) argues that the role of public relations should be to continuously demystify the client organization and its practices, transforming it into a more democratic institution for both internal and external publics. She notes that "a democratic institution will consistently communicate openly with its publics and will be prepared to change itself in that process" (p. 105).

Sriramesh and White (1992) address democratic requisites by linking societal culture and public relations in these two propositions:

> *Proposition 1:* Societal cultures that display lower levels of power distance, authoritarianism, and individualism, but have higher levels of interpersonal trust among workers, are most likely to develop . . . excellent public relations practices. . . .
>
> *Proposition 2:* Although such occurrences are rare, organizations that exist in societal cultures that do not display these characteristics conducive to the spawning of excellent public relations programs also may have excellent public relations programs if the few power holders of the organization have individual personalities that foster participative organizational culture even if this culture is atypical to mainstream societal culture. (p. 612)

Capitalistic in Heritage?

Both advertising and public relations are steeped in the capitalistic tradition. Holtzhausen (2000) says that public relations in the Western world is a product of both modernism and capitalism, originating to maintain the status of private and public organizations that have participated in the capitalist system.

> The organization itself is an ideological vehicle for capitalism. And the public relations practitioner is part of the ideological message. The purpose of ideologies, like all metanarratives, is to make people think alike and so assert power over society; therefore, the purpose of all ideologies is political. (p. 100)

However, Kruckeberg (1996) argues that although a democratic culture and government are important to the ideology of public relations, nothing inherently restricts implementation of public relations practice in nations having other than purely capitalistic economic systems.

In sum, arguments can be made that contemporary advertising and public relations are not solely Western (or U.S.) in their origin, nor can they be practiced effectively through an exclusively Western perspective; that they do not historically or inherently represent exclusively corporate interests but rather have served well, and can continue to serve well, many organizations—including governments

and nongovernmental organizations and charities—and these organizations'
causes throughout their histories; and that they are not solely (nor are they best
practiced as being) manipulative in nature. However, both advertising and public
relations have strong democratic traditions and capitalistic heritages. Given all of
this, what can be anticipated and what should be expected from today's advertising industry and from contemporary public relations practice in the postmodern,
postmillennial, post–Cold War era of transnational media and global communication in the age of an information revolution?

Postmodern, Postmillennial, Post–Cold War Era

Although the 20th century unquestionably gave birth to the most extraordinary
achievements in world history, its 100 years also were the most bloody and—
arguably—the most dysfunctional for many elements of society worldwide. Although much that occurred in the 1900s was good, a fundamental belief and
premise must be accepted that humankind must do far better in the third millennium for society even to continue. Basic questions that must be addressed and adequately resolved for the 21st century include these: What does it mean to be human and to be part of humankind in postmodern global society? What moral fields
must be developed or modified to ensure this humanity, this humanness? What
ethos—that is, moral and spiritual character—must be developed or modified in
global society to nurture this humanness? After late 20th-century victories of democracy and capitalism in former Eastern Bloc countries, what new forms of
democracy and capitalism can or must be developed, not only regionally but also
within a global ethos? Can and should democracy be culturally specific, and
should culturally specific capitalism be embraced in different parts of the world according to societal tradition and heritage? Indeed, some social problems must be
recognized as being so overwhelming, so critical, that all available resources must
be allocated to address them in the new century.

ENVIRONMENTAL CHALLENGES,
POPULATION GROWTH,
POVERTY AND HUNGER, WAR

Kennedy (1993) notes not only new and increasingly critical environmental challenges but also a corresponding increase in the world's population—replete with
rising demographic imbalances between rich and poor countries. Perhaps most
alarming of these is the population explosion. He observes,

> From the viewpoint of environmentalists . . . the earth is under a twofold
> attack from human beings—the excessive demands and wasteful habits of
> affluent populations of developed countries, and the billions of new mouths
> born in the developing world who (very naturally) aspire to increase their
> own consumption levels. (p. 33)

The Office of Population, Bureau for Global Programs, Field Support and Research, of the U.S. Agency for International Development (1996), reports that while the *rate* of the world population growth continues to fall, actual population numbers still are increasing and are expected to total 7.6 billion persons by the year 2020. Further, the share of the population represented by the more developed countries has declined from 27% of the world total in 1970 to 20% in 1996. If present trends continue, the more developed countries will make up only 16% of world population in little more than two decades. Andrew Belsey and Ruth Chadwick (1992) remind us that one fifth of the world's population—1 billion people—remain in dire physical need.

An inhospitable—perhaps irreversibly damaged—global environment, together with resultant poverty and hunger and war, can be ill afforded in the third millennium. All of the world's resources, and its people's best minds, must give priority to threats to the environment, to responsible management of the world's population, and to the elimination of poverty, hunger, and war. Advertisers would be naive to view such a growing population simply as increased markets, and public relations practitioners must consider the challenges that such 21st-century demographics pose in creating mutually beneficial relationships with culturally diverse publics as well as with global society at large.

Nevertheless, advertising and public relations practitioners can help address social problems that will occur through practitioners' expertise not only in communication but also in societal problem solving. In the 1980s, India had advertising billboards reminding, "A baby boom is the nation's doom." Increasingly, "social marketing" skills and public relations community- and relationship-building efforts of practitioners will need to reach "markets" and publics worldwide with messages that do far more than support the sale of products and services, many of which a majority of the world's population may not be able to afford and some of which may be harmful. These missions are more profound and far more difficult to achieve than advertising executives and public relations practitioners' simple attempt to sell products and services and justify the existence of their organizations within society.

THE MANAGEMENT OF CHANGE

Rapid change must be not only acknowledged but also proactively managed. Technology is advancing geometrically, and time and space are being compressed in ways that would have been unfathomable in past generations.

We must appreciate that we do not presently know where technology is going, that we do not know the societal effects of emerging technology, and that it is likely that this technology will affect different societies and cultures in different ways. For example, technology in less developed countries might well have different social outcomes from those in First World Western societies.

Carey (1989) notes Innis's observation that culture is fundamentally affected by communication technology, which can alter the structure of interests (the things thought about) by changing the character of symbols (the things thought with) and by changing the nature of community (the arena in which thought is developed). Referring to the technological age, Kruckeberg (1995–1996) observes,

> Life is more like taking [a] drive down a crowded avenue at 90 miles per hour. Response to feedback must be made far more quickly than many people may be able to "drive" comfortably and safely. The opportunity for prolonged deliberation in decision-making and feedback no longer exists, given the pressures of instantaneous transmission of communication and the accompanying expectations of those with whom one is communicating. (p. 36)

Holtzhausen (2000) looks forward to a postmodern age in which technology will not dominate humanity but rather will serve it. The ethically responsible society, Holtzhausen says, will support science and technology but will also emphasize imagination, sensitivity, emotion, humanity, and an appreciation of differences.

Such change has direct implications for the advertising and public relations industries. For example, in just four years, Internet advertising has grown from virtually nothing into a $5 billion business (Alsop, 2001). In London, several companies are developing technology to allow motion-picture advertisements to be projected onto the walls of subway tunnels (Ellison, 2001). "Cuecats"—small hand-held scanners that plug into personal computers to read bar codes on products as well as "cues" printed alongside ads and articles in newspapers, magazines, and catalogs—can automatically call up Web pages related to the products (Mossberg, 2000).

The head of the sensory-design research lab at Britain's Central St. Martin's College, explaining "sensory marketing," extols the benefits of reaching new shoppers and steady customers through their sense of smell. British Airways' first-class and business-class lounges at London's Heathrow Airport and New York's Kennedy Airport now spritz scent into the air to enhance British Airways' brand image (Ellison and White, 2000b).

Employers concerned about productivity will have to consider an additional threat: advertisers' view of the workplace as a place to target potential customers through the Internet. One United Kingdom advertising executive said that "Most advertisers concede there is a growing recognition that workers are spending more time taking care of personal business and are acting like consumers at the office" (Ellison, 2000a). More important questions about change, however, must address how transnational media and global communication in the age of information revolution will affect society itself.

TENSIONS FROM TECHNOLOGY, GLOBALISM, AND MULTICULTURALISM

Technology is significant not only in and of itself, but it has become the major intervening variable affecting the two other critical variables of the future—globalism and its converse, multiculturalism. The interaction of these three variables will create dynamic tensions in the future that will need examination and resolution.

Many of these tensions will need to be addressed by advertising executives and public relations practitioners on behalf of the organizations that they represent.

GOVERNMENTS, CORPORATIONS, AND PRIVATE CITIZENS

Fundamental changes will certainly occur in the relationships among governments, corporations, and private citizens. Schiller (1995) says that, among the 37,000 companies that predominate globally, the largest 100 transnational megafirms are the global power wielders.

> This world corporate order is a major force in reducing greatly the influence of nation states. As private economic decisions increasingly govern the global and national allocation of resources, the amount and character of investment, the value of currencies, and the sites and modes of production, important duties of government are silently appropriated by these giant private economic aggregates. (p. 21)

Schiller (1995) says these corporations promote deregulation and privatization of industry worldwide, notably in the telecommunications sector. One effect of this large-scale deregulation and massive privatization, Schiller says, is the increasing ineffectualness of national authority.

Corporations may become more powerful and influential than many nation-states. Corporations are capable of making unilateral decisions because these transnational organizations can cross frontiers with impunity to accomplish their goals. Further, it cannot be assumed that decisions made by transnational corporations will be within the moral field of Western culture or in the best interest of others. Governments will not be able to protect citizens' rights if governments' power— and the power of their citizens—pales in comparison to unaccountable corporations whose missions and goals can be totally self-serving.

Related issues of concern in the 21st century include tensions between indigenous cultures' sense of individualism and collectivity, traditions of egalitarianism versus authoritative governmental philosophies and infrastructures, conflicting worldviews among those in different societies, the changing nature of mass societies, and questions of ethics of the majority versus the ethics of the dominants.

NATIONALISM VERSUS GLOBALISM

The assumption of a homogenous global culture—whether through a neocolonial cultural imperialism or through a melding of what is good (or bad) in many or all cultures—can be assumed no more than can a revamped nationalism and metaphorical (if not literal) "ethnic cleansing," which latter scenario in the contemporary age some have likened to the pre–World War I Balkans. Bell (1988) observed pessimistically,

As we approach the twenty-first century, the problems of color, of tribalism, of ethnic differences—in Southeast Asia, the Middle East, the fratricidal hatred in the Muslim world—all bespeak an agenda of issues that contemporary sociology, least of all Marxism, is ill prepared to understand. We see, particularly in Marxism, how much our sociological categories were framed within the context of Western society, and how the themes of the Enlightenment, rationality, industrialization, consciousness, class development, the idea of "historic nations" and social evolution, became our prisms of understanding. And how irrelevant Marx, and even Weber and Durkheim, may be. (p. 441)

Merrill (1996) foresees a future era of conformity and authoritarianism, as described by Karl Mannheim. Mannheim talks of a historical cycle reminiscent of Nietzsche and Comte and distinguishes three stages of development—the medieval man in collective solidarity, the post-Renaissance man in individual competition, and the presently emerging man steeped in "group solidarity." It is this third category toward which we are presently drifting, and it applies equally to man in communist, fascist, and liberal-capitalist cultures, for the factor that Mannheim sees as uniting them all "is the phenomenon of Great Society which the industrial revolution has brought into being." He continues, "The pull of organizations . . . largely accounts for this drift toward conformity and authoritarianism" (p. 61).

Gilder (1992), however, predicts a new age of individualism that "will bring an eruption of culture unprecedented in human history." He continues, "Every film will be able to reach cheaply a potential audience of hundreds of millions of people around the world" (p. 54).

Stephen (1995) views fragmentation of the self as follows:

> The fragmentation of society has been mirrored by a fragmentation of self. In navigating the complex external world, the modern individual by necessity differentiates between the private or personal self and the public self. The public self, a kind of *Gesellschaft* personae . . . is tailored specifically to withstand the travails of presentation in multiple epistemic contexts. (p. 14)

And Bell (1988) early observed the rise of national tensions in almost every part of the world, as much in the (former) communist world as anywhere else, as greatly evidenced in the Balkans in the 1990s.

PAST VERSUS FUTURE

Tensions will remain between modern and traditional societies, as well as within the traditional societies themselves, particularly when the latter face overwhelming pressures to modernize. Stephen (1995) notes two characteristics that differentiate modern and traditional societies:

> The first dimension is pluralism. In traditional societies beliefs are consensual and communication functions mainly to convey information and to coordinate action. Modern societies are highly pluralistic. Beliefs are up for grabs and communication is used to create shared constructions of real-

ity—local pockets of consensus—that provide stability and bridge existentially isolated individuals. . . .

The second dimension is egalitarianism. If a society is predominantly hierarchical rather than egalitarian—as may more often be the case in traditional societies—interpersonal interaction occurs predominantly between individuals of unequal social power. (p. 16)

TENSIONS AMONG THE FIRST, SECOND, AND THIRD WORLDS

Although the Cold War may have been effectively won, the categorizations of the First, Second, and Third World may not yet be obsolete. However, with the effective removal of Marxist ideologies throughout much of the world, problems between the First World and the Third World may in fact have been clarified. Bellah, Madsen, Sullivan, Swidler, and Tipton (1991) note,

Now that East–West tensions are sharply diminishing, we can better understand that the deepest chasm is between the rich and the poor nations. . . . We have a long way to go before we understand the cultural dynamics of rapid social change and the terrible price that it has exacted in individual souls and in societies all over the globe. (p. 250)

Problems articulated in the 1970s regarding the flow of news and the balance of information between nations remain (Emery & Emery, 1988). World economic interdependence still places the heaviest economic burdens on the world's poorest nation-states (Bellah et al., 1991).

CLASS STRATIFICATION

Bell (1988) noted less cooperation and solidarity has occurred within the international working class in recent times than in the past 100 years. However, many social scientists see social class issues remaining in the 21st century. Brook and Boal (1995) warn about the contemporary technological age:

Automation in the name of progress and "inevitable" technological change is primarily to the benefit of that same class that not so long ago forced people off the land and into factories, destroying whole ways of life in the process: "labor-saving" devices have not so much reduced labor as they have increased profits and refined class domination. (p. viii)

Neill (1995) predicts that computerization of schools will not contribute to "high wages" or "good jobs," but in fact the U.S. class hierarchy will be intensified. Kruckeberg (1995) questions who will buy computers for the underclass of people and what will Third World peasants—with unfulfilled needs for food and fiber—have to say to one another electronically.

Or, will there be only increasing alienation and anomie—both for those availing themselves of communication technology and for a global underclass of people who cannot or will not accept telecomputers, powerbooks, electronic note pads, digital computer-linked cameras, portable faxes, cellular telephones and satellite uplinks? (p. 78)

Stephen (1995) notes that modern societies are characterized by a formal egalitarianism, but they are in fact stratified. Indeed, one characteristic of modernity, he says, has been the gradual unfolding of forms of behavior that enunciate class distinctions.

CONTROL OF TECHNOLOGY

Many of these dynamic tensions will be affected directly by policies related to the control of technology and its development and implementation. Will such control rest exclusively or predominantly with corporations and the marketplace in which they compete and influence, with governments, or with world citizenry? Will influence and decision-making related to development and implementation come primarily from the technologists and the corporations they represent and be market driven? Or will they come from the sundry professionals using (consuming) this technology or from global citizenry at large? How will issues of privacy versus access be addressed? Indeed, how will fundamental issues of education, not only of global leaders but also of the world's citizens, be addressed? That is, will generations of technocrats and their corresponding worldview replace or challenge the very foundations of society as held in trust by the liberal arts? Will global culture be a culture of technology, and will this culture imperialistically predominate in all areas of global society? For example, in early 2001, Microsoft centralized its marketing effort with a $200 million advertising campaign—the beginning of a nearly $500 million global marketing campaign (Buckman, 2001).

AN IDEOLOGICAL FOUNDATION FOR
ADVERTISING AND PUBLIC RELATIONS

To suggest that advertising and public relations can ameliorate the 21st-century problems identified in this chapter would be naive and presumptuous, although both can do much—independently and together—by contributing to the resolution of these problems. Kruckeberg (1995–1996) predicts,

> Organizations will need "keepers and reconcilers" of their values and belief systems up to and including their base ideologies. Those professionals will be critically needed who can examine, maintain and modify as necessary traditional organizational and societal values and beliefs that will be challenged in a McLuhanesque "global village" in which the values and belief systems of peoples throughout the world will ideologically confront one another. (p. 37)

He says that professionals will be critically needed who can examine, maintain, and modify as necessary indigenous organizational and societal values and belief systems in an age and communication milieu in which values, beliefs, and ideologies will be continually challenged. Tomorrow's public relations practitioners must define themselves globally as professionals through examination and articulation of their own values, belief systems, and ideology as a professional community.

Kruckeberg (2000) argues that public relations practitioners must "professionalize" on a global scale to provide a succinct definition of their role and function within global society as well as an articulate description of their worldview (that is, their ideology, values, and belief systems), and the same argument is made for advertising. This "professionalization," he says, will take practitioners away from the functionary role of a corporate "gunslinger" or "Samurai warrior," providing this specialized occupation with the necessary philosophical foundation to develop a "professional" worldview.

Grunig (2000) argues for a set of socially acceptable values for public relations, as well as a set of principles that can overcome possible power imbalances between the clients and publics of public relations practitioners.

CONCLUSION

Advertising and public relations are hardly a panacea for the social or global problems in the 21st century, but both can be used effectively to ameliorate some of the problems that we face. As powerfully persuasive and informative processes, advertising and public relations affect people of the world in many ways, especially in the advanced nations. However, if these professions become more readily accessible to all peoples and nations, if they are practiced humanely—not manipulatively—they may result in improved international relations and international communication. Ideally, both advertising and public relations should operate collaboratively with social, political, economic, and global organizations according to democratic principles and in tune with traditional values of a given society.

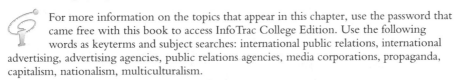 For more information on the topics that appear in this chapter, use the password that came free with this book to access InfoTrac College Edition. Use the following words as keyterms and subject searches: international public relations, international advertising, advertising agencies, public relations agencies, media corporations, propaganda, capitalism, nationalism, multiculturalism.

QUESTIONS FOR DISCUSSION

1. In what ways could historical and evolutionary factors differently affect how advertising and public relations are practiced in a given region or society? For example, how could cultural, governmental/regulatory, economic, geographic, and technological factors—as well as dominant ideological beliefs—influence the role, function, and strategies of public relations and advertising?

2. Is Kruckeberg (1996) correct that nothing inherently restricts implementation of public relations practice in nations having other than purely capitalistic economic systems? Why or why not?

3. Should democracy be culturally specific, and should culturally specific capitalism be embraced in different parts of the world according to societal tradition and heritage? Defend your answer, and discuss your answer's implications for advertising and public relations practice in those societies.

4. In what ways can advertising and public relations practitioners help address social problems that will occur in the 21st century? What implications would your answer have for the role of advertising and public relations and for the education of its practitioners?

5. Will the 21st century bring the evolution of a homogenous global culture or accentuate more pronounced multicultural differences among the world's peoples? What relationships exist among technology, globalism, and multiculturalism, and how will these variables affect the practice of public relations and advertising?

REFERENCES

Aalund, D. (2000, October 9). Is that lipstick I see on your collar, or just another flower ad? *Wall Street Journal,* p. B1.

Al-Enad, A. H. (1990). Public relations' roles in developing countries. *Public Relations Quarterly, 35*(1), 24–26.

Alsop, S. (2001, January 22). Give commercials a break. *Fortune, 143,* 50.

Beck, E. (2001, January 4). Ikea sees quirkiness as selling point in U.K. *Wall Street Journal,* p. B12.

Bell, D. (1988). *The end of ideology.* Cambridge: Harvard University Press.

Bellah, R. N., Madsen, R., Sullivan, W. M., Swidler, A., & Tipton, S. M. (1991). *The good society.* New York: Vintage Books.

Belsey, A., & Chadwick, R. (1992). Ethics and politics of the media: The quest for quality. In A. Belsey & R. Chadwick (Eds.), *Ethical issues in journalism and the media* (pp. 1–14). London: Routledge.

Boehm, Ed. (1989). *Behind enemy lines: WWII Allied/Axis propaganda.* Secaucus, NJ: Wellfleet Press.

Bravin, J. (2000, September 14). Hollywood launches messages of peace. *Wall Street Journal,* p. B17.

Brook, J., & Boal, I. A. (1995). Preface. In J. Brook & I. A. Boal (Eds.), *Resisting the virtual life: The culture and politics of information* (pp. vii–xv). San Francisco: City Lights.

Buckman, R. (2001, January 22). Microsoft ads push big-business software. *Wall Street Journal,* p. B9.

Campbell, R. (with Martin, C. R., & Fabos, B.). (2000). *Media and culture: An introduction to mass communication.* Boston: Bedford/St. Martin's.

Carey, J. W. (1989). Space, time, and communications: A tribute to Harold Innis. In J. W. Carey (Ed.), *Communication as culture* (pp. 142–172). Boston: Unwin Hyman.

Dumenco, S. (2000, December 18–25). Keyword: Sell. *New York, 33,* 54, 57.

Ellison, S. (2000a, October 9). U.K. advertisers focus online campaign on at-work Web surfers. *Wall Street Journal,* p. B13.

Ellison, S. (2000b, November 2). Ads for a Holocaust exhibit in London cause a stir. *Wall Street Journal,* pp. B1, B4.

Ellison, S. (2000c, December 14). Europeans await tech-ad onslaught to abate. *Wall Street Journal,* p. B6.

Ellison, S. (2001, January 10). Subway tunnels become latest frontier for ads. *Wall Street Journal*, p. A19.

Ellison, S., and White, E. (2000a, November 24). Marketers discover black Brazil. *Wall Street Journal*, pp. A11, A14.

Ellison, S., and White, E. (2000b, November 24). When there's more to an ad than meets the eye. *Wall Street Journal*, pp. A11, A14.

Emery, M., & Emery, E. (1988). *The press and America: An interpretive history of the mass media*. Englewood Cliffs, NJ: Prentice Hall.

Flagg, M. (2000, October 17). In today's Vietnam, the war is a selling point. *Wall Street Journal*, p. A19.

The German public relations business has not yet declared itself essential for industry and it still has to prove itself. (1987, April). *PR World*, p. 8.

Gilder, G. (1992). *Life after television*. New York: W. W. Norton & Co.

Grimes, A. (2000, October 26). Nike rescinds ad, apologizes to disabled people. *Wall Street Journal*, p. B20.

Grunig, J. E. (2000). Collectivism, collaboration, and societal corporatism as core professional values in public relations. *Journal of Public Relations Research, 12*(1), 23–48.

Gubernick, L. (2000, September 14). Hancock ad raises alarm in adoption community. *Wall Street Journal*, p. B1.

Heath, R. L. (2000). A rhetorical perspective on the values of public relations: Crossroads and pathways toward concurrence. *Journal of Public Relations Research, 12*(1), 69–91.

Holtzhausen, D. R. (2000). Postmodern values in public relations. *Journal of Public Relations Research, 12*(1), 93–114.

Kennedy, P. (1993). *Preparing for the 21st century*. New York: Vintage Books.

Kruckeberg, D. (1994, August). *A preliminary identification and study of public relations models and their ethical implications in select internal public relations departments and public relations agencies in the United Arab Emirates*. Paper presented at the meeting of the Association for Education in Journalism and Mass Communication conference, Atlanta, GA.

Kruckeberg, D. (1995). International journalism ethics. In J. C. Merrill (Ed.), *Global journalism: Survey of international communication* (pp. 77–87). New York: Longman.

Kruckeberg, D. (1995–1996, Winter). The challenge for public relations in the era of globalization. *Public Relations Quarterly, 40*(4), 36–38.

Kruckeberg, D. (1996, September). Answering the mandate for a global presence. *International Public Relations Review, 19*(2), 19–23.

Kruckeberg, D. (1999, August). *Overlaying First World public relations on Second and Third World societies*. Paper presented at the meeting of the Association for Education in Journalism and Mass Communication conference, New Orleans, LA.

Kruckeberg, D. (2000). Public relations: Toward a global professionalism. In J. A. Ledingham & S. D. Bruning (Eds.), *Public relations as relationship management: A relational approach to the study and practice of public relations* (pp. 145–157). Mahwah, NJ: Lawrence Erlbaum Associates.

Kruckeberg, D., Badran, B. A., Ayish, M. I., & Awad, A. A. (1994). *Principles of public relations*. Al-Ain: United Arab Emirates Press.

Mallinson, B. (1991). A clash of culture: Anglo-Saxon and European public relations. New versus old, or just dynamic interaction? *International Public Relations Review, 14*(3), 24–29.

Mathews, A. W. (2000, October 12). Advertisers find many Web sites too tasteless. *Wall Street Journal*, pp. B1, B14.

Merrill, J. C. (1996). *Existential journalism*. Ames: Iowa State University Press.

Mossberg, W. S. (2000, October 12). New ad scanner fails to prove itself helpful or convenient to use. *Wall Street Journal*, p. B1.

Neill, M. (1995). Computers, thinking, and schools in the "New World Economic Order." In J. Brook & I. A. Boal (Eds.), *Resisting the virtual life: The culture and politics of information* (pp. 181–194). San Francisco: City Lights.

Newsom, D., Turk, J. V., & Kruckeberg, D. (2000). *This is PR: The realities of public relations*. Belmont, CA: Wadsworth.

O'Connell, V. (2001, January 11). Edgy spots stir controversy, and results. *Wall Street Journal,* p. B13.

Office of Population, Bureau for Global Programs, Field Support, and Research, U.S. Agency for International Development. (1996, July). *World population profile: 1996.* Washington, DC.

Ovaitt, F., Jr. (1988). PR without boundaries: Is globalization an option? *Public Relations Quarterly, 33*(1), 5–9.

Porter, E., and Nelson, E. (2000, October 13). P&G reaches out to Hispanics. *Wall Street Journal,* p. B1.

Schiller, H. I. (1995). The global information highway: Project for an ungovernable world. In J. Brook & I. A. Boal (Eds.), *Resisting the virtual life: The culture and politics of information* (pp. 71–83). San Francisco: City Lights.

Sriramesh, K., & White, J. (1992). Societal culture and public relations. In J. E. Grunig (Ed.), *Excellence in public relations and communication management* (pp. 597–614). Hillsdale, NJ: Lawrence Erlbaum Associates.

Stephen, T. (1995). Interpersonal communication, history, and intercultural coherence. In F. R. Casmir (Ed.), *Communication in Eastern Europe: The role of history, culture, and media in contemporary conflicts* (pp. 5–25). Mahwah, NJ: Lawrence Erlbaum Associates.

Tsetsura, E. Y. (2000a). *Conceptual frameworks in the field of public relations: A comparative study of Russian and United States perspectives.* Unpublished master's thesis, Fort Hays State University, Hays, Kansas.

Tsetsura, E. Y. (2000b, March). *Understanding the "evil" nature of public relations as perceived by some Russian publics.* Paper presented at the meeting of the Educators Academy of the Public Relations Society of America, Miami.

11

❀

Communication
and Culture

CHRISTINE L. OGAN

Christine L. Ogan (PhD, University of North Carolina) is professor of journalism and associate dean for Graduate Studies and Research in the School of Informatics at Indiana University, Bloomington. Her research has a combined focus on communication technologies and international communication. Her work frequently addresses Turkey and the Turkish media. Her most recent work, *Communication and Identity in the Diaspora: Turkish Migrants in Amsterdam and Their Use of the Media,* is to be published in 2001 by Lexington Books.

WHAT IS CULTURE?

We may use the term *culture* in our everyday speech and expect that other people have the same understanding of it that we do. It is so common a concept that we often don't take the time to think about what we mean by it. Culture defines what it means to be a human being. It is all our behavior summed up, our whole life experience. Perhaps because it is so all-encompassing, Raymond Williams (1983) has called it "one of the two or three most complicated words in the English language" (p. 87).

In a good summary of the problem of duality of meaning in the concept as it is used today, Scannell, Schlesinger, and Sparks (1992) say the following:

> On the one hand there is a concern with artistic expression and creative, aesthetic, representational activity, and on the other with ways of living, the organization and nature of social activity. In both there is a concern with the

 For additional online resources, access the Global Media Monitor Web site that accompanies this book on the **Wadsworth Communication Cafe** Web site at http://communication.wadsworth.com.

transmission and reception of values and meanings, but the focus of attention and methods of approach are very different. The study of the arts as culture, drawing on literary and aesthetic traditions tends to a top-down view of culture embodied in the division between high and low culture. The study of culture as a way of life draws more on social history, anthropology and sociology and focuses on the structures of everyday life and its forms of interactions—"popular" culture. (p. 1)

In using the term as a concept referring to a "way of life," we speak of cultures at all levels and for all types of social collectives. Here, we will identify a few of those that will be important to the subsequent discussion in this chapter. At the broadest level, we could speak of human culture, but that is so vague as to be impossible to grasp. More frequently we refer to national culture, as if all of the people living within a particular nation-state shared the same culture. Of course culture existed before nations were formed. And many nations, such as those formed out of colonial boundaries in Africa, were created with artificial borders that included multiple cultures while dividing other cultures from one another.

Mass media are key components in any nation's culture. For some, they represent a low cultural form and are thus not worthy of serious study. People who think this way would not value a sitcom on television as much as an opera. Others, however, believe that the media, as popular cultural forms, must be examined because they are so pervasive and touch so many people. Lord David Puttnam (1998), former British junior minister of education, in an introduction to a speech by the Canadian minister of heritage to a European media conference, argued that one must look at the audiovisual industry as an important component of a nation's culture.

> Stories and images are among the principal means by which societies transmit their values and beliefs, from generation to generation, and community to community. As an industry we have developed the creation and marketing of these images to a point at which they confront us, intellectually and emotionally, in every aspect of our daily lives. . . . Culture is an essential element of the lifeblood of any nation. It sustains the conscience and vitality of a society. One measure of any community wishing to regard itself as truly civilized, is the quality and depth of its cultural achievement. It's that which defines our personal and our national identity.

CULTURE INDUSTRIES

The term *culture industries* was coined by Theodor Adorno and Max Horkheimer. These men were part of a group of people who formed the Frankfurt Institute for Social Research in 1923 in Germany. Before World War II, the Nazis exiled the group to the United States, but after the war most of them, including Adorno and Horkheimer, returned to Germany. They developed an approach to scholarship called critical theory, which was based on Marxist philosophy. Adorno said, in an essay published in English more than 20 years after his death in 1969, that he and

Horkheimer had first coined the term *culture industries* in their 1947 work, *Dialectic of Enlightenment*. The term was used to refer to "products which are tailored for consumption by masses, and which to a great extent determine the nature of that consumption, and are manufactured more or less according to plan" (1991, p. 98). The two believed that the real purpose of mass media was to provide ideological justification for the capitalistic societies where these industries developed. Mass culture (a term they chose not to use because it had an "agreeable" interpretation) was developed as a tool of capitalism for the social control of society, according to Adorno and Horkheimer.

Though scholars today do not dismiss the idea that the mass media are instruments of capitalism, the term *culture industries* carries a more positive meaning today. The United Nations Educational, Scientific and Cultural Organization (UNESCO) describes culture industries as important national economic resources that allow expressions of creativity to be "copied and boosted by industrial processes and worldwide distribution" (1999).

OTHER CULTURAL GROUPINGS

We may think of culture as the way of life of all human beings or of nations or of ethnic groups within or across national boundaries. But there are other specific types of cultures too. Businesses have cultures, and each business has its own set of cultural characteristics. Because global corporations employ people all over the world, it is likely that the culture of the corporation will conflict with the culture of the society where the employees live. If the society values harmonious family and personal relationships over personal achievement, and the transnational corporation established in this society values individual achievement and loyalty to the company for all its employees, then it is likely that some cultural conflict will arise in this environment.

Other groups have cultures too. Any organization to which we belong develops a culture if it manages to survive. An organization's culture is the glue that keeps people attached to it and allows members to identify with it. It is the set of meanings the members of the group share. We all belong to multiple groups, each with its own characteristic culture. These include schools, religious organizations, civic groups, and even neighborhood groups. And certainly each family has a culture that distinguishes it from other families. Each family has a set of traditions, a way of living and interacting. We have learned from animal behaviorists that many animal groupings also have cultures.

TRANSMISSION OF CULTURE

How is it we come to understand, articulate, and accept the culture of any group to which we belong? We know that it must be learned. We are born into a family, a community, a nation, but we must learn the culture of those groupings before we can become an integral part of them.

Clifford Geertz (1973) defined culture as "an historically transmitted pattern of meanings embodied in symbols, a system of inherited conceptions expressed in symbolic forms by means of which men communicate, perpetuate, and develop their knowledge about and attitudes toward life" (p. 89). The primary symbolic system used to transmit culture is that of language. Michael Schudson (1994) notes, "The importance of language as an aspect of culture can scarcely be over-estimated. Language is the fundamental human mass medium. It is the mass medium through which all other media speak" (p. 29).

Benedict Anderson (1983) described the way "print capitalism" in the form of newspapers created "imagined communities," where people came to believe that they shared a culture with people whom they may never have met face-to-face (pp. 10, 40). Ulf Hannerz (1996) noted that this awareness made people also realize that something existed beyond their local culture. While writing and print allowed people to develop a sense of we-ness, "simultaneously, it would have underlined a sense of cultural discontinuity which was very congruent with the political ideal of the nation-state." Hannerz continued, "As you are a citizen of one country and not another, and as territory belongs to one state but not the other, you identify with either one language or the other" (p. 21). So while written language increased the power to transmit one culture, thereby bringing people together, it differentiated people and nations from other cultures, thereby separating them.

Families used to be nearly the only transmitters of culture to young children by teaching the symbolic system, or language, to their children. And until the children learned to read in their native language, few outside cultural messages came through to the children. That all changed when first radio and then television entered the household. Joshua Meyrowitz (1985) articulates this view in his book *No Sense of Place.*

> Unable to read, very young children were once limited to the few sources of information available to them within and around the home: paintings, illustrations, views from a window, and what adults said and read to them. Television, however, now escorts children across the globe even before they have permission to cross the street. (p. 238)

Whether those cultural influences are detrimental or not is open to question, but television certainly sends messages that can conflict with the family culture. So children learn to negotiate multiple cultures from an early age.

This issue becomes more complicated when multiple languages are spoken. That can occur in the home, when a family has migrated from a place where a different language is spoken, and when multiple languages are spoken in the same country, as in Switzerland and Canada, for example.

Richard Collins (1990) believes that though language has played an important role in preserving the cultural distinction of the francophone citizens of Quebec, such small linguistic communities are always vulnerable to influences by the dominant language group through the mass media.

> Many in Quebec fear that modern communication technologies, particularly television, threaten the continued existence of their community, and thus

francophone society in North America. They argue (and their fears are shared by many in metropolitan France who believe the world francophone community is vulnerable to the pressures of English) that Quebec's anticipated fate is representative, and that larger and larger distinct societies will be threatened with loss of identity and assimilation as the "mass" embraced by mass communication expands with technical change; as the mass embraced by modern communication becomes larger and larger, so the critical mass required for a community's linguistic and cultural survival also increases. (p. 192)

Transnational television stations now surrounding the globe expand this issue. In most every country of the world it is possible to receive one or more (usually many more) television channels of news, entertainment, and sports that are broadcast in English and delivered locally via satellite. Some people fear that the existence of so much English-language broadcasting brings us ever closer to having English as the only world language for business, science, scholarship, and now news and entertainment. The pervasiveness of English is believed to threaten many other cultures. For example, about 80% of the electronically stored information in the world is written in English. And English is the primary language of the Internet, yet native English speakers constitute less than half of the online users. In some countries, like Germany and Turkey, all imported audiovisual media are dubbed into the local language. If the dubbing is of high quality, some viewers actually believe the content has been domestically produced. In other countries, like the Netherlands, English-language imports are subtitled instead. When audiences can hear the English spoken by the actors in the program, the Dutch believe that viewers will improve the quality of their spoken English.

HOW THE WEST DOMINATES IN PRODUCTION OF CULTURE

You may have heard it said that the United States is imperialistic when it comes to cultural products, specifically when it comes to films and television programs. No matter where you go in the world, you find that Hollywood films dominate the screens of local cinemas, and U.S. sitcoms and soap operas fill the program schedules of local television stations. And you may wonder why that is.

The easy answer to why so many U.S. films and television programs are aired internationally is that the United States produces more of them than any other country in the world. What's more, these programs and films are popular the world over. People really like the content. So why is that such a problem? Some scholars have conducted research on this issue.

As early as 1969, when Herbert Schiller, an American mass communications scholar, published *Mass Communication and the American Empire,* the U.S. domination of the world's media was noted. Schiller asserted in that book that the military-industrial complex in the United States was using its television programs and films to obtain world dominance in cultural products. In 1971 two Finnish scholars, Kaarle Nordenstreng and Tapio Varis, decided to document the flow of television programs in the world, by sending out questionnaires to program directors at television stations throughout the world. They asked people to calculate the number of domestically produced and imported television programs broadcast to audiences in their countries. Later they expanded the study to examine the international systems of sales and exchange. From the more than 50 countries included in the study (Nordenstreng & Varis, 1974), the researchers determined that the international flow of television programs was overwhelmingly one way, from the United States (and to a lesser extent Western Europe) to the rest of the world. The authors also concluded that the flow was dominated by entertainment content and that the one-way flow was based on historical conditions related to the introduction of television and economic resources and to demographic characteristics of the exporters and importers of programs. Television was an offshoot of the existing broadcast and film industries, and it developed first in the industrialized nations. Later, television hardware and software were exported to less developed countries. Though the poorest countries tended to be more dependent on foreign production, it did not explain all of the flow. For example, India produces the greatest number of feature-length films a year, yet it exports them at a much lower rate than does the United States.

> There are thus other factors besides the economy of a nation which influence the extent of inflow of TV material. The population size is naturally of crucial importance, since it largely determines such marketing conditions as the size of the TV audience, the general dominance of a national culture, and usually also a common or unifying language. (Nordenstreng & Varis, p. 54)

Tapio Varis replicated the study in 1983, and the general conclusion was that no major changes in the international flow of television programs and news had occurred since 1973 (Varis, 1985, p. 53). Varis did find a trend toward more regional exchanges in the second period, however. But the increased transnational concentration of media ownership and the unknown effect of direct broadcast satellites on program exchanges led Varis to be concerned that the flow of media products would continue to be one way.

In 1977, Jeremy Tunstall, a professor at City University, London, produced *The Media Are American,* another major publication that influenced thinking about the role of the United States in the world's media. Tunstall added historical context, as well as economic and cultural analysis, to reach his conclusions about American media domination. Though he dismissed Schiller's notion of an imperialist plot to subjugate the world, his research supported the finding of U.S. media dominance in the world. And he expressed concern about the extent of influence the exported news and entertainment might have.

> The central thesis of the present book, however, is that the media are not just one more example of any general thesis. The media are about politics, and commerce and ideas. This is a strange enough combination even when the media stay at home. But as an item of international trade the combination is even more unusual. When a government allows news importation it is in effect importing a piece of another country's politics—which is true of

no other import. The media also set out to entertain and intrigue—to make people laugh or cry—they have an emotional appeal unlike other products. And because the media also deal in ideas, their influence can be unpredictable in form and strength. (p. 263)

Other scholars also influenced the discussion of media and cultural imperialism at the time. Ariel Dorfman focused attention on the cultural messages contained in U.S. cartoon strips when he wrote *How to Read Donald Duck* in 1975. Arman Mattelart (1979) wrote about advertising and the commercial control of media industries. Still others, like Oliver Boyd-Barrett (1980) and Alan Wells (1972), wrote more theoretically about the concept of cultural and media imperialism. The trend in the literature of the period from the early 1970s to the mid-1980s was to view the United States as the destroyer of world cultures and world media economies. But most of the evidence that was brought to bear on the topic was economic evidence, not cultural proof. This is a problem, says John Tomlinson in his book, *Cultural Imperialism* (1991).

Because of the constant tendency to revert to an economic account, where cultural "effects" of media imperialism are posited, they are invariably problematic. Either they are simply assumed and allowed to function in the discourse as a self-evident concomitant of the sheer presence of alien cultural goods, or else they are inferred using fairly crude interpretative assumptions. (p. 34)

That happened because it was relatively easy to examine program schedules and determine how much imported content a station would broadcast. It was also relatively easy to count the number of foreign films screened at local theatres and compare them with the number of domestic films produced in a given year. It was even easy to determine profits or losses from film and television production over time. What was more difficult was trying to figure out if people were somehow personally affected by the cultural messages contained in the television programs and films.

In Tomlinson's view, we could assess blame to specific institutions—the mass media, the United States, or multinational capitalists—when accounting for the economic aspects of cultural imperialism. But dealing with the cultural domination is not so easy. Here, "it is not individual practices we are blaming, but a contextualizing structure: capitalism, not just as economic practices, but as the *central (dominant) positioning of economic practices* within the social ordering of collective existence" (Tomlinson, 1991, p. 168).

Perhaps what we are dealing with is a redefinition of the cultural context for individual nation-states and communities. The focus on economic development—generally under the umbrella of multinational capitalism—becomes the guideline for every autonomous system, and economic interdependence becomes the key to survival in the global system, while the strategies for preserving important elements of the cultures of the societies around the world have received much less attention.

We have little information concerning the individual effects of the consumption of Western cultural products. We know something about the effect on people's health when McDonald's and Kentucky Fried Chicken fare become the preferred meals in cultures where the local diet is relatively free of animal and other fats. It would be nice to so easily measure the effects of hip-hop music on the teenagers of a particular country where traditional music was based on a different tonal system and wasn't amplified so highly that conversation in a room where it was played became impossible. Or it would be even better if we could attach electrodes to people's heads when they watched *Friends* or the latest Steven Spielberg film to determine if attitudes and behavior changed as a result of exposure.

Most researchers have to resort to asking people questions about their reactions to certain imported content and then draw conclusions from what they *say* about their attitudes and behavior surrounding that content. The alternative is to conduct ethnographic studies through observation of small samples and draw conclusions about what relationship the researcher thinks a given behavior has with the consumption of imported media. Perhaps because of the major limitations in available methodologies, few studies have even focused on the issue. Empirical work has been limited to a few studies of the impact of the old television program *Dallas* on groups of Israeli Arabs, immigrants to Israel from Morocco and Russia, Israeli kibbutz residents, second-generation Americans in Los Angeles, and Japanese citizens (Katz & Liebes, 1985; Liebes & Katz, 1990). A second study was based on a self-selected sample of responses to an ad in a Dutch newspaper requesting information from people about why they liked *Dallas* (Ang, 1985). The Liebes and Katz study (1990) is the most extensive empirical study, but it included only 40 – 80 people from each community selected nonrandomly.

It would be wonderful to be able to analyze both the texts of cultural products and the reception of those texts by audiences in countries where charges of cultural imperialistic practices have been made, but alas, the enormity of this task makes it impossible. We are forced, instead, to limit our focus to particular programs, such as the internationally popular soap opera *The Young and the Restless* or to try to determine the overall impact of the volume of imported products through in-depth surveys. Or we could analyze the volume of texts exported from the United States and Europe on film or in television programs for the dominant cultural meaning. Though each of these methods taken alone is unsatisfactory, the accumulation of studies with limited focus could add to our understanding of the effects of imported cultural fare and could indeed help us to determine whether cultural imperialism exists and at what level.

The tentative conclusion from the limited research of the empirical work is that "audiences are more active and critical, their responses more complex and reflective, and their cultural values more resistant to manipulation and 'invasion' than many critical media theorists have assumed" (Tomlinson, 1991, pp. 49–50). So if Americans do export a large amount of media products, from news on television to feature-length films, we just don't know exactly what the cultural impact of consuming those products might be.

Marian Bredin (1996) has stated that the power of the media to bring cultural change to any ethnic group is quite limited. In a study of the role of communication technologies in aboriginal communities in remote regions of northern Canada, Bredin concluded that patterns of "local resistance and cultural persistence" prevent imported media from having powerful effects. Bredin said that such power cannot be attributed to imported media because such a conclusion ignores "the historical processes of contact and change which aboriginal groups have previously negotiated." She continued,

> These include "prehistoric" intertribal contact, migration and cultural diffusion, engagement in trade with Europeans, adoption of Christianity and syllabic literacy and the transition to permanent settlements and exposure to formal education. Taking these factors into account, it is clear that media cannot be isolated as the sole or even primary cause of cognitive, affective or behavioral changes among aboriginal people. (p. 165)

Despite our inability to understand exactly how U.S. media may affect people in other countries, the worries about U.S. dominance have not diminished. In fact, they have expanded to concerns about transnational control. In a reissue of his 1969 book, *Mass Communications and the American Empire,* Schiller noted in the 1992 retrospective that his description of cultural imperialism and those responsible for it had changed. The companies involved in the spread of cultural imperialism had grown into conglomerates that were based not only in the United States but also in Germany, Japan, France, Brazil, and England. Schiller wrote that this expansion of what he formerly referred to as American cultural imperialism has more recently become transnational corporate cultural domination.

> American cultural imperialism is not dead, but it no longer adequately describes the global cultural condition. Today it is more useful to view transnational corporate culture as the central force, with a continuing heavy flavor of U.S. media know-how, derived from long experience with marketing and entertainment skills and practices. (Schiller, 1992, pp. 14–15, 39)

WHAT CULTURES DO TO
DEFEND CULTURAL AUTONOMY

The diffusion of television programs, films, and other media to countries around the world is not a new phenomenon. Hollywood films have been popular in countries outside the United States for as long as they have been made. In the silent film era, it was even easier to export films, because language was not a factor. Countries with large domestic markets for their cultural products always had an advantage because they could pay for the production costs at home and look to the export markets as mostly profit. This enabled the big countries to charge less for those programs when selling them abroad and be competitive with other countries' exports. Small countries were at a disadvantage because they couldn't afford to produce many films or television programs and often had trouble covering costs because of the size of their domestic markets. They became vulnerable to the imported products, finding them cheaper than producing their own films and television programs.

Several strategies have been taken by countries with low production of films or television programs to protect their own cultural products. Those strategies include the following:

- Quotas
- Subsidies and grants
- Regional alliances
- Adaptation of programs
- Resistance measures

Quotas

The most significant policy for supporting domestic television production is that of the European Union. Drafted in 1984 (but adopted as policy in 1989 and revised in 1997) in a green paper titled *Television without Frontiers,* the European Union adopted a directive for its 15 member countries that called for all television stations to devote more than half of their schedules to European programs. The directive excluded news, sports, advertising, games, teletext, and teleshopping from consideration. France, the country that keeps closest watch on the preservation of its culture, was the strongest proponent of the adoption of this directive. France's protectionist cultural policy covers everything from cultural products like television and film to attempts at preventing foreign words from creeping into the French language. It is the only country in Europe to require television stations and film distributors to import European products. France also requires that no more than 40% of films screened in the country come from outside Europe. It also requires that 40% of the output on French broadcasting stations be French. Of late, however, France has had more trouble in maintaining sufficiently high amounts of French fiction on television or at the cinema. Collins (1999) cites a document from researchers in France that says that French fiction (produced only by France or in coproduction with other countries) used to account for 49% of broadcast fiction on three major channels, but in 1996 it accounted for only 25% (p. 163). And though the numbers of French films have increased from 97 in 1995 to 148 in 1998, the French share of the domestic film market dropped from 35% in 1995 to 27% in 1998. The American share of that market increased from 54% to 63%. French film critics have been blamed for being overcritical of domestic films while they praise the American products (Riding, 1999, December 14, p. E1).

The United States has taken the position that cultural products should be treated like any other goods traded in the market. In international trade talks, the United States has opposed the setting of quotas on film and television imports, viewing such quotas as trade barriers. However, other countries have been successful in obtaining a "cultural exception" for audiovisual products in the General Agreement on Tariffs and Trade (GATT), claiming that these are expressions of national identity and should be preserved. If no protection for these cultural expressions is provided, say those countries whose films and television programs are being threatened by imports, those industries might not survive. More than 130 countries are members of the World Trade Organization, created in 1995, successor to the 1947 GATT. The current GATT serves as the rule book for the WTO.

Subsidies and Grants

The United States opposes the use of government subsidies for development of films and television programs. But many countries take the position that without subsidies, their audiovisual sector will totally succumb to foreign imports. The 15 countries of the European Union are trying to harmonize their national subsidies to work together to increase protection for all of their film and television industries. But according to an analysis in *Screen Digest* ("Toward a Single European Market," 1999), "a European film industry only exists as a political ideal and has no concrete existence in reality" (p. 261). The article concludes that unless all of the countries open up their national subsidy and incentive mechanisms to all European producers, a single market will never develop. Yet even with subsidies, 16 of the top 20 box-office grossing films in Europe in 1999 were made in the United States. And 1 of the remaining 4 was a coproduction between the United States and Great Britain ("European Audiovisual Observatory," 2000).

Italy is a country internationally known for its films, and in 1998, for the first time ever, a foreign film won the Academy Award for best picture—the Italian film *Life Is Beautiful*. Subsidies have helped keep the Italian film industry afloat too. In 1999 the state invested $94 million in 70 films. And that same year the maximum budget eligible for financing was raised from $2.3 million to $4 million (Young, 1999, p. 19).

The European Union has been supplying grants for new production projects under a program called MEDIA (Measures to Encourage Development of the Audiovisual Industry). Now in its second 5-year program under MEDIA II, the program has as its aim to "strengthen the competitiveness of the European audiovisual industry" by providing financial assistance to television and film fiction, documentaries, animation, and multimedia production products (European Commission, 1999). The aid comes in the form of loans for no more than 50% of the development budgets of eligible European production companies. It also awards grants to projects, favoring those countries or regions with low production capacity and/or restricted geography or linguistic area. One of the selection criteria is a production's transnational potential. The European Union believes this program improves the competitive stature of its cultural products, especially when they come up against U.S. products in the marketplace.

Regional Alliances

National subsidies in many countries are usually carefully guarded and opened up only in the case of coproductions ("Toward a Single European Market," 1999, pp. 261–262). Coproduced films, usually ones that combine the talents and resources of two film production companies in two countries, have several advantages. They have a larger domestic market, that of two or more countries. They have appeal across cultures, not just within a particular culture. They usually have wider name recognition of principal actors, director, and so on. Statistics support their economic success.

The European MEDIA project is a regional alliance. Though loans and subsidies are its main means of supporting local projects, its existence as a regional organization displays moral support for local ventures.

Adaptation of Programs

For countries with smaller markets or fewer resources, film and television program production is too expensive to release many new products. In general, audiences prefer programs produced in their own language and set in their own cultural environment. In other words, they like local programs. The compromise that has been struck to address this dilemma is increasingly popular. It amounts to buying the rights to an imported television series or film and adapting it to the local culture and language. The producers, directors, writers, and actors are local. Only the format and the production values are imported. Soap operas travel particularly well when repackaged. *Good Times, Bad Times,* an Australian soap that has been remade for several European markets, accounted for nearly two thirds of German station RTL's advertising revenues in 1999 (Sacirbey, 1999). Game shows like *Jeopardy* and *Family Feud* have also done well in European adaptations.

Television programs have also been adapted by the U.S. television networks. *Who Wants To Be a Millionaire?* was one of the first big hits of the 21st century and originated in the United Kingdom. The several reality-based television programs appearing in the United States, including *Survivor* and *Big Brother,* had their beginnings in Europe. The latest of these adaptations, a British game show called *The Weakest Link,* airs on NBC. Anne Robinson, known for her mistreatment of guests on the show, hosts both the British and the U.S. versions.

Adopting game show and reality-based formats has the advantage of low production costs while tailoring the content to the culture of the local audience, wherever that is. The fact that U.S. producers are now purchasing international formats from Europe and elsewhere means that they are also seeking ways to create new programs at minimum expense.

RESISTANCE MEASURES

Some cultural groups try to resist being deluged by products from abroad by producing more products about themselves. This is a little different than offering subsidies or forming regional alliances, though the result may be the same. An example of how this has happened in Brazil might help explain the process.

Brazil has a very big television production and distribution system called TV Globo. It produces most of the television programs for the local market, but it also exports many programs to other countries. Within Brazil are groups of indigenous cultures that were present before Europeans arrived in the country to settle it. Today most of these native groups live in the Amazon rain forest, much as they did hundreds of years ago. As major parts of the forest are destroyed and settled by outsiders, the local residents see their way of life and their environment disappearing.

They also feel their cultural heritage will disappear unless they do something about it. The Kayapo, an indigenous group, have resisted the dominant culture and its media with their own media. Armed with video cameras, the Kayapo have been documenting their own cultural traditions by recording their stories, dances, history, and ceremonies on videotape. The older Kayapo had become concerned as younger ones abandoned the hunting-and-gathering culture of their ancestors for work in the lumber and mining industries. They also worried as they watched their children gaze at television in the evenings rather than listen to elders pass on culture through storytelling, details of ancestral customs, dream interpretation, and comments on changes in nature and the events of the day. So now they are making an electronic record to resist being overpowered by the mass media of Brazil.

But recording one's own video is not the only way to resist mass media. Marie Gillespie (1995) found that Punjabi families in Southall London used prerecorded Indian films in their homes for a similar purpose. British television and films did not focus much attention on their culture, so to pass on the cultural heritage to their children, parents regularly used the Indian films as a focus of family gatherings. The BBC has recently recognized the need to attend to minority culture media interests. In developing new digital radio and television channels, the corporation has plans for dedicating stations focused on black and Asian listeners (Ward, 2001). Television delivered by satellite is available to accomplish the same goal. It is even possible in the United States to pay a monthly fee to receive television channels from Arab countries, India, or Turkey on special satellite dishes.

In Israel the Mizrahi Jews, an ethnic minority made up of Sephardic Jews and their descendants, now have their own television channel (Briza), which is delivered along with a package of several domestic and imported channels on the Yes satellite network. The channel offers music from the Middle East; drama from Egypt, India, Turkey, and Spain; and local content that appeals to this minority group, who believe their interests are not well served on the Israeli national channels (Sappir, 2001). Briza's director, Ron Cahlili, said he is not bothered by the imports on his channel. He sees them as "an alternative to McDonald's—the American and English-dominated culture" (Sappir, 2001).

Resistance can come in other forms too. For Canada it comes in proposed legislation to keep Canadian advertisers from spending their money in split-run editions of U.S. magazines. Canada has a bigger problem than most countries in maintaining a unique culture. Sharing a 2,000-mile border with the United States and also a common language, it is barraged by signals from American television stations that spill over the border. And American films dominate the Canadian box office. Of the films shown in Canadian theaters, 96% are foreign. Three-fourths of the music played on Canadian radio does not originate in Canada. American magazines also circulate widely across the border, constituting four out of five titles on the newsstands ("Culture Wars," 1998). Bill C-55 was created to keep Canadian advertising dollars in Canada to support Canadian magazines. In 1998 the minister of Canadian heritage proposed the bill, which made it a criminal offense for Canadians to buy advertising in U.S. magazines produced predominantly for the American market.

Policies that resist foreign media domination have been developed in other countries too. Both China and India have a ban on direct broadcast satellite and the associated subscription fees. Though Asia was once thought to be an economic boom market for satellite television, international satellite television broadcasters like Rupert Murdoch have found that they have to supply programming free to domestic cable television companies and hotels, relying on advertising revenues for profits ("Asian Restrictions," 1999).

NOT ALL POP CULTURE IS AMERICAN

From the evidence presented, it would seem that the media really are American, and aside from a few pockets of resistance, others have had little success in battling with Hollywood or U.S. television producers and satellite broadcasters. But audiences around the world still prefer their local cultures and cultural products to imports. Take music, for example. Germany is the world's third-largest music market, following the United States and Japan. Local performers earn nearly half of the annual $3.5 billion in music sales in Germany. Spanish and Latin American artists generate more than half of music sales in Spain. And about half of French sales go to French rock groups ("Culture Wars," 1998). And in the United States, much international music is sold. Specifically, Spanish and Latin American artists are most popular.

Musical comedy, originally an American cultural form, has been looking to England for some of its best musicals since the mid-1970s. *The Phantom of the Opera, Joseph and the Amazing Technicolor Dreamcoat, Les Miserables,* and *Jesus Christ Superstar* are among them.

Much of the magazine and book publishing in the United States is also owned by foreign companies. The biggest U.S. publisher, Random House is owned by a German company, Bertelsmann, for example. HarperCollins is owned by Australian Rupert Murdoch, who became a U.S. citizen in order to purchase broadcast stations in this country.

ROLE OF JOURNALISTS
IN PRODUCTION OF CULTURE

Culture is at the core of what journalists do. Though objectivity is now widely recognized to be unachievable and probably undesirable, it was the aim of news production for decades. Journalists were expected to produce news without bias, as if they could detach themselves somehow from what they wrote. If that had been possible, perhaps we could think of news as a cultural-free product. The news event occurs. The journalist shows up on the scene and writes down the facts of the event. If it is a televised event, the camera records the details of the event or the interviews with the experts on videotape. The journalist then writes the story, and the next day it appears in the newspaper or it is aired that evening on television. If news were really produced that way, theoretically it could be translated into other languages and disseminated to audiences throughout the world and be understood in exactly the same way. The event would be understood as it actually happened.

But as John Fiske points out in his writing about television news culture, the empiricist concept of objectivity that has been under attack for most of this century doesn't exist. The concept of objectivity assumes a single truth, but Fiske (1987) says,

> "Truth" exists only in the (television) studio, yet that "truth" depends for its authenticity upon the eyewitness and the actuality film, those pieces of "raw reality" whose meanings are actually made by the discourse of the studio, but whose authenticating function allows that discourse to disguise its productive role and thus to situate the meanings in the events themselves. (pp. 288–289)

In other words, the television news producer deceives herself that truth exists and that the production of the news story is just a matter of organizing it for easy consumption by the audience.

Herbert Gans (1980), a sociologist who wrote a highly regarded book about the culture of news production based on an ethnographic study of CBS, NBC, *Newsweek,* and *Time,* said that "enduring values are built into news judgment; as a result, most values and opinions enter unconsciously" (p. 182). Those enduring values spring from the cultural orientation of the journalist. Gans groups the enduring values into eight clusters: ethnocentrism, altruistic democracy, responsible capitalism, small-town pastoralism, individualism, moderatism, social order, and national leadership (p. 42). Although some of these values travel across national and cultural boundaries, others are firmly grounded in American culture.

News culture is also revealed in news formats. As U.S. news has traveled the globe, first through international newspapers and newsmagazines, and later through television news, U.S. news formats have been picked up and copied by news organizations around the world. CNN, which appears in more than 200 countries, has perhaps had more influence on international broadcast news formats than any other single U.S. news organization. The use of stand-ups, voiceovers, outtakes, and sound bites has become ubiquitous in national television news programs everywhere. Whether we like it or not, this is another way that U.S. media culture has been adopted in other countries.

MANAGING CULTURAL CONFLICT

We are all well aware that cultures of the world don't always get along. Nations go to war with other nations; ethnic minorities within nations do battle with the dominant culture of the nation; and religious and racial differences reveal themselves in many different places. Our concern is what role the media play in ameliorating or exacerbating such conflicts internationally.

As the media become increasingly global—circulating news, information, and entertainment across borders—we might think that they would be able to help smooth out the differences between various cultural groupings. Benjamin Barber (1995), a political scientist, thinks that we need to understand two opposing trends in the world before we can understand what is happening on this front: globalization and fragmentation. Or as his book title says it, *Jihad vs. McWorld.*

> The first scenario rooted in race holds out the grim prospect of a retribalization of large swaths of humankind by war and bloodshed: a threatened balkanization of nation-states in which culture is pitted against culture, people against people, tribe against tribe, a Jihad in the name of a hundred narrowly conceived faiths against every kind of interdependence, every kind of artificial social cooperation and mutuality: against technology, against pop culture, and against integrated markets; against modernity itself as well as the future in which modernity issues. The second paints that future in shimmering pastels, a busy portrait of onrushing economic, technological, and ecological forces that demand integration and uniformity and that mesmerize peoples everywhere with fast music, fast computers and fast food—MTV, Macintosh, and McDonald's—pressing nations into one homogenous global theme park, one McWorld tied together by communications, information, entertainment, and commerce. Caught between Babel and Disneyland, the planet is falling precipitously apart and coming reluctantly together at the very same moment. (p. 4)

In a multicultural world where only about 20 of the world's states are homogeneous, many cultural groups feel they are buried by global culture and global corporations. Barber (1995) asserts that the search for local identity—"some set of common personal attributes to hold out against the numbing and neutering uniformities of industrial modernization and the colonizing culture of McWorld" (p. 9)—may end up as an open rebellion against a dominating group that seeks to wipe out that identity. If that is true, then the global media merely encourage cultural conflict, by sending the message that we are all alike, we are all consumers, and nothing makes us unique.

And just as the media have become more global, they are simultaneously taking on an increasingly local character. Cable television has acquired the technical ability to deliver hundreds of channels to our homes. And satellite dishes allow the reception of an equally large number of channels. The Internet provides millions of sites for media consumers. And as the cost to address smaller and smaller target audiences comes within reach, it is possible for people to tune out the global media and tune in media that address only our particular ethnic, religious, political, linguistic, and racial interests. So we stop learning about others and focus only on ourselves and those who are like us, allowing us more opportunity to feed our prejudices and ignorance.

One example of the role of television in this regard is that of MED-TV. MED-TV is a Kurdish-language television station that was broadcast from several different European countries until the British finally revoked the station's license in April 1999. The Kurds are a minority group who populate portions of Turkey,

Iraq, and Iran and who have never had a nation-state. They have been denied various rights in all three countries where they live. In Turkey they have never been permitted the right to schooling or mass media in their native language. Otherwise, they have full rights as Turkish citizens. The primary media in Turkey—both print and broadcast—are disseminated in Turkish. Ataturk, the founder of modern Turkey, believed that everyone who lived within the borders of the Turkish Republic should be identified as a Turk. That included the Kurdish population. The Kurds, for their part, have wanted to express their unique cultural and linguistic identity publicly. For about 16 years, the PKK, a Kurdish revolutionary group, has been waging a separatist war in southeastern Turkey. In 1994, MED-TV was established as a broadcasting voice to the Kurdish peoples wherever they live. Because Turkey would not grant permission for such a station, the organizers began broadcasting via satellite from London. The Turks said the British should close the station because it was owned by the PKK and was airing revolutionary messages. The Kurds denied any direct PKK connection with the station. The managers said they only wished to be able to transmit the Kurdish language and culture to their people. In April 1999 the Independent Television Commission in Britain agreed that the station had been broadcasting programs that might encourage acts of violence in Turkey (Kinzer, 1999) and closed down the station. The station's director, Hikmet Tabak, claimed that the decision was made following pressure by the Turkish government to close it down. Of late, several other Kurdish stations have sprung up in Europe to serve the Kurdish international community.

This case is clearly complex, but not unusual. Television may have been used to exacerbate a conflict between some Kurdish citizens in Turkey and the Turkish government. It might have encouraged a prolongation of the violence and acts of terror. The station claimed it was doing no such thing, that it was merely enriching the cultural experience of the Kurdish people by broadcasting in their language about subjects of interest to their cultural group. The Kurds have claimed that the national television stations in Turkey did not articulate their interests or celebrate their culture.

To further the communication about topics related to the Kurds, several Web sites have been opened. Establishing Web sites is also a common practice for other minority groups, especially when they feel that their voices are being suppressed by mainstream national or global media.

The Kurdish example is representative of the way cultures struggle to preserve a distinctive identity. In doing so, however, they may create more conflict with other cultural groups, rather than creating a climate for mutual cultural understanding.

HYBRID CULTURES AND THE MEDIA

In the United States, perhaps more so than in any other nation, a variety of ethnic groups have come together to live in the same geographic space. Here it has been called a melting pot, though the term has been frequently criticized. *Melting pot* referred what happened when a variety of cultural groups were brought together. As people migrated to the United States, each group lost some of its unique characteristics while it acquired characteristics of other cultures—mostly of the dominant, or "American," culture. The melting pot concept also brought a promise of a better life for immigrants. In exchange for giving up some of their cultural distinctiveness and assimilating into the dominant culture, they were given the same democratic rights and freedoms as other Americans, whether born here or naturalized citizens.

Of course, none of these groups ever became totally assimilated. They held on to the traditions of their cultural roots, some even keeping their language over generations. And the media helped them preserve those ties. Newspapers in a variety of languages circulated in the big cities. Blocks of time for radio or television broadcasting in other languages were purchased. Even whole television stations broadcast in other languages, particularly in areas where large numbers of immigrants from a particular culture lived. In recent times, Spanish-language broadcasting has been the most popular. According to the U.S. Census Bureau, Hispanics made up 11% of the population in 1997 and are projected to constitute a full quarter of the population by 2050. So there is a large audience for Spanish-language media in the United States. Univision Communications, a Spanish-language media company, broadcasts to 92% of Hispanic households through its 19 broadcast stations and its cable affiliates and cable company Galavision (McDonald, 1999).

Although immigrants may hold on to their cultural roots when they settle in another society, they also modify their traditions and behaviors in what has been called variously a process of hybridity (Bhabha, 1994), creolization (Hannerz, 1996), or glocalization (Robertson, 1994). Cultural identity is not fixed but fluid and dynamic, and that is true for everyone in a particular place, whether immigrant or native. As Stuart Hall (1992) has put it, the process of globalization has several consequences for cultural identity. As national identities decline and local identities are strengthened through resistance to globalization, new identities of hybridity also take the place of the old national identities (Hall, p. 300).

> Cultural identities come from somewhere, have histories. But, like everything which is historical, they undergo constant transformation. Far from being eternally fixed in some essentialized past, they are subject to the continuous "play" of history, culture and power. Far from being grounded in a mere "recovery" of the past, which is waiting to be found, and which, when found, will secure our sense of ourselves into eternity, identities are the names we give to the different ways we are positioned by, and position ourselves within, the narratives of the past. (Hall, 1997, p. 52)

Hall was writing primarily about the experience of migrants who live in the diaspora. They bring their histories with them when they migrate, but those histories change and develop as they blend with the culture where they find themselves and with their day-to-day experiences. Thus the terms *hybridity* or *creolization* refer to the mix of cultural frames for all of us. The dominant culture also takes on characteristics and traditions from the migrants to that culture. That is especially revealing as we look in a telephone directory for a list of restaurants in any given community. The world's cuisines are available in even small-town settings. And the term *fusion* has come to be applied to the mix of ingredients and cooking styles from two or more cultures to form new dishes.

Robertson (1994) writes that this process of fusion, or glocalization, occurs in the world's media too. He disputes the notion of media imperialism, arguing that cultural messages sent from the United States to other cultures are differentially received and interpreted according to the local cultural context; U.S.-produced films and television programs tailor their products to a global market because they need the international market to be profitable; seemingly national cultural resources, like Shakespearean plays, end up being interpreted and consumed in a local way and no longer belong to the culture where they originated; and ideas and cultural products flow from the "periphery" to the "center" (or from the Third World to the West) far more often than we have thought (p. 46).

Because it makes good business sense, many television program producers and filmmakers include characters from a variety of ethnic backgrounds, set plots in other cultural environments, and include storylines that deal with ethnic issues. Minority cultures form audiences too, and they buy products. It therefore becomes important to satisfy their interests to lure them to see the movie or tune in the channel or buy the newspaper or magazine. If media executives have come a little late to this realization, they are catering more to minority interests today.

WHAT WE CAN CONCLUDE

So in trying to sum up the issue of global culture as presented through the media, to make generalizations is difficult. We have seen that the United States dominates in the production of films and television programs. Journalism, American style, is also exported around the globe in broadcast and print formats. And yet, as powerful as the United States is in the global place of its cultural products, the people in other cultures have been able to preserve their own cultures and even do some influencing of their own. We are all born and raised into a nation, a community, and a family. And what we learn to value in these cultural environments sticks with us for life. Even if we leave our family, our community, and our nation, we never fully leave their cultures behind. And no matter how many television programs or films we watch, or how many books we read in our own language or other languages, we never totally abandon the cultures into which we were socialized. Rather, we learn to value new cultures and add them to the mix of what we already know. That's why it is so hard to understand and write about communication and culture. I often think that my life experiences in different cultures have caused me to leave little pieces of myself in various parts of the globe. And when I return to a certain place, I remember what it is I enjoyed about that place. The music in an Irish pub. The coffee in a little street café in Paris. The weekly market in any Turkish town or village. But also the farmer's market in Bloomington,

Indiana, and the basketball game in Indiana University's Assembly Hall. Reexperiencing the things I like in a particular culture reminds me that different personal needs are satisfied in different places by different cultures.

For more information on the topics that appear in this chapter, use the password that came free with this book to access InfoTrac College Edition. Use the following words as keyterms and subject searches: culture and communication, culture industries, cultural products, ethnic identity, mass communication, popular culture, global culture, international conflicts.

QUESTIONS FOR DISCUSSION

1. In this chapter our mass media have been described as culture industries. Does the use of that term concern you at all? What are the problems raised by the combination of business and culture?

2. This chapter has discussed several ways in which countries try to protect their cultural products. Why might that not be a good idea? What would change if countries took the opposite position and instead were happy to send and receive cultural products, such as books, television programs, and films, more freely?

3. How easy is it to change people's minds by exposing them to films or television programs with a different cultural perspective or set of values?

4. How might the media be used to resolve cultural conflict instead of exacerbating it?

5. How likely is it that the process of globalization might lead some day to one global culture with little or no local or regional variation on that culture? If that should happen, what might our mass media look like?

REFERENCES

Adorno, T. (1991). Culture industry reconsidered. In T. Adorno (Ed.), *The culture industry* (pp. 98–106). London: Routledge.

Anderson, B. (1983). *Imagined communities: Reflections on the origin and spread of nationalism.* London: Verso.

Ang, I. (1985). *Watching* Dallas: *Soap opera and the melodramatic imagination.* London: Methuen.

Asian restrictions and censorship of Internet and television. (1999, October 16). *The Economist.* Retrieved from LexisNexis online database (News Library).

Barber, B. (1995). *Jihad vs. McWorld.* New York: Times Books.

Bhabha, H. (1994). *The location of culture.* New York: Routledge.

Boyd-Barrett, O. (1980). *The international news agencies.* London: Constable.

Bredin, M. (1996). Transforming images: Communication technologies and cultural identity in Nishnawbe-Aski. In D. Howes (Ed.), *Cross-cultural consumption: Global markets, local realities* (pp. 161–177). New York: Routledge.

Collins, R. (1990). *Culture, communication, and national identity: The case of Cana-*

dian television. Toronto: University of Toronto Press.

Collins, R. (1999). European Union media and communication policies. In J. Stokes & A. Reading (Eds.), *The media in Britain: Current debates and developments* (pp. 158–169). London: Macmillan.

Culture wars. (1998, September 12). *The Economist,* p. 97.

Dorfman, A. (1975). *How to read Donald Duck: Imperialist ideology in the Disney comic* (A. Mattelart, Trans.). New York: International General.

The European Audiovisual Observatory presents its database on film admissions in Europe at the Cannes Market. (2000, May 10). European Audiovisual Observatory. Retrieved from the World Wide Web: http://www.obs.coe.int/oea/en/actu/doc_gen_actu_en.html

European Commission. (1999). *Commission report on the results obtained under the media II programme (1996–2000) from 1.1.96–30.6.98.* Retrieved from the World Wide Web: http://europa.eu.int/comm/dg10/avpolicy/whatsnew.html

Fiske, J. (1987). *Television culture.* London: Methuen.

Gans, H. J. (1980). *Deciding what's news: A study of* CBS Evening News, NBC Nightly News, Newsweek, *and* Time. New York: Vintage Books.

Geertz, C. (1973). *The interpretation of cultures.* New York: Basic Books.

Gillespie, M. (1995). *Television, ethnicity, and cultural change.* London: Routledge.

Hall, S. (1992). The question of cultural identity. In S. Hall, D. Held, & T. McGrew (Eds.), *Modernity and its futures* (pp. 272–316). Cambridge: Polity Press, in association with the Open University.

Hall, S. (1997). Cultural identity and diaspora. In K. Woodward, (Ed.), *Identity and difference* (pp. 51–59). London: Sage.

Hannerz, U. (1996). *Transnational connections: Culture, people, places.* London: Routledge.

Katz, E., & Liebes, T. (1985). Mutual aid in the decoding of *Dallas:* Preliminary notes from a cross-cultural study. In

P. Drummond & R. Paterson (Eds.), *Television in transition: Papers from the first international television studies conference* (pp. 187–204). London: British Film Institute.

Kinzer, S. (1999, April 13). Kurds are determined to restore TV station shut by the British. *New York Times,* p. A13.

Leonard, T. (2001, January 12). Anne Robinson looks for America's weakest link. *Daily Telegraph,* p. 3.

Liebes, T., & Katz, E. (1990). *The export of meaning: Cross-cultural readings of* Dallas. New York: Oxford University Press.

Mattelart, A. (1979). *Multinational corporations and the control of culture: The ideological apparatuses of imperialism* (Michael Chanan, Trans.). Sussex: Harvester Press.

McDonald, K. (1999, August 31). New Spanish-lingo programs to battle for Latino audience. *Daily Variety,* p. A27.

Meyrowitz, J. (1985). *No sense of place.* New York: Oxford University Press.

Nordenstreng, K., & Varis, T. (1974). *Television traffic—a one-way street?* Paris: UNESCO.

Puttnam, L. D. (1998, April 6). Introduction. *Proceedings of Audiovisual Conference.* Luxemburg: Office for Official Publications of the European Communities. Retrieved from the World Wide Web: http://europa.eu.int/eac/speeches/puttnam_en.html

Riding, A. (1993, December 15). The world trade agreement: The French strategy. *New York Times,* p. D19.

Riding, A. (1999, December 14). French fume at one another over U.S. films' popularity. *New York Times,* p. E1.

Robertson, R. (1994). Globalisation or glocalisation? *Journal of International Communication, 1*(1), 33–52.

Sacirbey, O. (1999, October 27). Germans want home-grown TV . . . with U.S. look. *Christian Science Monitor,* p. 1.

Sappir, S. L. (2001, January 15). Satellite TV's spicy dish. *Jerusalem Report,* p. 40.

Scannell, P., Schlesinger, P., & Sparks, C. (Eds.). (1992). Introduction. *Culture and Power.* London: Sage, pp. 1–14.

Schiller, H. (1969). *Mass communication and the American empire*. New York: A. M. Kelly.

Schiller, H. (1992). *Mass communications and American empire*. Boulder, CO: Westview.

Schudson, M. (1994). Culture and the integration of national societies. In D. Crane (Ed.), *The sociology of culture* (pp. 21–43). Cambridge: Blackwell.

Television without frontiers: Green paper on the establishment of the common market for broadcasting, especially by satellite and cable. (1984). Brussels: Commission of the European Communities.

Tomlinson, J. (1991). *Cultural imperialism: A critical introduction*. Baltimore: Johns Hopkins University Press.

Toward a single European market in film. (1999, October). *Screen Digest*, pp. 261–268.

Tunstall, J. (1977). *The media are American*. London: Constable.

UNESCO. (1999). Cultural industries: UNESCO sector for culture. Retrieved from the World Wide Web: http://www.unesco.org/culture/industries/index.html

Varis, T. (1985). *International flow of television programmes*. Paris: UNESCO.

Ward, A. (2001, January 19). BBC claims public support as it plans to invest pounds 300m in digital TV and radio. *Financial Times*, p. 4.

Wells, A. (1972). *Picture-tube imperialism? The impact of U.S. television on Latin America*. Maryknoll, NY: Orbis.

Williams, R. (1981). *The sociology of culture*. Chicago: University of Chicago Press.

Williams, R. (1983). *Keywords* (2nd ed.). New York: Oxford.

Young, D. (1999, August 16). Italo pic biz wrangles U.S. export declaration. *Variety*, p. 19.

NOTE

The author expresses her thanks to J. D. Denny for his assistance in supplying research for part of this chapter.

12

✹

Pedagogy, Critical Citizenship, and International Communication

M. MEHDI SEMATI

M. Mehdi Semati (PhD, University of Missouri—Columbia) is an assistant professor at Eastern Illinois University. His research addresses international communication, cultural studies, and communication theory. His writings have appeared as book chapters and as articles in journals such as *Critical Studies in Mass Communication, Journal of Popular Film and Television, Transnational Broadcasting Studies,* and *Journal of International Communication.*

This chapter addresses some aspects of teaching international communication as a field of inquiry and the role that global communication technologies can play in the classroom. Given the scope and the speed by which all facets of everyday life for most people are being affected by processes of globalization, pedagogy of international communication could take a more significant role. With globalization comes proximity to other cultures, traditions, peoples, and ways of living. The proliferation of culture and communication on a global scale, whether as a symptom or a cause of globalization, has had significant implications internationally. Indeed some people see cultural conflict as the primary source of

 For additional online resources, access the Global Media Monitor Web site that accompanies this book on the Wadsworth Communication Cafe Web site at http://communication.wadsworth.com.

tension in today's world. In this context, a critical pedagogy of international communication can play a positive role in and outside of the classroom by engaging students as citizens of a global community. If we accept that the popular media institutions, and the texts they produce are sites of everyday learning (Schwoch, White & Reilly, 1992), then a classroom devoted to the study of global communication can become a site for both learning the course content and acquiring skills in becoming critical consumers of global media in everyday life. In this chapter I report on my experience of teaching a class in international communication (during winter quarter 1998) that achieved these objectives.

In order to approach the material in a concrete manner, I chose a particular phenomenon to study throughout the term that would embody issues and problems that the course content intended to address. The phenomenon of global communication we chose to study was Cable News Network (CNN) and its role in the conduct of international communication, international relations, and international diplomacy. A particular broadcast of an "International Town Meeting" by CNN provided a concrete object of study that anchored much of our discussion throughout the term.

As I demonstrate in this chapter, approaching the material this way proved productive and heuristic. This particular subject provided an occasion to study, among other things, the following topics: the debate on the global flow of information (for example, the text of the International Town Meeting); media's role in international relations and public diplomacy (for example, the role of CNN in the conduct of diplomacy); methodological and theoretical issues (for example, introducing political economy and cultural studies as a different approach to CNN); and the social, political, and cultural significance of global communication.

More importantly, the course engaged students in constructing a fairly sophisticated argument about CNN. Here is an outline of that argument. The impact of CNN on the conduct of foreign policy has been termed "the CNN effect." The CNN effect thesis might explain events such as the International Town Meeting broadcast as an agent of acceleration, impediment, and agenda setting in the foreign policy decision-making process. The argument developed in the course suggests that what escapes analyses in the literature on the CNN effect is the fact that CNN is a televisual form, with its own logic. Through an analysis of the International Town Meeting, the class developed the view that the CNN effect may be better understood in terms of the theory of television proposed by Mary Ann Doane (1990), which addresses information, crisis, and catastrophe. The terms of this argument add up to a framework that recognizes CNN and the aesthetics associated with the "all-news" genre to operate within an unresolved tension between the categories of information, crisis, and catastrophe, and the maintenance of a paradoxical state of sustained and routinized crisis. The real "CNN effect" operates through the routinization of (international) conflict as compelling television and its use and abuse by policy makers, a process that undermines democratic processes. Paradoxically, this routinization amounts to a politicization of international politics and foreign policy decision-making processes prone to "miscalculations" such as the International Town Meeting, where the administration was forced to take into account public opinion contrary to its official policy.

As we concluded in class, such a phenomenon constitutes what we might call accidental democracy.

In order to accomplish our goals, I organized our inquiry into CNN in four progressive sections. In the first section, we simply followed the arguments and the literature on what is referred to as "the CNN effect." In the second section, we expanded the scope of our investigation to treat CNN as a televisual form. Here we asked questions about the specificity of television as a medium. In the third section, in order to draw from the materials students had studied in other communication courses, we approached CNN through Mary Ann Doane's theory. Finally, we discussed the implications of approaching CNN as such in terms of concerns with democracy and public participation in foreign policy decision-making processes.

With this introduction as a background, I now detail the approach we took in our study of global communication phenomena and the field of international communication. In the final section, I offer some concluding remarks on the teaching of international communication, global communication, pedagogy, and the notion of critical citizenship. In doing so, I hope to illustrate several points. First, a class in international communication can become more engaging if the content is approached in a topical and concrete fashion. Second, the content of such a class can be covered while drawing from other communication classes (for example, television criticism), which allows for a more integrated approach to a communication curriculum. Third, students are able to study particular international communication phenomena (such as CNN) in their wider cultural, political, social, and technological contexts. Finally, the topicality of the approach renders the study of international communication more relevant to students by drawing from the context of their social life.

THE INTERNATIONAL
TOWN MEETING AND CNN

On February 18, 1998, as the United States was preparing a military strike against Iraq for failing to meet the demands of the United Nations' weapon inspection team, CNN organized a "town hall meeting." According to a *New York Times* report, this event was organized at the request of the White House and scheduled for an early afternoon broadcast. Titled "Showdown with Iraq: An International Town Meeting," the meeting was held in the heartland of the United States (on the campus of Ohio State University), ostensibly so that the nation's foreign policies could be explained to the public. Although this public relations attempt proved to be a fiasco for the White House, it was a real bonanza for CNN.[1] What troubled the White House was that this "public relations disaster" was broadcast live to an international audience around the world.

The International Town Meeting was simulcast on CNN, CNN International, and CNN Radio Network, complete with commercial interruptions. Although the idea for the meeting was initially put forth by the National Security Council's communications staff member David Leavy, "like all high-profile administration doings, this one required multiple memos and meetings, implicating dozens of other officials in approving the idea and executing it" (Leavy, quoted in Bennet, 1998). Leavy's statement demonstrates that the White House constructed a role for CNN in the conduct of foreign policy. In viewing the International Town Meeting, it was difficult not to notice the presence of CNN: the beautiful aerial shot of the stage; the live "media event" broadcast around the world; CNN's logo plastered on all four sides of the cubical scoreboard on the arena ceiling; and so forth. The following day, a report in the *New York Times* told its readers that some White House officials were furious with CNN. "CNN did a horrible job with this," one administration aide said. Referring to the two CNN anchors, Judy Woodruff and Bernard Shaw, he added, "Judy and Bernie looked like they were deer caught in the headlights, and they had no control over the management of this" (Bennet, 1998). The topic of "serious criticism" in the press was not so much the foreign policy issues but CNN's role in the international political scene and the foreign policy decision-making process.[2]

For the purpose of my international communication class, this episode provided a concrete example and an occasion to introduce students to a critical engagement with a set of issues integral to the field of international communication. We began by addressing the question, How is one to understand the International Town Meeting?

THE CNN EFFECT

The concern about the overt impact of CNN on foreign policy has been described as "the CNN effect."[3] Under the auspices of the term *effect,* however, are included various dynamics of interaction. As Livingston (1997) has observed, the efforts to unpack the term *CNN effect* have largely failed, given the imprecise use of the term. This effect might be outlined and differentiated according to a set of analytically distinct categories. These categories could serve as a typology of CNN influence, which conceptualizes the CNN effect as accelerant, impediment, and agenda-setting agency (Livingston, 1997).[4]

When the CNN effect is conceptualized as an accelerant, the assumption is that the latest communication technologies deprive diplomats of the luxury of time for careful deliberation. Within the context of global satellite technologies, "real-time journalism," "parachute journalism," and "rooftop journalism" are among the labels applied to journalistic operation under the principle of speed. This principle requires instant analysis and response. As Nicholas Burns, State Department spokesperson, states, "In our day, as events unfold half a world away, it is not unusual for CNN State Department correspondent Steve Hurst to ask me for a reaction before we've had a chance to receive a more detailed report from our embassy and consider carefully our options."[5] It must be pointed out that there is nothing new about the press and communication technology becoming a factor in foreign policy equations. This trend has been present since the invention of the telegraph.[6] What is new is the speed, introduced by communication technologies, of "real-time" journalism as a factor in foreign policy equations.

Alternatively, when we conceptualize the CNN effect as an impediment to foreign policy, we attend to the dramatic and emotional impact of images. Here the concern is the public's emotional response to particular images (for example, gruesome pictures of death and destruction). For politicians and the military, the lesson learned from the Vietnam Conflict (applied to the Falklands, Grenada, Panama, and the Gulf War) was that unrestricted media access to a military operation may eventually prevent the public from accepting the official view of such an operation. (It is this factor that explains the presentation of the Gulf War as a "clean" war.) The public's support for war, for example, may be undermined by the media coverage of bloodshed. In the case of American intervention in Somalia in 1993, to cite another example, the picture of the body of an American soldier dragged through the streets of Mogadishu forced the Clinton administration to take into account the public's reaction to this particular policy and eventually to terminate the mission (see Seib, 1997).

Finally, the most familiar way to conceptualize the CNN effect is as an agenda-setting agency. Mohamed Sacirbey, Bosnian ambassador to the United Nations, once said, "If you look at how humanitarian relief is delivered in Bosnia you see that those areas where the TV cameras are most present are the ones that are the best fed, the ones that receive the most medicines. While on the other hand, many of our people have starved and died of disease and shelling where there are no TV cameras" (quoted in Seib, 1997, p. 90). When the images of starvation, bloodshed, and human misery flash across the television screens, television becomes the de facto "must-do-something" framework for policy makers. Consider the case of U.S. intervention in Somalia in 1992. Considering reelection, President George Bush was not inclined to commit any U.S. troops to an uncertain situation. Yet, it is alleged, the pressure of television, with its images of starvation and bloodshed, forced him into Somalia. Here are some comments by Marlin Fitzwater, Bush's press secretary, on this policy: "After the election, the media had the free time and that was when the pressure started building up. We heard it from every corner that something must be done. Finally, the pressure was too great. The President said, 'I just can't live with this for two months.' TV tipped us over the top at a time when the death rate [from starvation] was over a 100 a day" (quoted in Seib, 1997, p. 44).

It is clear that CNN, and other communication technologies in general, have complicated the conduct of foreign policy. That should not lead, however, to hasty conclusions and exaggerated claims based on limited evidence. To take the case of "humanitarian crises" (such as Bosnia, Somalia, Rwanda) for instance, the evidence is contradictory at best. Livingston (1997) has demonstrated that the majority of humanitarian operations are conducted without much media attention. As Livingston and Eachus (1995) have argued, the decision to intervene even in the case of Somalia was based more on diplomatic and bureaucratic operations than media coverage (notwithstanding the impact of the image I described above).

Nonetheless, the agenda-setting function of CNN's International Town Meeting seemed to be exploited by the administration. It is clear that the White House had Saddam Hussein in mind as an intended audience member, thus implicating CNN in the conduct of foreign policy. The press repeatedly reported that the purpose of the meeting was to "send a message" to Saddam Hussein. In a *USA Today* report, for example, Shafeeq Ghabra of Kuwait University was quoted as saying that the protests displayed during the meeting "could send the wrong message to Saddam" ("To Many Abroad," 1998). And as John Boehner, a Republican congressman from Ohio, put it, "If the Clinton administration's goal was to *send a message to Saddam via CNN,* this was an unmitigated disaster" ("U.S. Policy on Iraq," 1998; emphasis added).

At this point, I asked the students to consider what motivated the White House to choose the town hall meeting as a forum. It is well known that this meeting format is one of President Clinton's favorite forms of public communication (Denton & Holloway, 1996, p. 31). During the 1992 presidential elections such town hall meetings provided the candidates with free airtime and allowed them to target specific audiences who asked "soft" and "polite" questions. More importantly, these town hall meetings made politics more entertaining (Nimmo, 1994). Similarly, the talk show appearances during the same presidential campaign, argues Kerbel (1994), made it possible for politicians to avoid the press. The class concluded that television and certain assumptions about television were implicated in the conception and execution of this meeting as a conduit for foreign policy practices. Subsequently, we turned our attention to an analysis of CNN (and the International Town Meeting) as a televisual form.

CNN AS A TELEVISUAL FORM

In this section of the class, we examined how the logic of television might be implicated in the conception of the International Town Meeting and the reaction to its broadcast on CNN. This broadcast, which combined televisual elements from various formats of talk shows (for example, dramatic music, announcer, graphics, charts, hosts, and live studio audience), was heavily promoted by CNN. According to Malcolm Baroway, executive director of communications for Ohio State University, where the event took place, CNN wanted "to have an atmosphere as similar to a television studio as possible" (Bennet, 1998). The point is that even the White House had the specificity of the medium of television in mind in the conception of the International Town Meeting. In this context we considered CNN as a televisual form with its own logic and with a set of structural constraints and possibilities with which television as such operates. We discussed CNN and scheduling, CNN and the political economy of television news, and CNN as "talk."

CNN and Scheduling

In this section of the class, we looked at the daily scheduling of traditional broadcast channels and CNN in order to discover commonalities. The scheduling of CNN follows the logic of television in general.[7] It consists of half-hour and 1-hour segments, with commercial interruptions. In a way, CNN "packages" the world of news for its audience much the same way other channels do (I will discuss the specificity of CNN later). This temporal organization introduces some form of order (in the form of closure and reopening) to an otherwise chaotic world of events. To the extent that CNN follows the same temporal organization, which is a response to the same commercial imperatives, no distinction can be made between other broadcast networks and CNN.

More importantly, larger temporal organizations (such as early morning, daytime, prime time) structure CNN's content in much the same way as they structure the content of the broadcast networks. The 11:30 A.M. show, *CNN and Company With Mary Tillotson,* is an all-female roundtable discussion. The assumption of a mostly female audience is tied to the temporal organization of "daytime" television consumed mostly in a "domestic" setting. The afternoon scheduling is filled with a combination of news and talk shows (for example, *Burden of Proof,* resembling a quiz show of the broadcast networks, and *TalkBack Live,* of the Oprah Winfrey tradition found on traditional networks in the afternoon). The "prime time" and evening shows, mostly consisting of news, talk, and analysis, are the main attraction for "news junkies."

In the context of such a discussion of the logic of television in its temporal organizations, the class wanted to see how this logic might have dictated the conception of the International Town Meeting. Here is Walter Goodman (1998) of the *New York Times* reporting on the meeting:

> The dire moment came early during Wednesday's so-called town meeting at Ohio State University, devised by the Clinton administration to whip up enthusiasm for the bombing of Iraq, when Defense Secretary William Cohen displayed for the CNN camera a picture of an Iraqi mother and child who he said had been killed by nerve gas. He titled it, "Madonna and Child, Saddam Hussein Style." With that exhibit, Cohen exposed the White House's conception of the meeting. It was to be an appeal to the afternoon television audience, an easy target for sentiment.

Not only is the public conceived as an audience consuming television, but it is also presumed to be the daytime audience of broadcast networks: foreign policy as soap opera for the daytime audience. It should be pointed out that if the display of this photograph indicates that Cohen was after sentimentalism (and outrage), it both demonstrates the degree to which politicians subscribe to "the CNN effect" thesis and reflects their efforts to manage public opinion through CNN.

CNN and the Economics of Television

After considering the temporal organization of CNN as a logic of television, the class considered the marketing and promotional practices deployed by CNN and the traditional broadcast networks. Again the purpose was to discover the televisual logic structuring CNN's operation. The content in this section of the class made it possible to introduce political economy as a framework for studying media institutions and practices. The initial questions in this section revolved around issues of ownership and control in global communication. In that context we wanted to know to what extent CNN's content might be structured through operations that could be explained by the economic logic of television, as essentially business practices and decisions.

Among the issues raised was the circulation and recycling of video news segments among the various channels owned by Turner Broadcasting System (and Time Warner). The guiding principle behind the success of the "CNN family of networks" has been a simple one: "Take any given news item and air it again and again in different ways on each of the company's networks" (Flournoy & Stewart, 1997, p. 3).[8] The most visible case is that of the circulation of news cut to the "bit size" (this term is used by the tour guide for the CNN Center in Atlanta) for consumption on CNN Headline News. The recycling of news items among various channels is a business practice that makes the development of content cost efficient. In the world of media conglomerates, "synergistic" ownership allows the movement of characters, symbols, and stories across various corporate holdings.[9]

Moreover, various holdings of Turner Broadcasting Company (and Time Warner) do a considerable amount of cross-promotion. Such practices are well informed by the corporate logic. What CNN shares with broadcast networks in this regard is its relationship to corporate "synergy." That is, media conglomerates acquire smaller entities in order to support other units within the same corporation. Examples include the way CNN advertises for CNN/SI (CNN/Sports Illustrated) and CNNfn (CNN Financial Network); CNN Headline News promotes TNT (Turner Network Television); TNT promotes TBS Superstation; and so on. This support is not unlike the glaring cross-promotion made possible by cross-ownership of other networks: ABC's "family night" infomercials on Fridays promote the animated features made by its "parent company" Disney (such as *Hercules* and *Mulan*). The context is then widened from the circle of the CNN family of networks to include the entire entertainment complex owned by Time Warner.

CNN as "Talk"

In this section of the class, questions revolved around genres and codes of television. We wanted to know if the content of CNN could be explained by appealing to the categories, codes, and genres of television. Our intention was to move our discussion beyond CNN's self-declared categories of news and broadcast journalism. The most promising and obvious genre, or codification element, of television in this context was the consideration of CNN's content as "talk." By this I mean the extent to which CNN's content assumes an entertainment function for television. The majority of the content of all-news channels such as CNN is talk (analysis, debate, opinion, and the like) packaged as a program. The proliferation of all-news channels, along with talk radio and prime-time television newsmagazines, ensures plenty of talk (such as spin-doctoring and expert opinion), which passes as the content for news programs. Even a cursory look at these channels reveals that not only is talk the cheapest form of programming, but it is also becoming a form of entertainment posed as information. The endless commentary on a topic such as the Monica Lewinsky scandal on all-news channels, as well as traditional news outlets, has often been described as sensational (tabloid) journalism. The standard argument here is that entertainment (or the entertainment division of the networks) is creeping into the news. But why not turn the argument around? That is, the news industry is taking over the entertainment division of the networks. "The intrusion of the real," Mellencamp (1990a) argues, "is also the taking over of entertainment by the news division" (p. 57). In this context, notice the degree to which CNN these days feels comfortable lending its logo and even its crew and on-air personalities to Hollywood films such as *Contact* and *Air Force One* (or consider MSNBC in *Deep Impact*).[10] In a radio advertisement for the Fox News Channel aired by a local station (in Michigan) during the time this course was conducted, Fox news and talk shows were referred to as "powerful" programming, and the audience was invited to experience news as "contact sports."

The mechanism through which news items adopt an entertainment function (and form) is what we may call speculation. It is within the space of speculation that talk shows exist: if there is nothing to speculate about, there is nothing to "talk" about. One of the structural characteristics of all talk shows (or chat shows) is that the topic at hand is always already subject to speculation. No talk show, from the absurd type (such as the "carnivalesque" atmosphere of *The Jerry Springer Show*) to the most serious (Sunday morning chat shows such as CBS's *Face the Nation,* NBC's *Meet the Press,* ABC's *This Week*), can escape this logic.[11] In the case of the Sunday morning talk shows, which are the core of American broadcast journalism, the claim of objectivity dictates that all sides to a debate be present. When one speaks of talk (as in talk show) in the world of television, one is necessarily speaking of speculation.

One of the major consequences of understanding the content of CNN as such is that we are put in a position to ask questions about the events prior to their televisualization, for the difference between the real and the image produced by the media through simulation is considerable. Speculation renders the event, as Baudrillard (1995) would say, "sticky and unintelligible" (p. 32). That is to say, the real events are ontologically distinct from the informational media (virtual) events that claim to "represent" them. In other words, the "encrustation of the event in and by information" (that is, speculation) makes the event disappear insofar as it becomes subject to endless speculation and interpretation (Baudrillard, p. 48). In other words, what is lived in real time, with televisualization, is not the event but "the spectacle of the degradation of the event and its spectral evocation" (p. 48) in the endless commentary by "experts," "spin doctors" and "talking heads." This is one sense in which, Baudrillard argues, "the Gulf War did not take place" (this is the title of his book).

This aspect was not lost in the critical commentary on the International Town Meeting. Referring to the CNN broadcast, John Boehner, a Republican congressman from Ohio, complained, "This is a matter of global security and international peace, and they turned it into the Oprah Winfrey show. Not surprisingly, it didn't work" ("U.S. Policy on Iraq," 1998). This was not the only reference to the Oprah Winfrey show in the press. To give another example, Bennet (1998) stated, "After years of dabbling in the 'feel your pain' techniques of Oprah Winfrey, the Clinton White House wound up feeling plenty of its own Wednesday."

CNN AND DOANE'S TELEVISION THEORY

To enhance the theoretical richness of the students' approach to CNN, and to draw connections to other communication classes the students had had, this section of the class considered CNN from the perspective of a theory of television advocated by Mary Ann Doane (1990). Drawing on the theory, we considered the aesthetics associated with CNN in terms of the tension among the categories of information, crisis, and catastrophe. The class argued that in blurring the distinction among these categories, CNN capitalizes on the temporal mode as television's primary mode of operation.

In an essay on television, Doane (1990) locates television's operation and aesthetics in the temporal dimension. If photography operates in the "that-has-been" mode, television operates in the "this-is-going-on" mode, a perpetual "present-ness" (p. 222). Even when it imitates film (for example, fictional content in the past tense), television, with its commercial breaks and station identification, stitches the audience to the present. Given its organization of temporality, television, for legitimacy, is bound to and thrives on information, crisis, and catastrophe as three "different modes of apprehending the event" (p. 223).

The first of these—information—is characterized by its regularity. Information, Doane (1990) argues, "would specify the steady stream of daily 'newsworthy' events characterized by their regularity if not predictability" (p. 223). Although its content is always changing, "information, as a genre, is always *there*" (p. 223). One can always count on the weather report, financial update, sports headlines, and so on. Information is, "above all, that which fills time on television—using it up. Here time is flow: steady and continuous" (p. 223). Crisis has a different relationship to time in that it "involves a condensation of temporality" (p. 223). A consequential event of a particular duration, a crisis demands resolution within a particular time frame. Catastrophe's relationship to time, on the other hand, is that of "the instantaneous, the moment, the punctual." Without any extended duration, it "happens 'all at once.'" Because it "compresses" time, catastrophe is the gravest of all crises.

It is true that such distinctions may be difficult to maintain in practice, in that one may find events that threaten such a classificatory system. In a reply to this objection, Doane (1990) underlines what is precisely at stake theoretically.

> But what is more striking in relation to this inevitable taxonomic failure is that television tends to blur the differences between what seem to be absolutely incompatible temporal modes, between the flow and continuity of information and the punctual discontinuity of catastrophe. Urgency, enslavement to the instant and hence forgettability, would then be attributes of both information and catastrophe. Indeed, the obscuring of these temporal distinctions may constitute the specificity of television's operation. (p. 223)

Doane (1990) argues, "even television must have a way of compensating for its own tendency toward leveling of signification, toward banalization and nondifferentiation" (p. 224). If information is conceptualized in terms of flow and ubiquity, how is one to account for television's need for punctuation and differentiation? Apart from dramatizing information (graphics and visuals, dramatic music, and the rhetoric of the newscaster), "most effective, perhaps, is the crisis of temporality which signifies *urgency* and which is attached to the information itself as its single most compelling attribute" (p. 225).

If catastrophe is discontinuity within an otherwise continuous system, as "catastrophe theory" defines it, then the magnitude of the catastrophe correlates with the degree to which the catastrophe disrupts the daily routine of television programming (Doane, 1990, p. 232). With respect to the daily operation of television, Browne (1987) has argued that the position of the programs in the schedule of television is determined by the social order of the work world: "Television establishes its relation to the 'real,' not only through the codes of realistic representation, but through the schedule, to the socially mediated order of the workday and the workweek." That is, "television helps produce and render 'natural' the logic and rhythm of the social order" (p. 588). In the context of this argument, catastrophe represents that which escapes this structuring of temporality. In other words, catastrophe would signal the return of the repressed (Doane, 1990). In this way, we might say that CNN is in the business of bringing to our attention what is excluded from the social order. Just as a "catastrophe machine" (in the domain of mathematics) intends "to predictably produce unpredictable irregularities" (Doane, p. 234), CNN predictably and regularly brings to us unpredictable irregularities.

Let us return to the International Town Meeting in terms of the theory proposed by Doane (1990). To the extent that CNN scheduled the event, the meeting has the character of information (albeit as content and program for television). The information in this context addresses a political crisis. As such, the meeting is coverage of a crisis. The designation of the program (at least from the perspective of the White House) as a disaster reveals the propensity for CNN's content to approach catastrophe at any given moment. The disruption during the meeting, the unrest, the dissension, the asking of impolite questions, and things going wrong, much like any live television—all mark the potential for the collapse of information (already marked by urgency) into catastrophe. The routinization of such content (preplanning the coverage of a "crisis") marks the reversibility of this process: catastrophe is turned (tamed, or "domesticated") into information (it is just there, day or night). The round-the-clock coverage of the Gulf War is an example of this routinization of crisis, which we might call informationalization of the event. Operating across such categories, CNN reveals a new generic formation (all-news channel) that capitalizes on television's primary category, the temporal dimension. In the sense that the obscuring of temporal dimensions "may constitute the specificity of television's operation" (Doane, p. 223), we might say that CNN is a realization of the principle of operation of television.

THE REAL CNN EFFECT

In the last section of the class we discussed the implications of approaching CNN as a televisual form explained in terms of the theory presented by Doane (1990). This section provided an occasion to reflect on the content of the class as far as CNN was concerned. This self-reflexivity proved to be more useful than I had anticipated, in that it raised a series of questions that were epistemological in nature, questions that would have been highly abstract without concrete examples. These questions covered a range of topics, including the nature of claims, evidence, arguments, knowledge, inferences, and more. What needs to be pointed out in terms of my presentation in this chapter is that students had been engaged in a study that was both empirical/descriptive (for example, the CNN effect, CNN as Televisual) and theoretical (for example, CNN and Doane's theory). We had also asked questions that were empirical but beyond the scope of what we were able to answer. These particular questions had to do with the kinds of effects the routinization of conflict by CNN might have on audiences' knowledge, attitudes, and beliefs. Students came to understand that although we could not answer these questions definitively, we could engage in some reasonable speculation based on the available evidence (see below). Specifically, we explored the idea that through the "taming" of news on the one hand, and the use and abuse of news outlets such as CNN by decision makers in the political sphere on the other hand, CNN at once undermines and promises democratic potential (accidental democracy).

On the one hand, the news in a number of ways loses its urgency as that which calls for the undivided attention of the audience—the overall effect of which is what we may call the taming (domestication) of the news. These are the same characteristics we called televisual forms of CNN. First, CNN is just another television outlet in the domestic sphere (and workplace, airport, hotel, and so on). It is just there in all its ubiquity. Second, the chaotic and undifferentiated world of events is neatly organized and "brought to you" through the same temporal organizations of television in general (such as daytime television and prime-time television). Third, news is packaged in much the same way as non-news is packaged (for example, with commercial interruptions). Fourth, much of the content of CNN takes an entertainment function as talk (analysis, debates, speculation, and so on). Fifth, the recycling of news items among various CNN channels leaves the viewer with the impression of news as reruns (in much the same way that various retrospection or event anniversary programs do). Moreover, drawing on the work of Doane (1990), we can argue that CNN capitalizes on the specificity of television's operation in the temporal dimension, which is the obscuring of temporal distinctions (between catastrophe and information), by maintaining a daily, routinized schedule of crisis, catastrophe, and information. By operating in the space of the unresolved tension between categories of information, crisis, and catastrophe, confounded by the reproduction of the larger temporal organizations of television in everyday life (such as workday and weekday), CNN packages a world of conflict and chaos for assimilation into the texture of everyday life. In short, via these mechanisms the world of events (with political significance) is rendered inconsequential through the ordinariness of television.

On the other hand, because of its unlimited capacity to present matters of public concern to the public as news, CNN is increasingly used and abused by policy makers in pursuit of their own agenda. Let us return to the example of the International Town Meeting to illustrate this point. It is evident that the White House carefully chose the time, the format, and the medium (daytime, the town hall meeting format, and television/CNN). The reaction to the broadcast indicates that the White House had seriously miscalculated the degree to which a town hall format, broadcast on CNN as daytime television, can defy attempts to manage public opinion. In response to the complaints from the White House that CNN should have done a better job "controlling the crowd," Frank Sesno, CNN's Washington bureau chief, simply replied, "The White House wanted a town hall meeting and they got a town hall meeting" (Bennet, 1998).

Two particular reactions to the broadcast were notable in the press. First, the White House (and the press) was surprised by the probing, thoughtful, and vociferous reaction of the attendants to the meeting. One can only speculate as to what was expected, but a skeptical audience with intelligent questions was not it. As Robyn Meredith (1998) of the *New York Times* put it, the audience asked "tough, pointed questions of the sort that the national security advisers have not heard from Congress." They asked "probing" questions, according to Steven Erlanger (1998b) of the *New York Times*. Dan Balz and John Harris (1998) of the *Washington Post,* in an article titled "Hostility Disrupts Favored Clinton Forum," characterized the questioning as "hostile." Goodman (1998) best captured the correspondents' surprise to hear the audience asking substantive questions: "Now the most interesting question facing the correspondents, commentators and experts is what to make of the contradictory feelings of a public that refuses to be a herd."

Second, the meeting was generally held to be a public relations failure and declared a total disaster. One report announced that it had "all the makings of a major public relations disaster" (Balz & Harris, 1998). The Canadian Broadcasting Corporation declared the meeting a "public relations disaster." In Britain, Sky News characterized the meeting a "failure" of American leadership. France's LCI television declared the meeting "a disaster, a fiasco," one that Madeleine Albright (then Secretary of State) "will remember for a long time." Japan's public NHK television said the meeting had put the White House in a "tough" position ("To Many Abroad," 1998).

What the class observed was that the characterization of the event as a failure for the White House, the characterization of the International Town Meeting as a bonanza for CNN, and the utter surprise that participating citizens refused to ask polite questions reflected the degree to which CNN at once undermines and promises democratic potential. CNN undermines democratic potential not only by rendering matters of public concern inconsequential through the ordinariness of television but also by being manipulated by policy makers to manage public opinion. At the same time, the conception and the execution of the International Town Meeting demonstrate that CNN now spotlights the once-private (elite) world of diplomacy. More importantly, it is evident that the voice of the public can be heard, albeit through miscalculations and accidents such as the International Town Meeting and its broadcast on CNN.

CONCLUSION

In this chapter, I have reported some aspects of my experience in teaching an international communication class. The logic and the conviction behind teaching this class the way I did are that the popular (global) media are sites of everyday learning (Schwoch et al., 1992). Sights, sounds, narratives, images, and the texts they offer tell us about particular things in particular ways. They incline certain understandings of the world to the exclusion of others. They value particular ways of living at the expense of others. Another conviction behind this method is that academic material is much more meaningful to students when it connects to concrete topical examples and issues from their everyday living and their social, cultural, and political contexts. Such a pedagogical experience is meaningful in other ways. In such contexts students acquire skills in the critical consumption of global media and an awareness of themselves as political subjects. This is not to suggest that we ought to teach our students what particular values or political ideologies they should subscribe to (in my experience they reject such practices anyway). Rather, it is to suggest that the classroom experience ought to prepare them for the political dimensions of their lives by providing them with the tools to become critical consumers of global media and culture. Such a pedagogical practice leads to "critical citizenship" (Schwoch et al., 1992) by "open[ing] the eyes and ears of potential consumers of media culture to a more active, engaging, questioning way of reception and reading" (p. x). Learning, according to such a philosophy of pedagogy, "must include complex intellectual knowledge and skills that enhance the ability of a citizenry to continue to educate itself throughout its social life" (p. xi). With the ever-increasing globalization of all facets of media, culture, and everyday life, a classroom devoted to the study of the field of international communication and the topic of global communication provides an excellent forum for promoting critical citizenship.

For more information on the topics that appear in this chapter, use the password that came free with this book to access InfoTrac College Edition. Use the following words as keyterms and subject searches: global community, media effects, international town meeting, journalism, agenda setting, television talk shows, international news, economics of broadcasting.

QUESTIONS FOR DISCUSSION

1. What other communication classes (or related fields) can you draw from to address the issues raised in this class?

2. What specific theories, arguments, and investigations that you have read elsewhere can be consulted to study the issues of concern in your international communication class?

3. What current news story (or stories) would be appropriate to study that would explicitly embody many of the topics in your international communication class?

4. What specific issues or areas of investigation that you studied in this class do you find especially relevant to your past experience and your future?

5. Why is studying international communication important today? How do you think your international communication class can help you live your life outside the classroom?

NOTES

1. This characterization is taken from the *New York Times* report by James Bennet (1998). The press coverage cited throughout this paper was obtained through a Lexis-Nexis search using "international town meeting" as keywords (pagination thus does not apply). I have included in the bibliography of this chapter the sources I cite throughout the chapter, as well as some additional readings my students did in this and other communication classes relevant to our discussion. For more national and international reaction to this broadcast see "To many abroad," from *USA Today;* Barton Gellman (1998), of the *Washington Post;* and Steve Erlanger (1998), of the *New York Times.*

2. As I was watching this broadcast, I was reminded of an essay by Meaghan Morris (1993) on the television coverage of the Australian Bicentenary called *Australia Live: Celebration of a Nation.* She argues that in contrast to the event itself, the Australian broadcast became a topic of "serious criticism." Many commentators agreed that the broadcast did not celebrate a nation in a "traditional or substantive sense of that term." Instead, it celebrated "its own technical demonstration that four hours of live television could simultaneously be produced and consumed around the globe without too many disasters" (pp. 19–20). Similarly, the role of CNN, rather than the foreign policies being proposed, became the topic of "serious criticism."

3. Other designations include "CNN curve" and "CNN factor" (Livingston, 1997, p. 291).

4. Needless to say, one may further differentiate effects. Livingston (1997) discusses the media-as-impediment category as (a) an "emotional inhibitor" and (b) a "threat to operational security." As it will become clear, my purpose is broader in scope, and these distinctions will be subsumed and addressed in the larger context of my approach.

5. Quoted in Livingston (1997, p. 294). For other statements and examples attesting to this issue, see Neuman (1996), Seib (1997), and Livingston (1997).

6. For a history of communication technologies and their relationship to foreign policy, see Neuman (1996).

7. Parts of the schedule discussed in here is the schedule of CNN at the time of the town meeting broadcast.

8. The "CNN family of networks" includes the following:

CNN networks	Launch year
CNN	1980
CNN Headline News	1981
CNN Radio	1982
CNN International	1985
CNN World Report news exchange	1987
CNN Newsource	1987
Noticiero Telemundo—CNN	1988
CNN Airport Network	1992
CNN Interactive (Internet)	1995
CNNfn (Financial Network)	1995
CNN/SI (Sports Illustrated)	1996
CNN en Español	1997

Note. From Flournoy & Stewart, 1997, p. 3.

9. For an insightful analysis of marketing strategies by media corporations, see McAllister (2000).

10. The story of the alleged sexual misconduct by the president completely eclipsed the coverage of the "crisis in the Gulf." But in a move that complicated the conduct of foreign policy considerably, Hollywood released a film *(Wag the Dog)* in which a president, with the help of a Hollywood producer, fabricates a war in order to detract from his sexual scandal. The "Wag the Dog factor" was a serious dilemma for the president. Here is a report from the *Washington Post* by Fred Hiatt (1998), describing the foreign policy dilemma:

But the president's tough words [for Saddam Hussein], in an interview with PBS's Jim Lehrer, like the crisis itself, received almost no attention—because they came in the same interview as Clinton's first partial denial of having sex with a White House intern and inducing her to lie about it. That issue grabbed not only the headlines, but pretty much the whole rest of the paper, too. Which sums up Clinton's dilemma here (or, at least, one of his dilemmas). The time has come for the United States to issue a clear ultimatum to Saddam Hussein and then, if he does not back down, to take military action, with or without allies. But if the president does so now, who will believe—here or overseas—that he is not just creating a crisis to keep Kenneth Starr at bay?

Are we not justified reading this move by Hollywood as a revenge on the news industry by the entertainment industry?

11. Fallows (1996), in his illuminating essay on the public and their view of the press, discusses the consequences of the proliferation of "reporter talk shows."

REFERENCES

Balz, D., & Harris, J. (1998, February 19). Hostility disrupts favored Clinton forum. *Washington Post*. Retrieved March 22, 1998, from LexisNexis online database (News Library).

Baudrillard, J. (1995). *The Gulf War did not take place*. Bloomington: Indiana University Press.

Bennet, J. (1998, February 19). Bad vibes from the heartland launch fleet of finger-pointers. *New York Times*. Retrieved March 22, 1998, from LexisNexis online database (News Library).

Bennett, W. L. (1989). Marginalizing the majority: Conditioning public opinion to accept managerial democracy. In M. Margolis & G. Mauser (Eds.), *Manipulating public opinion* (pp. 320–361). Pacific Grove, CA: Brooks/Cole.

Bennett, W. L., & Manheim, J. (1993). Taking the public by storm: Information, cuing, and the democratic press in the Gulf Conflict. *Political Communication, 10*, 331–351.

Brown, C. H. (1967). *The correspondents' war*. New York: Charles Scribner's Sons.

Browne, N. (1987). Political economy of television (super) text. In H. Newcomb (Ed.), *Television: The critical view* (4th ed., pp. 585–599). New York: Oxford University Press.

Chomsky, N. (1991). *Deterring democracy*. London: Verso Books.

Dayan, D., & Katz, E. (1994). Defining media events: High holidays of mass communication. In Horace Newcomb (Ed.), *Television: The critical view* (5th ed., pp. 332–351). New York: Oxford University Press.

Denton, R., & Holloway, R. (1996). Clinton and the town hall meetings: Mediated conversation and the risk of being "in touch." In R. Denton, Jr., and R. Holloway (Eds.), *The Clinton presidency: Images, issues, and communication strategies* (pp. 17–41). London: Praeger.

Doane, M. A. (1990). Information, crisis, catastrophe. In P. Mellencamp (Ed.), *Logics of television* (pp. 222–239). Bloomington: Indiana University Press.

Erlanger, S. (1998a, February 16). Trying to schedule a war presents logistical problems. *New York Times*. Retrieved March 22, 1998, from LexisNexis online database (News Library).

Erlanger, S. (1998b, February 19). Top Clinton aides find doubt on Iraq at campus in Ohio. *New York Times*. Retrieved March 22, 1998, from LexisNexis online database (News Library).

Fallows, J. (1996, February). Why Americans hate the media. *Atlantic Monthly, 45–64*.

Flournoy, D., & Stewart, R. (1997). *CNN: Making news in the global market*. London: University of Luton Press.

Gellman, B. (1998, February 19). U.S. officials heckled at Iraq seminar. *Washington Post*. Retrieved March 22, 1998, from LexisNexis online database (News Library).

Goodman, W. (1998, February 21). On sex and on bombs: A time for irresolution. *New York Times*. Retrieved March 22, 1998, from LexisNexis online database (News Library).

Herman, E. (1993). The media's role in U.S. foreign policy. *Journal of International Affairs, 47*(1), 23–45.

Hiatt, F. (1998, January 25). . . . And a crisis in Iraq. *Washington Post.* Retrieved March 22, 1998, from LexisNexis online database (News Library).

Kerbel, M. (1994). *Edited for television.* Boulder, CO: Westview Press.

Livingston, S. (1997). Beyond the "CNN effect": The media–foreign policy dynamic. In P. Norris (Ed.), *Politics and the press: The news media and their influence* (pp. 291–318). London: Lynne Rienner.

Livingston, S., & Eachus, T. (1995). Humanitarian crises and U.S. foreign policy: Somalia and the CNN effects reconsidered. *Political Communication, 12,* 413–429.

Malek, A. (1988). New York Times' editorial position and the U.S. foreign policy: The case of Iran. *Gazette: International Journal for Mass Communication Studies, 42,* 105–119.

Malek, A. (Ed.) (1997). *News media and foreign relations: A multifaceted perspective.* Norwood, NJ: Ablex.

McAllister, M. (2000). From flick to flack: The increased emphasis on marketing by media entertainment corporations. In R. Anderson and L. A. Strate (Eds.), *Critical studies in media commercialism* (pp. 101–122). New York: Oxford University Press.

Mellencamp, P. (1990a). *Indiscretions: Avant-garde film, video, and feminism.* Bloomington: Indiana University Press.

Mellencamp, P. (1990b). TV time and catastrophe, or beyond the pleasure principle of television. In P. Mellencamp (Ed.), *Logics of television* (pp. 240–266). Bloomington: Indiana University Press.

Meredith, R. (1998, February 19). 6,000 Ohioans prove to be a tougher audience than Congress. *New York Times.* Retrieved March 22, 1998, from LexisNexis online database (News Library).

Morris, M. (1990). Banality in cultural studies. In P. Mellencamp (Ed.), *Logics of television* (pp. 14–43). Bloomington: Indiana University Press.

Morris, M. (1993). Panorama: The live, the dead, and the living. In G. Turner (Ed.), *Nation, culture, text: Australian cultural and media studies* (pp. 19–58). New York: Routledge.

Morse, M. (1986). The television news personality and credibility: Reflections on the news in transition. In T. Modleski (Ed.), *Studies in entertainment: Critical approaches to mass culture* (pp. 55–79). Bloomington: Indiana University Press.

Morse, M. (1990). An ontology of everyday distraction: The freeway, the mall, and television. In P. Mellencamp (Ed.), *Logics of television* (pp. 191–221). Bloomington: Indiana University Press.

Mowlana, H. (1997). The media and foreign policy: A framework for analysis. In A. Malek (Ed.), *News media and foreign relations: A multifaceted perspective* (pp. 29–41). Norwood, NJ: Ablex.

Neuman, J. (1996). *Lights, camera, war: Is media technology driving international politics?* New York: St. Martin's Press.

Nimmo, D. (1994). The electronic town hall in campaign '92: Interactive forum or carnival of Buncombe. In R. Denton, Jr. (Ed.), *The 1992 presidential campaign: A communication perspective* (pp. 207–226). London: Praeger.

Prince, S. (1993). Celluloid heroes and smart bombs: Hollywood at war in the Middle East. In R. Denton, Jr. (Ed.), *The media and the Persian Gulf War* (pp. 235–256). London: Praeger.

Said, E. (1988). *Covering Islam: How the media and the expert determine how we see the rest of the world.* New York: Pantheon.

Sayyid, B. S. (1997). *A fundamental fear: Eurocentrism and the emergence of Islam.* London: Zed Books.

Schweid, B. (1998, February 19). Albright defends U.S. policy on Iraq. *Washington Post.* Retrieved March 22, 1998, from LexisNexis online database (News Library).

Schwoch, J., White, M., & Reilly, S. (1992). *Media knowledge: Readings in popular culture, pedagogy, and critical citizenship.* Albany: State University of New York Press.

Seib, P. (1997). *Headline diplomacy: How news coverage affects foreign policy.* London: Praeger.

Shapiro, M. J. (1997). *Violent cartographies: Mapping cultures of war.* Minneapolis: University of Minnesota Press.

Sturken, M. (1995). The television image and collective amnesia: Dis(re)membering the Persian Gulf War. In P. d'Agostino and D. Tafler (Eds.), *Transmission: Toward a post-television culture* (pp. 135–149). Thousand Oaks, CA: Sage.

To many abroad, public forum a fiasco. (1998, February 19). *USA Today.* Retrieved March 22, 1998, from Lexis-Nexis online database (News Library).

Turner, C., Daniszewski, J., & Wright, R. (1998, February 23). UN, Iraq reach an 11th-hour deal. Retrieved March 22, 1998, from LexisNexis online database (News Library).

U.S. policy on Iraq draws fire in Ohio. (1998, February 19). *CNN Online.* Retrieved March 22, 1998, from the World Wide Web: http://www.cnn.com/WORLD/9802/18/town.meeting.folo/index.html

Virilio, P. (1986). *Speed and politics.* New York: Semiotext(e).

Wark, M. (1994). *Virtual geography: Living with global media events.* Bloomington: Indiana University Press.

Žižek, S. (1993). *Tarrying with the negative: Kant, Hegel, and the critique of ideology.* Durham, NC: Duke University Press.

13

✵

Patterns in Global Communication: Prospects and Concerns

LEO A. GHER

Leo A. Gher (MS, Southern Illinois University at Carbondale) is associate professor and director of the Brown Media Management Lab, Southern Illinois University at Carbondale. A Fulbright Fellow to Croatia, a former chief executive of an international media corporation, and a chief financial officer of a wireless company, he is CEO of Avery Media International, whose clients include Arab Radio and TV, Egyptian Radio and Television, ENOKI—Japan, Lithuanian Broadcasting, and others. Gher was the organizer of Global Fusion 2000 conference. In addition to published articles and book chapters, he has coedited (with H. Amin) *Civic Discourse and Digital Age Communications in the Middle East* and authored *Digital Media and the Arab World: Millennium Issues for a New World Order.*

O n February 2, 1996, the United States Congress passed a laissez-faire Communications Act, which was the manifest beginning of a new world order for global media. This American legislation was not the democratizing revolution of the information age envisioned by the writers of the 1980 *MacBride Report,* but it was a sign of things to come. In the era of broadcasting just past, traditional networks dominated the distribution systems of sovereign nations. CBS was the model in the United States; the BBC, in the United Kingdom; Gostelradio, in the Soviet Union; and in such countries as China, India, Finland, Egypt, and many others, communications networks were ruled or regulated by

 For additional online resources, access the Global Media Monitor Web site that accompanies this book on the Wadsworth Communication Cafe Web site at http://communication.wadsworth.com.

governmental institutions. Although it is true that certain programs from one country were often aired on other nation's systems, the control of content was always held within state bureaucracies or by the citizen-owners of the nation. As the new millennium began, a de facto free marketplace consisted of dominant, global communications networks that are accountable only to corporate stockholders or the chief executive officers of international conglomerates.

The passage of the 1996 Communications Act is a somewhat arbitrary benchmark, given that many of the world's entertainment giants have, for a long time, been busy creating deals in preparation for their piece of a world-network entertainment oligarchy. The original visionary of global media, Ted Turner, saw the future of a new world order when he created CNN in June 1980. Rupert Murdoch followed suit in Australia, India, and the United Kingdom, and so too have such companies as Time Warner, Viacom, Disney, and Westinghouse.

But in recent years, unique superplayers have emerged on the world stage, mainly through protective mergers or hostile acquisitions. Vertical business cartels have been formed to secure capital or dominate a marketplace: telephone companies have joined with television networks; entertainment giants have merged with online powerhouses; banking conglomerates have united with cable operators; computer software interests have partnered with satellite distributors. Other companies have forged horizontal alliances to control specialized business sectors: a telephone company from one nation consolidates resources with a similar business in another nation, or two, or three. One clear example of a new-world-order communications merger took place in 1995, when Arab Media Corporation joined forces with the Kirch Television of Germany, Saudi prince Waleed Ben Talal (owner of EuroDisney), and the Richardson Broadcasting Consortium of South Africa to provide capital for a venture called MultiChoice. According to the *International Herald Tribune,* the group's first act was to purchase a majority interest in the media properties of film-television mogul and president of Italy, Silvio Berlusconi. This entertainment consortium has extended its reach to five continents. It also owns several of the world's largest film, television, and music libraries, and it controls entertainment production, distribution, and exhibition facilities all over the world. An example of horizontal partnering occurred in the winter of 2000 when Britain's Vodafone AirTouch acquired Germany's Mannesmann for US$163 billion, the highest-valued merger/takeover at the time (Ewing & Kunii, 2000).

The information revolution, at least our generation's information revolution, seems to have come to a denouement, appropriately enough, in the final days of the 20th century. Some future historian will probably place its life span within the final 25 years of the second millennium of the Christian calendar. It has been called it a global movement, but of course all information revolutions (newspaper, telegraph, telephone, cinema, radio, television) have had a significant planetary impact. That this revolution, or any of its immediate forerunners, will have had a greater impact on humanity than Gutenberg's printing press is highly unlikely.

However, this information revolution has indeed had profound effects on the world community, and certainly, recent changes in entertainment and information services have occurred at a faster pace than ever before. But societies everywhere are now faced with four critical questions about the meaning of such change: Is humanity better off as a result of the transformation? Who are the winners and the losers? What immediate concerns should industry leadership address? And what are the prospects for the future development of media and communication in the new world order?

The purpose of this concluding chapter of this book is threefold. First, the status of the communication industry's global infrastructure will be reviewed; second, issues of privacy and information warfare will be examined; and third, the interdependent connections of global economics, transnational media corporations, and vanishing national culture in 21st-century media will be explored.

THE STATUS OF INFRASTRUCTURE
IN THE COMMUNICATIONS INDUSTRY

The term *information revolution* is often misunderstood, and to some people, it is intrinsically confusing. Different writers have called this time of change the communications age or the era of new media. Some authors have dubbed it the computer generation, and of course, there's the popular designation *information superhighway.* Nicholas Negroponte probably described it most appropriately when he called it the digital revolution, because the fundamentals of this latest paradigm shift may be found in the transformation from mechanical and analog information processing to digital processing. No matter what industry sector is examined— radio or television, Internet or intranet, telephony, hobby games, e-commerce, or computerization—a majority of communication businesses are now, or will shortly be, supported by a digital infrastructure. One of the most important developments of the digital revolution has been wireless technology, first achieved through the use of global satellites. These space-based systems are now the established infrastructure of the modern global communications industry.

The Global Satellite System

In 1965 the first commercial satellite was launched into orbit. With the rollout of services, that initial geosynchronous satellite could handle only 240 voice circuits at a single time. Orbiting satellites now carry approximately 40% of transnational voice traffic and virtually all television exchange among countries. Throughout 1998 and 1999, numerous personal communications satellite systems were launched, using low earth orbits (LEOs), which minimize transmission delays. John Evans (1998) reports that three to five voice-type satellite systems and possibly a dozen data-oriented systems could begin operations. At the beginning of the new millennium, more than 200 geostationary satellites and more than 150 LEO satellites orbited the earth, constituting a planetary infrastructure fully capable of providing direct voice, data, radio, and television services to the 6 billion citizens of the planet (Ricardo's Geo-Orbit 2000).

In the past few years the communications satellite industry has witnessed the largest buildup of space-based potential in its history. These satellites provide commercial C, FSS Ku, BSS Ku, and L band services around the world and presently house an estimated 5,000 transponders. In addition, Iridium had launched all of its 66 satellites into low earth orbit before filing for Chapter 11 reorganization, while Globalstar and Orbcomm are also providing LEO constellation satellite services. More satellites were launched in the 1990s than in the industry's 43-year history. Currently, more than 50% of the world's in-orbit transponders are C-band transponders, but the Ku-band frequency is the preferred frequency for future projects because launch protocols are simpler and less costly. Some satellite providers will use Ka-band frequencies to link their LEO satellite system to downlink gateways and for intersatellite communication between spacecraft (Boeke & Fernandez, 1999).

Asia–Pacific Rim

A number of prominent satellites have been established to serve the Asia–Pacific region. They include *AsiaSat, InSat, KoreaSat, NStar, Palapa, APStar, MeaSat, Thaicom, IntelSat 801, ChinaStar, SinoSat,* and *Telkom,* among others. During the 1990s more satellites were ordered for the Asia-Pacific Rim than for any other part of the world, and the Peoples Republic of China launched several Western-built satellites to increase its national capacity. Japan owns the most domestic satellites, and two Japanese businesses are preparing to launch trans-Pacific satellites in the immediate future. More than 20 satellites serve as trans-Pacific or trans-Indian links, joining North America and Europe to Asia (Boeke & Fernandez, 1996).

The Middle East

In the Middle East, NileSat, *Amos 1,* and the ArabSat DBS (direct broadcast satellite) platform have added considerable capacity to information and entertainment services. Arab countries have participated in IntelSat for many years, but primary service is provided by the Arab Satellite Communications Organization (ArabSat), which includes Algeria, Bahrain, Djibouti, Iraq, Jordan, Kuwait, Lebanon, Libya, Mauritania, Morocco, Oman, Qatar, Somalia, Sudan, Syria, Tunisia, the Palestine Liberation Organization, the United Arab Emirates, Yemen, South Yemen, Saudi Arabia, and Egypt. Because of increased demand for transponders, several generations of ArabSat birds (or satellites) have been put into operation; most of these satellites offer 34 transponders each (22 C-band and 12 Ku-Band), with an expected life span of 12 years (Amin, 1996). ArabSat services include news exchanges, educational broadcasting, emergency communications, domestic telecommunications, and data transmission such as email and newspaper publications (al-Saadon, 1990).

Africa

Historically, Africa has been the most neglected market for space-based communications services, but the players within the continent have been stimulated by PanAmSat's *PAS 4* satellite, which began beaming programming from its high-powered Ku-band downlink to South Africa. ArabSat also has some interest in the

African region, but mainly in the North, where Arabic is the predominant language. According to Boeke and Fernandez (1996), those who wish to use an African satellite will be required to share *IntelSat 805* as required by the Regional African Satellite Communication Organization. Africastar now offers DTH (direct-to-home) digital audio to the continent, and organizations or companies like IntelSat and PanAmSat are currently providing Africa with better and more high-power transmissions services.

Europe

In Europe, Nordic countries are developing several DTH Hot Birds for service in the eastern region, in part thanks to the high-power capacity of *Amos 1* and satellites owned by PanAmSat, IntelSat, and EutelSat. These satellite fleets make television, Internet, and telecommunications services available to smaller receivers. Europe, moreover, has always been the pioneer in the fields of DBS and DTH, and those services are flourishing throughout the continent. With more than 40 satellites in orbit and more waiting to be launched, Europe enjoys many choices and advanced services. The costs of such services, however, are the highest in the world. Popular satellites are the SES Astra fleet and EutelSat's Hot Birds, which are regularly sold out. Colocating satellites in the same orbital slot is popular in Europe because customers can access more network programming with a single antenna. Presently, six Astra birds are at 19.2°E, with two additional satellites ready to join that constellation, and by employing its consortium power, EutelSat is gaining on its competition with the Hot Bird slot at 13.0°E, where five satellites provide DTH programming ("*Via Satellite*'s global satellite survey," 1996).

South America

Argentina, Brazil, and Mexico have satellite systems in operation, and Argentina and Brazil have new satellites on order that will provide expanded coverage. Latin America is sustained by a variety of trans-Atlantic satellites, including, among others, 11 IntelSat and 2 PanAmSat birds, and thanks to the continued deregulation of the telecommunications sector, Argentina is becoming the region's satellite center. For the most part, individual users are also permitted to access IntelSat directly, a growing trend for several countries on the continent. This enlightened policy is making life easier for entrepreneurial corporations in the satellite industry, which provides financial growth and business opportunity for the nations involved.

North America

The North American satellite scene has been changing rapidly and is undergoing a dramatic transformation in the opening years of the new millennium. The often-discussed World Trade Organization agreement has opened up the telecommunications market for a variety of services from different countries, and the formation of a Pan-American market for satellite services has emerged. United States and Latin American operators are forming partnerships; Canadian companies are offering services to U.S. businesses, and U.S. satellites have been authorized to cover Canada at the same time. The United States, nevertheless, continues to monopolize the North American satellite market, and it claims more geosynchronous satellites and more C-band and Ku-band transponders than any other country.

In 1996 the U.S. Federal Communications Commission made preparatory authorizations to empower AT&T, Hughes, and General Electric to go ahead with expansion arrangements. In 1997, *Loral, Orion, GE 4,* and *EchoStar* were certified to serve the domestic market, and *TeleSat,* Canada's Nimiq DBS bird, was forced, for competitive reasons, to seek partnerships with other DBS service providers (Boeke & Fernandez, 1999). Hughes/PanAmSat, GE Americom, and Loral Skynet have expanded beyond their traditional American market to Europe, Latin America, and the Asia-Pacific and have satellite fleets that rival the IntelSat system. North America, the Asia–Pacific region, and Europe are now in a virtual tie in the number of satellites serving each region.

Compressed digital satellite technology has become the true success story of the communications revolution. Where once transoceanic cables provided the industry's primary infrastructure, orbital satellite systems currently dominate. As Boeke and Fernandez (1999) report, "Satellites are blanketing all areas of the world, both developed and developing. In this sense, satellites already do and will continue to provide backbone telecommunications connectivity around the world" (p. 5).

More satellites will be launched in the first decade of the 21st century, of course, but the industry is entering a period of maturation in which second- and third-generation technologies are being implemented. Businesses are experiencing a transformation from geostationary-based systems to low-earth-orbit constellations, and many governmental operators are exiting the market, either by auctioning off, privatizing, or not replacing existing satellites. As a result, the market for space-based telecommunications services will become highly commercialized, providing ubiquitous coverage around the world.

Global Internet Services

As the new millennium begins, the Internet is undeniably bound to national telephone systems, which are unevenly distributed around the globe, and attempts to measure the infrastructure of the Internet are difficult at best. The preeminent economies[1] of such nations as the United States, Canada, England, Japan, and Germany have perfected sophisticated, fiber-optic telephone (and cable) infrastructures, which support high-speed connectivity and full penetration of the market, and digital wireless systems are becoming more and more popular in all developed countries.

In a Nua survey in 2001, the global population of online users of the Internet had reached 407.1 million. The United States and Canada accounted for almost 167 million users, or 41% of the online population. The United Kingdom, Japan, and Germany made up the other 5 highest-ranked wired nations of the world, and the next top 10 countries were Australia, France, Sweden, Italy, Spain, the Netherlands, Taiwan, China, Finland, and Norway—this total group accounted for 90% of the universe (Nua, 1999). In other words, the remaining 195 sovereign nations garnered only 10% of the world's online population. Totals for online user populations in other parts of the world are Africa, 2.6 million; Asia–Pacific, 69 million; and South America, 10.7 million (Nua, 2000).

Efforts to systematically gauge the size and status of the Internet at any specific moment are tricky—the mere act of stopping to measure causes inaccuracies in the measurement. Down through the years, the growth of the Internet was estimated at a somewhat steady 10% per month. But in 1994, Internet growth exploded. Given a comparable sustained growth rate, aggregate worldwide users of the Internet should exceed 700 million by 2005 (Nua, 1999).

In the first statistically valid research of Internet users, O'Reilly and Associates reported that in the United States "the total number of users who have direct Internet access is 5.8 million" (Peck, 1995). Out of approximately 100 million American households, virtually all (99%) have a telephone connection, and at the close of the 20th century the number of U.S. households with home computers was estimated to have surpassed 60 million, with 45 million having access to Internet services (Quarterman, 1996). With the implementation of PCS (personal communication services) technology in 1997, maximized penetration of telephone and television services, and the utilization of computer convergence technology, the United States has become the first fully integrated digital telecommunication market in the world.

However, the picture is far different for both expectant and base economies of the world. Investment in communication infrastructure is considerably slower, and the growth of the essential components (computer accessibility, telephony networks, new media technology, and Internet connectivity) to give their citizenry access to online services is far behind countries with preeminent or developed economies. Nonetheless, some expectant economies have had balanced growth in the number of people linking to the Internet. One regional example of slow growth is the Middle East, where, according to the Dabbagh Information Technology Group, an estimated 72% of users now access the Internet at home. The report also states that 22% go online primarily at work, 4% at academic institutions, and 2% in cybercafes (DITnet, 1999). In its entirety, however, only 1.9 million people in the Middle East are now online, which is approximately 0.5% of its population of 350 million (Nua, 2000). But new media services are being introduced. Telephone long-distance lines grew around 10% a year over the last decade, with the highest growth in Egypt and Oman. Around 80% of the current capacity of the local telephone networks in the Arab world is already being used; 95% are automatic switching systems, with 50% of that group being digital. The international traffic for telegrams and telexes services has declined 50% and 40%, respectively, over the last 10 years, but international telephone traffic has increased 150%. Saudi Arabia and the United Arab Emirates are among the busiest countries in the world in this respect (Gher & Amin, 1999).

At the end of 1999, Arab states had an average of 4 telephone lines per 100 inhabitants, which is approximately one tenth of the average in developed countries. This ratio varies in the region from a high of 30:100 in the United Arab Emirates to less than 1:100 in the Sudan. Most Arab states rely heavily on coaxial-cabled telephone lines to link computer owners to the Internet. Many regions of the world are like the Middle East, where communications infrastructure progress has been piecemeal, growing only at an arithmetic pace. This unhurried pace is a problem and will cause a sharp economic crisis for expectant or base economies, because nations with preeminent or developed economies are growing at a geometric pace, and, obviously, the gap is widening moment by moment.

Nations with base economies are another matter altogether. Most sub-Saharan Africa countries and much of Asia, excluding Pacific Rim nations and India, are without up-to-date telephone infrastructure. Such countries face many difficult problems: unemployment remains high; the number of poor continues to rise; and many people have yet to share in the fruits of even 20th-century economics (World Bank, 1999). Countries with base economies are now confronted by inexorable worldwide dynamics. As World Bank economist, John Page, argues, "the global economy is developing so rapidly that nations or regions that fail to make the required structural adjustment to compete for market share and capital investment are now liable to remain irrevocably poor" (Miller, 1996). On the other hand, some signs of optimism may be found. Once low-earth-orbit satellite systems become fully operational, both expectant economies and base economies will be able to bypass the enormous build-out costs of land-based communications infrastructure and will be capable of entering the new world order with one quantum leap to space-based communications systems.

To say the least, global telecommunications has been transformed. Developed nations, world news services, and international business conglomerates have taken advantage of digital technologies and are far ahead of most other countries. The communication revolution is no longer a revolution—it has reached a state of maturation. Electronics manufacturers, of course, will build better toys, terrestrial broadcasters will implement high-definition television, Microsoft and Apple will redesign computer operating systems over and over, and marketers will create a never-ending demand for new products—but the basics of compressed, digital technologies are now well established and widely accepted.

PRIVACY AND INFORMATION WARFARE

With an elemental shift of life cycle to maturation, the communications industry now faces two intriguing and pointed issues—privacy and information warfare. In a 1928 judgment, Justice Louis Brandeis wrote, "The evil incident to invasion of the privacy of the telephone is far greater than that involved in tampering with the mails." The transformation from analog to digital, or from wired to wireless technologies, does not lessen the concerns about privacy and information warfare.

In the 1990s the Federal Bureau of Investigate (FBI) initiated several programs that would not only ensure access to digital infrastructures but would also increase the government's ability to capture communications of all kinds. The earliest projects were designed to inspect digital telephone and pager communications, but later activities have been extended proportionately with the increased use of the Internet. Many U.S. lawmakers were appropriately cautious about institutionalizing such projects, but European governmental and police groups took up the idea quickly (Rogers, 1999).

Governmental Intrusion

For more than a decade, news sources have informed the public about a surveillance system called Echelon, which has been cooperatively operated by the security services of the United States, the United Kingdom, Canada, Australia, and New Zealand. Under a covenant known as UKUSA, the system entitles these countries to observe and analyze telephone, fax, email, and Internet communications. Echelon is, of course, able to monitor email and e-commerce from any part of the world, but the huge volume of messaging makes it impossible to scrutinize individual messages. To solve the problem, Echelon employs special computer programming known as a dictionary. The dictionary is programmed by security services to search communications for key words, special phrases, or names of senders and recipients. Currently, the five governments use different dictionaries, each with its own specialized set of parameters. When a communication is flagged for its content by any of the dictionaries, it is automatically singled out for detailed analysis.

Echelon monitoring terminals are located around the world. The New Zealand and Yakima, Washington, stations oversee trans-Pacific satellite traffic, while the Sugar Grove, Virginia, station, along with Morwenstow in Britain, watches the Atlantic region. The Geraldton, Australia, station monitors the southern Asia region and some trans-Pacific satellite communications, and the Shoal Bay, Darwin, station oversees most of the Southeast Asian territories. All Echelon terminals monitor geostationary satellites in the Clark Belt above the equator quite easily, but it is more difficult for the terminals to observe low-earth-orbit satellites such as those used in Iridium, Globalstar, and Orbcomm fleets.

Furthermore, domestic law that forbids government spying on its own citizenry has been one barrier for the Echelon group to overcome. Member nations circumvent this problem by simply spying for each other, then handing over intriguing data to partner nations. Because much of the process is automated, the system is open to abuse. It is estimated that 80% of the intercepted communications at the Geraldton station are forwarded to the CIA (Central Intelligence Agency) or NSA (National Security Agency) in Washington, D.C., without ever being examined locally.

Initial funding for Echelon was authorized during the Cold War era, when the Soviet Union was seen as an eminent danger to Western democracies. That threat, of course, has greatly diminished, but the system was expanded in the 1990s when organized crime and drugs cartels were targeted for investigation. The end of the Cold War has moved national attention from the capitalist—communist ideological war to the economic battlefront, in which information is the new currency. There is evidence that much of the surveillance being carried out by the UKUSA group is now economic in nature and that the sharing of data is selective. Countries, organizations, and even individuals not within the Echelon alliance are at risk, and are subject to abuses of privacy law.

The U.S. government, meanwhile, has been in the process of establishing a 21st-century electronic surveillance system called FIDNet (Federal Intrusion Detection Network) that would monitor government computer systems and communications networks for any signs of international terrorist hacker attacks. Data assembled would be sent to the FBI, which would then thwart the hacker attacks. The process could easily be extended to the private sector ("EPIC Warns," 1999). If government funding is appropriated, the Justice Department could, hypothetically, observe anyone's computer or communications network as part of its efforts to insulate federal computers.

Invasion of privacy in the digital age is not the exclusive franchise of governments; corporations are just as culpable. Recently, Microsoft began shipping communication software that permitted their operators to chat with America Online (AOL) users. AOL immediately revised its software to limit messages from hacker attacks. AOL and Microsoft redesigned their software on an hour-to-hour basis— AOL to impede, Microsoft to circumvent. Cisco Systems, in another part of cyberspace, carelessly let it be known that their QoS (quality of service) programming could be sorted to block access to particular Internet activities. Open access groups are worried that anti–open access groups might use Cisco's QoS software to block cable modem users from seeing specific Web sites.

In another interesting development, Wink Technologies has been partnering with dozens of broadcast, satellite, cable, and television companies that plan to include Wink technology in future consumer products. The reason these companies are attracted to Wink is that its software has the capacity to monitor user behaviors: viewing habits, online surfing actions, and even purchasing trends. After monitoring, Wink programming directs the data back to whoever is paying for the service. The idea is to focus highly targeted advertising or direct marketing to online users. In sum, the federal government hopes to spy on its population to protect it from transnational crackers; AOL wants to safeguard its online customers from Microsoft programmers and constricted access to Web sites by Cicso System hackers; and Wink Technologies is creating software that makes it simple for content providers to gather information on everyone (Rogers, 1999).

International Information Warfare

For the citizens of the 21st century, working in a global network of electronic commerce and online information, future war is not likely to come from a nuclear bomb or environmental disaster but by email. Computer hackers can spread cyber viruses that strike without warning, destroying a company's sensitive files, and cyber terrorists can scatter propaganda around the world in microseconds using the World Wide Web. In both the near term and the long term, cyber attacks will be the price paid for the freedom to surf the information superhighway. It is not a case of whether it will happen but when. An individual or a group hoping to cause damage now has the capability to incapacitate and cripple society without firing a single shot or launching a lone missile.

For many years, techno-evangelists have been hyping the benefits of the digital age, but they have steadfastly turned a blind eye to its hazards, and recently the online community has been visited by the dark side of the World Wide Web. With premeditation, crackers have constructed viruses that have disrupted and damaged governments and businesses on a planetary scale. The Chernobyl Sleeper virus rested silently and submissively in computer systems for months, before activating itself on the anniversary of the Russian nuclear accident. The Melissa virus, on the other hand, hit like a lightning bolt. Acquiring access through email, this destructive virus flooded the recipient's PC and destroyed files, before replicating itself across the Internet ("EPIC Warns," 1999). In the summer of 2000, the innocuous Love Bug virus attacked computers on every continent. After a worldwide investigation to find the perpetrators of this electronic disease, it was determined that the program's creators posted the virus on the World Wide Web by accident, an accident that caused $10 billion in damage to businesses and individuals everywhere.

Showing off for their peers by breaking into secured targets is the initial goal of most computer hackers, but many malevolent crackers in cyberspace are out to do serious damage. For example, Irish Republican Army (IRA) supporters at the University of Texas revealed details of British army bases in Northern Ireland on the Internet. In denial-of-service attacks, Tamil Tigers swamped Sri Lanka's embassies with email, causing their computer systems to crash. During the Serbian bombing campaign of 1999, NATO computers were attacked by a daily flood of 2,500 virus-laden emails. The United States may be the world's only superpower, but it has been particularly susceptible to cyber attacks. The U.S. Defense Department registered 250,000 attacks on its Web sites in 1996 alone; 62% were successful. The defense establishment struggles against more than 80 similar assaults every week, and the U.S. government, as a countermeasure, has committed more than $2.3 billion a year to protect its computer networks from sabotage (Rogers, 1999). Most developed nations of the world are following the U.S. lead, and many experts now suggest that the next e-market boom will be driven by corporations specializing in e-security, rather than those focusing on e-commerce, operating systems providers, or software programming.

International Debate Concerning
Free Access to New Media

In many expectant and base economies, information cannot be freely exchanged via the Internet. While claiming to protect the public from pornography or cultural invasion, many of these nations tightly control the right of entry to modern entertainment and information services. The governments of Saudi Arabia, Tunisia, Bahrain, Iran, and the United Arab Emirates, for example, block access to some foreign television channels and Web sites. Iraq and Libya have not yet linked to the Internet, and Syria, the only country in the Middle East that has made physical connection to the World Wide Web, has prohibited local access to its citizens.

But the outgrowth of tools to counter censorship and defeat surveillance—tools such as encryption, anonymous remailing, anticensorship proxy servers, and wireless communications—seems to be outpacing the machinery of government control. Moreover, many people in countries where media censorship is enforced are already using the Internet to overcome restraints on information. Local organizations are disseminating news more effectively than ever, newspapers are posting stories online that were censored in print editions, and cybercafes are appearing everywhere in nations that restrict home access to the Internet.

GLOBAL ECONOMICS, TRANSNATIONAL MEDIA CORPORATIONS, AND VANISHING CULTURE

During the past 25 years, many changes have occurred that require fresh thinking about the new world order in the communication industry and about global economics and cultural identity. Humanity is entering a post–communications revolution period, a time filled with punctuated uncertainties. Ideas and beliefs, organizations and institutions, are being metamorphosed—they shift, they crack, and they break apart, and it is natural for people to feel great stress and a desire to return to the past, when the old certainties were the foundations of society, economics, and government. But in this new millennium, the community of nations cannot rebuild the past.

As we enter this period, societies are being driven in two opposing directions. A constricting force drives people into isolation, and an expanding force drives economies toward globalization. The dynamics of constriction are created by the ethnocentric and populist themes of lost cultural identity and a return to traditional values, while the dynamics of expansion are being powered by transnational commercialism and a new media environment.

The breakup of the Soviet Union in 1989 may be seen as a case study of the constricting force at work. Such countries as Estonia, Latvia, Lithuania, and Poland, among others, wished to break away from their domineering commonwealth to revitalize a lost national unity and to rediscover their cultural identity. At the end of the 1990s, Yugoslavia followed a similar pattern, when such countries as Slovenia, Croatia, Bosnia-Herzegovina, and Albania severed their relationship with another overlord to reinstitute their own national character. In the summer of 2000, native Fijians insisted that Fiji must be governed only by the indigenous peoples of the islands; Isatubu peoples sought independence from the Solomon Islands; Tamil tribes fought for freedom from Sri Lanka; and other comparable battles were waged in many regions of the world. It is an easily recognizable and very old pattern of society—it is the reawakening of tribalism.

Cultural Impact

Concerns expressed by peoples outside of Western civilization about the digital age are genuine and valid. As seen through their eyes, the consistent flow of pop-culture media from the West is a threat to their culture and traditions. Although such tensions have existed for hundreds of years, the sudden and addictive impact of videogames, music CDs, computer software, stereotyping films, racial profiling, and Western television programming has intensified the defensiveness of societies in many countries. Such societies are notably protective of old traditions, religious proprieties, and conservative values and are justifiably proud of their cultural legacies, preserved through the use of language, customs, culture, and their own media (Schleifer, 1992). Numerous countries have responded to this infiltration, imagined or real, through severe rules of censorship. In the West, freedom of expression is a basic right, protected by constitutional authority. But in many nations outside the Western sphere of influence, this type of censorship is easily tolerated, even expected, as a form of civic responsibility within a legitimate social framework.

For peoples of non-Western heritage, stereotyping in film and television continues to be a source of cultural, religious, and ethnic degradation. Although such stereotyping itself is intrinsically harmful, the larger problem can be seen only in the context of American entertainment dominance. Nearly 90% of films and television programs exhibited worldwide are American in origin, and these entertainment products are the main perpetrators of stereotyping imagery. No peoples are exempt, but Arabs, Iranians, and Turks have been particularly villainized in American action-adventure films.

Economic Impact

Global economics and digital communications systems encourage sovereign states to expand their reach outward and to create external partnerships to compete in the contemporary economy. It has not always been that way, however. In the Cold War era, economics and politics were bipolar—the mainstay in the West was the United States, and in the East, it was the Soviet Union. Both superpowers were willing to accept the responsibility of being the wellspring for international economics. For example, after World War II, American economic policy provided billions of dollars to Germany and Japan to rebuild their economies. That plan continued in the last half of the 20th century in the form of balance-of-trade policy. The 1995 U.S. deficit of $145 billion was the mirror image of the Japanese trade surplus of $130 billion. All Pacific Rim countries (the Asian Tigers) made up the difference, but the fundamentals are the same—China's $17 billion trade deficit with Japan in 1994 was financed by its $20 billion surplus with the United States, and so on. In a similar manner, the USSR provided economic support for Eastern European client-states and many other countries. But with the collapse of the Soviet Union, the world was left with only one superpower and only one reservoir for global economics, the United States.

In recent years, many business experts have envisioned three major trading blocs (the European Union, NAFTA, and Pacific Rim partners) as substitutes for the old bipolar system. These trading blocs would be large enough to support expectant and base national economies, but the tripolar powers would have to be willing to finance the process, just as the United States and the USSR did after World War II. This has not occurred. To its credit, Germany has taken up the responsibility of resurrecting the East German economy, but Japan has been entirely unwilling to accept any negative balance of trade, however limited it might be. In their turn, Europe, Japan, the Asian Tigers, and now China have all used the American market to jump-start their economic and national development. But without easy access to global markets and modern communication systems, economic progress and growth are difficult if not impossible for countries with expectant or base economies. However, it should be obvious to all that the American market, as big as it is, cannot be the world's sole source of economic energy much longer.

At this time in history, the fundamental assets of capitalism—land, labor, natural resources, and cash—are entirely fungible; resources are moved unhindered and virtually instantly from country to country as needed. In a free market economy, any nation or consortium can compete if its fundamentals are in place, and the most important fundamental for creating economic wealth in today's economy is human brainpower. Such man-made, brainpower industries as electronic computing, information management, and telecommunications are already dominant in world marketplaces. All sovereign states must make key structural changes to meet the challenges of the coming brainpower revolution. No peoples are exempt—not those of Britain, Germany, Japan, Estonia, Fiji, India, Kenya, Egypt, Brazil, Vietnam, Russia, or America.

What is required for the man-made, brainpower economy of tomorrow? Free enterprise, an open market, an educated population, superior communications infrastructure, and 10,000 public and private sector partnerships are the key ingredients. This type of partnering is the linchpin for survival in future times.

CONCLUSION

As humankind enters the 21st century, it is facing a civilization with one superpower and numerous transnational media consortia, which are responsible to no sovereign state or world body. There are 3 preeminent economic powers and about 20 nations with developed economies—the clear winners of the information revolution. Some 50 sovereign states with expectant economies must make institutional or structural adjustments if they expect to compete in the marketplaces of the new world order. This leaves an estimated 150 nations with base economies as the undeniable losers of the information revolution, and with the constricting force fully active in the world, that number will increase over time as jingoistic groups break away from their current federal affiliations.

Civilization is changing, re-creating itself at a geometric pace, and the time lapse between each reconstruction is shrinking dramatically. Once the period of reconstruction proceeded at a millennium's pace, then in hundreds of years, then in decades, and now it has shrunk to less than a human life span. The next revolution will probably take less than 10 years to complete. Obviously, the kingdom of 1950s television has completely disappeared, and the "Tiffany network" of Walter Cronkite news has splintered into hundreds of information channels. How individuals use entertainment and information services has changed forever.

In the meantime, as a direct result of digital technology, individuals have given up a great deal of privacy, and nations have lost a considerable measure of security and sovereignty. It is clear that the utopian hopes for this recent information revolution have been only partially fulfilled. However, some wonderful advancements have been made. The planet has been encased by fleets of space-based satellites that have the capacity to provide entertainment and information services to the earth's entire population, and compressed, digital technology makes it cost effective for any nation or consortium to compete for commercial, financial, and industrial resources.

To be successful, the next revolution must build upon the infrastructure of the global electronic media now in place. The coming change will be a brainpower revolution, in which man-made resources will be used in every part of the world, not just in the West. Such a change will take leadership—a higher-level leadership—and institutional commitments from all to build a system of public-access computer networks. This goal can be achieved by making sure that digital telecommunication access is available everywhere. Individually owned or leased computer hardware would no longer be required; only a link to the public-access computer networks would be necessary. Online computing services would be priced as tiered rates of the telephone company. But such a system must be seen as a public commitment, not a private one, because the supply-demand protocols of free enterprise capitalism will not normally commit to long-term structural investments. Building roads, constructing sewers, laying telephone lines, launching satellites, and educating the population are the public responsibilities of local, national, and, in the near future, world governments. With such advanced communication networks, the job of educating "the other half" of the world's population may begin.

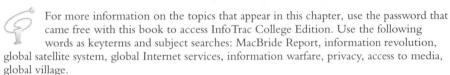 For more information on the topics that appear in this chapter, use the password that came free with this book to access InfoTrac College Edition. Use the following words as keyterms and subject searches: MacBride Report, information revolution, global satellite system, global Internet services, information warfare, privacy, access to media, global village.

QUESTIONS FOR DISCUSSION

1. Do you think that Marshall McLuhan's concept of the global village has been achieved? Why? Why not? Cite evidence from this chapter.

2. In what ways are Western media organizational strategies similar to or contrary to those of other regions of the world?

3. What economic growth patterns and telecommunication infrastructure support systems can you identify among the various regions of the world?

4. How have privacy rights and communications security been compromised at the beginning of the third millennium? Make two forecasts about the resolutions to these critical problems.

5. What are the cultural and religious repercussions of acquiring new electronic technology and media in developing countries?

NOTE

1. This writer favors redefining such expressions as *First World, Second World,* and *Third World* and *industrialized, developing,* and *underdeveloped* for characterizing the economies of the today's sovereign nations. The decision is not motivated by political correctness, but because the terms are anti-quated and lack meaning in the 21st-century economic world. More useful descriptors might be as follows:

■ *Preeminent economy*—a dominant world power in terms of gross domestic product (GDP), upon which other nations depend for commercial trade, market leadership, international security, and government stability. Examples are the United States, the United Kingdom, Germany, and Japan.

- *Developed economy*—a significant world leader in terms of GDP, upon which regional partner-nations rely for commerce, authority, constancy, and defense. Examples include the original members of the European Union, Canada, France, Scandinavian states, and the Asian Tigers.

- *Expectant economy*—a serious regional principal, with an uneven but normally

upward-trending GDP, often dominant in a specialized, business sector; administrative policy is frequently fluid. Examples are Poland, India, Mexico, Brazil, Saudi Arabia, and China.

- *Base economy*—a nation whose gross domestic product is stagnant or shrinking and that relies on the international community for aid; governmental institutions are unstable. Examples include most nations of sub-Saharan Africa, Afghanistan, Iraq, Cuba, the breakaway states of Indonesia, and Russia.

REFERENCES

Amin, H. Y. (1996). Broadcasting in the Arab World and the Middle East. In A. Wells (Ed.), *World Broadcasting*. London: General Hall Press.

Boeke, C., & Fernandez, R. (1996, July). A global satellite survey. *Via Satellite, 11*(7), 16–26.

Boeke, C., & Fernandez, R. (1999, July). Satellite trends and statistics, 1998. *Via Satellite, 14*(9), 18–29.

DITnet. (1999). Retrieved June 2000 from the World Wide Web: http://www.ditnet.co.ae/

EPIC warns that FBI surveillance plan marks the return of cold war mentality. (1999, August 2). *Multimedia Week, 8*(29).

Evans, John V. (1998, April). New satellites for personal communications. *Scientific American*, p. 70.

Ewing, J., & Kunii, I. M. (2000, May 22). DoCoMo rising. *Business Week— European Edition*, p. 18.

Gher, L. A., & Amin, H. Y. (1999, February). New and old media access and ownership in the Arab world. *Gazette, 61*(1), 61.

MIDS. (1996, March). Internet demographic survey. *Matrix Information and Directory Services, 6*, 3.

Miller, J. (1996). *God has ninety-nine names*. New York: Simon & Schuster.

The new Saudi press barons. (2000, June 11). *International Herald Tribune* (news release), p. 4.

Nua Internet Surveys. (1999, October). Retrieved March 2000 from the World Wide Web: http://www.nua.ie/surveys/

Nua Internet Surveys. (2000, March). Retrieved March 2000 from the World Wide Web: http://www.nua.ie/surveys/

Peck, D. (1995, October 31). Defining Internet opportunities. *O'Reilly and Associates, Online Research Group, 31.*

Quarterman, J. S. (1996, February). Third MIDS Internet demographic survey. *Matrix Information and Directory Services.*

Ricardo's Geo-Orbit. (2000, May). Global GEO Satellites. Retrieved June 2000 from the World Wide Web: http://www.geo-orbit.org

Rogers, G. K. (1999, July 22). Security versus privacy. *Bangkok Post.* Retrieved May 2000 from the World Wide Web: http://scoop.bangkokpost.co.th/bangkokpostnews/data070799/070799_database19.html

al-Saadon, H. T. (1990). The role of Arab-Sat in television program exchange in the Arab World (Doctoral dissertation, Ohio State University, 1990). *Dissertation Abstracts International, 59,* 4218A.

Schleifer, S. A. (1992). *Global media, the new world order, and the significance of failure: Media in the midst of war.* Cairo, Egypt: Adham Center Press.

Via Satellite's global satellite survey. (1996, July). *Phillips Business Information, 11*(7), 16–26.

World Bank. (1999, September). Middle East/North Africa Status Report, 1999. Retrieved June 2000 from the World Wide Web: http://wbln0018.worldbank.org/mna/mena.nsf

List of Acronyms

ABC: American Broadcasting Company

ABU: Asia–Pacific Broadcasting Union

AFP: Agence-France Presse

ANR: All News Radio

AP: Associated Press

APC: Association for Progressive Communication

APTN: Associated Press Television News

ArabSat: Arab Satellite Communications Organization (members are the 22 nations of the Arab League)

ASBU: Arab States Broadcasting Union

ASCO: Arab Satellite Communications Organization

ASEAN: Association of Southeast Asian Nations

AT&T: American Telephone and Telegraph

BBC: British Broadcasting Corporation

CANA: Caribbean News Agency

CARICOM: Caribbean Community

CBS: Columbia Broadcasting System

CBU: Caribbean Broadcasting Union

CCTV: China Central Television

CIA: Central Intelligence Agency

CIS: Commonwealth of Independent States

CNN: Cable News Network

CNNfn: CNN Financial Network

CNNI: CNN International

CNN/SI: CNN/Sports Illustrated

COE: Council of Europe

COMSAT: Communication Satellite Corporation

CSCE: Conference on Security and Co-operation in Europe

DBS: direct broadcast satellite

DJN: Dow Jones Newswires

DPA: Deutsche Press Agency

DTH: direct-to-home

DVD: digital video disc

DW-TV: Deutsche Welle Television

EBU: European Broadcasting Union

EC: European Community

EEC: European Economic Community

EU: European Community

EutelSat: European Telecommunications Satellite Organization

FAO: Food and Agriculture Organization

FCC: Federal Communications Commission

FDI: foreign direct investment

GATS: General Agreement on Trade in Services

GATT: General Agreement on Tariffs and Trade

GDP: gross domestic product

GNN: Global News Network

GNP: gross national product (total amount of goods and services produced within a country)

HDTV: high-definition television

IANS: India Abroad News Service

IBI: International Broadcast Institute

IBU: International Broadcasting Union

IC: international communication

ICAO: International Civil Aviation Organization

IGOs: international governmental organizations, or intergovernmental organizations

IIC: International Institute of Communication

ILO: International Labor Organization

IMF: International Monetary Fund

IMO: International Maritime Organization

INGOs: international nongovernmental organizations

INS: International News Service

IntelSat: International Telecommunications Satellite Organization

IPI: International Press Institute

IPR: intellectual property right

ISDN: Integrated System Digital Networks

ISPs: Internet service providers

ITAR-TASS: Information Telegraph Agency of Russia–Telegraph Agency of the Soviet Union

ITU: International Telecommunication Union (a UN specialized agency)

LDCs: less developed countries

LECs: local exchange carriers

LEOs: low earth orbits

MDCs: more developed countries

MENA: Middle East News Association

MSO: multiple system operator

MTV: Music Television

NAFTA: North American Free Trade Agreement

NAM: Non-Aligned Movement

NATO: North Atlantic Treaty Organization

NBC: National Broadcasting Company

NGBT: Negotiating Group on Basic Telecommunications

NGOs: nongovernmental organizations

NHK: Nippon Hansai Kyoki (Japan Broadcasting Corporation)

NICs: newly industrialized countries

NIIO: New International Information Order

NSF: National Science Foundation

NTIA: National Telecommunications Information Administration

NWEO: new world economic order

NWICO: new world information and communication order

NWIO: new world information order

NWO: new world order

OECD: Organization for Economic Co-operation and Development

OIRT: Organization for International Radio and Television

OPEC: Organization of Petroleum Exporting Countries

OPECD: Organization for Economic Co-operation and Development

PAHO: Pan American Health Organization

PanAmSat: Pan American Satellite

PRSA: Public Relations Society of America

PTT: Post, Telegraph and Telephone

QoS: quality of service

RASCOM: Regional African Satellite Project

RFE/RL: Radio Free Europe/Radio Liberty

SNTV: Sports News Television

TASS: Telegraph Agency of the Soviet Union

TDF: transborder data flow

TNC: transnational corporation

TNMC: transnational media corporation

TNT: Turner Network Television

UCC: Universal Copyright Convention

UN: United Nations

UNCTAD: United Nations Conference on Trade and Development

UNDP: United Nations Development Program

UNESCO: United Nations Educational, Scientific and Cultural Organization

UNICEF: United Nations Children's Fund

UNIDO: United Nations Industrial Development Organization

UPI: United Press International

UPU: Universal Postal Union

USAID: United States Agency for International Development

USIA: United States Information Agency

VCR: video cassette recorder

VOA: Voice of America

WAP: wireless application protocol

WARC: World Administrative Radio Conference

WHO: World Health Organization

WIPO: World Intellectual Property Organization

WTN: World Television Network

WTO: World Trade Organization

Suggested Readings

Abshire, D. M. (1976). *International broadcasting: A new dimension of western diplomacy.* Beverly Hills, CA: Sage.

Akwule, R. (1992). *Global telecommunications: The technology, administration, and politics.* Boston: Focal Press.

Albarran, A. B. (1998). *Global media economics: Commercialization, concentration, and integration of world media markets.* Ames: Iowa State University Press.

Albarran, A. B., & Goff, D. H. (Eds.). (2000). *Understanding the Web: Social, political, and economic dimensions of the Internet.* Ames: Iowa State University Press.

Alexander, A., Owers, J., & Carveth, R. (Eds.). (1998). *Media economics: Theory and practice* (2nd ed.). Mahwah, NJ: Lawrence Erlbaum Associates.

Alger, D. (1998). *Megamedia: How giant corporations dominate mass media, distort competition, and endanger democracy.* Lanham, MD: Rowman & Littlefield.

Allen, D. (Ed.). (1996). *Women transforming communications: Global intersections.* Thousand Oaks, CA: Sage.

Alleyne, M. D. (1995). *International power and international communication.* New York: St. Martin's Press.

Alleyne, M. D. (1997). *News revolution: Political and economic decisions about global information.* New York: St. Martin's Press.

Altschull, J. H. (1984). *Agents of power.* White Plains, NY: Longman.

Bagdikian, B. H. (1997). *The media monopoly* (5th ed.). New York: Beacon Press.

Barker, C. (1999). *Television, globalization, and cultural identities.* London: Open University Press.

Barnouw, E., & Barnouw, E. (1998). *Conglomerates and the media.* New York: New Press.

Becker, T. D., & Slaton, C. D. (2000). *The future of teledemocracy: Visions and theories—Action experiments—Global practices.* Westport, CT: Greenwood.

Boyd, D. A. (1999). *Broadcasting in the Arab world: A survey of the electronic media in the Middle East* (3rd ed.). Ames: Iowa State University Press.

British Broadcasting Corporation. (1982). *Voice for the world: The work of the BBC external service*. London: BBC.

Browne, D. R. (1999). *Electronic media and industrialized nations: A comparative survey*. Ames: Iowa State University Press.

Browne, R. B., & Fishwick, M. W. (1998). *The global village: Dead or alive?* Bowling Green, Ohio: Bowling Green Popular Press.

Burniske, R. W., & Monke, L. (1999). *Breaking down the digital walls: Learning to teach in a post-modern world*. Albany: State University of New York Press.

Burns, R. (1998). *Television: An international history of the formative years*. Edison, NJ: Institute of Electrical Engineers.

Campbell, R. (with Martin, C. R., & Fabos, B.). (2000). *Media and culture: An introduction to mass communication*. Boston: Bedford/St. Martin's.

Carey, A., & Lohrey, A. (Eds.). (1997). *Taking the risk out of democracy: Corporate propaganda versus freedom and liberty*. Urbana: University of Illinois Press.

Carruthers, S. L. (2000). *The media at war: Communication and conflict in the 20th century*. New York: St. Martin's Press.

Cate, F. H. (1997). *Privacy in the information age*. Washington, DC: Brookings Institution Press.

Chinoy, M. (2000). *China live: People power and the television revolution* (Updated ed.). Lanham, MD: Rowman & Littlefield.

Chomsky, N. (1991). *Deterring democracy*. London: Verso Books.

Cooper, K. (1942). *Barriers down*. New York: Farrar & Rinehart.

Cooper-Chen, A., & Kodama, M. (1997). *Mass communication in Japan*. Ames: Iowa State University Press.

Craige, B. J. (1996). *American patriotism in a global society*. New York: State University of New York Press.

Croteau, D., & Hoynes, W. (2001). *The business of media: Corporate media and the public interest*. Thousand Oaks, CA: Pine Forge Press.

DeFleur, M. L., & Ball-Rokeach, S. (1989). *Theories of mass communication* (5th ed.). New York: Longman.

Derne, S. (2000). *Movies, masculinity, and modernity: An ethnography of men's filmgoing in India*. Westport, CT: Greenwood.

Diamond, L. (1994). *Political culture and democracy in developing countries: Textbook edition*. Boulder, CO: Lynne Rienner.

Diehl, P. F. (1997). *The politics of global governance: International organizations in an interdependent world*. Boulder, CO: Lynne Rienner.

Dizard, W. P., Jr. (1989). *The coming information age* (3rd ed.). New York: Longman.

Donahue, R. T. (1998). *Japanese culture and communication: Critical cultural analysis*. Lanham, MD: University Press of America.

D'Souza, D. (1996). *The end of racism: Principles for a multiracial society*. New York: Free Press.

Ducatel, K., Webster, J., & Herrmann, W. (Eds.). (2000). *The information society in Europe: Work and life in an age of globalization*. Lanham, MD: Rowman & Littlefield.

Dutton, W. H. (Ed.). (1996). *Information and communication technologies: Visions and realities*. Oxford: Oxford University Press.

Ebo, B. (2001). *Cyberimperialism? Global relations in the new electronic frontier*. Westport, CT: Praeger.

Emerson, T. I. (1970). *The system of freedom of expression*. New York: Random House.

Epstein, E. (2000). *News from nowhere: Television and the news*. Lanham, MD: Rowman & Littlefield.

Ess, C. (Ed.). (2001). Culture, technology, communication: Towards an intercultural global village. Albany: State University of New York Press.

Eugster, E. (1983). *Television programming across national boundaries: The EBU and OIRT experience*. Dedham, MA: Artech House.

Fardon, R., & Furniss, G. (Eds.). (2000). *African broadcast cultures: Radio in transition*. Westport, CT: Praeger.

Featherstone, M. (Ed.). (2000). *Global modernities*. Thousand Oaks, CA: Sage.

Flournoy, D., & Stewart, R. (1997). *CNN: Making news in the global market*. London: University of Luton Press.

Fortner, R. S. (1993). *International communication: History, conflict, and control of the global metropolis*. Belmont, CA: Wadsworth.

Frederick, H. H. (1986). *Cuban-American radio wars*. Norwood, NJ: Ablex.

Frederick, H. H. (1993). *Global communication and international relations*. Belmont, CA: Wadsworth.

Friedland, L. A. (1992). *Covering the world: International television news services*. New York: 20th Century Fund.

Garnham, N. (1990). *Capitalism and communication: Global culture and the economics of information*. Thousand Oaks, CA: Sage.

George, J. (1994). *Discourse of global politics: A critical (re)introduction to international relations*. Boulder, CO: Lynne Rienner.

Gerbner, G., Mowlana, H., & Nordenstreng, K. (1993). *The global media debate: Its rise, fall, and renewal*. Norwood, NJ: Ablex.

Gershon, R. A. (1996). *The transnational media corporation: Global messages and free market competition*. Mahwah, NJ: Lawrence Erlbaum Associates.

Gher, L. A., & Amin, H. Y. (Eds.). (1999). *Civic discourse in the Middle East and digital age communications*. Norwood, NJ: Ablex.

Gillett, S. E., & Vogelsang, I. (Eds.). (1999). *Competition, regulation, and convergence: Current trends in telecommunications policy research*. Mahwah, NJ: Lawrence Erlbaum Associates.

Ginneken, J. V. (1999). *Understanding global news: A critical introduction*. Thousand Oaks, CA: Sage.

Goldstein, R. J. (Ed.). (2000). *The war for the public mind: Political censorship in 19th-century Europe*. Westport, CT: Praeger.

Gross, P. (1996). *Mass media in revolution and national development: The Romanian laboratory*. Ames: Iowa State University Press.

Gudykunst, W. B. (Ed.). (1993). *Communication in Japan and the United States*. Albany: State University of New York Press.

Gudykunst, W. B., & Mody, B. (Eds.). (2001). *Handbook of international and intercultural communication* (2nd ed.). Thousand Oaks, CA: Sage.

Gudykunst, W. B., & Nishida, T. (1994). *Bridging Japanese/North American differences*. Thousand Oaks, CA: Sage.

Gurtov, M. (1999). *Global politics in the human interest* (4th ed.). Boulder, CO: Lynne Rienner.

Hachten, W. A. (1992). *The world news prism: Changing media of international communication* (3rd ed.). Ames: Iowa State University Press.

Hachten, W. A. (1993). *The growth of media in the Third World, African failure, Asian successes*. Ames: Iowa State University Press.

Hafez, K. (Ed.). (1999). *Islam and the West in the mass media: Fragmented images in a globalizing world*. Cresskill, NJ: Hampton Press.

Halbert, D. J. (1999). *Intellectual property in the information age: The politics of expanding ownership rights*. Westport, CT: Praeger.

Hamelink, C. J. (1994). *The politics of world communication*. London: Sage.

Hamelink, C. J. (1995). *World communication*. London: Zed Books.

Hart, M. (2000). *The American Internet advantage: Global themes and implications of the modern world*. Lanham, MD: University Press of America.

Herbert, J. (2000). *Practicing global journalism: The effects of globalization and the media convergence*. Boston: Butterworth-Hienemann.

Herman, E., McChesney, R. W., & Herman, E. S. (1998). *The global media: The missionaries of global capitalism*. Herndon, VA: Cassell Academic.

Hill, K. A., & Hughes, J. E. (1998). *Cyberpolitics: Citizen activism in the age of the Internet*. Lanham, MD: Rowman & Littlefield.

Hilliard, R. L., & Keith, M. C. (1996). *Global broadcasting systems*. Boston: Focal Press.

Holmes, P. A. (1999). *Broadcasting in Sierra Leone*. Lanham, MD: University Press of America.

Inglehart, R. (1990). *Culture shift in advanced industrial society*. Princeton, NJ: Princeton University Press.

International Commission for the Study of Communication Problems. (1980).

Many voices, one world: communication and society, today and tomorrow. New York: UNESCO.

Jandt, F. E. (1998). *Intercultural communication: An introduction* (2nd ed.). Thousand Oaks, CA: Sage.

Johnston, C. B. (1998). *Global news access: The impact of new communications technologies.* Westport, CT: Greenwood.

Jones, T. D. (1998). *Human rights: Group defamation, freedom of expression, and the law of nations.* Boston: Martinus Nijhoff.

Kamalipour, Y. R. (Ed.). (1995, 1997). *The U.S. media and the Middle East: Image and perception.* Westport, CT: Greenwood/Praeger.

Kamalipour, Y. R. (Ed.). (1999). *Images of the U.S. around the world: A multicultural perspective.* Albany: State University of New York Press.

Kamalipour, Y. R. (Ed.). (2001). *Media, sex, violence, and drugs in the global village.* Lanham, MD: Rowman & Littlefield.

Kamalipour, Y. R., & Carilli, T. (Eds.). (1998). *Cultural diversity and the U.S. media.* Albany: State University of New York Press.

Kamalipour, Y. R., & Mowlana, H. (Eds.). (1994). *Mass media in the Middle East: A comprehensive handbook.* Westport, CT: Greenwood.

Kamalipour, Y. R., & Thierstein, J. P. (Eds.). (2000). *Religion, law, and freedom: A global perspective.* Westport, CT: Greenwood.

Karim, K. H. (2000). *The Islamic peril: Media and global violence.* Montreal, Canada: Black Rose Books.

Kennedy, P. (1993). *Preparing for the 21st century.* New York: Vintage Books.

Keohane, R. O., & Nye, J. S. (1971). *Transnational relations and world politics.* Cambridge: Harvard University Press.

Ku, C., & Diehl, P. F. (Eds.). (1998). *International law: Classic and contemporary readings.* Boulder, CO: Lynne Rienner.

Lai, D. (1997). *Global perspectives: International relations, U.S. foreign policy, and the view from abroad.* Boulder, CO: Lynne Rienner.

Ledbetter, J. (1997). *Made possible by: The death of public broadcasting in the United States.* London: Verso Books.

Lee, C. C. (1980). *Media imperialism reconsidered: The homogenizing of television culture.* Beverly Hills, CA: Sage.

Lengel, L. B. (Ed.). (1999). *Culture and technology in the new Europe: Civic discourse in transformation in post-socialist nations.* Norwood, NJ: Ablex.

Lent, J. A. (1999). *Women and mass communication in the 1990's: An international, annotated bibliography.* Westport, CT: Greenwood.

Li, H. (1998). *Image, perception, and the making of U.S.–Chinese relations.* Lanham, MD: University Press of America.

Lindahl, R. (1978). *Broadcasting across borders: A study on the role of propaganda in external broadcasts.* Göteborg, Sweden: C. W. K. Gleerup.

Loader, B. D. (Ed.). (1997). *The governance of cyberspace.* London: Routledge.

Lull, J. (2000). *Media, communication, culture: A global approach.* Irvington, NY: Columbia University Press.

Mackenzie, H. (1999). *The directory of the armed forces radio service series.* Westport, CT: Greenwood.

Malek, A., & Kavoori, A. P. (Eds.). (2000). *The global dynamics of news: Studies in international news coverage and news agenda.* Westport, CT: Praeger.

Mansell, R., & Wehn, U. (1998). *Knowledge societies: Information technology for sustainable development.* Oxford: Oxford University Press.

McChesney, R. W. (1999). *Rich media, poor democracy: Communication politics in dubious times.* Urbana: University of Illinois Press.

McChesney, R. W., Wood, E. M., & Foster, J. B. (Eds.). (1998). *Capitalism and the information age: The political economy of the global communication revolution.* New York: Monthly Review Press.

McLuhan, M., Fiore, Q., & Agel, J. (1997). *War and peace in the global village.* New York: Wired Books.

McLuhan, M., & Powers, B. R. (1992). *The global village: Transformation in world life and media in the 21st century.* New York: Oxford University Press.

McPhail, T. C. (1987). *Electronic colonialism: The future of international broadcasting and communication.* Newbury Park, CA: Sage.

McQuail, D. (1992). *Media performance: Mass communication and the public interest.* London: Sage.

McQuail, D. (2000). *McQuail's mass communication theory* (4th ed.). Thousand Oaks, CA: Sage.

McWilliams, W. C., & Piotrowski, H. (1997). *The world since 1945: A history of international relations.* Boulder, CO: Lynne Rienner.

Meadows, M. (2001). *Voices in the wilderness: Images of aboriginal people in the Australian media.* Westport, CT: Greenwood.

Melkote, S. R. (1998). *International satellite broadcasting and cultural implications.* Lanham, MD: University Press of America.

Melody, W. H. (Ed.). (1997). *Telecom reform: Principles, policies, and regulatory practices.* Lyngby: Technical University of Denmark.

Merrill, J. C. (Ed.). (1995). *Global journalism: Survey of international communication* (3rd ed.). White Plains, NY: Longman.

Mickelson, S. (1983). *America's other voice: The story of Radio Free Europe and Radio Liberty.* New York: Praeger.

Mittelman, J. H. (Ed.). (1996). *Globalization: Critical reflections.* Boulder, CO: Lynne Rienner.

Mohammadi, A. (Ed.). (1997). *International communication and globalization.* Thousand Oaks, CA: Sage.

Moore, R. L. (1999). *Mass communication law and ethics* (2nd ed.). Mahwah, NJ: Lawrence Erlbaum Associates.

Moore, R. L., Farrar, R. T., & Collins, E. L. (1997). *Advertising and public relations law.* Mahwah, NJ: Lawrence Erlbaum Associates.

Mostert, A. (n.d.). *A brief history of Radio New York Worldwide.* New York: Radio New York Worldwide.

Mowlana, H. (1990). *The passing of modernity: Communication and the transformation of society.* New York: Longman.

Mowlana, H. (1996). *Global media in transition: The end of diversity?* Thousand Oaks, CA: Sage.

Mowlana, H. (1997). *Global information and world communication.* London: Sage.

Naficy, H. (1993). *The making of exile cultures: Iranian television in Los Angeles.* Minneapolis: University of Minnesota Press.

Nazer, H. M. (1999). *Power of a third kind: The Western attempt to colonize the global village.* Thousand Oaks, CA: Sage.

Neuman, J. (1996). *Lights, camera, war: Is media technology driving international politics?* New York: St. Martin's Press.

Ngwainmbi, E. K. (1999). *Exporting communication technology to developing countries: Sociocultural, economic, and educational factors.* Lanham, MD: University Press of America.

O'Heffernan, P. (1991). *Mass media and American foreign policy: Insider perspectives on global journalism and the foreign policy process.* Westport, CT: Greenwood.

Olson, S. R. (1999). *Hollywood planet: Global media and the competitive advantage of narrative transparency.* Mahwah, NJ: Lawrence Erlbaum Associates.

Over, W. (1999). *Human rights in international public sphere: Civic discourse for the 21st century.* Westport, CT: Praeger.

Paraschos, E. E. (1998). *Media law and regulation in the European Union: National, transnational, and U.S. perspectives.* Ames: Iowa State University Press.

Perry, N. (1998). *Hyperreality and global culture.* New York: Routledge.

Pettman, R. (1996). *Understanding international political economy, with readings for the fatigued.* Boulder, CO: Lynne Rienner.

Price, M. E., & Verhulst, S. G. (Eds.). (1999). *Broadcasting reform in India: Media law from a global perspective.* New York: Oxford University Press.

Prosser, M. H. (Ed.). (2000). *Civic discourse and discourse conflict in Africa.* Norwood, NJ: Ablex.

Prosser, M. H., & Sitaram, K. S. (Eds.). (1999). *Civic discourse: Intercultural, international, and global media.* Norwood, NJ: Ablex.

Quester, G. H. (1990). *The international politics of television*. Lexington, MA: Lexington Books.

Qvist, P. O., & von Bagh, P. (2000). *Guide to the cinema of Sweden and Finland*. Westport, CT: Praeger.

Ryan, M. P. (1998). *Knowledge diplomacy: Global competition and the politics of intellectual property*. Washington, DC: Brookings Institution Press.

Said, E. (1988). *Covering Islam: How the media and the expert determine how we see the rest of the world*. New York: Pantheon.

Samovar, L. A., & Porter, R. E. (2001). *Communication between cultures* (4th ed.). Belmont, CA: Wadsworth.

Sassen, S. (1988). *The mobility of labor and capital*. Cambridge: Cambridge University Press.

Sayyid, B. S. (1997). *A fundamental fear: Eurocentrism and the emergence of Islam*. London: Zed Books.

Schlesinger, A. M., Jr. (1992). *The disuniting of America: Reflections on a multicultural society*. New York: W. W. Norton & Co.

Seib, P. (1997). *Headline diplomacy: How news coverage affects foreign policy*. London: Praeger.

Shapiro, M. J. (1997). *Violent cartographies: Mapping cultures of war*. Minneapolis: University of Minnesota Press.

Shaw, M. (1996). *Civil society and media in global crises: Representing distant violence*. New York: Books International.

Sitaram, K. S., & Prosser, M. H. (Eds.). (1998). *Civic discourse: Multiculturalism, cultural diversity, and global communication*. Norwood, NJ: Ablex.

Sitaram, K. S., & Prosser, M. H. (Eds.). (2000). *Civic discourse: Communication, technology, and cultural values*. Norwood, NJ: Ablex.

Smolla, R. A. (1992). *Free speech in an open society*. New York: Alfred A. Knopf.

Sparks, C., & Tulloch, J. (Eds.). (2000). *Tabloid tales: Global debates over media standards*. Lanham, MD: Rowman & Littlefield.

Sreberny-Mohammadi, S., Winseck, D., McKenna, J., & Boyd-Barrett, O. (Eds.).

(1998). *Media in global context: A reader*. New York: Oxford University Press.

Stevenson, R. L. (1993). *Communication, development, and the Third World: The global politics of information*. New York: University Press of America.

Stevenson, R. L. (1994). *Global communication in the 21st century*. New York: Longman.

Tanno, D. V., & Gonzalez, A. (Eds.). (1998). *Communication and identity across cultures*. Thousand Oaks, CA: Sage.

Taylor, P. M. (1997). *Global communications, international affairs, and the media since 1945*. New York: Routledge.

Tehranian, M. (1990). *Technologies of power: Information machines and democratic prospects*. Norwood, NJ: Ablex.

Tehranian, M. (1999). *Global communication and world politics: Domination, development, and discourse*. Boulder: Lynne Rienner.

Tehranian, M. (Ed.). (1999). *Worlds apart: Human security and global governance*. London: I. B. Taurus.

Tehranian, M., Hamikzadeh, F., & Vidale, M. (Eds.). (1977). *Communications policy for national development: A comparative perspective*. London: Routledge, Kegan & Paul.

Tehranian, M., & Tehranian, K. (Eds.). (1992). *Restructuring for world peace: On the threshold of the 21st century*. Cresskill, NJ: Hampton Press.

Teich, A. H. (2000). *Technology and the future* (8th ed.). Boston: Bedford/St. Martin's.

Thussu, D. K. (1998). *Electronic empires: Global media and local resistance*. New York: Oxford University Press.

Thussu, D. K. (2000). *International communication: Continuity and change*. New York: Oxford University Press.

Tomlinson, J. (1991). *Cultural imperialism: A critical introduction*. Baltimore: Johns Hopkins University Press.

Turow, J. (1997). *Breaking up America: Advertisers and the new media world*. Chicago: University of Illinois Press.

UNESCO. (1999). *World communication and information report, 1999–2000*. Paris: UNESCO.

Valdivia, A. N. N. (1995). *Feminism, multi-culturalism, and the media: Global diversities.* Thousand Oaks, CA: Sage.

Van Belle, D. A. (2000). *Press freedom and global politics.* Westport, CT: Praeger.

Van Dijk, J. (1999). *The network society: An introduction to the social aspects of new media.* Thousand Oaks, CA: Sage.

Veseth, M. (1998). *Selling globalization: The myth of the global economy.* Boulder, CO: Lynne Rienner.

Vincent, R. C., Nordenstreng, K., & Traber, M. (Eds.). (1999). *Towards equity in global communication: MacBride update.* Cresskill, NJ: Hampton Press.

Wang, J. (2000). *Foreign advertising in China: Becoming global, becoming local.* Ames: Iowa State University Press.

Wark, M. (1994). *Virtual geography: Living with global media events.* Bloomington: Indiana University Press.

Weiss, T. G., & Gordnker, L. (Eds.). (1996). *NGOs, the UN, and global governance.* Boulder, CO: Lynne Rienner.

Wells, A. (Ed.). (1996). *World broadcasting.* London: General Hall Press.

Willis, J. (Ed.). (1999). *Images of Germany in the American media.* Westport, CT: Praeger.

Wilson, K. G. (2000). *Deregulating tele-communications: U.S. and Canadian tele-communication, 1840–1997.* Lanham, MD: Rowman & Littlefield.

Wood, J. (1994). *History of international broadcasting.* Edison, NJ: Institute of Electrical Engineers.

Wood, J. (1999). *History of international broadcasting* (vol. 2). Edison, NJ: Institute of Electrical Engineers.

World Commission on Culture and Development. (1995). *Our creative diversity.* Paris, UNESCO.

Youm, K. H. (1996). *Press law in South Korea.* Ames: Iowa State University Press.

Index